THE NEW
CAMBRIDGE MODERN HISTORY

ADVISORY COMMITTEE

SIR GEORGE CLARKE   SIR JAMES BUTLER   J.P.T. BURY
THE LATE E.A.BENIANS

VOLUME XIV

ATLAS

THE NEW CAMBRIDGE MODERN HISTORY

ATLAS

EDITED BY

H. C. DARBY

Emeritus Professor of Geography in the University of Cambridge

AND

HAROLD FULLARD

Cartographic Editor, George Philip & Son Ltd

CAMBRIDGE UNIVERSITY PRESS

CAMBRIDGE

LONDON · NEW YORK · MELBOURNE

Published by the Syndics of the Cambridge University Press
The Pitt Building, Trumpington Street, Cambridge CB2 1RP
Bentley House, 200 Euston Road, London, NW1 2DB
32 East 57th Street, New York, NY 10022, USA
296 Beaconsfield Parade, Middle Park, Melbourne, 3206, Australia

Library of Congress catalogue card number: 57-14935

ISBN 0 521 07708 7

First published 1970
Reprinted (with corrections) 1978

Printed in Great Britain
by George Philip Printers Ltd, London

CONTENTS

List of Maps	*page* vii	
Preface	xvii	
Acknowledgements	xix	
List of Abbreviations	xxiii	

MAPS   I

Subject Index   289

LIST OF MAPS

THE WORLD

PAGE		SCALE
1	The World on Globes, 1459–c1530	
	The World, 1459, according to Fra Mauro	
	The World, 1492, according to Martin Behaim	
	The World, c1530, according to an anonymous Nuremberg globe	
2–3	The Old World, c1500	1:45M
4–5	The World: Exploration to 1529	1:130M
6–7	Expanding Knowledge of the World, c1500–c1800	
	The World, c1500	1:270M
	The World, c1600	1:270M
	The World, c1700	1:270M
	The World, c1800	1:270M
8–9	The World: Europe Overseas, 1714	1:130M
10–11	The World: Europe Overseas, 1763	1:130M
12–13	The World: European Possessions and States of European Origin, 1830	1:130M
14–15	The World: European Possessions and States of European Origin, 1878	1:130M
16–17	The World, 1914	1:130M
18–19	The World, 1926	1:130M
20–1	The World, 1950	1:130M
22–3	The World: Achievement of Independence, 1945–68	1:130M
24–5	North-west and north-east passages: Selected voyages to first complete navigation	1:24M
26	North Polar Regions: Exploration	1:40M
27	South Polar Regions: Exploration	1:40M

WARS AND TREATY SETTLEMENTS

28	The Peasants' War, 1524–6	1:5M
29	The Anglo-Dutch Wars, 1652–74	1:4M
30–1	The Thirty Years' War, 1618–48	
	30a The Bohemian War, 1618–20 and the Palatinate War, 1621–3	1:10M
	b The Lower Saxon-Danish War, 1625–9 and the Polish-Swedish War, 1625–9	1:10M
	31a The Swedish War, 1630–4	1:10M
	b The Franco-Swedish War, 1635–48	1:10M
32a	Treaty of Westphalia, 1648	1:15M
b	Treaty of Pyrenees, 1659	1:15M
33a	Wars of Louis XIV, 1667–98	1:15M
b	Treaties of Aix-la-Chapelle, Nijmegen, and Rijswick, 1668–97	1:15M
34	War of Spanish Succession, 1701–14	1:15M
35	Treaties of Utrecht, 1713, Rastatt and Baden, 1714	1:15M
36a	The Northern War, 1655–60	1:15M
b	Treaties of Roskilde, Copenhagen, Oliva, and Kardis, 1658–61	1:15M
37a	The Great Northern War, 1700–21	1:15M
b	Treaties of Stockholm, 1719 and Nystad, 1721	1:15M
38a	War in S.E. Europe, 1683–1739	1:15M
b	Treaties of Carlowitz, Passarowitz and Belgrade, 1699–1739	1:15M
39	War of Austrian Succession, 1740–8	1:7½M
40	The Seven Years' War, 1756–63 (The Third Silesian War)	1:5M

LIST OF MAPS

PAGE   SCALE

Page	Map	Scale
41	The Seven Years' War Overseas, 1756–63	
	a North America and West Indies	1:40M
	b Spain and Africa	1:40M
	c India	1:40M
42	Treaty Settlements in Europe, 1735–63	1:15M
43	Treaty Settlements Overseas, 1713–63	
	a North America and West Indies	1:40M
	b West Africa	1:40M
	c India	1:40M
44–5a	War in Europe, 1789–1815	1:15M
b	Egyptian Campaign, 1798–9	1:15M
46a	Russian Campaign (Advance) 1812	1:10M
b	Russian Campaign (Retreat) 1812	1:10M
c	Peninsular War, 1807–14	1:10M
47a	The Waterloo Campaign, June 16–18, 1815	1:600,000
b	British and French Naval Movements, March–October, 1805	1:60M
48	Treaty Settlements in Europe, 1795–1812	1:15M
49	Treaty Settlements in Europe, 1814–15	1:15M
50a	War Overseas, 1790–1816	1:30M
b	Treaty Settlements Overseas: India, 1790–1816	1:30M
c	Treaty Settlements Overseas: South Africa, 1795–1814	1:30M
51a	The Crimean War, 1853–5	1:8M
b	The Sevastopol Campaign	1:2M
52–3	The First World War, 1914–18	1:20M
54	The Western Front, 1914–18	1:4M
55a	German Losses in Africa, 1920	1:85M
b	German Losses in the Pacific, 1920	1:85M
56–7	Treaty Settlements in Europe, 1919–26	1:10M
58–9	Europe at the height of German domination, November, 1942	1:15M
60	Europe: Movements of people, 1939–45	1:17½M
61	Europe: Movements of people, 1944–52	1:17½M
62–3	The Second World War, 1939–45	1:130M

EUROPE

Page	Map	Scale
64–5	Europe: Physical	1:20M
66–7	Europe: Ecclesiastical, c1500	1:12M
68–9	Europe: Universities to 1830	1:12M
70–1	Europe, c1500	1:15M
72–3	Europe, c1648	1:15M
74–5	Europe, c1721	1:15M
76–7	Europe, c1812	1:15M
78–9	Europe, c1815	1:15M
80–1	Europe, c1914	1:15M
82–3	Europe, c1926	1:15M
84–5	Europe, after 1945	1:15M
86–7	Europe: Railways, 1870	1:15M
88	West and Central Europe: Population, c1870	1:15M
89	Central Europe: Railway Development to 1870	1:8M
90	West and Central Europe: Population Changes, 1870–1925 (after Haufe)	1:15M

LIST OF MAPS

PAGE   SCALE

91 West and Central Europe: Population, 1914   1:15M
92 West and Central Europe: Industries, 1914   1:15M
93 Europe: Industrial Changes, 1870–1965
       Coal, 1870   1:60M
       Coal, 1965   1:60M
       Pig Iron and Ferro-Alloys, 1870   1:60M
       Pig Iron and Ferro-Alloys, 1965   1:60M
       Petroleum, 1965   1:60M
       Electric Energy, 1965   1:60M

THE BRITISH ISLES

94a Ireland in the 16th–18th centuries   1:4M
  b Ireland, 1922   1:4M
95a Scotland in the 16th–17th centuries   1:4M
  b Scotland in the 18th century   1:4M
96   England and Wales during the Civil War, 1642–6
       a May 1–December 9, 1643   1:6M
       b November, 1644–December, 1645   1:6M
97   England, Wales and S. Scotland: Some Economic Distributions in the 18th century 1:4M
98   British Isles: Population, 1801 (Ireland, 1821)   1:6M
99   British Isles: Population, 1851   1:6M
100 British Isles: Parliamentary Representation before 1832   1:6M
101a British Isles: Parliamentary Representation after 1832   1:6M
  b British Isles: Population, 1831   1:20M
102a England, Wales and Southern Scotland: Textile industries, 1851   1:6M
  b England, Wales and Southern Scotland: Metal industries, 1851   1:6M
103a England, Wales and Southern Scotland: Textile industries, 1901   1:6M
  b England, Wales and Southern Scotland: Metal industries, 1901   1:6M
104 British Isles: Population, c1911   1:6M
105a London, c1700   1:50,000

FRANCE

105b Paris, c1700   1:50,000
106 Burgundian Lands, 1363–1477   1:5M
107 France, c1500   1:7½M
108–9 Northern and Eastern frontiers of France, 1552–1766   1:2½M
110 France, 1585–98   1:7½M
111 Eastern frontier of France under Louis XIV, 1643–1715   1:5M
112a France, 1632: Post roads   1:10M
  b France, 1789: Custom and Tax areas   1:10M
113a France, 1789: Pays d'Election and Pays d'Etat   1:10M
  b France, 1789: Law and language   1:10M
114a France, 1789: Ecclesiastical   1:10M
  b France, 1802: Ecclesiastical   1:10M
115a France, 1789: Gouvernements   1:10M
  b France, 1815: Départements   1:10M
116 Paris, 1789   1:25,000
117 Eastern frontier of France, 1814–71, and Franco-German War, 1870–1   1:5M

ix

LIST OF MAPS

CENTRAL EUROPE

PAGE		SCALE
118–19	Hanseatic League and the Baltic, 1370–c1500	1:10M
120	Spread of German settlements eastwards by the 15th century	1:10M
121	The Imperial Circles, c1512	1:10M
122–3	Central Europe, c1500	1:5M
124–5	Central Europe, c1560	1:5M
126	Central Europe, c1560: Religious situation	1:10M
127	Central Europe, c1618: Religious situation	1:10M
128	Confessional Leagues, 1530–47	1:7½M
129a	Edict of Restitution, 1629	1:7½M
b	Changes in population in the Empire, 1618–48	1:7½M
130–1	Central Europe, c1648	1:5M
132–3	Central Europe, c1786	1:8M
134	Central Europe and Northern Italy, 1797	1:8M
135	Central Europe and Northern Italy, 1803	1:8M
136	Central Europe and Northern Italy, 1806	1:8M
137	Central Europe and Northern Italy, 1810	1:8M
138a	The rise of Prussia, 1411–1618	1:10M
b	The rise of Prussia, 1618–1713	1:10M
139a	The rise of Prussia, 1713–95	1:10M
b	The rise of Prussia, 1795–1815	1:10M
140a	Germany, 1828: Customs Unions	1:10M
b	Germany, 1834–66: the Zollverein	1:10M
141a	Germany, 1867–88: the New Zollverein	1:10M
b	The formation of the German Empire, 1864–71	1:10M
142	Prussia and Austria, 1815–66	1:10M
143a	The Schleswig-Holstein Question after October 1864	1:3M
b	The Schleswig-Holstein Question, 1914–20	1:3M
144	The Habsburg Empire, c1556	1:15M
145	Austrian Habsburgs and the Empire to 1648	1:8M
146	The Habsburg Empire, 1648–1914	1:8M
147	The disruption of the Habsburg Empire: Linguistic, 1920	1:8M
148a	Central Europe to 1939	1:12M
b	Central Europe, 1945	1:12M

NORTHERN EUROPE

149	Scandinavia and the Baltic, 1523–1660	1:12M

THE NETHERLANDS

150a	The Netherlands under Charles V, 1506–55	1:4M
b	The Netherlands, 1574–89	1:4M
151a	The Netherlands, 1590–1607	1:4M
b	The Netherlands, 1609–48	1:4M
152	The Netherlands and Belgium, 1814–39	1:3M
153a	The Netherlands: Land reclamation, 1300–1966	1:3M
b	The Delta area: Land reclamation, 1300–1966	1:1M

LIST OF MAPS

SWITZERLAND

PAGE		SCALE
154	Growth of the Swiss Confederation, 1291–1797	1:2M
155	Switzerland and the Sonderbund War, 1847	1:2M

ITALY

156a	Italy, c1500	1:7½M
b	Growth of Florence to 1454	1:5M
157	The Growth of the House of Savoy, 1416–1748	1:3M
158a	Growth of Venice, Seawards to 1797	1:10M
b	Growth of Venice, Landwards to 1797	1:5M
159	Alpine Barrier to c1750	1:5M
160	Italy, 1713–48	1:7½M
161	Italy, 1815–1924	1:7½M

IBERIAN PENINSULA

162a	Iberian Peninsula: Mesta Routes	1:10M
b	Iberian Peninsula: The Reconquest to 1492	1:10M
163a	Iberian Peninsula, 1492	1:10M
b	The Spanish Civil War, 1936–9	1:10M

THE BALKANS AND THE NEAR EAST

164–5	The growth of the Ottoman Empire to 1683	1:15M
166–7	The decline of the Ottoman Empire, 1683–1924	1:15M
168	Balkan Peninsula, c1830	1:8M
169a	Growth of Serbia, 1817–1913; and formation of Yugoslavia, 1918–20	1:8M
b	Growth of Greece, 1830–1922	1:8M
170a	Balkan Peninsula, 1878–1912	1:10M
b	Balkan Peninsula, 1912–13	1:10M
171a	Balkan Peninsula: Linguistic, 1920	1:10M
b	Balkan Peninsula, 1920–3	1:10M
172a	Conflicting claims in Macedonia, c1912	1:10M
b	Major ethnic groups in Macedonia, 1912 and 1926	1:2½M
173	Palestine, 1920–51	1:2½M
174	The Middle East to 1926	1:22½M
175	The Middle East to c1960	1:22½M

EASTERN EUROPE AND RUSSIA

176a	Decline and dissolution of the Baltic Orders, 1466–1583	1:8M
b	Danzig, 1454–1938, and the Polish Corridor, 1938	1:1½M
177a	Poland, 1569–1772	1:12M
b	Partitions of Poland, 1772–95	1:12M
178a	Poland, 1815–1914	1:12M
b	Poland: Linguistic, 1920	1:12M

LIST OF MAPS

PAGE   SCALE

179a Poland, 1916–38   1:12M
   b Poland, 1945   1:12M
180–1 The expansion of Russia in Europe, 1300–1689   1:15M
 182 Russia under Peter the Great, 1689–1725   1:20M
 183 The expansion of Russia in Europe, 1725–1855   1:20M
 184 The expansion of Russia in Europe and Asia, 1598–1914   1:45M
 185 Russia in Asia: Population, 1910   1:45M
186a The expansion of Russia in the Caucasus, 1761–1914   1:10M
   b The expansion of Russia in Turkestan, 1825–1914   1:20M
 187 Jewish population in Central Europe and Russia, c1900   1:15M
 188 Russia in Europe: Economic, c1860   1:20M
 189 Russia in Europe: Economic, 1913   1:20M
 190 Russia in Europe: Population, 1910   1:20M
 191 Western Russia, 1914–23   1:15M
 192 Russia: Mining and Industry, 1913   1:45M
 193 Russia: Mining and Industry, 1960   1:45M

NORTH AMERICA

194–5a Atlantic coast colonies, c1650, and the Iroquois   1:5M
    b Cape Cod-Boston District   1:1½M
 196 Spanish, British, French in Eastern N. America, 1603–1763 (before Treaty of Paris) 1:17½M
 197 North-east America to 1763: British and French rivalry (before Treaty of Paris)   1:7½M
198a North America, 1756   1:35M
   b North America, 1763 (after Treaty of Paris)   1:35M
 199 The American Revolution, 1775–83   1:8M
200a United States, 1783–1803   1:20M
   b United States: Density of population, c1790   1:20M
201a California: The gold and silver rush, 1849–59   1:5M
   b North America: Colonial economy in the 18th century   1:20M
 202 United States: Territorial expansion from 1803   1:25M
 203 United States: Exploration of the West, 1803–53   1:20M
204a United States: Railroads and Overland mail, c1860   1:35M
   b United States: Rates of travel, c1860   1:35M
 205 United States: Population, 1860   1:25M
 206 United States: Slavery to c1860   1:25M
 207 The American Civil War, 1861–5   1:10M
208a United States: Areas of virgin forest, 1650   1:35M
   b United States: Areas of virgin forest, 1850   1:35M
209a United States: Areas of virgin forest, 1926   1:35M
   b United States: Gold, silver, oil and gas, c1930   1:35M
210a United States: Cotton growing, 1859   1:25M
   b United States: Cotton growing, 1919   1:25M
211a United States: Cotton spinning, 1840   1:25M
   b United States: Cotton spinning, 1926   1:25M
212a United States: Iron and steel, 1858   1:25M
   b United States: Iron and steel, 1908   1:25M
 213 United States: Economic, c1900   1:25M
 214 United States: Coloured population, 1900   1:25M

xii

LIST OF MAPS

PAGE   SCALE

215 United States: Population, 1900   1:25M

216 European emigration to U.S., 1851–1910

       1851–60   1:60M

       1861–70   1:60M

       1871–80   1:60M

       1881–90   1:60M

       1891–1900   1:60M

       1901–10   1:60M

217 United States: Foreign-born population, 1900   1:25M

218 United States: Presidential elections, 1904–20

       a 1904   1:50M

       b 1908   1:50M

       c 1912   1:50M

       d 1920   1:50M

219a Alaskan boundary dispute, 1898–1903   1:7M

  b Maine boundary dispute, 1783–1842   1:7M

220 Canada: Exploration, 1768–1905   1:30M

221a Eastern Canada: Settlement in the 18th and early 19th century 1:15M

  b Canada: Westward expansion of settlement   1:15M

222 Canada: Development of provinces

       a Canada, 1862   1:50M

       b Canada, 1867   1:50M

       c Canada, 1882   1:50M

223 Canada: Development of provinces

       a Canada, 1898   1:50M

       b Canada, 1912   1:50M

       c Canada, 1949   1:50M

224a Canada: Origin of the population, 1911   1:30M

  b Canada: Population, 1951   1:30M

LATIN AMERICA

225a Maya and Aztec civilisations   1:15M

  b Conquest of Mexico, 1519–21   1:3M

226a North America: The exploration of the South-west to 1618 1:15M

  b North America: The South-west, annual rainfall   1:70M

227 Mexico, 1824–67   1:25M

228 West Indies: Exploration to 1525   1:20M

229 West Indies, 1525–1650   1:20M

230 West Indies, 1650–1763   1:20M

231 West Indies, 1763–1830   1:20M

232 West Indies, 1830–1910   1:20M

233a Central America: Population, c1950   1:40M

  b South America: Exploration, 1799–1917   1:40M

234 The Inca Empire and the Conquest of Peru   1:30M

235 South America, c1650   1:40M

236 South America in the 18th century   1:40M

237 South America, 1800–30   1:40M

238 South America, 1830–1956   1:40M

239 South America: Population, c1950   1:40M

240a Panama Canal   1:1½M

LIST OF MAPS

AFRICA

PAGE   SCALE

240b   Suez Canal   1:1½M

241   North Africa: Caravan routes in the 19th century   1:30M

242   Africa to c1830   1:50M

243   Africa: Exploration, 1830–89   1:50M

244   Africa, c1880   1:50M

245   Africa, c1885   1:50M

246   Africa, 1914   1:50M

247   Africa, 1926   1:50M

248   Africa, c1950   1:50M

249   Africa to 1968   1:50M

250   Africa: Christian mission stations, c1920   1:50M

251   Africa: Population, c1950   1:50M

252   West Africa to 1800   1:15M

253   West Africa, 1880–1900   1:20M

254   North-west Africa: European advance to c1912   1:20M

255   East Africa, c1960   1:15M

256a   South Africa: The Great Trek, 1836–46   1:12½M

    b   The Boer War, 1899–1902   1:12½M

257   South Africa, 1854–1910   1:12½M

258a   Union of South Africa: Minerals and railways, c1910   1:15M

    b   Union of South Africa: Coloured and Asiatic population, 1951   1:15M

259a   Union of South Africa: Bantu population, 1951   1:15M

    b   Union of South Africa: White population, 1951   1:15M

INDIA AND THE FAR EAST

260   Portuguese in the East, c1580   1:50M

261   European activity in the East, c1650   1:40M

262–3   East Indies, 1700–1820   1:22½M

264–5   East Indies, 1820–1914   1:22½M

266   India to c1707   1:25M

267   India, 1756–1805   1:25M

268   India, 1805–58   1:25M

269   Indian Mutiny, 1857–9   1:15M

270   India, 1858–1947   1:25M

271   India: Linguistic, c1950   1:25M

272   India: Religions, c1950   1:25M

273   The Mohammedan World, c1950   1:85M

274   China during the Manchu (Ch'ing) dynasty, 1644–1912   1:30M

275a   Treaty ports in China   1:30M

    b   Leased Territories in China:

        Weihaiwei   1:3M

        Kwantung   1:3M

        Tsingtao (Kiaochow)   1:3M

        Hong Kong   1:3M

        Kwangchow   1:3M

276a   Japan in the Far East, 1870–1942   1:30M

    b   Japan in the Far East, 1942–5   1:275M

LIST OF MAPS

PAGE		SCALE
277	The Far East until *c*1939	1:40M
278–9	India and the Far East: Population, *c*1950	1:30M
280a	Expansion of Buddhism	1:85M
b	Chinese in South-east Asia, *c*1939	1:40M
281a	New Zealand: Settlement to 1950	1:8M
b	New Zealand: Population, *c*1950	1:17½M
282–3	The Pacific to 1922	1:60M
284–5	Australia: Exploration, 1521–1903	1:25M
286–7a	Australia: Settlement, 1830–1950	1:25M
286–7a	Australia: Settlement to 1950	1:25M
b	Australia: Development of the states:	
	Australia, 1829	1:120M
	Australia, 1836	1:120M
	Australia, 1853	1:120M
	Australia, 1859	1:120M
	Australia, 1863	1:120M
288	Australia: Population, *c*1950	1:25M

PREFACE

The making of any atlas is an exercise in compromise—between, amongst other things, the scales of maps, the choice of names, the availability of information and the cost of production. This is especially true of a historical atlas. The present atlas has been designed with the aim of making it easily portable, convenient for frequent use and able to stand upon a bookshelf. Even so, the scales of the majority of the maps compare favourably with those of atlases of a much larger format because there are many double-page maps and because insets have only rarely been included on a page.

In planning the atlas we have tried to balance the amount of space given to maps of Europe by nearly as many maps dealing with non-European lands—with North America, Latin America, Africa, the Far East, Australasia and the world as a whole. A substantial number of maps showing economic and social conditions has been included. We wish we could have included even more, but, only too often, we have drawn a blank in our search for reliable economic information for some areas at a number of periods. To have increased such economic maps by even a small number would have involved extensive research programmes impossible within the limits within which we worked. Maps showing exploration, major wars and treaty settlements have also been included.

Some historical atlases have adopted a basic chronological plan; others have grouped maps of similar areas together. Each method can be defended, but we have followed the latter method in the belief that it facilitates reference to individual areas at different periods. The maps within each group, so far as is possible, have been arranged in chronological sequence and have been produced on the same scale to enable easy comparison between them.

Instead of a topographical index of names, a subject index has been assembled based mainly upon area and chronology. The treatment of place-names always presents difficulties to atlas makers because spellings so often change with shifting political boundaries. We have tried to follow the spellings generally in use in English historical writing. Each map has been newly compiled and has been reproduced using the latest cartographic techniques; type-faces and colours have been selected with the aim of presenting information in as clear a manner as possible. Although designed to serve the needs of readers of *The New Cambridge Modern History*, the atlas is also intended to illustrate school or university courses on modern history.

PREFACE

We are grateful for advice at various stages of the work to the editors of, and contributors to, *The New Cambridge Modern History*. Professor R. M. Hatton and Professor D. B. Horn have very kindly given us help over specific maps. We also owe warm thanks to the cartographic staff of Messrs. George Philip and Son Ltd. Finally, we are greatly indebted to Mr G. R. Versey who has given much general assistance in the preparation of the maps and index.

H. C. DARBY
HAROLD FULLARD

King's College, Cambridge
Michaelmas, 1969

ACKNOWLEDGEMENTS

Among the works consulted in the preparation of this
atlas, the following have been especially useful.

J. T. Adams, *Atlas of American History* (New York, 1943).

H. Ammann und Karl Schib, *Historischer Atlas der Schweiz* (Aarau, 1958).

АТЛАСЬ АЗІАТСКОЙ РОССІИ [*Atlas of Asiatic Russia*] (St. Petersburg, 1914).

Atlas Narodov Mira (Moscow, 1964).

Official Year Books of the Commonwealth of Australia (Melbourne, 1901-8).

J. N. L. Baker, *A History of Geographical Discovery and Exploration* (London, 1931).

J. G. Bartholomew, *The Survey Atlas of England and Wales* (London, 1903).

——*Atlas of the World's Commerce* (London, 1907).

——*A Literary and Historical Atlas of Asia* (London, 1913).

I. Bowman, *The New World* (Yonkers, N.Y., 1921).

H. Butterfield, *et al.*, *A Short History of France* (Cambridge, 1961).

The Cambridge Modern History, 14 vols. (Cambridge, 1902-12).

Atlas of Canada (Ottawa: Dept. of Interior, 1915).

Ceskoslovenský Vojenský Atlas (Praha, 1965).

J. W. Chalmers, W. J. Eccles and H. Fullard, *Philip's Historical Atlas of Canada* (London, 1966).

Chambers's Encyclopaedia (London, 1959).

J. H. Clapham, *An Economic History of Modern Britain*, 3 vols. (Cambridge, 1926-38).

The Columbia Lippincott Gazetteer of the World (New York, 1962).

H. C. Darby (ed.), *An Historical Geography of England before A.D.* 1800 (Cambridge, 1936).

I. Darlington and J. Howgego, *Printed Maps of London c.* 1553-1850 (London, 1964).

C. C. Davies, *An Historical Atlas of the Indian Peninsula* (Oxford, 1949).

АТЛАС ИСТОРИИ ГЕОГРАФИЧЕСКИХ ОТКРЫТИИ И ИССЛЕДОВАНИИ [*Atlas of the History of Geographical Discoveries and Explorations*] (Moscow, 1959).

G. Droysen, *Allgemeiner Historischer Handatlas* (Leipzig, 1886).

Encyclopaedia Britannica, Eleventh Edition (New York, 1910-11).

J. Engel (ed.), *Grosser Historischer Weltatlas*, Teil III (Neuzeit) (Munchen, 1962).

J. D. Fage, *An Atlas of African History* (London, 1958).

T. W. Freeman, *Ireland* (London, 1950).

——*The Conurbations of Great Britain* (Manchester, 1959).

H. Fullard and H. C. Darby, *The University Atlas* (London, 1967).

The Geographical Journal (London since 1893).

The Geographical Review (New York, since 1916).

M. Gilbert, *Recent History Atlas* (London, 1966).

Greek Refugee Settlement (League of Nations, Geneva, 1926).

Helmut Haufe, *Die Bevölkerung Europas* (Berlin, 1936).

A. Herrmann, *Historical and Commercial Atlas of China* (Harvard-Yenching Institute, 1935).

——*An Historical Atlas of China* (Chicago, 1966).

W. A. Heurtley, *et al.*, *A Short History of Greece* (Cambridge, 1965).

Historical Atlas of the Muslim Peoples (London, 1957).

Historical Atlas of the U.S.S.R. for Secondary Schools, 3 vols. (Moscow, 1949-52).

Keith Johnston, *A Sketch of Historical Geography* (London, 1909).

C. Joppen, *Historical Atlas of India* (London, 1928).

C. Joppen and H. L. O. Garrett, *Historical Atlas of India* (London, 1938).

H. H. Kagan, *The American Heritage Pictorial Atlas of United States History* (New York, 1966).

Julius Klein, *The Mesta: A study in Spanish Economic History* (Harvard, 1920).

E. Kremling, *IRO Weltwirtschaftsatlas* (Munchen, 1961).

E. Lehmann, *Historisch-Geographisches Kartenwek* (Leipzig, 1960).

P. I. Lyashchenko, *History of the National Economy of Russia to the* 1917 *Revolution* (New York, 1949).

B. R. Mitchell and P. Deane, *Abstract of British Historical Statistics* (Cambridge, 1962).

R. Muir and George Philip, *Philip's Historical Atlas Medieval and Modern* (London, 1927).

G. P. Murdock, *Africa: Its Peoples and their Culture History* (New York, 1959).

Naval Intelligence Division, *Geographical Handbooks:* Belgium, China Proper, France, Germany, Greece, Netherlands and Yugoslavia (London, Admiralty, 1942-5).

H. Newbolt, *The Year of Trafalgar* (London, 1905).

A. E. Nordenskiöld, *Facsimile Atlas to the early History of Cartography* (London, 1889).

C. Oman, *Nelson* (London, 1947).

C. O. Paullin and J. K. Wright, *Atlas of the Historical Geography of the United States* (Washington and New York, 1932).

A. Petermanns, *Mitteilingen* (Gotha, since 1855).

Philip's Atlas of Modern History, prepared under the direction of the Historical Association (London, 1964).

Philip's Chamber of Commerce Atlas (London, 1912).

K. Ploetz, *Auszug aus der Geschichte* (Wurzburg, 1960).

R. L. Poole, *Historical Atlas of Modern Europe* (Oxford, 1902).

F. W. Putzger, *Historischer Weltatlas* (Bielefeld und Berlin, 1961).

E. Reich, *A New Student's Atlas of English History* (London, 1903).

W. Van Royen and O. Bowles, *The Mineral Resources of the World* (New York, 1952).

F. Schrader, *Atlas de Géographie Historique* (Paris, 1907).

W. R. Shepherd, *Historical Atlas* (Pikesville, Maryland, 1956).

W. Smith, *An Economic Geography of Great Britain* (London, 1953).

Axel Sømme, *A Geography of Norden* (Oslo, 1960).

O. H. K. Spate, *India and Pakistan* (London, 1954).

L. Dudley Stamp and S. H. Beaver, *The British Isles* (London, 1954).

The Statesman's Yearbook (London, since 1864).

League of Nations, Statistical Yearbooks (various titles), (United Nations, New York).

A. J. Toynbee and E. D. Myers, *Historical Atlas and Gazetteer* (Oxford, 1959).

R. F. Treharne, *Bibliography of historical atlases and hand-maps for schools* (London, Historical Association, 1939).

R. F. Treharne and H. Fullard, *Muir's Historical Atlas Medieval and Modern* (London, 1962).

United Nations Yearbooks.

United States Census of Population, 1960 (U.S. Department of Commerce).

E. W. Walker, *Historical Atlas of South Africa* (Oxford, 1922).

Weltatlas: Die Staaten der Erde und ihre Wirtschaft (Gotha, 1964).

Westermanns Atlas zur Weltgeschichte (Braunschweig, 1956).

LIST OF ABBREVIATIONS

Ab.	Abbey	Helv.	Helvetia
Abp.	Archbishopric	Hung.	Hungary
Arch.	Archipelago		
Arg.	Argentina	Indep.	Independent
Aust.	Austrian	I, Is	Island, Islands
Austral.	Australia	Ital.	Italian, Italy
Auton.	Autonomous		
		Jap.	Japan
B.	Battle, Bay, Bight		
Bdy.	Boundary	K.	Kingdom
Bech.	Bechuanaland		
Belg.	Belgian, Belgium	L.	Lake, Lordship
Bol.	Bolivia	Ld.	Land
Bp.	Bishopric	Ldg.	Landgraviate
Br.	Britain, British	Liech.	Lichtenstein
Bran.	Brandenburg	Lux.	Luxembourg, Luxemburg
Brun.	Brunswick		
Bulg.	Bulgaria	Mand.	Mandate
		Mar.	Margraviate, Marquisate
C.	Cape, County	Mass.	Massachusetts
Cent.	Central, Century	Md.	Maryland
Chin.	Chinese	Mex.	Mexico
Co.	Company	Mod.	Modura
Col.	Colony	Mont.	Montenegro
Conf.	Confederation	Mt.	Mount
Conn.	Connecticut	Mts.	Mountains
Courl.	Courland		
Cz.	Czechoslovakia	N.	North, Northern
		N.C.	North Carolina
D.	Duchy	N.H.	New Hampshire
D.C.	District of Columbia	N.J.	New Jersey
Del.	Delaware	N.Y.	New York
Den.	Denmark	N.Z.	New Zealand
		Neth.	Netherlands
Ec.	Ecuador		
El.	Electorate	Occup.	Occupation, Occupied
Eng.	England, English	Ottom. Emp.	Ottoman Empire
Fr.	France, French	P.	Pass
		Pal.	Palatinate
G.	Gulf	Par.	Paraguay
Ga.	Georgia	Pen.	Peninsula
Geb.	Gebirge	Pol.	Poland, Polish
Gen.	Genoa	Pom.	Pomerania
Ger.	Germany	Port.	Portugal, Portuguese
German C.	German Confederation	Pr.	Principality, Prince
Gr.	Grand	Prot.	Protection, Protectorate
Gr. D.	Grand Duchy	Prov.	Province
Gr. Pr.	Grand Principality	Pruss.	Prussia
Gt.	Great	Pt.	Port.
Habsb.	Habsburg	R.	River
Han.	Hanover		

LIST OF ABBREVIATIONS

Rep.	Republic	**Sw.**	Switzerland
R.I.	Rhode Island	**Swiss C.**	Swiss Confederation
Rum.	Rumania		
		T.	Treaty
S.	San, Seigneurie, South	**Terr.**	Territory
Sa.	Sierra	**Trib.**	Tributary
Sav.	Savoy	**Turk.**	Turkey, Turkish
Sax.	Saxon, Saxony	**Tusc.**	Tuscany
S.C.	South Carolina		
Scot.	Scotland	**U. of S.A.**	Union of South Africa
Sd.	Sound		
Serb.	Serbia	**Va.**	Virginia
Sp.	Spain	**V.C.**	Viscounty
Span.	Spanish	**Ven.**	Venice
St.	State	**Vt.**	Vermont
St. Sta.	Saint, Santa		
Str.	Strait	**Yug.**	Yugoslavia

THE WORLD, 1459
(after a Map by Fra Mauro)

THE WORLD, 1492
(after a Globe by Martin Behaim)

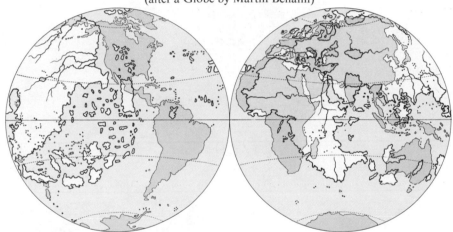

THE WORLD, *c.*1530
(after an anonymous Globe, probably made at Nuremberg)

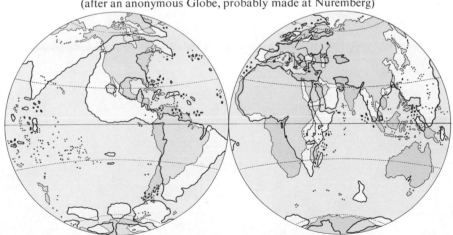

The World as known today is superimposed in grey

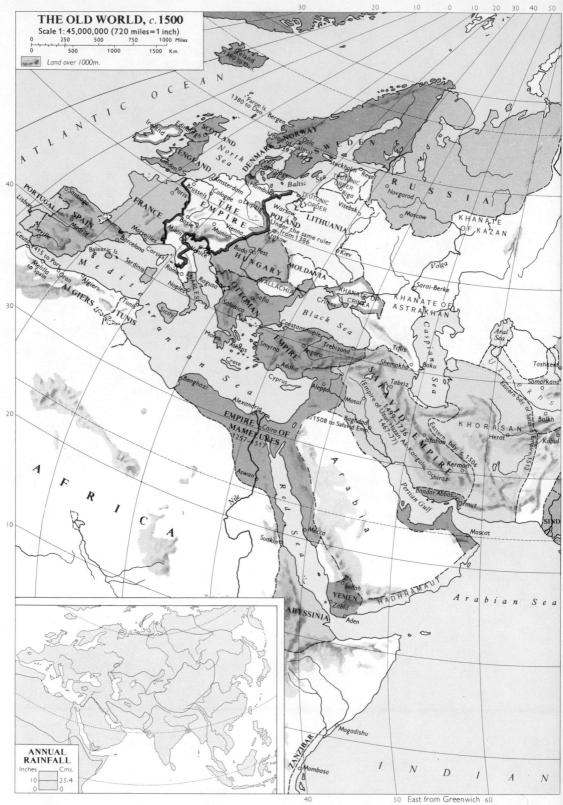

THE OLD WORLD, *c.*1500
Scale 1: 45,000,000 (720 miles=1 inch)

0   250   500   750   1000 Miles
0   500   1000   1500 Km.

Land over 1000m.

ATLANTIC OCEAN

Iceland
1380 to Den.

Faroe Is.
1380 to Den.

Bergen

Ireland
Edinburgh
SCOTLAND
ENGLAND
London
Amsterdam
Brussels
Cologne
Paris
Basle
Milan
Marseilles
Barcelona
Corsica
Rome
Naples
Ragusa
Venice

North
Sea

Oslo
Copenhagen
Hamburg
Leipzig
Vienna
Munich

NORWAY
Union of
Calmar
1397–1523
SWEDEN
DENMARK
Stockholm
Reval
Baltic Sea
Riga
Vitebsk
TEUTONIC
ORDER
TEUTONIC
ORDER
Warsaw
POLAND
Under the same ruler
from 1386
Krakow
Buda
Pest
HUNGARY
MOLDAVIA
WALLACHIA

Novgorod

Moscow

RUSSIA

KHANATE
OF KAZAN

Volga
Sarai-Berke

KHANATE OF
ASTRAKHAN

PORTUGAL
Lisbon
Santiago
Oporto
Seville
Madrid
SPAIN
Ceuta 1415 to Port.
Oran
Melilla
to Spain
Algiers
ALGIERS
Tunis
TUNIS
Balearic Is.
Sardinia
Sicily

FRANCE
THE EMPIRE
CHARLES

Mediterranean Sea

Morea
Athens
Crete

OTTOMAN
EMPIRE
Sofia
Salonica
Constantinople
Smyrna
Angora
Adalia
Cyprus
Aleppo

Black Sea
Crimea
KHANATE OF
CRIMEA
Trebizond
Tiflis
Shemakha
Baku
Tabriz

Caspian Sea

Aral Sea
Uzbeks
Tashkent
Samarkand
Balkh

KHORASAN
Herat
Kabul
Eastern bdy of Safavid Empire 1512

Eastern bdy. c.1506

Benghazi

Alexandria
Cairo
EMPIRE OF
MAMELUKES
1257–1517
Aswan

Nile
Red Sea

1508 to Safavid Emp.
Mosul
Baghdad
SAFAVID
EMPIRE
1499–1736
(Empire of Uzun Hasan Ak-Koyunlu 1467–77)
Isfahan
Kerman
Shiraz
Bandar Abbas
Ormuz

Persian Gulf

Mecca
Suakin

Arabia

Mascat

SIND

AFRICA

ABYSSINIA

Sadah
YEMEN
Zabid
Aden

HADHRAMAUT

Arabian Sea

ZANZIBAR
Mogadishu

Mombasa

INDIAN

ANNUAL
RAINFALL

Inches   Cms.
10 ——— 25.4
0 ——— 0

40   50   East from Greenwich   60

East from Greenwich

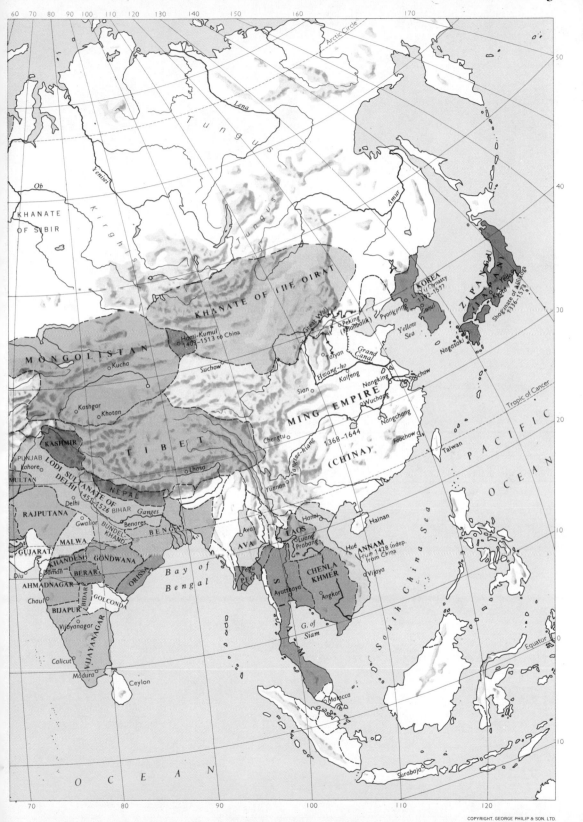

60 70 80 90 100 110 120 130 140 150 160 170

Arctic Circle

50

KHANATE
OF SIBIR

Ob

Yenisei

Lena

T u n g u s

T u n g u s

Amur

40

Kirghiz

KHANATE OF THE OIRAT

Great Wall

KOREA
Yi Dynasty
1392–1597
Seoul

Pyongyang

Z I P A N G U

Yedo

Kyoto

Shogunate of Ashikaga
1336–1573

30

MONGOLISTAN

Hami-Kumul
1403–1513 to China

Kucha

Suchow

Peking
(Khambalik)

Taiyan

Yellow
Sea

Nagasaki

Grand
Canal

Kashgar

Khotan

Hwang-ho

Kaifeng

Sian

Nangking

Wuchang

Suchow

PACIFIC

KASHMIR

T I B E T

MING EMPIRE

Chengtu

Yangtse-kiang

Nanchang

20

PUNJAB
Lahore

MULTAN

LODI SULTANATE OF
DELHI 1451–1526

Delhi

NEPAL

Lhasa

1368–1644

(CHINA)

Yünnan

Foochow

Taiwan

OCEAN

Tropic of Cancer

RAJPUTANA

Gwalior

BUNDEL-
KHAND

BIHAR

Benares

Ganges

BENGAL

Hanoi

Aval

LAOS
Luang
Prabang

Hainan

10

MALWA

GUJARAT

Diu

KHANDESH
Daman

GONDWANA

AVA

ANNAM
from 1428 indep.
from China

Hué

Vijaya

BERAR

ORISSA

Bay of

Pegu
PEGU

CHENLA
KHMER

AHMADNAGAR

Chaul

BIDAR

GOLCONDA

Bengal

Ayutthaya

Angkor

S
I
A
M

BIJAPUR

Vijayanagar

VIJAYANAGAR

Calicut

Madura

Ceylon

G. of
Siam

South China Sea

Equator

0

Malacca

Surabaja

O C E A N

10

70 80 90 100 110 120

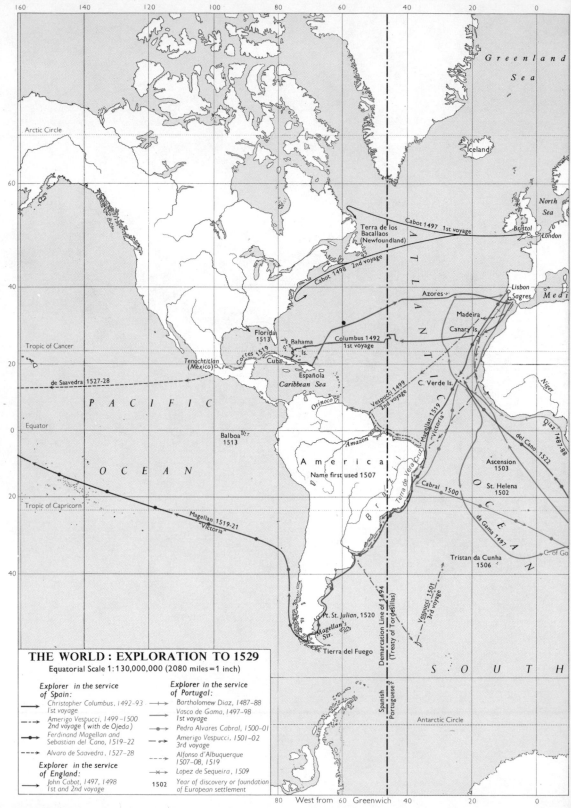

THE WORLD: EXPLORATION TO 1529
Equatorial Scale 1:130,000,000 (2080 miles = 1 inch)

Explorer in the service of Spain:
Christopher Columbus, 1492–93 1st voyage
Amerigo Vespucci, 1499–1500 2nd voyage (with de Ojeda)
Ferdinand Magellan and Sebastian del Cano, 1519–22
Alvaro de Saavedra, 1527–28

Explorer in the service of England:
John Cabot, 1497, 1498 1st and 2nd voyage

Explorer in the service of Portugal:
Bartholomew Diaz, 1487–88
Vasco de Gama, 1497–98 1st voyage
Pedro Alvares Cabral, 1500–01
Amerigo Vespucci, 1501–02 3rd voyage
Alfonso d'Albuquerque 1507–08, 1519
Lopez de Sequeira, 1509

1502 Year of discovery or foundation of European settlement

MERCATOR'S PROJECTION

Greenland Sea

Arctic Circle

Iceland

North Sea

Cabot 1497 1st voyage

Bristol
London

Terra de los Bacallaos (Newfoundland)

Cabot 1498 2nd voyage

Azores

Lisbon
Sagres

Medi

Madeira

Canary Is.

Florida 1513

Bahama Is.

Columbus 1492 1st voyage

Tropic of Cancer

de Saavedra 1527–28

Tenochtitlan (Mexico)

Cortes 1519

Cuba

Española

Caribbean Sea

Española

C. Verde Is.

Vespucci 1499 2nd voyage

Orinoco

PACIFIC

Balboa 1513

Amazon

America
Name first used 1507

Equator

OCEAN

Magellan 1519 "Victoria"

Diaz 1487–88

del Cano 1522

Ascension 1503

Cabral 1500

St. Helena 1502

da Gama 1497

G. of Go

Tristan da Cunha 1506

Tropic of Capricorn

Magellan 1519–21 "Victoria"

Brazil

Terra de Vera Cruz

Vespucci 1501 3rd voyage

Demarcation Line of 1494 (Treaty of Tordesillas)

Pt. St. Julian, 1520

Magellan's Str.

Tierra del Fuego

SOUTH

Spanish Portuguese

Antarctic Circle

80   West from 60 Greenwich   40   20   0

Baltic Sea

Danube

Black Sea

Caspian Sea

Mediterranean Sea

Nile

Volta

Volga

Indus

Ganges

PACIFIC

Ormuz, 1515

Diu

d'Albuquerque 1507-08

Aden, 1524

1519

1519

Socotra

Goa, 1510

Calicut, 1498

Cochin

da Gama, 1498

Colombo, 1518

de Sequeira 1509

Malindi

Mombasa

Seychelles 1505

Sumatra

St. Lazaro Arch. 1521

Magellan April 1521

Brunei 1521

Malacca 1511

Borneo

Celebes

Ladrone Is.

de Saavedra 1527-28

Caroline Is. 1528

OCEAN

Spice Is., 1511 (Moluccas)

Magellan 1521 Victoria

INDIAN

Moçambique 1507

Sao Lourenço (Madagascar)

Mascarenhas 1505

OCEAN

Java

Timor

del Cano (after Magellan's death) 1521-22 "Victoria"

od Hor...

ERN

OCEAN

Demarcation Line of 1529 (Treaty of Saragossa)

Portuguese

Spanish

East from Greenwich

COPYRIGHT. GEORGE PHILIP & SON. LTD.

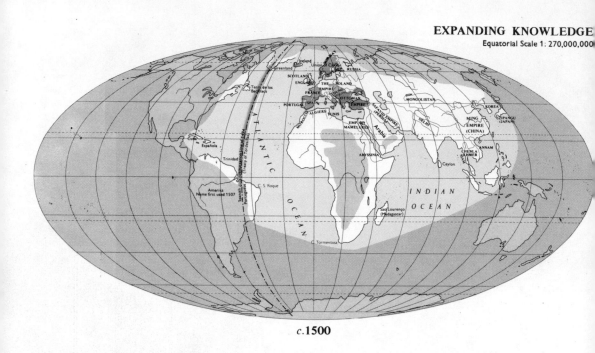

*c.*1500

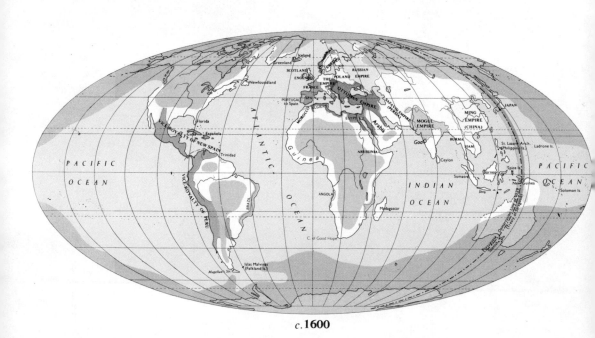

*c.*1600

OF THE WORLD
(4320 miles = 1 inch)

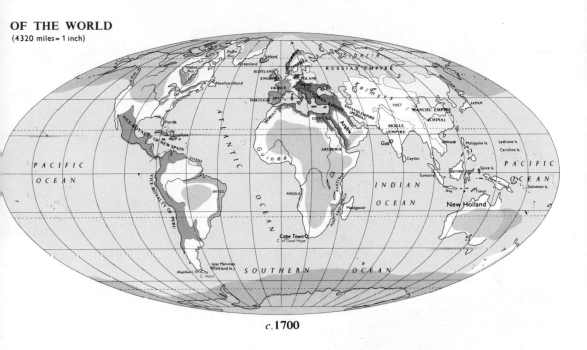

*c.*1700

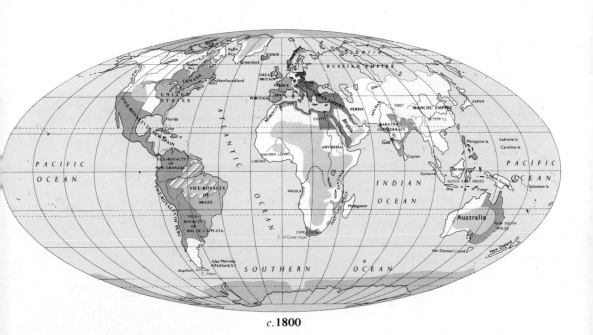

*c.*1800

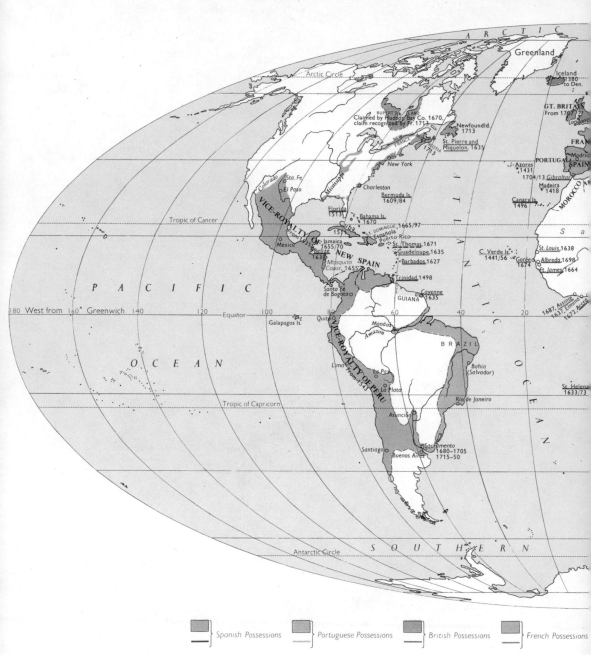

ARCTIC

Greenland

Arctic Circle

Iceland
1380
to Den.

GT. BRITAIN
From 1707
London

RUPERT'S LAND
Claimed by Hudson Bay Co. 1670,
claim recognized by Fr. 1713

Newfoundld.
1713

NEW
FRANCE

St. Pierre and
Miquelon, 1635

FRAN

NOVA
SCOTIA
1713

Azores
1431

PORTUGAL

Madrid

SPAIN

New York

1704/13 Gibraltar

Colorado
Sta. Fe

Madeira
1418

MOROCCO

El Paso

Charleston

Bermuda Is.
1609/84

Canary Is.
1496

Tropic of Cancer

VICE-ROYALTY OF

Florida
1513

Bahama Is.
1670

Cuba

S a

C. Verde Is.
1441/56

St. Louis 1638

151

ST. DOMINGUE

1665/97

Jamaica
1655/70

Española

Puerto-Rico

Goree
1674

Albreda 1698

Mexico

St. Thomas, 1671

St. James 1664

Belize
1638

NEW SPAIN

Guadeloupe, 1635

Masquito
Coast, 1655

Barbados 1627

Trinidad, 1498

1687, Assini

1637, Elmina

1672, Accra

Santa Fe
de Bogota

Cayenne
1635

GUIANA

P A C I F I C

180 West from 160 Greenwich 140

120

Equator 100

80

60

40

20

Galapagos Is.

Quito

Mandus

VICE-ROYALTY OF PERU

Amazon

B R A Z I L

O C E A N

Lima

From 1543

La Paz

Bahia
(Salvador)

St. Helena
1633/73

La Plata

Tropic of Capricorn

Rio de Janeiro

Asunción

O C E A N

Sacramento
1680–1705
1715–50

Santiago

Buenos Aires

Antarctic Circle

S O U T H E R N

Spanish Possessions   Portuguese Possessions   British Possessions   French Possessions

OVERSEAS, 1714

(2080 miles = 1 inch)

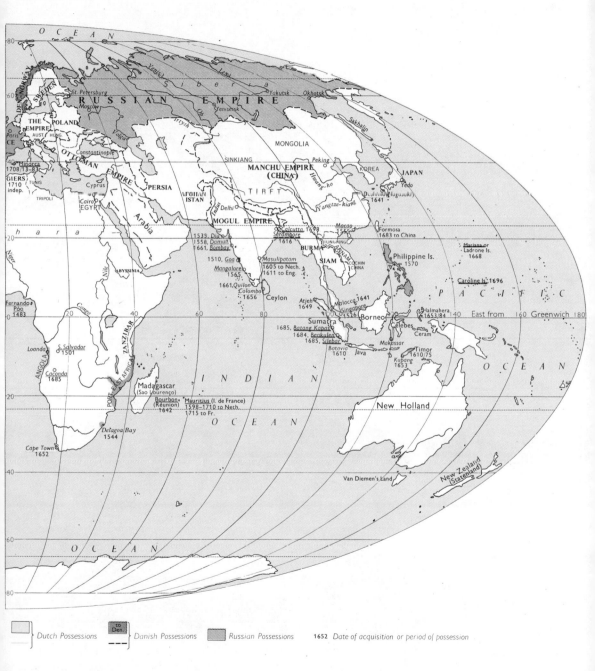

O C E A N
80
SWEDEN St. Petersburg Yenisey Lena Yakutsk Okhotsk
60 DEN. RUSSIAN EMPIRE Siberia Sakhalin
THE POLAND Moscow Yeniseisk
EMPIRE AUST. HUNG. Irtysh Ob
Paris Volga MONGOLIA
CE OTTOMAN SINKIANG Peking KOREA JAPAN
40 Minorca Constantinople MANCHU EMPIRE Edo
1708/13-83 EMPIRE (CHINA) Hwang-ho Deshima (Nagasaki)
GIERS TUNIS Cyprus PERSIA AFGHAN TIBET 1641
1710 ISTAN Delhi Yangtze-kiang Macao Formosa
indep. TRIPOLI Cairo Indus 1555 1683 to China
EGYPT MOGUL EMPIRE Calcutta 1698 HONG-KONG
Arabia 1535, Diu Serampore BURMA ANAM
h a r a 1558, Damun 1616 Masulipatam SIAM COCHIN Mariana or
20 Niger ABYSSINIA 1661, Bombay 1605 to Neth. CHINA Ladrone Is.
1510, Goa 1611 to Eng. Philippine Is. 1668
Congo Mangalore 1570
1565 Atjeh Malacca 1641 Caroline Is. 1696
Fernando 1661, Quilon 1649 Singapore P A C I F I C
Poo Colombo Ceylon Sumatra 1526 Borneo Halmahera
1483 20 40 60 80 1656 100 Celebes 1653/84 140 East from 160 Greenwich 180
Loanda S. Salvador 1685, Batang Kapas Ceram
1501 1684, Benkulen Makassar
ANGOLA 1685, Silebar Timor O C E A N
Caconda Batavia Java 1610/75
1685 I N D I A N 1610 Kupang
Madagascar 1653
(Sao Lourenço) O C E A N New Holland
20 Bourbon Mauritius (I. de France)
(Réunion) 1598-1710 to Neth.
Delagoa Bay 1642 1715 to Fr. O C E A N
1544 Van Diemen's Land New Zealand
Cape Town (Statenland)
1652
40
60
O C E A N
80

Dutch Possessions   to Den. --- Danish Possessions   Russian Possessions   1652 Date of acquisition or period of possession

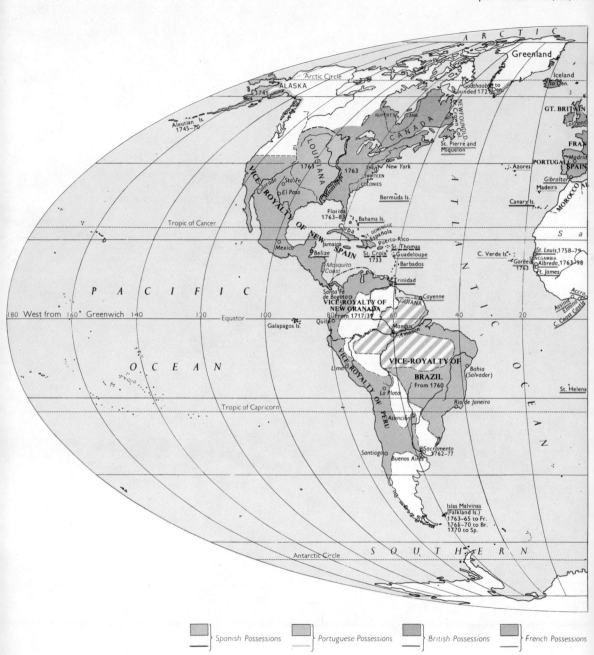

ARCTIC

Greenland

Arctic Circle

ALASKA

1741

Iceland
to Den.

Godthaab to Den.
founded 1721

GT. BRITAIN

London

NEWFOUNDLD.
Br. Crown Col.

CANADA

FRAN

RUPERT'S LAND

St. Pierre and
Miquelon

PORTUGAL

Madrid
SPAIN

Aleutian Is.
1745–70

LOUISIANA

1763

1763

New York

THE
THIRTEEN
COLONIES

Azores

Gibraltar

Colorado

Sta. Fe

Madeira

MOROCCO AL

El Paso

Mississippi

Bermuda Is.

Canary Is.

S a

Tropic of Cancer

Florida
1763–83

Bahama Is.

VICE-ROYALTY OF NEW SPAIN

Cuba

A
T
L
A
N
T
I
C

St. Louis, 1758–79

Mexico

Jamaica

Española

S. DOMINGUE

Puerto Rico

SENEGAMBIA

C. Verde Is.

Albreda, 1763–98

1763

Belize

Masquito
Coast

St. Croix
1733

St. Thomas

Guadeloupe

Barbados

Goree

Ft. James

Trinidad

Santa Fé
de Bogotá

Cayenne

GUIANA

Accra

Assini

Elmina

180 West from 160° Greenwich 140

VICE-ROYALTY OF
NEW GRANADA
From 1717/39

Quito

120

Equator

100

Galapagos Is.

80

60

Mandus
Amazon

40

20

C. Coast Castle

VICE-ROYALTY OF
BRAZIL
From 1760

Bahia
(Salvador)

P A C I F I C

Lima

VICE-ROYALTY OF PERU

O C E A N

St. Helena

Tropic of Capricorn

La Plata

Rio de Janeiro

O
C
E
A
Z

Asuncion

Sacramento
1762–77

Santiago

Buenos Aires

Islas Malvinas
(Falkland Is.)
1763–65 to Fr.
1766–70 to Br.
1770 to Sp.

Antarctic Circle

S O U T H E R N

OVERSEAS, 1763

(2080 miles = 1 inch)

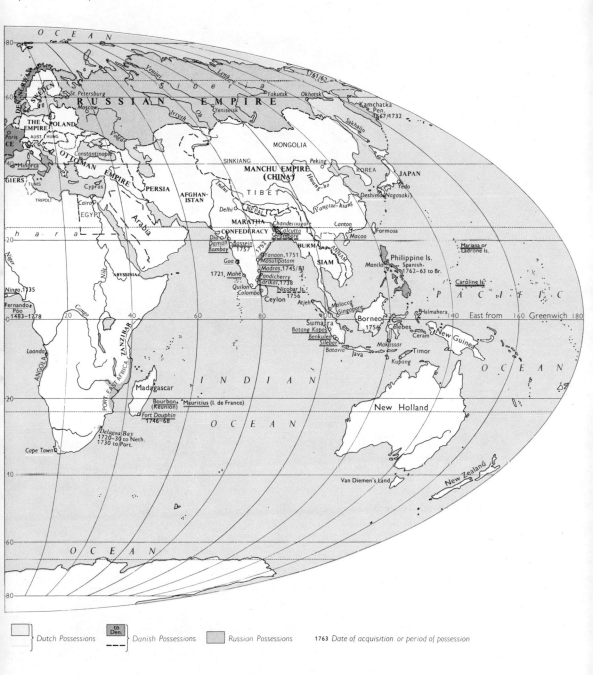

O C E A N
80

RUSSIAN EMPIRE
Siberia
1761/62
St. Petersburg
Moscow
Yakutsk
Okhotsk
Kamchatka
Pen.
1767/1732

SWEDEN
DENMARK

Yenisei
Lena

THE
EMPIRE
POLAND
AUST. HUNG.
CE
Paris

OTTOMAN
Constantinople
EMPIRE

MONGOLIA

Irtysh
Ob
Yenisseisk
Volga

KOREA
JAPAN
Yedo
Deshima Nagasaki

GIERS
TUNIS
TRIPOLI
Cyprus
Cairo
EGYPT
h a r a

PERSIA
AFGHAN-
ISTAN
Arabia

SINKIANG
MANCHU EMPIRE
(CHINA)
TIBET
NEPAL
Delhi
Hwang-ho
Peking

Yangtze-kiang
Canton
Macao
Formosa

MARATHA
CONFEDERACY
Diu
Daman Bassein
Bombay 1757
Goa
1721, Mahé
Quilon
Colombo
Ceylon

Chandernagore
Serampore
Calcutta
BURMA
ANNAM
SIAM

Yanaon, 1751
Masulipatam
Madras, 1745/81
Pondicherry
Karikal, 1738
Nicobar Is.
1756
Atjeh

Mariana or
Ladrone Is.

Philippine Is.
Spanish.
Manila 1762-63 to Br.

Caroline Is.

P A C I F I C

Niger

Ningo, 1735
Fernando
Póo
1483-1778

Congo

ABYSSINIA

ZANZIBAR

Malacca
Singapore
Borneo
1756
Sumatra
Batang Kapas
Benkulen
Silebar
Batavia
Java
Makassar
Kupang
Ceram
Timor

Halmahera

New Guinea

O C E A N

Loanda
ANGOLA

PORT. EAST AFRICA

Madagascar
Bourbon
(Reunion)
Mauritius (I. de France)

Fort Dauphin
1746-68

Cape Town

Delagoa Bay
1720-30 to Neth.
1730 to Port.

I N D I A N

O C E A N

New Holland

East from 160 Greenwich 180

Van Diemen's Land
New Zealand

O C E A N

Dutch Possessions   Danish Possessions   Russian Possessions   1763 Date of acquisition or period of possession

COPYRIGHT. GEORGE PHILIP & SON. LTD.

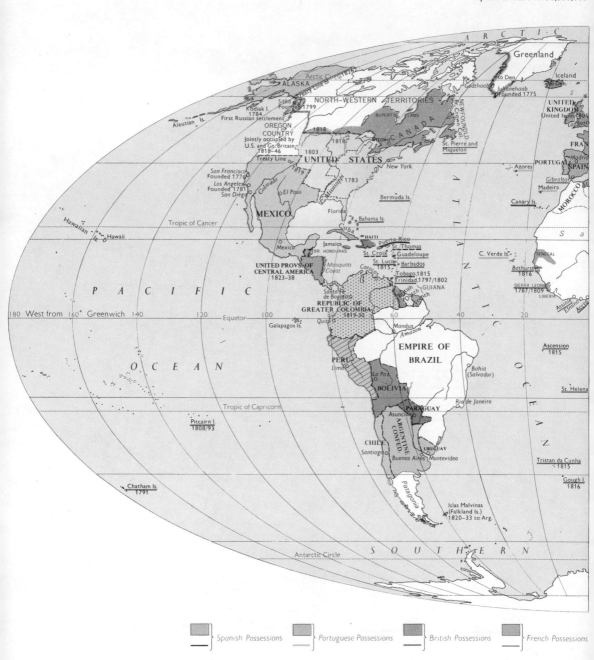

THE WORLD: EUROPEAN POSSESSIONS

Equatorial Scale 1:130,000,000

AND STATES OF EUROPEAN ORIGIN, 1830

(2080 miles=1 inch)

O C E A N

NORWAY
SWEDEN
1809
St. Petersburg
DEN.
GER.
CONFED.
POLAND
Moscow
RUSSIAN EMPIRE
Yenisei
Lena
Siberia
Yakutsk
Okhotsk
Kamchatka Pen.
Sakhalin
Kuril Is.
Irtish
Ob
Yeniseisk
MONGOLIA
SINKIANG
Peking
KOREA
JAPAN
Yedo
Constantinople
OTTOMAN EMPIRE
Crete
MANCHU EMPIRE (CHINA)
Hoang-ho
Deshima (Nagasaki)
1641-1859
RIA
30/48
Malta
1800
TUNIS
Cyprus
PERSIA
AFGHAN-ISTAN
TIBET
Ryu Kyu Is.
TRIPOLI
1822-40 to Egypt
Cairo
Delhi
NEPAL
Yangtze-kiang
Canton
Formosa
FEZZAN
EGYPT
1811 autonomous
Arabia
Indus
Chandernagore, 1815
Macao
Philippine Is.
h a r a
NUDIA
1820/22 to Egypt
Nile
ABYSSINIA
Diu
Daman
Bombay
INDIA
Calcutta
Serampore
Yanaon
SIAM
Mariana or Ladrone Is.
neg (Ft. Fredensborg)
1784
Congo
20
40
Goa
Mahe
Laccadive Is.
1791/1855
Pulicat
Pondicherry
Karikal
Andaman Is.
1789-96
Nagpur
ANNAM
Poulo Condore
1787
Caroline Is.
ernando
Poo
1827-43
ZANZIBAR
PORT E ST AFRICA
60
Maldive Is.
1815
Ceylon
1798/1815
Nicobar Is.
Pattani
1824
Malacca
1795/1819
Singapore
Borneo
Celebes
Halmahera
140
East from
160
Greenwich 180
P A C I F I C
Loando
ANGOLA
Seychelles
1769 to Fr.
1794 to Br.
Chagos Is.
1784
Sumatra
1824, Batang Kapas
1824, Benkulen
DUTCH EAST INDIES
Makassar
New Guinea
Timor
O C E A N
Sainte Marie
1818
Madagascar
I N D I A N
Batavia
Java
Bourbon,
(Réunion)
1810-14 to Br.
1814 to Fr.
Mauritius (I. de France)
1810
O C E A N
WESTERN AUSTRALIA
1829
NEW SOUTH WALES
1788
Delagoa Bay
Port Natal
1824-39
Cape Town
CAPE COL.
1806/14
Perth
Lord Howe I.
1788 to N.S.W.
Sydney
Crozet Is.
1772
Kerguelen
1772
VAN DIEMEN'S LAND
NEW ZEALAND
1814/40
Auckland Is.
1806
Macquarie Is.
1811 to Tasmania
Campbell I.
1810
O C E A N

Dutch Possessions

to Den. Danish Possessions

United States' Possessions

Russian Possessions

or period of possession

Spanish Possessions   Portuguese Possessions   British Possessions   French Possession

1842 *Date of acquisition or period of possession*   B. *Belgium*, BH. *Bhutan*, C. *Costa Ric*

MOLLWEIDE'S EQUAL AREA PROJECTION

AND STATES OF EUROPEAN ORIGIN, 1878

(2080 miles = 1 inch)

--- Danish Possessions   United States' Possessions   Dutch Possessions   Russian Possessions

G. Guatemala, H. Honduras, N. Netherlands, NIC. Nicaragua, O.F.S. Orange Free State, S. Salvador

British Empire ⟩ French Possessions ⟩ Spanish Possessions ⟩ Portuguese Possessions ⟩ United States' Possession

1914 *Date of acquisition*   A. *Albania*, B. *Belgium*, BH. *Bhutan*, C. *Costa Rica*, D.R. *Dominican Rep.(from 1905 U.S. special rights)*, G. *Guatemala*

P. *Panama (1903 indep.Rep*

MOLLWEIDE'S INTERRUPTED EQUAL AREA PROJECTION

1914

(2080 miles=1 inch)

H. *Honduras,* Haiti (from 1915 U.S. special rights), N. *Netherlands,* NIC. *Nicaragua* (1909/12 U.S. special rights, 1912 milit. occup.),
under U.S. Protection), S. *Salvador*

THE WORLD,

Equatorial Scale 1:130,000,000

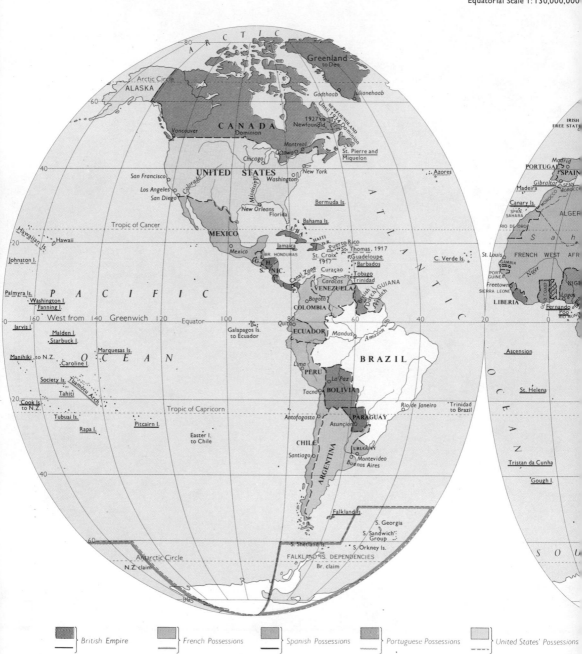

ARCTIC

80

Arctic Circle

ALASKA

60

Greenland
to Den.

Godthaab

Julianehaab

CANADA

Vancouver

Dominion

NEWFOUNDLAND
1927 to Dominion
Until 1933
Newfoundld.

Montreal

Ottawa

St. Pierre and
Miquelon

Chicago

UNITED STATES

New York

Washington

.:: Azores

MADRID
PORTUGAL SPAIN

IRISH
FREE STATE

San Francisco

Los Angeles
San Diego

Colorado

Mississippi

Madeira

Gibraltar
SPAIN

MOROCCO

New Orleans

Florida

Bermuda Is.

Canary Is.
SPAN
SAHARA

MOROCCO
ALGER

Tropic of Cancer

MEXICO

Bahama Is.

RIO DE ORO

Sah

Hawaiian Is.

Hawaii

Mexico

CUBA

HAITI

Puerto Rico

St. Thomas, 1917

St. Croix
1917

Guadeloupe

Barbados

C. Verde Is.

St. Louis

GAMBIA

FRENCH WEST AFR

Johnston I.

BR. HONDURAS

G.H.
S. NIC.

Curaçao

Tobago
Trinidad

Caracas

PORT
GUINEA
SIERRA LEONE

Freetown

NIG

Palmyra Is.

Washington I.
Fanning I.

Canal Zone

VENEZUELA

British
Dutch
French

GUIANA

LIBERIA

GOLD COAST

Lagos

Fernando
Poo

160

West from 140 Greenwich 120

Equator 100

COLOMBIA

Bogotá

60

40

20

P A C I F I C

Jarvis I.

Galapagos Is.
to Ecuador

Quito

ECUADOR

Mandus

Amazon

40

Ascension

Malden I.
Starbuck I.

Marquesas Is.

O C E A N

Manihiki
to N.Z.

Caroline I.

Lima

PERU

BRAZIL

St. Helena

Society Is.

Tahiti

Tuamotu Arch.

La Paz

BOLIVIA

Cook Is.
to N.Z.

Tacna

Rio de Janeiro

Trinidad
to Brazil

Tubuai Is.

Tropic of Capricorn

Antofagasta

PARAGUAY

Rapa I.

Pitcairn I.

Asunción

URUGUAY

Tristan da Cunha

Easter I.
to Chile

CHILE

Santiago

ARGENTINA

Montevideo
Buenos Aires

Gough I.

40

Falkland Is.

S. Georgia

S O U

60

Antarctic Circle

N.Z. claim

S. Shetland Is.

S. Sandwich
Group

S. Orkney Is.

FALKLAND IS. DEPENDENCIES

Br. claim

80

British Empire
French Possessions
Spanish Possessions
Portuguese Possessions
United States' Possessions

A. Albania, B. Belgium, BH. Bhutan, C. Costa Rica, CZ. Czechoslovakia, D.R. Dominican Rep., E. Estonia, G. Guatemala, H. Honduras,

1926

(2080 miles = 1 inch)

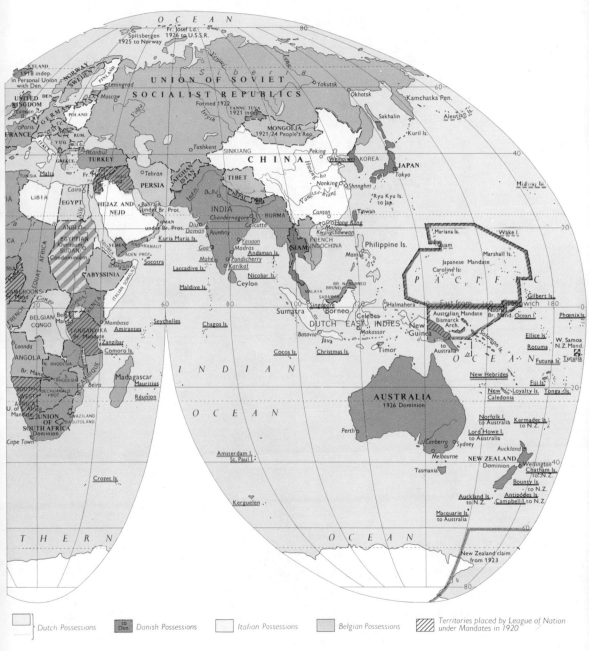

O C E A N

Fr. Josef Ld.
1926 to U.S.S.R.
Spitsbergen
1925 to Norway

ICELAND
1918 indep.
in Personal Union
with Den.

NORWAY SWEDEN FINLAND

UNITED KINGDOM
(London)

DEN.

U N I O N   O F   S O V I E T

Moscow   S i b e r i a   Yakutsk

Leningrad

FRANCE Paris

GERMANY POLAND CZ. AUS. HUNG.

S O C I A L I S T   R E P U B L I C S

Formed 1922

Okhotsk   Kamchatka Pen.

ITALY YUG. BULG. RUM.

Volga   Irtysh

Sakhalin   Kuril Is.

Aleutian Is.

Istanbul GREECE TURKEY

MONGOLIA
1921/24 People's Rep.

TANNU TUVA
1921 indep.

SINKIANG   Peking   Weihaiwei   KOREA

JAPAN

TUNISIA Malta

Tashkent

Fr. Mor.

PERSIA AFGHANISTAN

C H I N A

Hwang-ho

Tokyo

Midway Is.

Cairo   Tehran

TIBET

Nanking   Shanghai

Ryu Kyu Is.
to Jap.

LIBYA   EGYPT

HEJAZ AND
NEJD

Bahrein
under Br. Prot.

NEPAL

Indus

Delhi   BHUTAN

Yangtze-kiang

Canton   Taiwan

ANGLO-
EGYPTIAN
SUDAN
Condominium

OMAN
under Br. Prot.

Diu
Daman

INDIA   Chandernagore   BURMA

Kweichowkwan
Hong Kong
Macao

Kuria Muria Is.

FRENCH
INDOCHINA

Philippine Is.

Mariana Is.

Wake I.

YEMEN HADRAMAUT

ABYSSINIA

ADEN PROT.

Socotra

ITALIAN SOMALILD.
SOMALI.

Bombay

Goa   Madras

Mahe

Andaman Is.

Pondicherry
Karikal

Manila

Guam

Japanese Mandate

Marshall Is.

Laccadive Is.

Nicobar Is.

SIAM

Caroline Is.

P A C I F I C

CAMEROONS
Mand.

FRENCH
EQUAT. AFRICA

Congo

BELGIAN
CONGO

Beira Mand.

Maldive Is.

Ceylon

BR. N. BORNEO

MALAYA BRUNEI

SARAWAK

Halmahera

East from

Greenwich   180

Gilbert Is.

Mombasa
Br. Mandate

TANGANYIKA

Seychelles

Amirantes

Chagos Is.

Singapore   Borneo

Sumatra

Celebes

Makassar

Australian Mandate
Bismarck
Arch.

New
Guinea

Nauru
Br. Mand.

Ocean I.

Phoenix Is.

Ellice Is.

Rotuma

W. Samoa
N.Z. Mand.

Tutuila

ANGOLA

Zanzibar

Comoro Is.

Batavia

Java

Timor

Solomon Is.

to
Australia

Futuna Is.

Loanda

N. RHODESIA

Br. Mand.

S. RHODESIA

Madagascar

Mauritius

Cocos Is.

Christmas Is.

O C E A N

New Hebrides

Fiji Is.

SOUTH
WEST
AFRICA
U. of S. Africa
Mandate

BECHUANALAND
PROT.

SWAZILAND

UNION
OF
SOUTH AFRICA
Dominion

BASUTOLAND

Réunion

A U S T R A L I A
1926 Dominion

New
Caledonia

Loyalty Is. Tonga Is.

Cape Town

Perth

Canberra   Sydney

Norfolk I.
to Australia

Kermadec Is.
to N.Z.

Lord Howe I.
to Australia

Amsterdam I.
St. Paul I.

Melbourne

Auckland

NEW ZEALAND
Dominion

Wellington
Chatham Is.
to N.Z.

Crozet Is.

I N D I A N   O C E A N

Tasmania

Bounty Is.
to N.Z.

Kerguelen

Auckland Is.
to N.Z.

Antipodes Is.
Campbell I. to N.Z.

Macquarie Is.
to Australia

T H E R N

O C E A N

New Zealand claim
from 1923

Dutch Possessions	Danish Possessions (to Den)	Italian Possessions	Belgian Possessions	Territories placed by League of Nation under Mandates in 1920

L. *Lithuania*, LA. *Latvia*, N. *Netherlands*, NIC. *Nicaragua* (*until 1933 milit. occup.*), P. *Panama*, PAL. *Palestine*, S. *Salvador*, TJ. *Transjordan*

THE WORLD,

Equatorial Scale 1:130,000,000

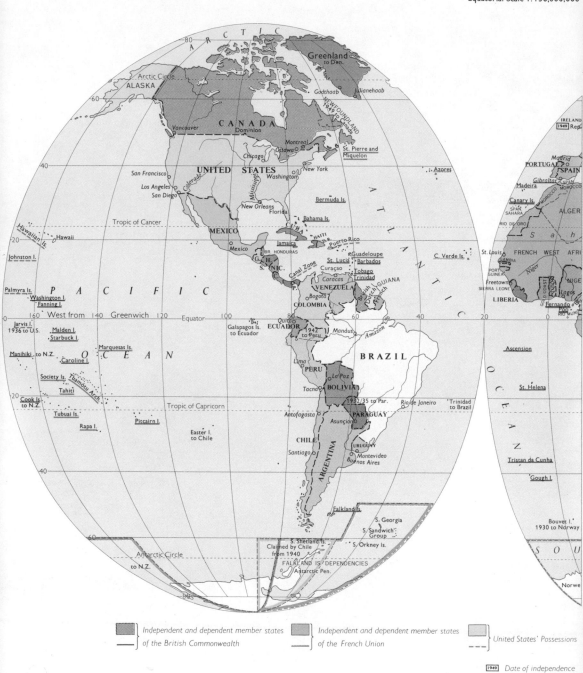

ARCTIC
80
Greenland
to Den.
Arctic Circle
ALASKA
60
Godthaab
Julianehaab
NEWFOUNDLAND
1949 Canada
CANADA
Dominion
Vancouver
Montreal
St. Pierre and
Miquelon
Ottawa
Chicago
40
San Francisco
UNITED STATES
New York
Washington
Los Angeles
Colorado
Azores
San Diego
Bermuda Is.
New Orleans
Tropic of Cancer
Florida
MEXICO
Bahama Is.
20
Hawaiian Is.
Hawaii
CUBA
HAITI
Mexico
Jamaica
D.R.
Puerto Rico
Johnston I.
BR. HONDURAS
Guadeloupe
G. H.
St. Lucia
Barbados
S. NIC.
Curaçao
Tobago
Palmyra Is.
Canal Zone
Trinidad
Washington I.
P.
VENEZUELA
DUTCH GUIANA
Fanning I.
French
PACIFIC
COLOMBIA
0
160 West from 140 Greenwich 120
Equator 100
80
60
40
20
Jarvis I.
Quito
1942
1936 to U.S.
Galapagos Is.
ECUADOR
to Peru
Mandus
Amazon
Malden I.
to Ecuador
Starbuck I.
Manihiki to N.Z.
Marquesas Is.
BRAZIL
Caroline I.
OCEAN
PERU
Lima
La Paz
Society Is.
Tuamotu Arch.
BOLIVIA
Tahiti
Tacna
Rio de Janeiro
Trinidad
20
Cook Is.
1932/35 to Par.
to Brazil
to N.Z.
Tropic of Capricorn
Antofagasta
PARAGUAY
Tubuai Is.
Pitcairn I.
Asunción
Rapa I.
Easter I.
URUGUAY
to Chile
CHILE
Montevideo
Santiago
Buenos Aires
ARGENTINA
40
Falkland Is.
S. Georgia
S. Sandwich
Group
60
S. Shetland Is.
S. Orkney Is.
Claimed by Chile
from 1940
Antarctic Circle
FALKLAND IS. DEPENDENCIES
to N.Z.
Antarctic Pen.

IRELAND
1949 Rep.
Madrid
PORTUGAL
SPAIN
Madeira
Gibraltar
SPAIN
MOROCCO
Canary Is.
ALGER
SPAN.
SAHARA
RIO DE ORO
Sahar
FRENCH WEST AFRI
St. Louis
GAMBIA
C. Verde Is.
PORT.
GUINEA
NIGE
Freetown
SIERRA LEONE
GOLD COAST
Lagos
LIBERIA
Fernando
RIO MUNI

Ascension

St. Helena

Tristan da Cunha

Gough I.

Bouver I.
1930 to Norway

SOU

Norwe

Independent and dependent member states
of the British Commonwealth

Independent and dependent member states
of the French Union

United States' Possessions

1949 Date of independence

A. Albania, B. Belgium, BH. Bhutan, C. Costa Rica, CAM. Cambodia, C.Z. Czechoslovakia, D.R. Dominican Rep., G. Guatemala,

1950

(2080 miles=1 inch)

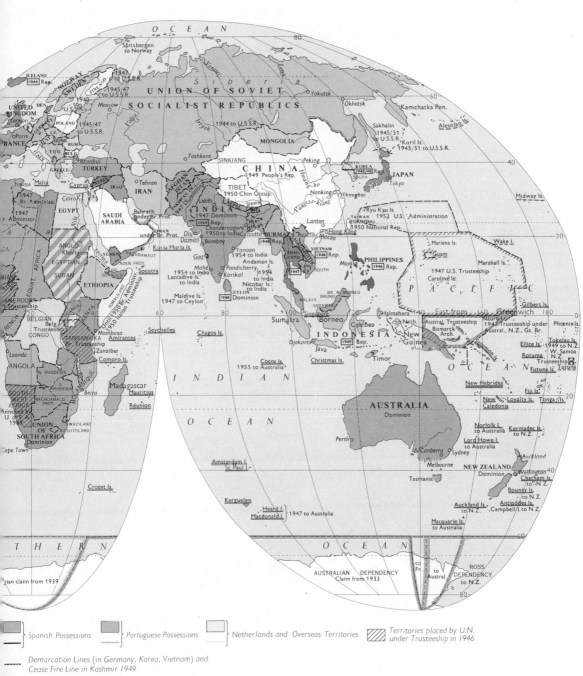

O C E A N
Spitsbergen
to Norway

ICELAND
1944 Rep.
NORWAY
SWEDEN
FINLAND 1947 to U.S.S.R.
1945/47 to U.S.S.R.
1940
UNITED KINGDOM
DEN.
U.S.S.R.
Moscow
UNION OF SOVIET
SOCIALIST REPUBLICS
Yakutsk
Okhotsk
Kamchatka Pen.
London
Paris
POLAND 1945/47 to U.S.S.R.
Volga
Irtysh
1944 to U.S.S.R.
Aleutian Is.
FRANCE
YUG.
RUM.
BULG.
Istanbul
TURKEY
Tashkent
SINKIANG
Peking
MONGOLIA
Sakhalin 1945/51 to U.S.S.R.
Kuril Is. 1945/51 to U.S.S.R.
TUNISIA Malta
GREECE
Cyprus
IRAQ
IRAN
Tehran
AFGHAN-ISTAN
CHINA
1949 People's Rep.
NORTH KOREA 1945/48
SOUTH
Rad
JAPAN
Tokyo
Midway Is.
1947 Br. Administr.
Cairo
SAUDI ARABIA
Bahrain under Br. Prot.
PAKISTAN 1950 Dominion
Delhi
TIBET 1950 Chin Occup.
Nanking
Shanghai
Hwang-ho
Yangtse-kiang
Ryu Kyu Is. 1952 U.S. Administration
EGYPT
r. Administr.
OMAN under Br. Prot.
INDIA 1947 Dominion
SIKKIM
TAIWAN (FORMOSA) 1950 National Rep.
Wake I.
YEMEN
HADHRAMAUT
Diu 1950 to India
Bombay
Daman
Chandernagore 1950 to India
Calcutta
BURMA 1948 Rep.
Canton
Hong Kong
Macao
Mariana Is.
Guam
ANGLO-EGYPTIAN SUDAN
Khartoum
ERITREA
ADEN PROT.
Goa
Yanaon 1954 to India
Andaman Is.
VIETNAM 1946 Rep.
THAI-LAND
SOUTH
Manila
PHILIPPINES 1946 Rep.
Marshall Is.
Socotra
SOMALILAND
Mahé 1954 to India
Pondicherry
Karikal 1954 to India
Nicobar Is.
1947
1947 U.S. Trusteeship
Caroline Is.
ETHIOPIA
Laccadive Is. 1954 to India
CEYLON 1948 Dominion
BR. N. BORNEO
MALAYA
SARAWAK
P A C I F I C
Maldive Is. 1947 to Ceylon
Seychelles
Chagos Is.
Sumatra
Borneo
Celebes
Halmahera to Neth.
Austral. Trusteeship
Bismarck Arch.
Nauru 1947 Trusteeship under Austral., N.Z., Gt. Br.
Gilbert Is.
Phoenix Is.
BELGIAN CONGO
Belg. Trusteeship
TANGANYIKA Br. Trusteeship
Mombasa
Amirantes
Zanzibar
Comoro Is.
Djakarta
INDONESIA 1949 Rep.
Java
New Guinea
PAPUA
Solomon Is.
Ellice Is. 1949 to N.Z.
W. Samoa N.Z. Trusteeship
Rotuma N.Z.
Tutuila
Loanda
ANGOLA
N. RHODESIA
S. RHODESIA
Madagascar
Mauritius
Cocos Is. 1955 to Australia
Christmas Is.
Timor
I N D I A N
O C E A N
New Hebrides
Fiji Is.
Futuna Is.
SOUTH WEST AFRICA
Annexed by U.S.A. 1949
BECHUANALAND PROT.
UNION OF SOUTH AFRICA Dominion
Beira
MOZAMBIQUE
SWAZILAND
BASUTOLAND
Réunion
AUSTRALIA Dominion
New Caledonia
Loyalty Is.
Tonga Is.
Cape Town
Amsterdam I.
St. Paul I.
Perth
Canberra
Sydney
Melbourne
Norfolk I. to Australia
Lord Howe I. to Australia
Kermadec Is. to N.Z.
Crozet Is.
Kerguelen
Heard I.
Macdonald I. 1947 to Australia
Tasmania
NEW ZEALAND Dominion
Wellington
Auckland
Chatham Is. to N.Z.
Bounty Is. to N.Z.
Antipodes Is.
Auckland Is. to N.Z.
Campbell I. to N.Z.
Macquarie Is. to Australia
S O U T H E R N
O C E A N
to Fr.
to Austral.
AUSTRALIAN DEPENDENCY Claim from 1933
ROSS DEPENDENCY to N.Z.
gian claim from 1939

Spanish Possessions
Portuguese Possessions
Netherlands and Overseas Territories
Territories placed by U.N. under Trusteeship in 1946

Demarcation Lines (in Germany, Korea, Vietnam) and Cease Fire Line in Kashmir 1949

H. Honduras, I. Israel, J. Jordan, L. Lebanon, N. Netherlands, NIC. Nicaragua, P. Panama, S. Salvador, Sikkim (1947 independent, 1950 Indian Prot.)

THE WORLD: ACHIEVEMENT

Equatorial Scale 1:130,000,000

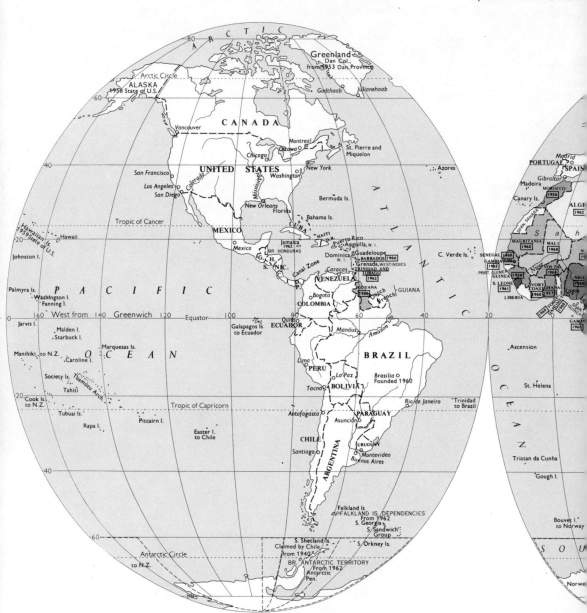

All states which attained independence after 1945 are coloured;

1946 *Date of independence after 1945*

A. *Albania*, B. *Belgium*, BH. *Bhutan*, BU. *Burundi*, C. *Costa Rica*, CAM. *Cambodia*, CZ. *Czechoslovakia*, D.R. *Dominican Rep.*, G. *Guatemala*,

W.I. *West Indies, Associated States*

MOLLWEIDE'S INTERRUPTED EQUAL AREA PROJECTION

OF INDEPENDENCE, 1945–68

(2080 miles = 1 inch)

names of small islands which became independent are underlined in red

—— Demarcation Lines (in Germany, Korea, Vietnam) and Cease Fire Line in Kashmir 1949

H. Honduras, I. Israel, J. Jordan, L. Lebanon, M. Malawi, N. Netherlands, NIC. Nicaragua, P. Panama, R. Rwanda, S. Salvador, Sikkim (Indian Prot.),

with United Kingdom from 1967

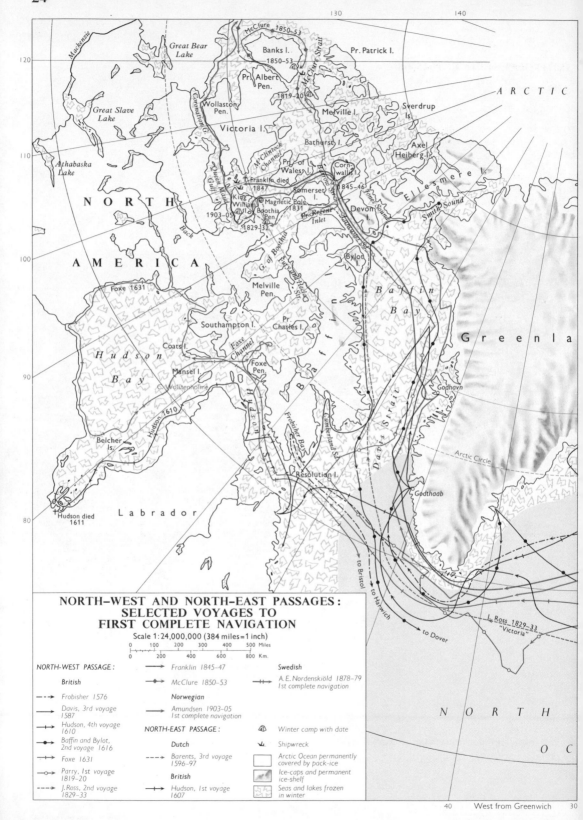

**NORTH–WEST AND NORTH-EAST PASSAGES:
SELECTED VOYAGES TO
FIRST COMPLETE NAVIGATION**

Scale 1:24,000,000 (384 miles=1 inch)

0   100   200   300   400   500 Miles
0   200   400   600   800 Km.

NORTH-WEST PASSAGE:

British

- - -→ *Frobisher 1576*
———→ *Davis, 3rd voyage 1587*
↦→ *Hudson, 4th voyage 1610*
●—●→ *Baffin and Bylot, 2nd voyage 1616*
++—→ *Foxe 1631*
○—○→ *Parry, 1st voyage 1819–20*
-·-·→ *J. Ross, 2nd voyage 1829–33*

———→ *Franklin 1845–47*
◆—◆→ *McClure 1850–53*

Norwegian

———→ *Amundsen 1903–05 1st complete navigation*

NORTH-EAST PASSAGE:

Dutch

- - -→ *Barents, 3rd voyage 1596–97*

British

++—→ *Hudson, 1st voyage 1607*

Swedish

++—→ *A. E. Nordenskiöld 1878–79 1st complete navigation*

⛺ *Winter camp with date*

⚓ *Shipwreck*

▢ *Arctic Ocean permanently covered by pack-ice*

▨ *Ice-caps and permanent ice-shelf*

▨ *Seas and lakes frozen in winter*

† Barents died 1597

Kara Sea

North Pole

Franz Josef Land

O C E A N

Noyaya Zemlya

Kolguyev I.

B a r e n t s   S e a

White Sea

N. Dvina

Spitsbergen (Svalbard)

Kola Pen.

Greenland Sea

Bear I.

Trømsø

A.E. Nordenskiöld 1878–79 "Vega"

L. Onega

L. Ladoga

Jan Mayen

Hudson 1607

Barents 1596–97

S c a n d i n a v i a

G. of Bothnia

G. of Finland

N o r w e g i a n

S e a

Christiania (Oslo)

Baltic Sea

Vistula

Denmark Str.

Iceland
Reykjavik

Hudson 1610

Oder

Frobisher 1576

Faroe Is.

Shetland Is.

Franklin 1845–47 "Erebus", "Terror"

North Sea

Amundsen 1903–05 "Gjöa"

Parry 1819–20 "Hecla", "Griper"

Amsterdam

Foxe 1631

Rhine

Hudson 1607

Harwich

Baffin and Bylot 1616

B r i t i s h   I s l e s

Dover

Davis 1587

London

Bristol

A T L A N T I C

Dartmouth

O C E A N

Rhône

E U R O P E

East from Greenwich

140 150 West from 160 Greenwich 170 180 170 East from 160 Greenwich 150 140

PACIFIC OCEAN
Bering Sea
Sea of Okhotsk

U. S.
Alaska
Yukon
1878-79

Wrangel I.
de Long 1879-81
Jeannette
Chelyuskin 1933-34

S i b e r i a

U. S. S. R.

Point Barrow
1903-05
Amundsen "Gjöa"
Amundsen Airship 1926 Norge

Mackenzie
Gt. Bear L.

Beaufort Sea

Amundsen 1926 Airship "Norge"
Baf. defined 1925
Wilkins 1928

New Siberian Is.
de Long died 1881

Sedov 1937-40
Sibiriakov 1932

Lena

1905
Banks I.
Victoria I.
Pr. Patrick I.
Melville I.
Magnetic Pole 1960
Pr. of Wales I.
1903-05
Sverdrup Is.
Axel Heiberg I.
Devon
Ellesmere I.

ARCTIC OCEAN

North Pole

Nansen 1893-96 Fram
Severnaya Zemlya

Yenisei

C A N A D A

Peary 1909

Byrd 1926
Cagni 1901

Franz Josef Land

Ob

Baffin Bay
Peary 1891-92
Davis Str.
Godhavn
Godthaab
Nansen 1888
French expedition 1949-51
Wegener 1930-31
Koch-Wegener 1912-13
Ice-centre Station
Papanin 1937-41

G r e e n l a n d

Spitsbergen (Svalbard)
Bear I.
Greenland Sea
Jan Mayen

Novaya Zemlya

Barents Sea

A. E. Nordenskiöld 1878-79
Vardö
Murmansk
Kola Pen.
White
Arkhangelsk

ICELAND
Reykjavik

Amundsen 1903-05 "Gjöa"

Norwegian Sea
Tromsö

N O R W A Y
SWEDEN
FINLAND
G. of Bothnia

Arctic Circle

ATLANTIC OCEAN

30 20 10 0 10 20 30

40 50 60 70 80 90 100 110 120 130 140

NORTH POLAR REGIONS : EXPLORATION

Scale 1:40,000,000 (640 miles=1 inch)

0 200 400 600 800 Miles
0 200 400 800 1200 Km.

EXPLORATION:

North-West Passage:

→ Amundsen (Norwegian) 1903-05 1st complete navigation

North-East Passage:

→ A.E.Nordenskiöld (Swedish) 1878-79, 1st complete navigation

→ de Long (U.S.) 1879-81

● Track of the "Sibiriakov" (U.S.S.R.) 1932

→ Track of the "Chelyuskin" (U.S.S.R.) 1933-34

Polar Regions:

→ Nansen (Norwegian) 1893-96

+ Cagni (Italian) 1901

→ Peary (U.S.) April 6th, 1909 Pole reached for the 1st time

→ Byrd (U.S.) May 9th, 1926 Pole first reached by aeroplane

→ Amundsen (Norwegian) by airship 1926

→ Wilkins (Australian) by aeroplane 1928

→ Track of the "Sedov" (U.S.S.R.) 1937-40

--- Track of expedition under Papanin (U.S.S.R.) 1937-41

Greenland:

● Nansen (Norwegian) 1888 Greenland crossed for the 1st time

● Peary (U.S.) 1891-92

◇ Koch-Wegener (Danish-German) 1912-13

■ Wegener (German) 1930-31

····· French expedition 1949-51

····· Expeditions over land or ice

Winter camp with date
Shipwreck

Arctic Ocean permanently covered by pack-ice

Ice-caps and permanent ice-shelf

Seas and lakes frozen in winter

SPHERES OF INFLUENCE:

U.S. U.S.S.R.
Canada Norway
Denmark

COPYRIGHT. GEORGE PHILIP & SON, LTD.

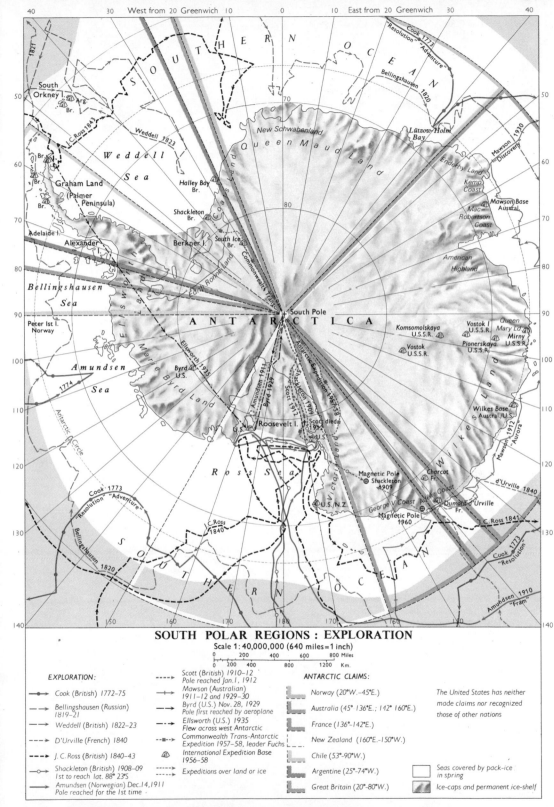

SOUTH POLAR REGIONS : EXPLORATION

Scale 1 : 40,000,000 (640 miles = 1 inch)

0   200   400   600   800 Miles
0   200   400   600   800   1200 Km.

EXPLORATION:

→ Cook (British) 1772–75

→ Bellingshausen (Russian) 1819–21

→ Weddell (British) 1822–23

–→ D'Urville (French) 1840

–•–→ J. C. Ross (British) 1840–43

–○→ Shackleton (British) 1908–09
1st to reach lat. 88° 23'S

→ Amundsen (Norwegian) Dec.14,1911
Pole reached for the 1st time

––→ Scott (British) 1910–12
Pole reached Jan.1, 1912

–↑→ Mawson (Australian)
1911–12 and 1929–30

→ Byrd (U.S.) Nov. 28, 1929
Pole first reached by aeroplane

–•–•– Ellsworth (U.S.) 1935
Flew across west Antarctic

–■–■– Commonwealth Trans-Antarctic
Expedition 1957–58, leader Fuchs

⌂ International Expedition Base
1956–58

⋯⋯⋯ Expeditions over land or ice

ANTARCTIC CLAIMS:

Norway (20°W.–45°E.)

Australia (45° 136°E.; 142° 160°E.)

France (136°–142°E.)

New Zealand (160°E.–150°W.)

Chile (53°–90°W.)

Argentine (25°–74°W.)

Great Britain (20°–80°W.)

The United States has neither made claims nor recognized those of other nations

☐ Seas covered by pack-ice in spring

▨ Ice-caps and permanent ice-shelf

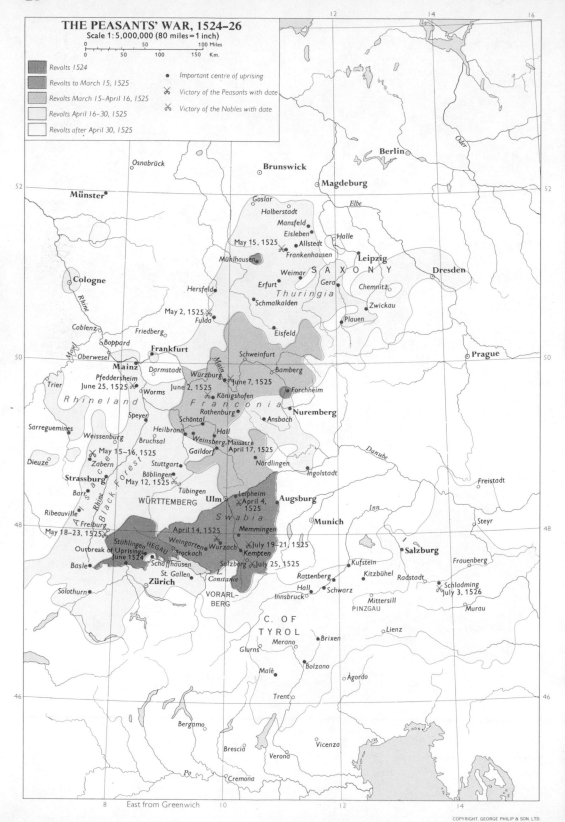

THE PEASANTS' WAR, 1524–26
Scale 1:5,000,000 (80 miles = 1 inch)

0   50   100   150 Km.
0   50   100 Miles

Revolts 1524
Revolts to March 15, 1525
Revolts March 15–April 16, 1525
Revolts April 16–30, 1525
Revolts after April 30, 1525

• Important centre of uprising
✗ Victory of the Peasants with date
✗ Victory of the Nobles with date

Osnabrück
Brunswick
Münster
Magdeburg
Berlin
Oder
Goslar
Halberstadt
Mansfeld
Eisleben
Halle
May 15, 1525
Allstedt
Mühlhausen
Frankenhausen
Leipzig
Dresden
Weimar
S A X O N Y
Cologne
Hersfeld
Erfurt
Gera
Chemnitz
Thuringia
Rhine
Schmalkalden
Zwickau
Coblenz
May 2, 1525
Fulda
Eisfeld
Plauen
Prague
Friedberg
Boppard
Oberwesel
Frankfurt
Schweinfurt
Mosel
Mainz
Darmstadt
Würzburg
June 7, 1525
Bamberg
Trier
Pfeddersheim
June 25, 1525
Worms
June 2, 1525
Königshofen
Forchheim
Rhineland
Speyer
Rothenburg
Ansbach
Nuremberg
Franconia
Schöntal
Sarreguemines
Weissenburg
Heilbronn
Hall
Bruchsal
Weinsberg, Massacre
April 17, 1525
Dieuze
May 15–16, 1525
Zabern
Gaildorf
Nördlingen
Stuttgart
Ingolstadt
Danube
Strassburg
Böblingen
May 12, 1525
Freistadt
Barr
Tübingen
Ulm
Leipheim
April 4, 1525
Augsburg
Ribeauville
WÜRTTEMBERG
Swabia
Inn
Steyr
Freiburg
April 14, 1525
Memmingen
Munich
May 18–23, 1525
Stühlingen HEGAU
Weingarten
Wurzach
July 19–21, 1525
Salzburg
Outbreak of Uprising
June 1524
Stockach
Kempten
July 25, 1525
Kufstein
Frauenberg
Basle
Schaffhausen
Sulzberg
Rattenberg
Kitzbühel
Radstadt
St. Gallen
L.
Constance
Hall
Schwarz
Schladming
July 3, 1526
Solothurn
Zürich
VORARL-
BERG
Innsbruck
Mittersill
PINZGAU
Murau
C. OF
TYROL
Lienz
Merano
Brixen
Glurns
Malè
Bolzano
Àgordo
Trent
Bergamo
Vicenza
Brescia
Verona
Po
Cremona

East from Greenwich

COPYRIGHT. GEORGE PHILIP & SON. LTD.

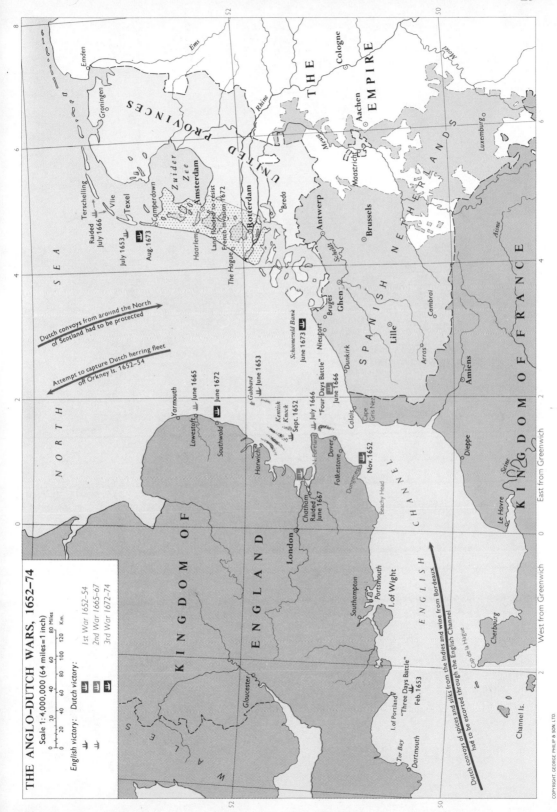

THE ANGLO-DUTCH WARS, 1652–74

Scale 1:4,000,000 (64 miles=1 inch)

0 20 40 60 80 Miles
0 20 40 60 80 100 120 Km.

English victory: Dutch victory:
⚓ ⚓ ⚓   ⚓ ⚓ ⚓

1st War 1652–54
2nd War 1665–67
3rd War 1672–74

THE EMPIRE

Cologne
Aachen
Luxemburg

UNITED PROVINCES

Emden
Groningen
Ems
Rhine
Terschelling
Vlie
Texel
Raided July 1666
July 1653 ⚓
Aug. 1673 ⚓
Camperdown
Zuider Zee
Amsterdam
Haarlem
Land flooded to resist French invasion 1672
The Hague
Rotterdam
Breda

SPANISH NETHERLANDS

Antwerp
Brussels
Ghent
Bruges
Schelde
Nieuport
Dunkirk
Lille
Arras
Cambrai
Amiens
Maastricht
Meuse
Schoneveld Bank June 1673 ⚓

KINGDOM OF FRANCE

Aisne
Moser
Dieppe
Le Havre
Seine
Cherbourg
Channel Is.
East from Greenwich
West from Greenwich

NORTH SEA

Dutch convoys from around the North of Scotland had to be protected →

← Attempt to capture Dutch herring fleet off Orkney Is. 1652–54

Yarmouth
June 1665 ⚓
June 1672 ⚓
Lowestoft
Southwold
Harwich
Gabbard ⚓ June 1653
Kentish Knock Sept. 1652 ⚓
July 1666 ⚓ "Four Days Battle" June 1666
N. Foreland
Dover
Folkestone
Dungeness ⚓ Nov. 1652
Calais
Cape Gris Nez
Beachy Head
Chatham Raided June 1667
London

KINGDOM OF ENGLAND

Gloucester
Southampton
Portsmouth
I. of Wight

WALES

I. of Portland
Tor Bay
Dartmouth

ENGLISH CHANNEL

"Three Days Battle" Feb. 1653

Dutch convoys of spices and silks from the Indies and wine from Bordeaux had to be escorted through the English Channel →

Cap de la Hague

COPYRIGHT GEORGE PHILIP & SON. LTD.

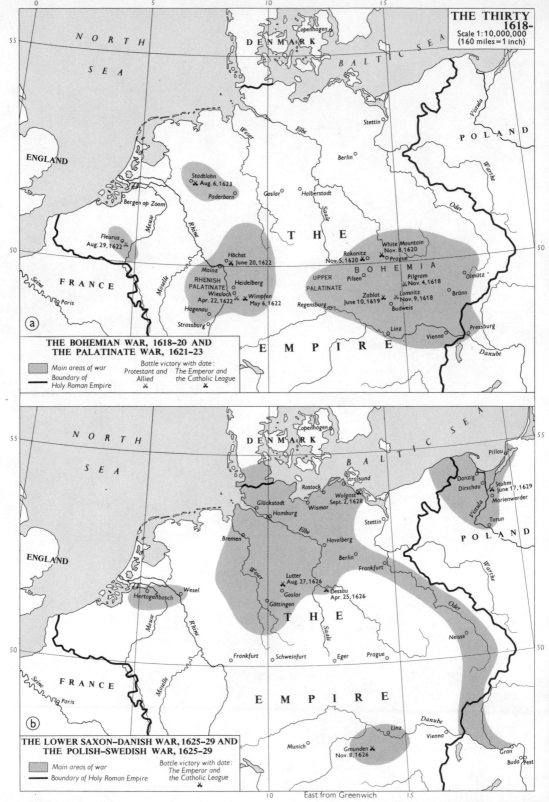

THE THIRTY
1618-
Scale 1:10,000,000
(160 miles = 1 inch)

N O R T H

S E A

DENMARK

B A L T I C   S E A

Copenhagen

ENGLAND

Stettin

POLAND

Berlin

Weser

Elbe

Saale

Oder

Vistula

Warthe

Stadtlohn
Aug. 6, 1623

Paderborn

Goslar

Halberstadt

T H E

Bergen op Zoom

Meuse

Rhine

Fleurus
Aug. 29, 1622

White Mountain
Nov. 8, 1620
Prague

Rakonitz
Nov. 5, 1620

FRANCE

Höchst
June 20, 1622

Mainz

RHENISH
PALATINATE

Heidelberg

Wiesloch
Apr. 22, 1622

Wimpfen
May 6, 1622

Hagenau

Strassburg

B O H E M I A

UPPER
PALATINATE

Pilsen

Regensburg

Zablat
June 10, 1619

Budweis

Pilgram
Nov. 4, 1618

Lomnitz
Nov. 9, 1618

Olmütz

Brünn

Seine

Paris

Moselle

(a)

Linz

Vienna

Pressburg

E M P I R E

Danube

**THE BOHEMIAN WAR, 1618–20 AND
THE PALATINATE WAR, 1621–23**

Main areas of war

**Boundary of
Holy Roman Empire**

Battle victory with date:
*Protestant and   The Emperor and
Allied   the Catholic League*
✕   ✕

N O R T H

S E A

DENMARK

B A L T I C   S E A

Copenhagen

Pillau

Rostock

Stralsund

Danzig

Dirschau

Stuhm
June 17, 1629

Marienwerder

Glückstadt

Wismar

Wolgast
Sept. 2, 1628

Homburg

Stettin

Torun

ENGLAND

Bremen

Havelberg

Vistula

POLAND

Warthe

Hertogenbosch

Wesel

Weser

Elbe

Berlin

Frankfurt

Oder

Meuse

Rhine

Lutter
Aug. 27, 1626

Goslar

Dessau
Apr. 25, 1626

Göttingen

Saale

T H E

Neisse

FRANCE

Frankfurt

Schweinfurt

Eger

Prague

Seine

Moselle

(b)

E M P I R E

Munich

Gmunden
Nov. 8, 1626

Linz

Danube

Vienna

Gran

Buda
Pest

Paris

**THE LOWER SAXON–DANISH WAR, 1625–29 AND
THE POLISH–SWEDISH WAR, 1625–29**

Main areas of war

Boundary of Holy Roman Empire

Battle victory with date:
*The Emperor and
the Catholic League*
✕

East from Greenwich

COPYRIGHT. GEORGE PHILIP & SON. LTD.

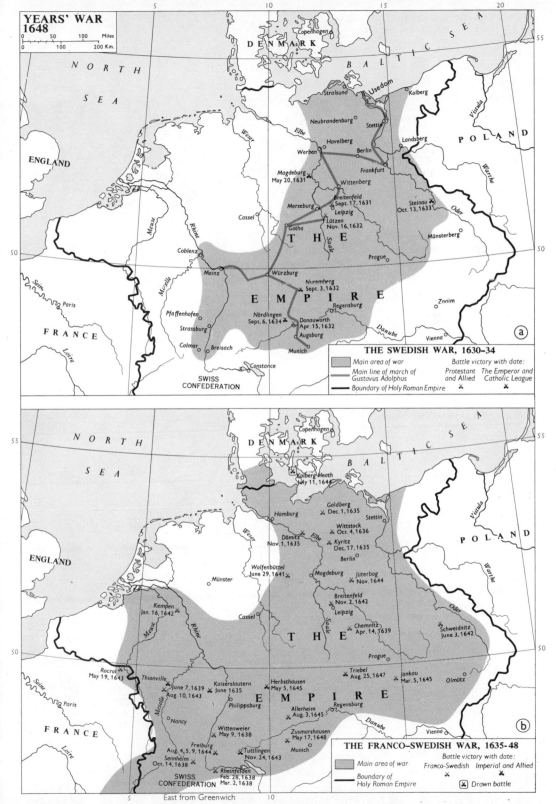

YEARS' WAR
1648

Miles
100
0   100   200 Km.

NORTH SEA

BALTIC SEA

DENMARK

Copenhagen

POLAND

ENGLAND

Stralsund   Usedom
Kolberg
Neubrandenburg   Stettin
Landsberg
Havelberg   Berlin
Werben
Frankfurt

Magdeburg
May 20, 1631   Wittenberg
Breitenfeld
Sept. 17, 1631   Steinau
Merseburg   Leipzig   Oct. 13, 1633
Gotha   Lützen
Nov. 16, 1632   Münsterberg

Coblenz   **THE**   Prague

Mainz   Würzburg
Nuremberg
Sept. 3, 1632   Znnim
Pfaffenhofen   **EMPIRE**   Regensburg
Nördlingen   Donauwörth
Sept. 6, 1634   Apr. 15, 1632
Strassburg   Augsburg   Vienna
Colmar   Breisach   Munich

Constance   (a)

SWISS CONFEDERATION

THE SWEDISH WAR, 1630–34

Main area of war   Battle victory with date:
Main line of march of   Protestant   The Emperor and
Gustavus Adolphus   and Allied   Catholic League
Boundary of Holy Roman Empire   ✕   ✕

NORTH SEA

BALTIC SEA

DENMARK

Copenhagen

Kolberg-Heath
July 11, 1644

POLAND

ENGLAND

Goldberg
Hamburg   Dec. 1, 1635   Stettin
Wittstock
Oct. 4, 1636
Dömitz   Kyritz
Nov. 1, 1635   Dec. 17, 1635
Berlin
Wolfenbüttel
June 29, 1641   Magdeburg   Jüterbog
Münster   Nov. 1644
Breitenfeld
Nov. 2, 1642   Schweidnitz
Kempen   Leipzig   June 3, 1642
Jan. 16, 1642   Cassel   **THE**
Chemnitz
Apr. 14, 1639
Prague

Rocroi   Triebel   Jankau
May 19, 1643   Aug. 25, 1647   Mar. 5, 1645
Thionville   **EMPIRE**   Olmütz
June 7, 1639   Kaiserslautern   Herbsthausen
Aug. 10, 1643   June 1635   May 5, 1645
Nancy   Philippsburg   Regensburg
Allerheim
Aug. 3, 1645
Wittenweier   Zusmarshausen   Vienna
May 9, 1638   May 17, 1648   (b)
Freiburg   Munich
Aug. 4, 5, 9, 1644   Tuttlingen
Sennheim   Nov. 24, 1643
Oct. 14, 1638   Rheinfelden
Feb. 28, 1638
Mar. 2, 1638

SWISS CONFEDERATION

East from Greenwich

THE FRANCO–SWEDISH WAR, 1635-48

Main area of war   Battle victory with date:
Franco-Swedish   Imperial and Allied
Boundary of   ✕   ✕
Holy Roman Empire   ✕ Drawn battle

COPYRIGHT. GEORGE PHILIP & SON, LTD.

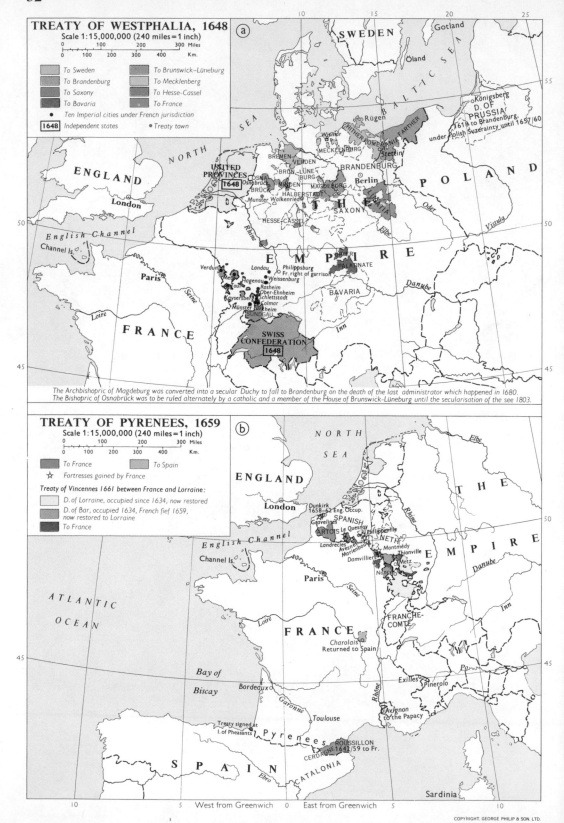

TREATY OF WESTPHALIA, 1648

Scale 1:15,000,000 (240 miles = 1 inch)

0 100 200 300 Miles
0 100 200 300 400 Km.

- To Sweden
- To Brandenburg
- To Saxony
- To Bavaria
- To Brunswick–Lüneburg
- To Mecklenberg
- To Hesse-Cassel
- To France
- Ten Imperial cities under French jurisdiction
- 1648 Independent states
- Treaty town

SWEDEN
Gotland
Öland
NORTH SEA
BALTIC SEA
Rügen
Wismar
HITHER POMERANIA FARTHER
Königsberg
D. OF PRUSSIA
1618 to Brandenburg, under Polish Suzerainty until 1657/60
MECKLENBURG
Stettin
BREMEN VERDEN
BRANDENBURG
BRUN-LÜNE BURG
Berlin
POLAND
ENGLAND
London
UNITED PROVINCES
1648
OSNA BRÜCK
Osnabrück
MINDEN
MAGDEBURG
Münster Wolkenried
HALBERSTADT
HESSE-CASSEL
T H E
SAXONY
Oder
Elbe
Vistula
English Channel
Channel Is.
Rhine
E M P I R E
Verdun
Landau
Philippsburg
Fr. right of garrison
PALATINATE
Paris
Metz Hagenau
Toul Weissenburg
Rosheim
Ober-Ehnheim
Kaysersberg Schlettstadt
Colmar
Münster Türkheim
SUNDGAU
BAVARIA
Danube
Seine
Loire
Inn
FRANCE
SWISS CONFEDERATION
1648

The Archbishopric of Magdeburg was converted into a secular Duchy to fall to Brandenburg on the death of the last administrator which happened in 1680.
The Bishopric of Osnabrück was to be ruled alternately by a catholic and a member of the House of Brunswick-Lüneburg until the secularisation of the see 1803.

TREATY OF PYRENEES, 1659

Scale 1:15,000,000 (240 miles = 1 inch)

0 100 200 300 Miles
0 100 200 300 400 Km.

- To France
- To Spain
- ☆ Fortresses gained by France

Treaty of Vincennes 1661 between France and Lorraine:
- D. of Lorraine, occupied since 1634, now restored
- D. of Bar, occupied 1634, French fief 1659, now restored to Lorraine
- To France

NORTH SEA
ENGLAND
London
Dunkirk
1658-62 Eng. Occup.
Gravelines
SPANISH
ARTOIS
Le Quesnoy
NETH
Landrecies
Avesnes Philippeville
Marienbourg
Montmédy
Damvilliers
Thionville
Metz
Nancy
T H E
E M P I R E
Rhine
Danube
Inn
English Channel
Channel Is.
FRANCHE-COMTE
ATLANTIC OCEAN
Paris
Seine
Loire
FRANCE
Charolais
Returned to Spain
Bay of
Biscay
Bordeaux
Garonne
Toulouse
Rhône
Exilles
Pinerolo
Avignon
to the Papacy
Treaty signed at
I. of Pheasants
P y r e n e e s
ROUSSILLON
CERDAGNE 1642/59 to Fr.
S P A I N
CATALONIA
Ebro
Sardinia

10 5 West from Greenwich 0 East from Greenwich 5 10

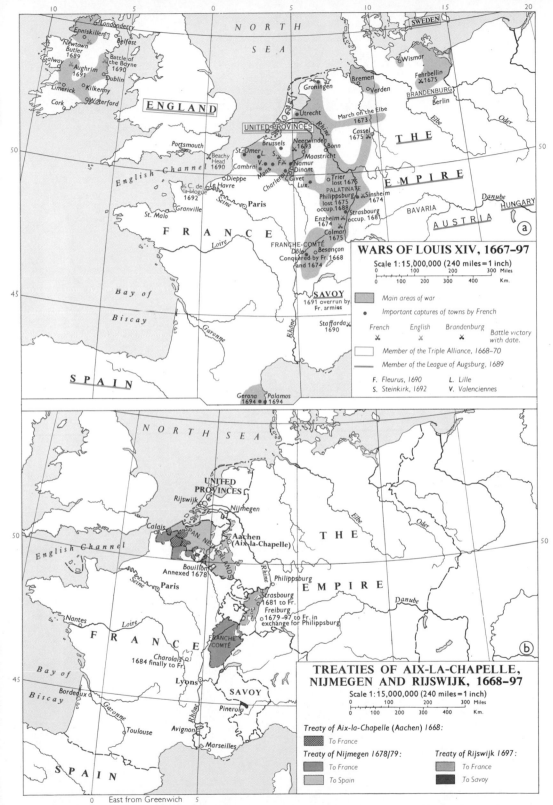

WARS OF LOUIS XIV, 1667–97

Scale 1:15,000,000 (240 miles = 1 inch)

0 100 200 300 Miles

0 100 200 300 400 Km.

Main areas of war

● Important captures of towns by French

French ✗ English ✗ Brandenburg ✗ Battle victory with date.

Member of the Triple Alliance, 1668–70

Member of the League of Augsburg, 1689

F. Fleurus, 1690 L. Lille
S. Steinkirk, 1692 V. Valenciennes

TREATIES OF AIX-LA-CHAPELLE, NIJMEGEN AND RIJSWIJK, 1668–97

Scale 1:15,000,000 (240 miles = 1 inch)

0 100 200 300 Miles

0 100 200 300 400 Km.

Treaty of Aix-la-Chapelle (Aachen) 1668:
  To France

Treaty of Nijmegen 1678/79:
  To France
  To Spain

Treaty of Rijswijk 1697:
  To France
  To Savoy

COPYRIGHT. GEORGE PHILIP & SON. LTD.

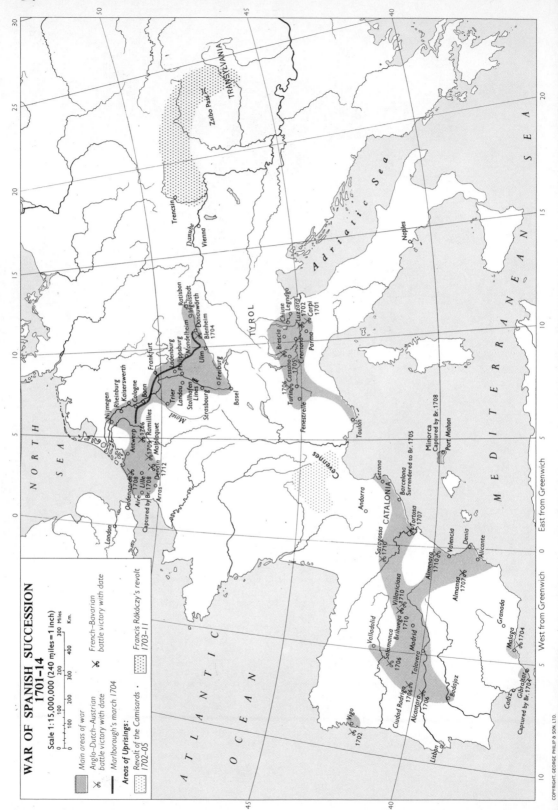

WAR OF SPANISH SUCCESSION
1701–14

Scale 1:15,000,000 (240 miles=1 inch)

0   100   200   300 Miles
0 100 200 300 400   Km.

✗ Anglo–Dutch–Austrian
   battle victory with date

✗ French–Bavarian
   battle victory with date

— Marlborough's march 1704

Areas of Uprisings:

· Revolt of the Camisards
   1702–05

   Francis Rákóczy's revolt
   1703–11

   Main areas of war

COPYRIGHT. GEORGE PHILIP & SON, LTD.

TRANSYLVANIA
Zsibo Pass
Trencsin
Danube
Vienna

Adriatic Sea

Naples

Ratisbon
Höchstädt
Ingolstadt
Donauwörth
Philippsburg
Ladenburg
Blenheim
Nördlingen
1704
Wondelsheim
Ulm
TYROL
Frankfurt
Freiburg
Trier
Landau
Stollhofen
Lines
Strasbourg
Basel
Moselle

Chiuse
Brescia Legnago
Luzzara
Cremona 1702
Carpi
Parma 1701
Turin Cassano
1706 1705
Fenestrelle
Toulon

Nijmegen
Rheinburg
Kaiserswerth
Cologne
Bonn
Antwerp 1706 Ramillies
1709 Malplaquet
Oudenarde Denain
1708 1712
Aire Lille
1708 1708
Arras–Captured by Br. 1708

NORTH SEA

London

Cévennes

Andorra

Gerona
Barcelona
Surrendered to Br. 1705
Tortosa
1707
Saragossa
1710
CATALONIA

Valencia
Denia
Almenara
1710 Alicante

Minorca
Captured by Br. 1708
Port Mahon

MEDITERRANEAN SEA

Valladolid
Salamanca Villaviciosa
1706 Brihuega 1710
Madrid 1710 Almansa
Talavera 1707
Ciudad Rodrigo
1706
Alcántara Badajoz
1706

Granada

Málaga
1704

Cádiz
Gibraltar
Captured by Br. 1704

Vigo
1702

Lisbon

ATLANTIC OCEAN

East from Greenwich

West from Greenwich

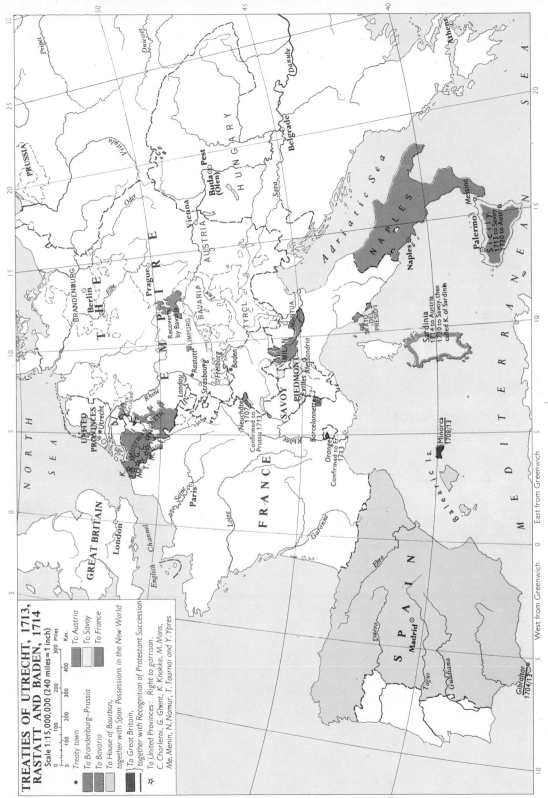

TREATIES OF UTRECHT, 1713, RASTATT AND BADEN, 1714

Scale 1:15,000,000 (240 miles=1 inch)

0 100 200 300 400 Km.

0 100 200 300 Miles

• Treaty town

To Austria

To Savoy

To France

To Brandenburg-Prussia

To Bavaria

To House of Bourbon, together with Span Possessions in the New World

To Great Britain, together with Recognition of Protestant Succession

To United Provinces: Right to garrison:
C. Charleroi, G. Ghent, K. Knokke, M. Mons,
Me. Menin, N. Namur, T. Tournai and Y. Ypres

☆

PRUSSIA

Pripet

Dniester

Vistula

Oder

BRANDENBURG

Berlin ○

THE

Elbe

Prague ○

EMPIRE

Danube

Buda ○ Pest
(Ofen)

HUNGARY

Sava

Belgrade

Vienna ○

AUSTRIA

BAVARIA

Inn

TYROL

Recovered by Bavaria

Rastatt

Freiburg

Baden

Strasbourg

Landau

LIMPURG

LOWER GELDERS

UPPER GELDERS

Rhine

UNITED PROVINCES

Utrecht

AUSTRIAN NETH.

K. G. T. M. N. C.

Me.

Y.

NORTH SEA

GREAT BRITAIN

London ○

English Channel

Seine

Paris ○

F R A N C E

Loire

Garonne

Rhône

Neuchâtel
Confirmed to Prussia 1713

SAVOY

PIEDMONT

Exilles Alessandria

MILAN

MANTUA

Barcelonnette

Orange
Confirmed to Fr. 1713

Adriatic Sea

N A P L E S

Naples ○

Messina

Palermo ○

SICILY
1713 to Savoy, then 1720 to Austria

STATO DEI PRESIDI

Sardinia
1714 to Austria
1720 to Savoy, then called K. of Sardinia

Balearic Is.

Minorca
1708/13

M E D I T E R R A N E A N   S E A

Athens ○

S P A I N

Madrid ○

Duero

Ebro

Tagus

Guadiana

Gibraltar
1704/13

West from Greenwich

East from Greenwich

36

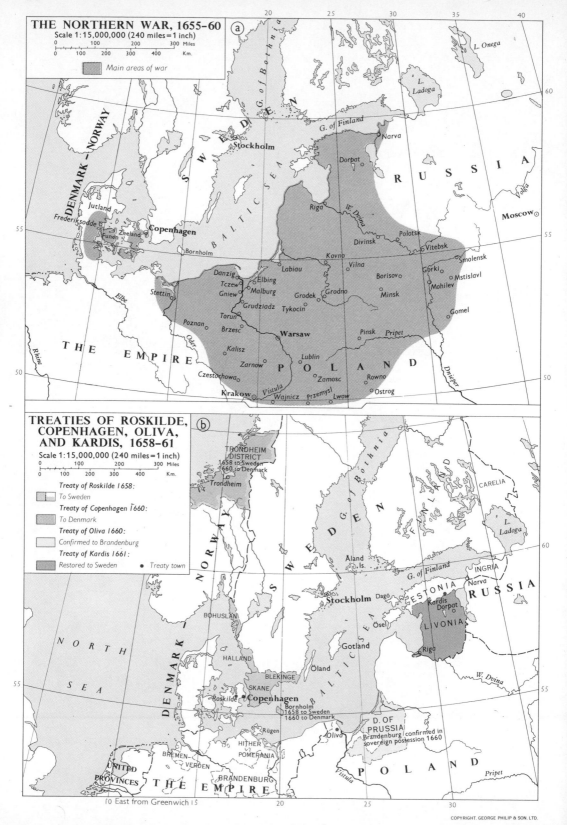

THE NORTHERN WAR, 1655-60
Scale 1:15,000,000 (240 miles=1 inch)

Main areas of war

TREATIES OF ROSKILDE, COPENHAGEN, OLIVA, AND KARDIS, 1658-61
Scale 1:15,000,000 (240 miles=1 inch)

Treaty of Roskilde 1658:
To Sweden

Treaty of Copenhagen 1660:
To Denmark

Treaty of Oliva 1660:
Confirmed to Brandenburg

Treaty of Kardis 1661:
Restored to Sweden

• Treaty town

COPYRIGHT. GEORGE PHILIP & SON. LTD.

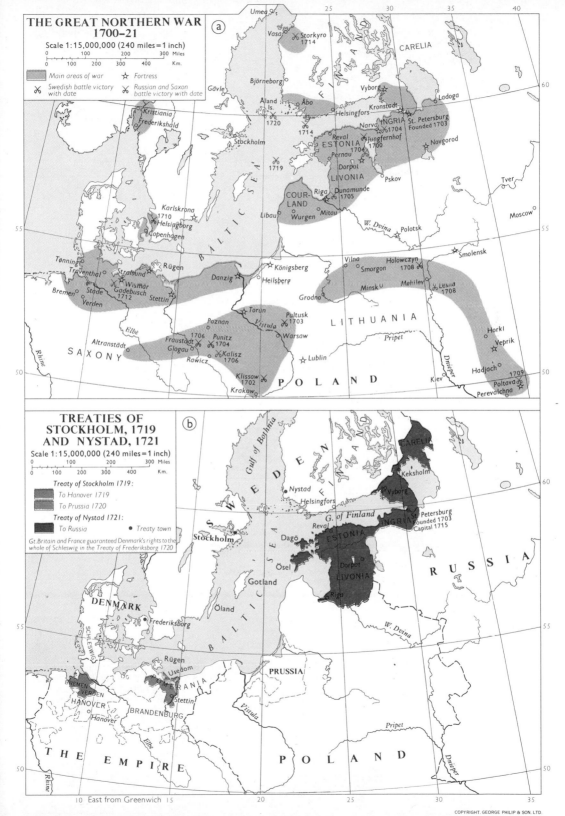

THE GREAT NORTHERN WAR 1700–21

Scale 1:15,000,000 (240 miles = 1 inch)

0   100   200   300 Miles
0   100   200   300   400 Km.

▨ Main areas of war   ☆ Fortress
✵ Swedish battle victory with date
✕ Russian and Saxon battle victory with date

Umeå
Vasa
Storkyro 1714
CARELIA
Björneborg
Gävle
Åland Is. 1720
Åbo
Helsingfors
Vyborg
Kronstadt
Ladoga
Kristiania
Frederikshald
1714
Narva 1704
INGRIA
St. Petersburg Founded 1703
Stockholm
Reval
Jungfernhof 1700
Novgorod
ESTONIA 1704
Pernau
Dorpat
1719
LIVONIA
Pskov
Tver
Riga
Dunamunde 1705
COUR-LAND
Mitau
Libau
Wurgen
W. Dvina
Polotsk
Moscow
Karlskrona 1710
Helsingborg
Copenhagen
BALTIC SEA
Vilna
Smorgon
Holowczyn 1708
Smolensk
Tønning
Traventhal
Stralsund
Rügen
Königsberg
Heilsberg
Danzig
Grodno
Minsk
Mehilev
Lesna 1708
Bremen
Stade
Wismar
Gadebusch 1712
Stettin
Verden
Torun
Pultusk 1703
Vistula
Warsaw
LITHUANIA
Pripet
Horki
Veprik
Elbe
Poznan
Fraustadt 1706
Punitz 1704
SAXONY
Glogau
Rawicz
Kalisz 1706
Lublin
Dnieper
Hadjach
Poltava 1709
Perevalchna
Altranstädt
Klissow 1702
Krakow
POLAND
Kiev

TREATIES OF STOCKHOLM, 1719 AND NYSTAD, 1721

Scale 1:15,000,000 (240 miles = 1 inch)

0   100   200   300 Miles
0   100   200   300   400 Km.

Treaty of Stockholm 1719:
▨ To Hanover 1719
▨ To Prussia 1720

Treaty of Nystad 1721:
▨ To Russia   • Treaty town

Gt. Britain and France guaranteed Denmark's rights to the whole of Schleswig in the Treaty of Frederiksborg 1720

Gulf of Bothnia
SWEDEN
FINLAND
CARELIA
Keksholm
Nystad
Helsingfors
Vyborg
St. Petersburg Founded 1703 Capital 1715
Stockholm
G. of Finland
Reval
INGRIA
RUSSIA
Dagö
ESTONIA
Ösel
Dorpat
LIVONIA
Gotland
Riga
Öland
W. Dvina
DENMARK
Frederiksborg
BALTIC SEA
SCHLESWIG
Rügen
Usedom
PRUSSIA
POMERANIA
Stettin
BREMEN
VERDEN
HANOVER
Hanover
BRANDENBURG
Vistula
Pripet
Dnieper
THE EMPIRE
POLAND
Rhine
Elbe

10   East from Greenwich   15

COPYRIGHT. GEORGE PHILIP & SON. LTD.

38

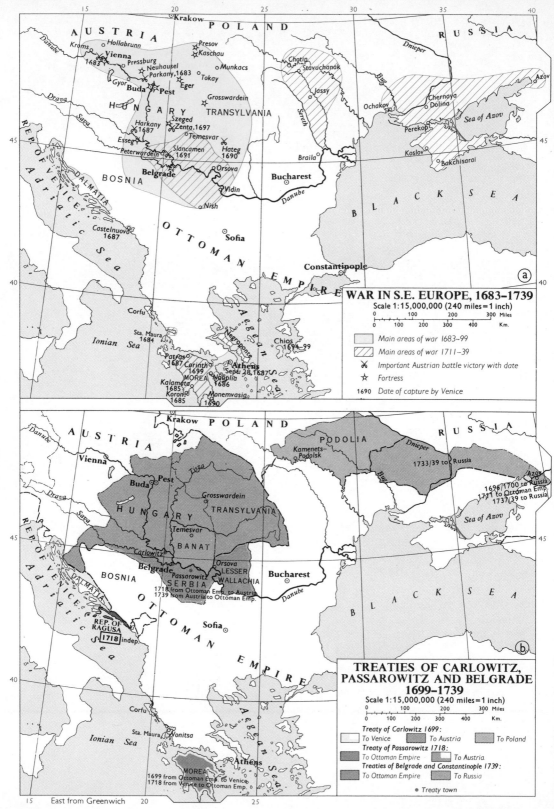

WAR IN S.E. EUROPE, 1683–1739
Scale 1:15,000,000 (240 miles = 1 inch)
0 100 200 300 400 Miles
Km.

Main areas of war 1683–99
Main areas of war 1711–39
Important Austrian battle victory with date
Fortress
1690 Date of capture by Venice

TREATIES OF CARLOWITZ, PASSAROWITZ AND BELGRADE 1699–1739
Scale 1:15,000,000 (240 miles = 1 inch)
0 100 200 300 400 Miles
Km.

Treaty of Carlowitz 1699:
To Venice   To Austria   To Poland
Treaty of Passarowitz 1718:
To Ottoman Empire   To Austria
Treaties of Belgrade and Constantinople 1739:
To Ottoman Empire   To Russia
Treaty town

East from Greenwich

COPYRIGHT. GEORGE PHILIP & SON. LTD.

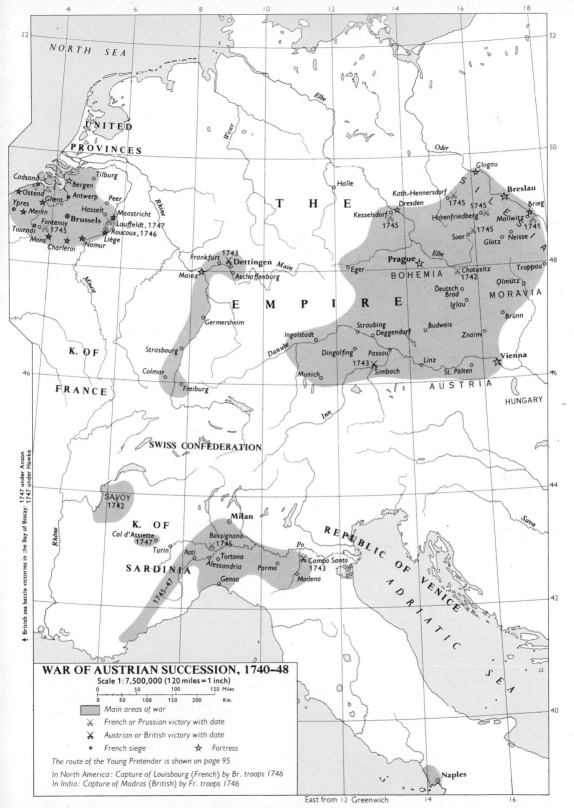

NORTH SEA

UNITED
PROVINCES

Cadsand
Ostend Bergen
Ghent Antwerp Peer
Ypres Hasselt
Menin
Fontenoy Brussels Maastricht
Tournai 1745 Lauffeldt, 1747
Mons Liège Roucoux, 1746
Charleroi Namur

K. OF

FRANCE

Rhine
Meuse

THE   E

Halle

Frankfurt 1743
Mainz **Dettingen** Main
Aschaffenburg

Germersheim

E   M   P   I   R   E

Strasbourg

Colmar

Freiburg

Danube

SWISS CONFEDERATION

Elbe

Oder

SILESIA

Glogau
Breslau
Kath-Hennersdorf
Dresden 1745 1745
Kesselsdorf Hohenfriedberg Brieg
1745 Mollwitz 1741
Soor 1745 Neisse
Glatz

Prague
Eger Chotusitz
BOHEMIA 1742
Deutsch Olmütz
Brod MORAVIA
Iglau
Brünn

Straubing Budweis
Ingolstadt Deggendorf Znaim
Dingolfing Passau
1743 Linz Vienna
Munich Simbach St. Pölten

AUSTRIA

HUNGARY

Inn

Rhone

Troppau

British sea battle victories in the Bay of Biscay: 1747 under Anson / 1747 under Hawke

SAVOY
1742

K. OF
Col d'Assiette
1747
Turin
SARDINIA
1745-47

Milan

Bassignano
1745
Asti
Tortona
Alessandria
Parma
Genoa
Modena

Po
Campo Santo
1743

REPUBLIC OF VENICE

ADRIATIC SEA

Sava

Naples

East from 12 Greenwich

WAR OF AUSTRIAN SUCCESSION, 1740-48
Scale 1:7,500,000 (120 miles = 1 inch)

0   50   100   150 Miles
0   50   100   150   200 Km.

▨   Main areas of war

✕   French or Prussian victory with date

✕   Austrian or British victory with date

•   French siege   ✧ Fortress

The route of the Young Pretender is shown on page 95

In North America: Capture of Louisbourg (French) by Br. troops 1746
In India: Capture of Madras (British) by Fr. troops 1746

40

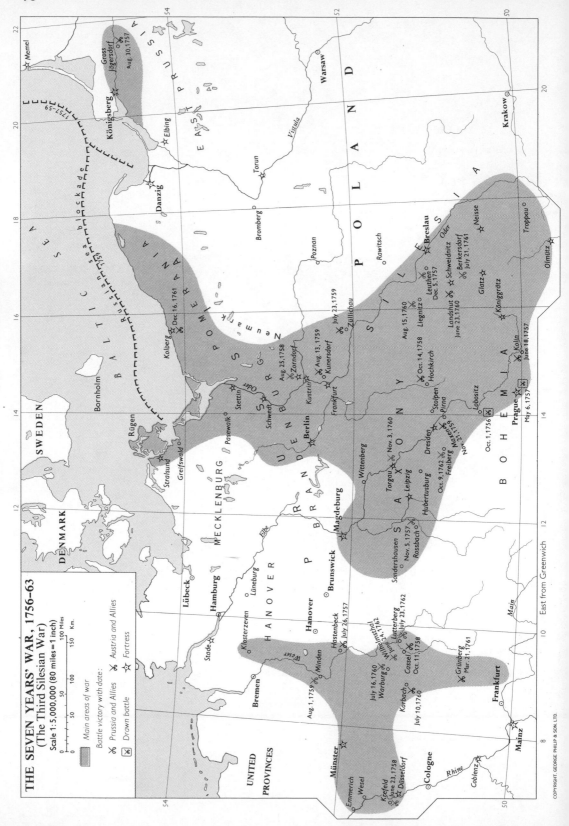

THE SEVEN YEARS' WAR, 1756–63
(The Third Silesian War)

Scale 1:5,000,000 (80 miles=1 inch)

| 0 | 50 | 100 | 150 Miles |

| 0 | 50 | 100 | Km. |

Main areas of war

Battle victory with date:
✗ Prussia and Allies   ✗ Austria and Allies
⊠ Drawn battle   ✰ Fortress

COPYRIGHT. GEORGE PHILIP & SON LTD.

East from Greenwich

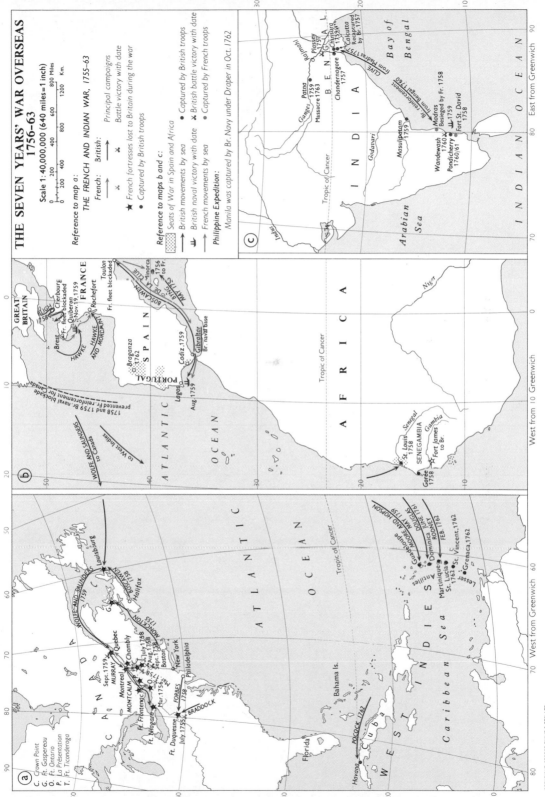

THE SEVEN YEARS' WAR OVERSEAS 1756–63

Scale 1: 40,000,000 (640 miles=1 inch)

0   200   400   600   800 Miles
0   200   400   600   800   1000   1200 Km.

Reference to map a:

THE FRENCH AND INDIAN WAR, 1755–63

French: British: — Principal campaigns
✗   ✗   Battle victory with date
★ French fortresses lost to Britain during the war
● Captured by British troops

Reference to maps b and c:

Seats of War in Spain and Africa
↓ British movements by sea   ● Captured by British troops
↑ French movements by sea   ✗ British battle victory with date
Philippine Expedition: ↑ Captured by French troops
● British naval victory with date

Manila was captured by Br. Navy under Draper in Oct. 1762

(a) Map labels:
C. Crown Point
G. Ft. Gospereau
O. Ft. Ontario
P. La Présentation
T. Ft. Ticonderoga

CANADA   Louisburg   WOLFE AND SAUNDERS 1759   Halifax   BOSCAWEN 1758
Murray   Sept.1759   Quebec   Chambly   July 1758
MURRAY   MONTCALM   1759   Montreal   Ft. Frontenac   Aug.1758
Ft. Niagara   July 1759   FORBES 1758   New York   Philadelphia   Boston
Mar.1756   Ft. Duquesne   BRADDOCK   July 1755   Bahama Is.
Florida   Havana   POCOCK 1762   Cuba   WEST INDIES   Caribbean Sea
ATLANTIC OCEAN   Tropic of Cancer
Lesser Antilles   Guadeloupe 1759   Dominica 1761   Martinique 1762
St. Lucia 1762   St. Vincent, 1762   Grenada, 1762
KEPPEL 1762   BARRINGTON AND HOPSON 1759   DOUGLAS 1761   MONCKTON 1762   RODNEY

West from Greenwich 60   West from Greenwich 70

(b) GREAT BRITAIN   FRANCE   SPAIN   PORTUGAL   AFRICA
Brest   Cherbourg 1758   Fr. fleet blockaded   Rochefort   Toulon   Fr. fleet blockaded
HAWKE Nov.19,1759   HAWKE AND MORDAUNT   Quiberon   Minorca   1756 to Fr.
BOSCAWEN   DE LA CLUE 1759   BYNG   MAYS   Braganza 1762   Gibraltar Br. naval base
Cadiz,1759   Lagos, Aug.1759   Gibraltar,1759
1758 and 1759 Br. naval blockade prevented Fr. reinforcement for Canada
WOLFE AND SAUNDERS to Canada   to West Indies
ATLANTIC OCEAN   Tropic of Cancer
Niger   St. Louis 1758   SENEGAMBIA   Senegal   Gambia   Fort James to Br.
Gorée 1758

West from 10 Greenwich

(c) INDIA   BENGAL   Bay of Bengal   INDIAN OCEAN   Arabian Sea
Rohilkand   Plassey 1757   Chinsura 1759   Calcutta Recaptured by Br. 1757
CLIVE from Madras 1757   Ganges   Patna 1759   Massacre 1763   Chandernagore 1757
Godavari   Br. reinforcement from Bengal 1760   Madras 1759/60   Besieged by Fr. 1758
Masulipatam 1759   Wandewash 1760   Pondicherry 1760/61   Fort St. David 1758   Indus
Tropic of Cancer

East from Greenwich

COPYRIGHT GEORGE PHILIP & SON LTD.

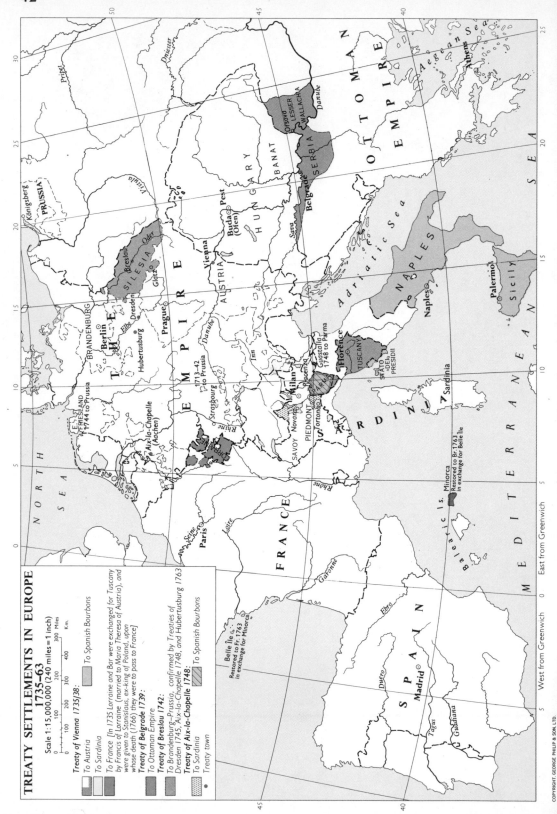

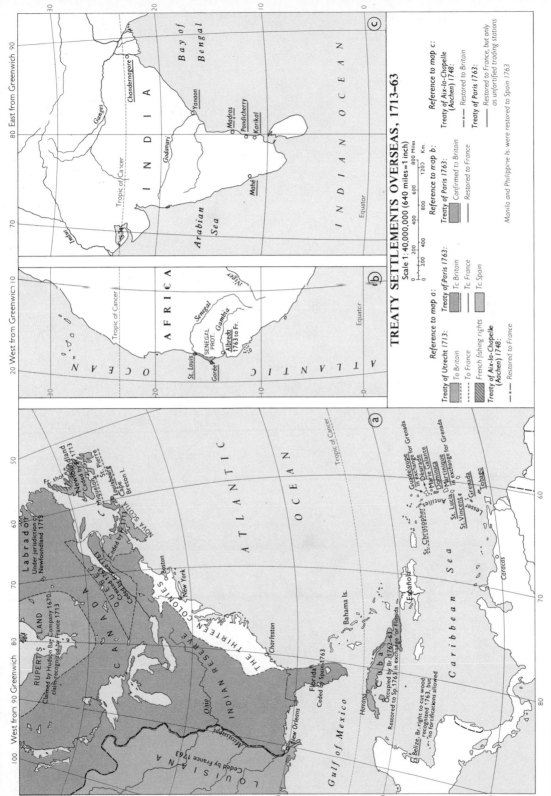

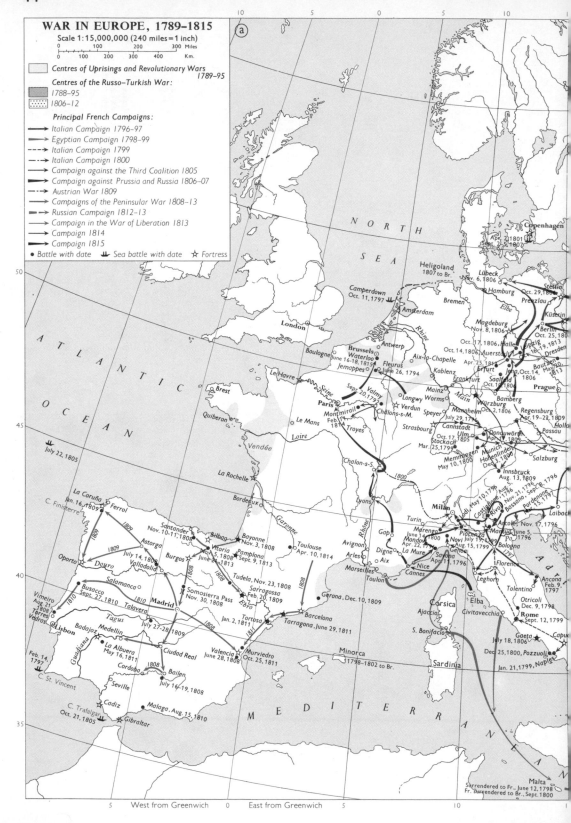

WAR IN EUROPE, 1789–1815

Scale 1:15,000,000 (240 miles=1 inch)

| | 100 | 200 | 300 Miles |
| | 100 | 200 | 300 | 400 | Km. |

Centres of Uprisings and Revolutionary Wars 1789–95

Centres of the Russo–Turkish War:
1788–95
1806–12

Principal French Campaigns:
→ Italian Campaign 1796–97
→ Egyptian Campaign 1798–99
--→ Italian Campaign 1799
-·-→ Italian Campaign 1800
→ Campaign against the Third Coalition 1805
→ Campaign against Prussia and Russia 1806–07
-·-→ Austrian War 1809
→ Campaigns of the Peninsular War 1808–13
→ Russian Campaign 1812–13
→ Campaign in the War of Liberation 1813
→ Campaign 1814
→ Campaign 1815

● Battle with date   ⚓ Sea battle with date   ☆ Fortress

(a)

NORTH SEA

ATLANTIC OCEAN

MEDITERRANEAN

West from Greenwich   0   East from Greenwich   5   10

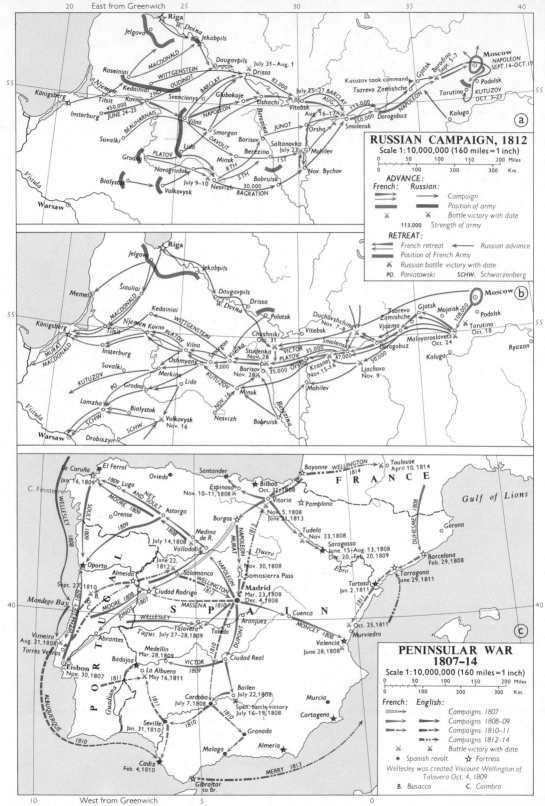

East from Greenwich

RUSSIAN CAMPAIGN, 1812
Scale 1:10,000,000 (160 miles = 1 inch)

0   50   100   200 Miles
0   100   200   300 Km.

ADVANCE:
French: Russian:
⟶   Campaign
▬▬   Position of army
✕   Battle victory with date
113,000   Strength of army

RETREAT:
⟵   French retreat   ⟵   Russian advance
▬▬   Position of French Army
✕   Russian battle victory with date
PO. Poniatowski   SCHW. Schwarzenberg

PENINSULAR WAR 1807–14
Scale 1:10,000,000 (160 miles = 1 inch)

0   50   100   150   200 Miles
0   100   200   300 Km.

French: English:
▭▭▭   Campaigns 1807
▬▬▬   Campaigns 1808–09
▭▬▶   Campaigns 1810–11
▬ ▬ ▬   Campaigns 1812–14
✕   Battle victory with date
•   Spanish revolt   ☆ Fortress
Wellesley was created Viscount Wellington of
Talavera Oct. 4, 1809
B. Busaco   C. Coimbra

Gulf of Lions

West from Greenwich

COPYRIGHT. GEORGE. PHILIP & SON. LTD.

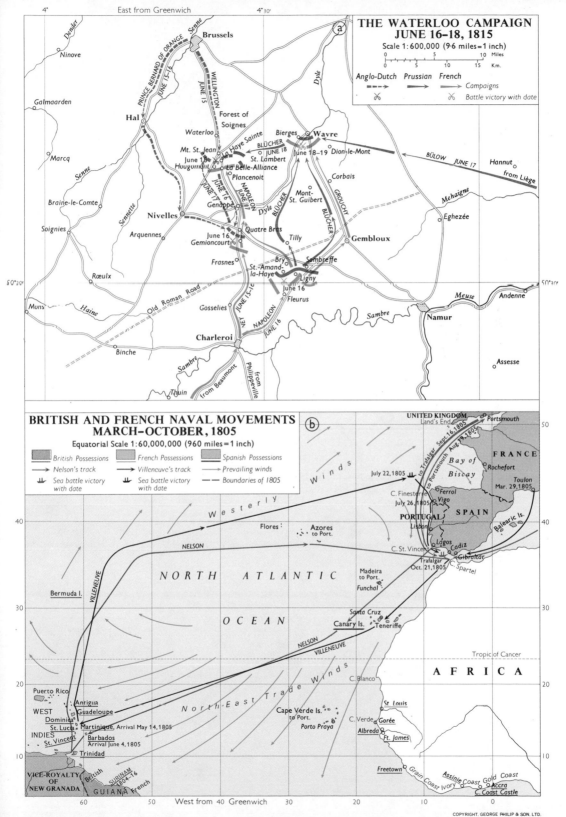

THE WATERLOO CAMPAIGN
JUNE 16–18, 1815

Scale 1:600,000 (9·6 miles=1 inch)

0 ___ 5 ___ 10 Miles
0 __ 5 __ 10 __ 15 Km.

Anglo-Dutch Prussian French

→ Campaigns
✄ Battle victory with date

BRITISH AND FRENCH NAVAL MOVEMENTS
MARCH–OCTOBER, 1805

Equatorial Scale 1:60,000,000 (960 miles=1 inch)

British Possessions   French Possessions   Spanish Possessions

→ Nelson's track
→ Villeneuve's track
→ Prevailing winds
Sea battle victory with date
Sea battle victory with date
— — Boundaries of 1805

COPYRIGHT. GEORGE PHILIP & SON, LTD.

TREATY SETTLEMENTS IN EUROPE
1795-1812

Scale 1:15,000,000 (240 miles = 1 inch)

0   100   200   300 Miles
0   100   200   300   400 Km.

To France: Annexations
1795-98 | 1801-05 | 1806 | 1807-08 | 1809-12

Passed under French Influence
1795-98 | 1801-05 | 1806 | 1807-08 | 1809-12

——— Demarcation line between France and Prussia at the T. of Basle 1795

To Britain:
To Russia: 1807 | 1809 | 1812

1810 Date of acquisition or period of possession   • Treaty town

The Settlements include the treaties of: Basle 1795, Tolentino and Campo
Formio 1797, Lunéville 1801, Amiens 1802, Pressburg 1805, Tilsit 1807,
Fredrikshamn and Schönbrunn (Vienna) 1809, and Bucharest 1812
Intermediate stages before the final control by France are omitted.

COPYRIGHT. GEORGE PHILIP & SON. LTD.

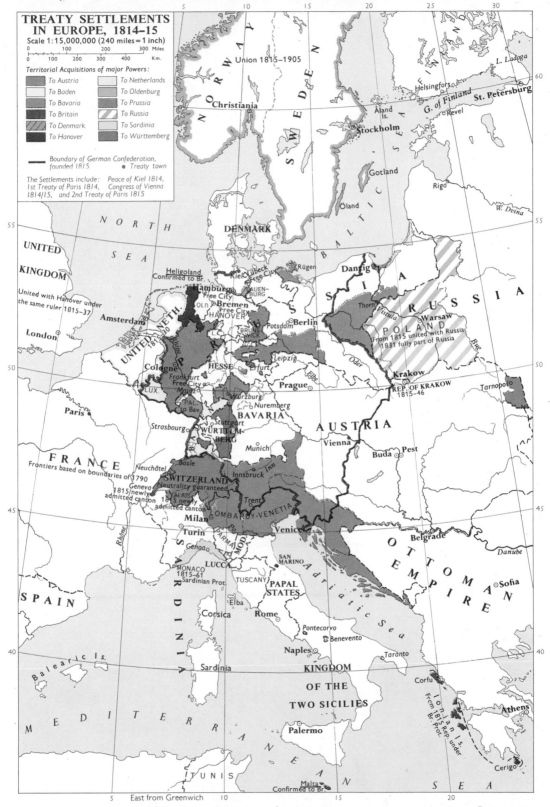

TREATY SETTLEMENTS IN EUROPE, 1814–15

Scale 1:15,000,000 (240 miles = 1 inch)

0 100 200 300 Miles
0 100 200 300 400 Km.

Territorial Acquisitions of major Powers:

To Austria
To Baden
To Bavaria
To Britain
To Denmark
To Hanover

To Netherlands
To Oldenburg
To Prussia
To Russia
To Sardinia
To Württemberg

— Boundary of German Confederation, founded 1815
• Treaty town

The Settlements include: Peace of Kiel 1814, 1st Treaty of Paris 1814, Congress of Vienna 1814/15, and 2nd Treaty of Paris 1815

COPYRIGHT. GEORGE PHILIP & SON, LTD.

50

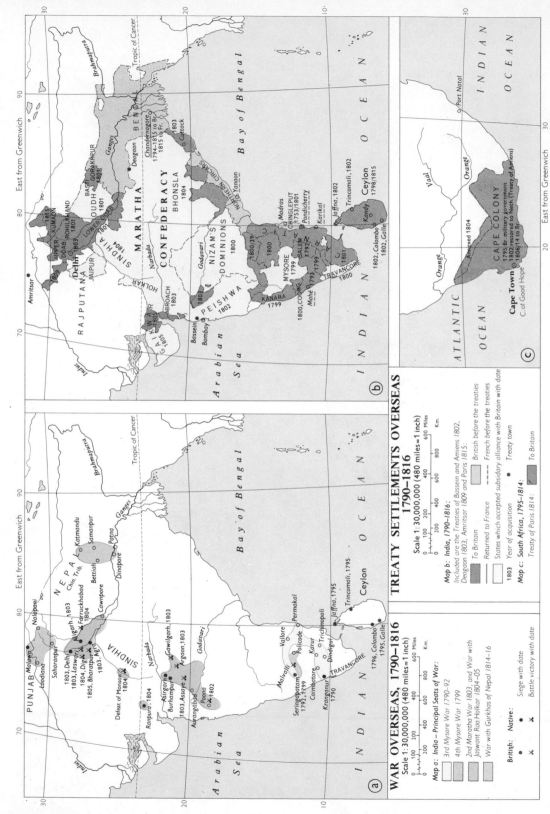

WAR OVERSEAS, 1790–1816

Scale 1:30,000,000 (480 miles=1 inch)

Map a: India – Principal Seats of War:

3rd Mysore War 1790–92
4th Mysore War 1799
2nd Maratha War 1803, and War with Jaswant Rao Holkar 1804–05
War with Gurkhas of Nepal 1814–16

British: ● Native: ○ Siege : ✕
× Native ✕ Battle victory with date

TREATY SETTLEMENTS OVERSEAS 1790–1816

Scale 1:30,000,000 (480 miles=1 inch)

Map b: India, 1790–1816:
Included are the Treaties of Bassein and Amiens 1802, Deogoon 1803, Amritsar 1809 and Paris 1815:

To Britain
Returned to France
1803 Year of acquisition
British before the treaties
French before the treaties
States which accepted subsidiary alliance with Britain with date
● Treaty town

Map c: South Africa, 1795–1814:
Treaty of Paris 1814: To Britain

COPYRIGHT GEORGE PHILIP & SON LTD.

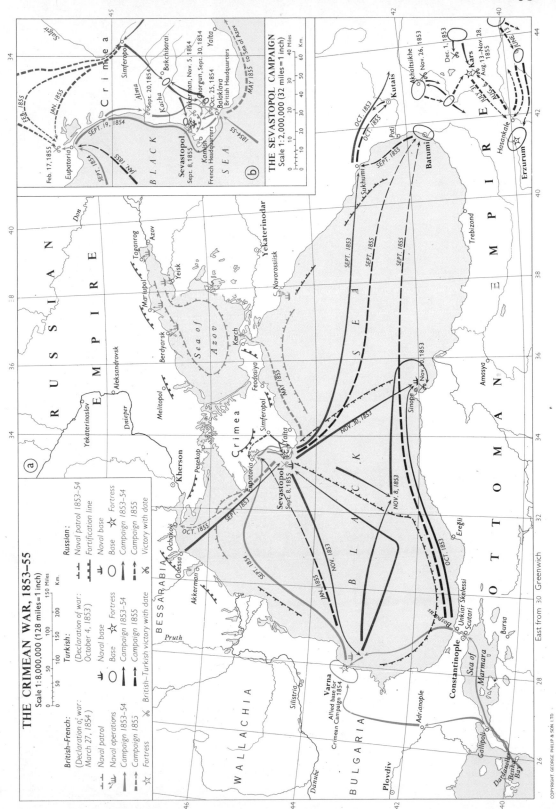

THE CRIMEAN WAR, 1853–55

Scale 1:8,000,000 (128 miles=1 inch)

0 50 100 150 200 Km.
0 50 100 150 Miles

British-French:
(Declaration of war:
March 27, 1854)

⚓ Naval patrol
⚓ Naval operations
Campaign 1853–54
Campaign 1855
☆ Fortress

Turkish:
(Declaration of war:
October 4, 1853)

◔ Naval base
☆ Fortress
Campaign 1853–54
Campaign 1855
✗ British–Turkish victory with date

Russian:
Naval patrol 1853–54
Fortification line
◔ Naval base
◔ Base ☆ Fortress
Campaign 1853–54
Campaign 1855
✗ Victory with date

(a)

THE SEVASTOPOL CAMPAIGN

Scale 1:2,000,000 (32 miles=1 inch)

0 10 20 30 40 Miles
0 10 20 30 40 50 60 Km.

(b)

RUSSIAN EMPIRE

OTTOMAN EMPIRE

BLACK SEA

Sea of Azov

WALLACHIA

BESSARABIA

BULGARIA

Crimea

Sevastopol

Constantinople

Varna
Allied base for
Crimean Campaign 1854

Kars

Batumi

Erzurum

East from 30 Greenwich

COPYRIGHT GEORGE PHILIP & SON LTD

THE FIRST WORLD WAR, 1914–18

Scale 1:20,000,000 (320 miles=1 inch)

0	100	200	300	400 Miles
0	200	400	600 Km.	

‑‑‑‑‑ Frontlines in August 1914

‑ ‑ ‑ Russo-German front at the beginning of 1915

—— Frontlines in November 1918

Central Powers at the outbreak of war

States subsequently allied to Central Powers

States neutral throughout the war

—— Max. extent of advance of Central Powers

⚓ Sea battle with date

➔ Campaigns 1918

Entente Powers at the outbreak of war

States neutral at the outbreak of war, later joining the Entente

10 East from Greenwich 15

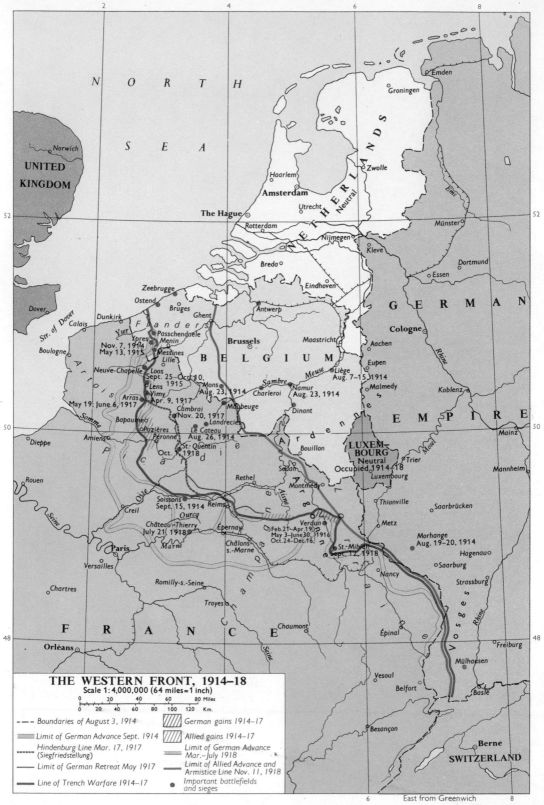

THE WESTERN FRONT, 1914–18

Scale 1 : 4,000,000 (64 miles=1 inch)

0   20   40   60   80 Miles

0   20   40   60   80   100   120 Km.

- - - - Boundaries of August 3, 1914
░░░░ Limit of German Advance Sept. 1914
▓▓▓▓ Hindenburg Line Mar. 17, 1917 (Siegfriedstellung)
——— Limit of German Retreat May 1917
━━━ Line of Trench Warfare 1914–17

▨ German gains 1914–17
▨ Allied gains 1914–17
═══ Limit of German Advance Mar.–July 1918
━━━ Limit of Allied Advance and Armistice Line Nov. 11, 1918
● Important battlefields and sieges

East from Greenwich

COPYRIGHT. GEORGE PHILIP & SON, LTD.

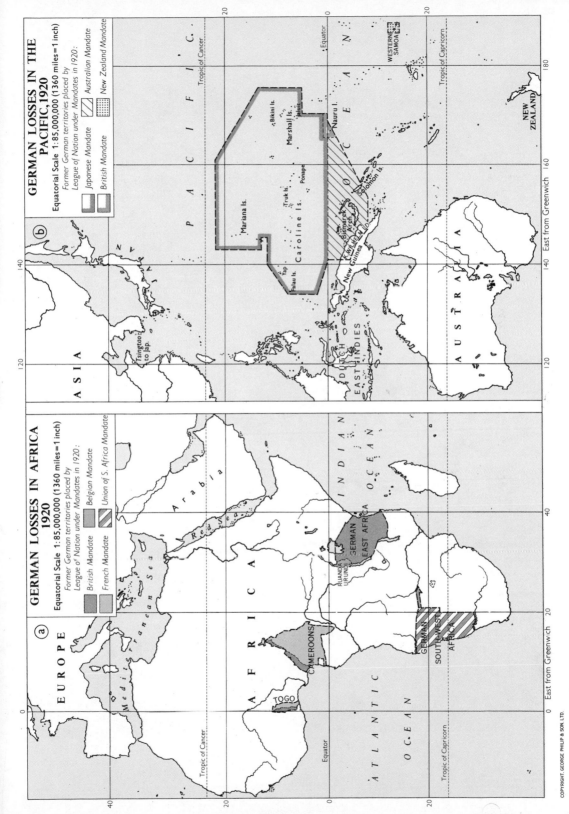

GERMAN LOSSES IN THE PACIFIC, 1920

Equatorial Scale 1:85,000,000 (1360 miles=1 inch)
Former German territories placed by
League of Nation under Mandates in 1920:

- Japanese Mandate
- British Mandate
- Australian Mandate
- New Zealand Mandate

GERMAN LOSSES IN AFRICA 1920

Equatorial Scale 1:85,000,000 (1360 miles=1 inch)
Former German territories placed by
League of Nation under Mandates in 1920:

- British Mandate
- French Mandate
- Belgian Mandate
- Union of S. Africa Mandate

TREATY SETTLEMENTS IN EUROPE 1919–26

Scale 1:10,000,000 (160 miles=1 inch)

0 50 100 150 200 Miles
0 100 200 300 Km.

Ceded by Germany

Ceded by Austro-Hungary

Ceded by Bulgaria

Ceded by Russia

Areas ceded by Turkey in the Middle East are shown on pp. 166/167 and 174.

German demilitarized area west and 50km. east of the Rhine and demilitarized "Zone of the Straits" in Turkey

Zone of Allied Occupation

Sanctions areas occupied 1920–25

Ruhr Basin under French Occupation 1923–25

Neutral zone of 10 kilometres with bridge-heads

Plebiscite areas with date of plebiscite

Internationalized rivers

Date of independence   1918

Boundaries 1914

Boundaries 1926

SWEDEN

NORWAY

FINLAND   1917/20

Trondheim

Bergen

Oslo

Oulu

Vaasa

Tampere

Turku

Helsinki

Vyipuri (Vyborg)

Boundary 1920

Lake Onega

Lake Ladoga

Petrograd (1924 Leningrad)

Lake Pskov

Narva

ESTONIA   1918/20

Tallinn

Tartu (Dorpat)

Åland Is. 1921 neutral under Finnish Sovereignty

Gulf of Finland

Gulf of Bothnia

Stockholm

Gotland

Öland

Bornholm

Göteborg

Copenhagen

DENMARK

Kiel

Schleswig

Feb. 10, 1920 to Denmark

Mar. 14, 1920 to Germany

Rügen

BALTIC SEA

NORTH SEA

Hamburg Free harbour for Czechoslovakia

Bremen

Stettin Free harbour for Czechoslovakia

LATVIA   1918/20

Riga

Demarcation line 1920–38

LITHUANIA   1918/20

Kaunas

Memel

Vilna

Grodno

1917 to Lith. 1920/23 to Pol.

Memel Terr. 1919–23 under allied administr. 1923 to Lith. 1924 auton. region

Königsberg

Marienwerder

Allenstein

July 11, 1920 to Germany

Danzig 1919 Free City

1919 to Pol.

Smolensk

UNION OF SOVIET SOCIALIST REPUBLICS

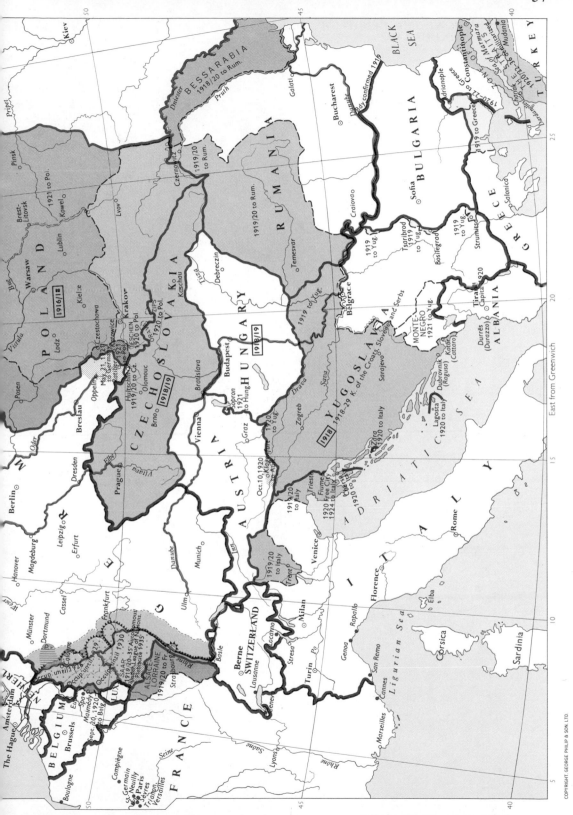

Kiev

POLAND 1916/18

Pinsk
Brest-Litovsk
Kowel
1921 to Pol.
Warsaw
Lublin
Lodz
Kielce
Posen
Czestochowa
Vistula
Bug

BESSARABIA 1918/20 to Rum.

Dniester
Pruth
Galati
Czernowitz
1919/20 to Rum.
1919/20 to Rum.

Breslau
Oppeln
May 21, 1921 to German plebiscite to Germany
Ratibor
Hultschin 1919/20 to Cz.
Beuthen
TESCHEN 1920 to Pol.
Krakow
1920 to Pol.
CZECHOSLOVAKIA 1918/19
Olomouc
Brno
Debreczin
Kaschau
Tisza
Bucharest
Danube
Duly confirmed 1919
BLACK SEA

RUMANIA
Temesvar
Craiova
1919/20 to Rum.
1919 to Yug.

Dresden
Elbe
Vltava
Prague
Vienna
Bratislava
Sopron 1921 to Hung.
Graz
1920
Budapest
HUNGARY 1918/19
Danube
1919 to Yug.
Belgrade
Drava
Sava
Zagreb
Sarajevo
YUGOSLAVIA 1918
K. of the Croats, Slovenes and Serbs
Nish
Tsaribrod 1919 to Yug.
Bosilegrad 1919 to Yug.
Strumitsa 1919 to Yug.

BULGARIA
Sofia
Adrianople
Constantinople
Sea of Marmara
TURKEY
Greece
1919 to Greece
1920 to Greece
Mudania
1920/22 to Turkey
Chonak E.
Dardanelles

Berlin
Leipzig
Magdeburg
Erfurt
Hanover
Weser
Cassel
Münster
Dortmund
Frankfurt
Cologne
Occup. until 1926
Occup. until 1929
Occup. until 1930
SAAR 1919/20-35 Aug. 1935 League of Nations. Plebiscite 1935
ALSACE LORRAINE 1919/20 to Fr.
Strasbourg
Rhine
Ulm
Munich
Inn
Danube
AUSTRIA
Oct. 10, 1920 Klagenfurt
Trieste
1919/20 to Italy
Fiume 1920 Free City 1924 to Italy
Zara 1920 to Italy
Lagosta 1920 to Italy
ADRIATIC SEA
Dubrovnik (Ragusa)
Kotor (Cattaro)
MONTE-NEGRO 1921 to Yug.
Durrës (Durazzo)
ALBANIA
Tirana Capital 1920
GREECE
Salonica

NETHERLANDS
Amsterdam
The Hague
BELGIUM
Brussels
Eupen
Malmedy Sept. 20, 1920 to Belg.
Spa
LUX.
Compiègne
St. Germain
Neuilly
Paris
Sèvres
Trianon
Versailles
Seine
Boulogne
FRANCE
Lyons
Rhône
Saône
Marseilles
Cannes
San Remo
Nice
Geneva
Berne SWITZERLAND
Lausanne
Basle
Locarno
Stresa
Turin
Po
Genoa
Rapallo
Ligurian Sea
Corsica
Sardinia
Milan
Trent
1919/20 to Italy
Venice
Florence
Elba
Rome
ITALY

East from Greenwich

EUROPE AT THE HEIGHT OF
GERMAN DOMINATION, NOV. 1942

Scale 1:15,000,000 (240 miles=1 inch)

0   100   200   300 Miles

0   100   200   300   400
Km

Hitler's Germany with Austria and
Prot. of Bohemia-Moravia
Subject terr. under German
Administration
Territories under Ger. Occupation
Italy with annexed territories
Axis Powers: Germany and Italy
Powers co-operating with Axis
Territories occupied by Axis

Limit of German advance Dec. 1941
Furthest extent of Axis-Powers
Nov. 1942
France, Vichy governed
Unconquered terr. of U.S.S.R.
Nov. 1942
Terr. of the Allied Powers
Neutral Countries
Boundary of Germany in 1937

60

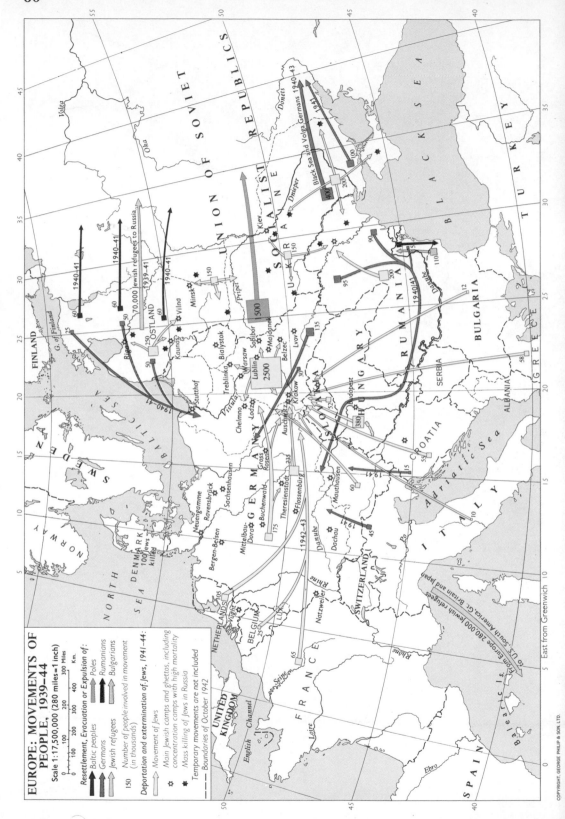

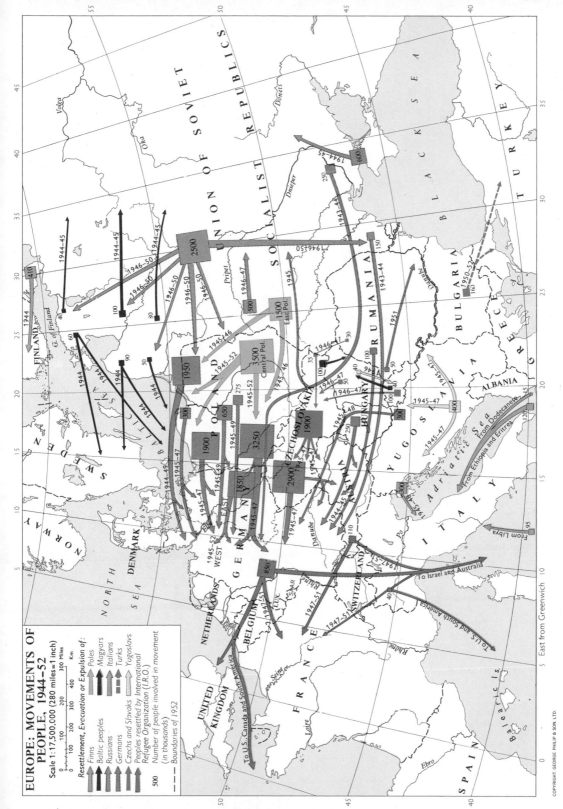

EUROPE: MOVEMENTS OF PEOPLE, 1944–52

Scale 1:17,500,000 (280 miles=1 inch)

Resettlement, Evacuation or Expulsion of:

Finns · Poles
Baltic peoples · Magyars
Russians · Italians
Germans · Turks
Czechs and Slovaks · Yugoslavs

Peoples resettled by International Refugee Organization (I.R.O.)

500 Number of people involved in movement (in thousands)

— — — Boundaries of 1952

61

COPYRIGHT GEORGE PHILIP & SON LTD.

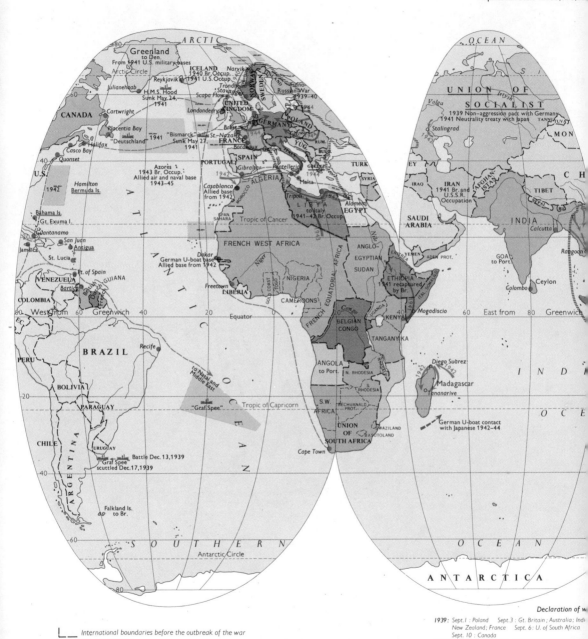

THE SECOND WORLI

Equatorial Scale 1:130,000,00

Declaration of w

1939: Sept.1 : Poland   Sept.3 : Gt. Britain ; Australia; Indi
New Zealand ; France   Sept. 6: U. of South Africa
Sept. 10 : Canada
1940: Apr. 9: Norway   May 10: Netherlands; Belgium
1941: Apr.6: Yugoslavia; Greece   June 22: U.S.S.R.
Dec. 9: China; Free French Government under de Gau
Dec. 11: U.S. ; Cuba; Dominican Rep.; Guatemala;
Nicaragua; Haiti   Dec. 12: Honduras; Salvador
Dec. 17: Czechoslovakia (In Exile)
1942: Jan. 13: Panama   Jan. 15: Luxembourg (in Exile)
May 22: Mexico   Aug. 23: Brazil
Dec. 1: Ethiopa

International boundaries before the outbreak of the war

The Axis Powers:

- 1939
- 1940
- 1941
- After Dec. 8, 1941
- Axis bases

Furthest extent of Axis powers at the end of 1942

Main area of German U-boat activity

Main area of German naval operations

YUG. States invaded by Germany (underlined in red)

Japanese advances

A. Albania, B. Belgium, BH. Bhutan, C. Costa Rica, EC. Ecuador, G. Guatemale

WAR, 1939–45

2080 miles=1 inch)

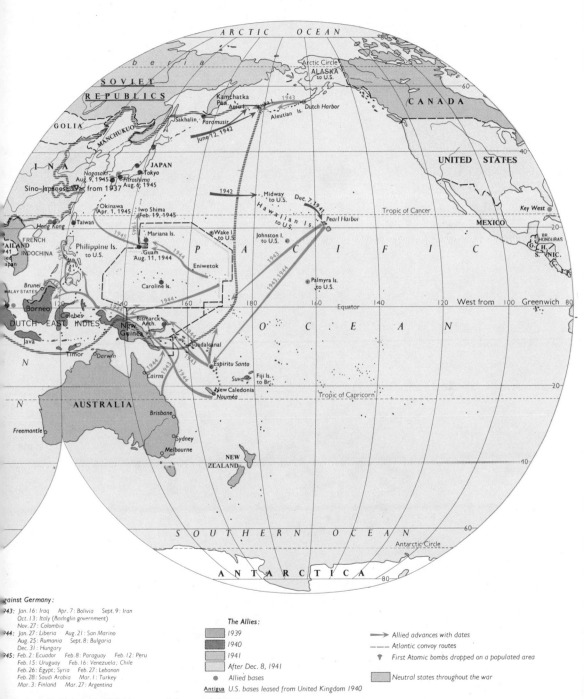

ARCTIC OCEAN

beria

SOVIET REPUBLICS

GOLIA

MANCHUKUO

Sakhalin, Paramusir
June 12, 1942

Kamchatka Pen.
Attu I. 1943
Aleutian Is.
Dutch Harbor

ARCTIC CIRCLE
Arctic Circle
ALASKA
to U.S.

CANADA

Nagasaki,
Aug. 9, 1945
Hiroshima
Aug. 6, 1945
Tokyo
JAPAN

Sino-Japanese War from 1937

INA

UNITED STATES

1942
Midway
to U.S.
Dec. 7, 1941

Tropic of Cancer

Key West

MEXICO

Okinawa
Apr. 1, 1945
Iwo Shima
Feb. 19, 1945

Hawaiian Is.
Pearl Harbor

Hong Kong
Taiwan

FRENCH
AILAND
41
INDOCHINA
led
apan

Philippine Is.
to U.S.

Mariana Is.
Guam
Aug. 11, 1944
Eniwetok

Wake I.
to U.S.
Johnston I.
to U.S.

P   A   C   I   F   I   C

BR.
HONDURAS
G.H.
S. NIC.

Brunei
MALAY STATES
Borneo
Celebes
DUTCH EAST INDIES
Java
Timor
Darwin

New Guinea
Bismarck Arch.

Caroline Is.

Guadalcanal

Espiritu Santo

Palmyra Is.
to U.S.

O   C   E   A   N

Equator

West from   Greenwich

Cairns

New Caledonia
Nouméa

Suva
Fiji Is.
to Br.

Tropic of Capricorn

AUSTRALIA

Brisbane

Freemantle

Sydney
Melbourne

NEW
ZEALAND

SOUTHERN   OCEAN

Antarctic Circle

ANTARCTICA

gainst Germany:

943: Jan.16: Iraq   Apr. 7: Bolivia   Sept. 9: Iran
      Oct.13: Italy (Badoglio government)
      Nov. 27: Colombia
944: Jan.27: Liberia   Aug. 21: San Marino
      Aug. 25: Rumania   Sept. 8: Bulgaria
      Dec. 31: Hungary
945: Feb. 2: Ecuador   Feb. 8: Paraguay   Feb. 12: Peru
      Feb.15: Uruguay   Feb.16: Venezuela; Chile
      Feb. 26: Egypt; Syria   Feb. 27: Lebanon
      Feb. 28: Saudi Arabia   Mar. 1: Turkey
      Mar. 3: Finland   Mar. 27: Argentina

The Allies:

	1939
	1940
	1941
	After Dec. 8, 1941
● Allied bases

Antigua U.S. bases leased from United Kingdom 1940

→ Allied advances with dates
--- Atlantic convoy routes
⚓ First Atomic bombs dropped on a populated area

Neutral states throughout the war

H. Honduras, N. Netherlands, NIC: Nicaragua. P. Panama, S. Salvador,

ATLANTIC

OCEAN

NORWEGIAN

SEA

January: 0°C (32°F)

Reykjavik

Iceland

Faroe Is.

Shetland
Is.

Orkney
Is.

Hebrides

Scotland

Edinburgh

Beech

NORTH

SEA

Oslo

Stockholm

Skagerrak

Vänern

Vättern

Gotland

BALTIC

Kattegat

Beech

Jutland

Funen

Zealand

Elbe

Berlin

Magdeburg

Oder

Vistula

Ireland

C. Clear

Wales

England

London

Thames

Land's End

English Channel

Cologne

Frankfurt

Harz

Saale

Erz. Geb.

Prague

Sudetes

Bay of
Biscay

C. Finisterre

Bordeaux

Cantabrian Mts.

Duero

Pyrenees

Seine

Paris

Loire

Central

Massif

Vosges

Black Forest

Danube

Munich

Vienna

Budapest

ALPS

Lyons

Rhône

Milan

Po

Venice

Drava

Sava

APENNINES

Dinaric Alps

Lisbon

Tagus

Madrid

Ebro

Beech

Castile

Aragon

Barcelona

Marseilles

Florence

Adriatic Sea

C. St. Vincent

Sierra Morena

Seville

Valencia

Balearic Is.

Corsica

Rome

Sardinia

Naples

Sierra Nevada

Str. of Gibraltar

MEDITERRANEAN

Tyrrhenian
Sea

Sicily

Ionian
Sea

E. Rif

Great Atlas

Maritime Atlas

C.
Bon

Malta

Saharan Atlas

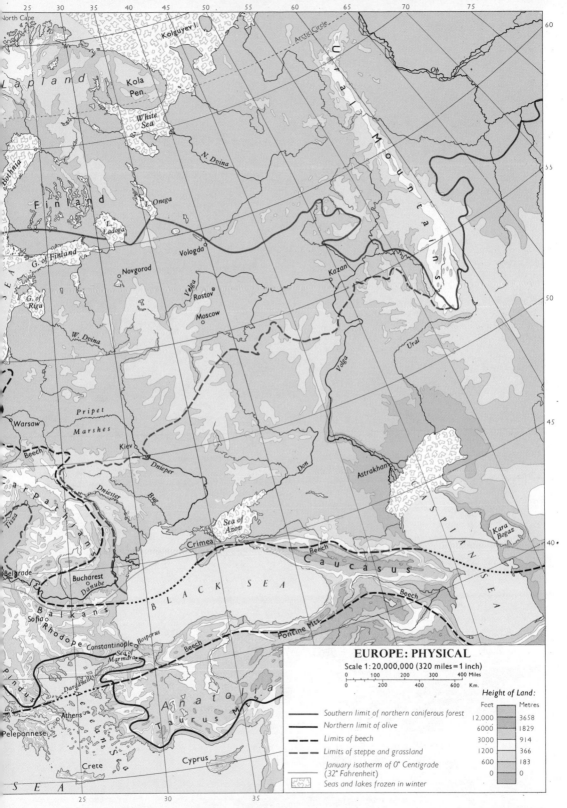

EUROPE: PHYSICAL

Scale 1 : 20,000,000 (320 miles = 1 inch)

```
0    100    200    300    400 Miles
0        200        400        600  Km.
```

Southern limit of northern coniferous forest

Northern limit of olive

Limits of beech

Limits of steppe and grassland

January isotherm of 0° Centigrade
(32° Fahrenheit)

Seas and lakes frozen in winter

Height of Land:

Feet	Metres
12,000	3658
6000	1829
3000	914
1200	366
600	183
0	0

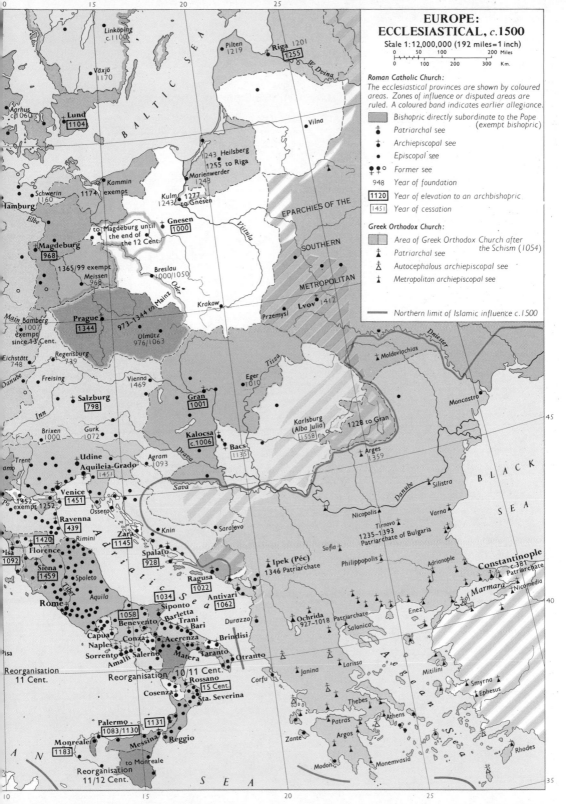

EUROPE:
ECCLESIASTICAL, c.1500
Scale 1:12,000,000 (192 miles=1 inch)

0   50   100   200 Miles
0   100   200   300 Km.

Roman Catholic Church:

The ecclesiastical provinces are shown by coloured areas. Zones of influence or disputed areas are ruled. A coloured band indicates earlier allegiance.

Bishopric directly subordinate to the Pope *(exempt bishopric)*

✝ Patriarchal see

✝ Archiepiscopal see

• Episcopal see

⚰ ○ Former see

948 Year of foundation

☐1120 Year of elevation to an archbishopric

☐1451 Year of cessation

Greek Orthodox Church:

Area of Greek Orthodox Church after the Schism (1054)

✝ Patriarchal see

Ⓐ Autocephalous archiepiscopal see

✝ Metropolitan archiepiscopal see

Northern limit of Islamic influence c.1500

COPYRIGHT. GEORGE PHILIP & SON. LTD.

▲ Stockholm   ● Åbo (Turku) moved to Helsingfors   ● Dorpat   ▲ St. Petersburg   ● Moscow   ● Kazan
1739 1753   1640   1827   1632 1656 1801   1724   1755   1804

EUROPE:
UNIVERSITIES TO 1830

Scale 1:12,000,000 (192 miles=1 inch)

University	Academy of Sciences	
●		Foundation before 1400
●	▲	Foundation 1400–1600
●	▲	Foundation after 1600

1367   Year of foundation

1793   Year of cessation

BALTIC SEA

W. Devina

Lund 1668
Copenhagen
1478 1743

Vilna 1578 1831

Königsberg 1544

Kiel 1665
Rostock 1419
Greifswald 1456

Bützow 1760 1789

Elbe

Berlin 1701/1812
Frankfurt 1506 1811

Vistula

Helmstedt 1576 1809
Wittenberg 1502 1817

Oder

Breslau 1702

Göttingen 1694 1806
1734 Halle
1379 1816
Erfurt Jena 1558
Fulda 1804
Leipzig 1409

Krakow 1364

Lvov 1784

Dniester

Würzburg 1402, 1582
Bamberg 1648 1803
Prague 1348 1759

Olmütz 1573 1778

Erlangen 1743
Ingolstadt 1459 1800

Danube

Tyrnau 1635 1770

Tissa

Dillingen 1549 1804
Landshut 1800 1826
Linz 1669 1803
Pressburg 1467

Vienna 1365

Buda (Ofen) 1389 1777 1526

Munich 1759

Inn

Salzburg 1623 1810

Graz 1585

Innsbruck 1763,1792 1810

Drava

Fünfkirchen 1367 1526

Sava

Danube

BLACK SEA

Vicenza 1204
Treviso 1318
Padua 1222 1779
Parma 1502
Ferrara 1391
Reggio 1188 1200 1712
Bologna

S. of Marmara

Adriatic Sea

Florence 1349 1582
Pisa 1338
Arezzo 1215
Urbino 1564
Siena 1300
Perugia 1276
Camerino 1727

Rome 1303 1603

Aegean Sea

Naples 1224
Salerno 1173

AN
SEA

Palermo 1621 1637
Messina 1549
Catania 1434

10   15   20   25

50

45

40

35

EUROPE, c.1500

Scale 1:15,000,000 (240 miles=1 inch)

0 100 200 300 Miles
0 100 200 300 400 Km.

- - - Boundary of the Holy Roman Empire
Church Lands
Lands of the Union of Calmar
Electorate of Brandenburg
Saxony (Electorate and Duchy)
Lands of the House of Habsburg
Bohemia and Hungary, united under the same crown from 1490
Venetian Lands

EUROPE, c.1648

Scale 1:15,000,000 (240 miles=1 inch)

0   100   200   300 Miles
0   100 200 300 400 Km.

Boundary of the Holy Roman Empire
Church Lands
Electorate of Brandenburg
Electorate of Saxony
Lands of the House of Habsburg (Austrian Branch)
Spanish Lands
Venetian Lands
1648 Date of independence

Faroe Is.
to Den.

Shetland Is.

Orkney Is.

Särna

NORWAY

Bergen

Christiania

DENMARK
United 1380-1814

SW

Göteborg

Copenhagen
Malmö
Bornholm

NORTH
SEA

Heligoland

Lübeck
Hamburg
1648
to Sweden
Stettin

1648
Sweden
Bremen
BRANDENBURG
Berlin

HEBRIDES
SCOTLAND
Edinburgh

Under the same ruler from 1603

Durham
York

I. OF MAN

IRELAND
Dublin

ENGLAND
WALES

Oxford Cambridge
Bristol London

Amsterdam
UNITED PROVINCES
1648

T H E

Brunswick
Magdeburg
SAXONY
Dresden

Calais Brussels
SPANISH NETHERL.
Aachen Cologne
Mainz
Trier
Frankfurt
Nuremberg
E M P I R E

BOHEMIA
Prague

ATLANTIC OCEAN

English Channel

Channel Is.

BRITTANY
Nantes

NORMANDY
Paris
Seine
Orléans
Loire Tours

Verdun
Strassburg
Basle
FRANCHE COMTÉ
Charolais
SWISS
Berne
CONFEDERATION
1648
Geneva

Danube
BAVARIA
Munich
Salzburg

AUSTRIA
ST
TYROL
CARINTHIA
CARNIOL
Trieste

FRANCE

Bordeaux
Garonne Toulouse

Lyons
Rhône

SAVOY
Turin
Milan

Venice

Ferrara

San Marino

Adriatic

La Coruña

Oporto

NAVARRE
Pamplona

Andorra
ROUSSILLON
1642/59 to Fr.

Avignon to the Papacy
Marseilles

Genoa
Florence

PAPAL STATES

Lisbon
PORTUGAL
1580-1640

Duero
Valladolid
Saragossa
Ebro

Madrid
CASTILE
Toledo
Tagus

SPAIN
ARAGON

Barcelona

Corsica
1557/59
to Genoa

1557/59
to Spain

Rome
Benevento
Naples
Salerno

Guadiana

Valencia

Balearic Is.

Sardinia
to Spain

Cagliari

NA

Seville
GRANADA
Granada

1580-1640 to Sp.
Tangier 1640-62 to Port.
Ceuta
1580 to Spain
Gibraltar
Melilla
Oran

MOROCCO

ALGIERS

Algiers Bugia

Oran

MEDITERRANEAN

Bona Biserta
Tunis

TUNIS

Palermo
Sicily
to Spain

Malta
to Knights of St. John

5 West from Greenwich 0 East from Greenwich 5 10

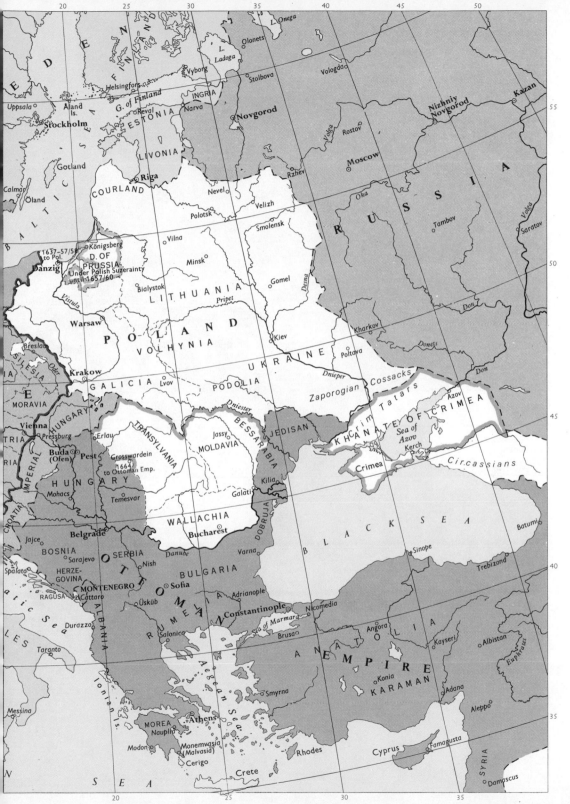

20   25   30   35   40   45   50

E D E N

S W E D E N

L. Onega

Olonets

FINLAND

L. Ladoga

Vyborg

Stolbova

Vologda

Helsingfors

G. of Finland

INGRIA

Novgorod

Nizhniy Novgorod

Kazan

55

Uppsala

Åland Is.

Reval

Narva

ESTONIA

Stockholm

LIVONIA

Volga

Rostov

Moscow

R U S S I A

Gotland

Riga

Nevel

Oka

Tambov

Saratov

Calmar

Öland

COURLAND

Polotsk

Velizh

Smolensk

50

BALTIC SEA

1637-57/59 to Pol.

Königsberg

D. OF PRUSSIA

Danzig

Vilna

Minsk

Desna

Don

Under Polish Suzerainty until 1657/60

Bialystok

LITHUANIA

Gomel

Vistula

Pripet

Warsaw

P O L A N D

Kiev

Kharkov

Donets

Breslau

VOLHYNIA

U K R A I N E

SILESIA

Oder

Krakow

GALICIA

Lvov

PODOLIA

Poltava

Dnieper

Zaporogian Cossacks

Don

45

MORAVIA

Dniester

Jassy

BESSARABIA

JEDISAN

Crim Tatars

KHANATE OF CRIMEA

Azov

Vienna

Pressburg

HUNGARY

Erlau

TRANSYLVANIA

MOLDAVIA

Sea of Azov

TRIA

IMPERIAL

Buda (Ofen)

Pest

Grosswardein 1664 to Ottoman Emp.

Kerch

Crimea

Circassians

RIA

HUNGARY

Mohacs

Temesvar

Kilia

Galati

CROATIA

WALLACHIA

DOBRUJA

B L A C K S E A

Belgrade

Bucharest

Batumi

BOSNIA

SERBIA

Danube

Varna

Sinope

Jajce

Nish

Sarajevo

HERZE-GOVINA

O T T O M A N

BULGARIA

40

Spalato

RAGUSA

Cattaro

MONTENEGRO

Sofia

Trebizond

Durazzo

ALBANIA

R U M E L I A

Üsküb

Adrianople

Nicomedia

Salonica

Constantinople

Brusa

Sea of Marmara

Angora

A N A T O L I A

Kayseri

Albistan

Euphrates

Taranto

Aegean Sea

E M P I R E

KARAMAN

Konia

Adana

Aleppo

35

Messina

Ionian Sea

MOREA

Nauplia

Athens

Smyrna

Adana

Modon

Monemvasia (Malvasia)

Rhodes

Cyprus

Famagusta

SYRIA

Cerigo

Crete

Damascus

N   S E A

20   25   30   35

EUROPE, *c.*1721

Scale 1:15,000,000 (240 miles=1 inch)

0   100   200   300 Miles

0   100   200   300   400 Km.

—— Boundary of the Holy Roman Empire

Church Lands

Venetian Lands

Brandenburg–Prussia

Lands of the House of Habsburg (Austrian Branch)

Gt. Britain and Hanover, united under the same ruler since 1714

Poland and El. of Saxony, united under the same ruler 1697–1763

1710   Date of independence

Faroe Is.
to Den.

Shetland Is.

Orkney Is.

Hebrides

SCOTLAND

Edinburgh

IRELAND

Dublin

I. OF MAN

GREAT BRITAIN
From 1707

York

WALES

ENGLAND

Norwich

Oxford   Cambridge

Bristol   London

Bergen

NORWAY

Christiania

SWE...

Göteborg

Aalborg

DENMARK

Copenhagen

Malmö

Bornholm

NORTH SEA

to Sweden

Heligoland
1721 to Den.

1667/76
to Den.

Hamburg

Stettin

Bremen

HANOVER

BRANDENBURG

Minden

Magdeburg

Berlin

THE

SAXONY

Leipzig

Dresden

BOHEM...

Prague

E M P I R...

Amsterdam

UNITED PROVINC...

Brussels

1714
to...

Aachen

Cologne

Austria

Trier

Frankfurt

Nuremberg

Danube

BAVARIA

Munich

AUS...

Salzburg

STY...

Calais

English Channel

Channel Is.

BRITTANY

NORMANDY

Paris

Seine

Orléans

Nantes

Loire

Tours

FRANCE

Limoges

Bordeaux

Garonne

Toulouse

1713–42
to Bran.

Strasbourg

Basle

FRANCHE
to Prussia
COMTÉ

SWISS
CONFEDERATION

Berne

Innsbruck

TYROL

CARINTHIA

Trent

CARNIOLA

La Coruña

Oporto

Braganza

Duero

Valladolid

Burgos

Ebro

Saragossa

Pamplona

Andorra

ROUSSILLON

PORTUGAL

Lisbon

Tagus

Madrid

Toledo

Guadiana

SPAIN

CATALONIA

Barcelona

Valencia

Lagos

Seville

Cartagena

Granada

Lyons

SAVOY

1713/48
to Savoy

PIEDMONT

1714
to Savoy

Milan

1714
to Aust.

Venice

Orange
Confirmed
1713

Avignon
to the Papacy

1713 to Fr.

Genoa

Florence

San Marino

Bologna

Adri...

PAPAL STATES

Marseilles

S
A
R
D
I
...

Rhône

1714
to Aust.

Corsica
to Genoa

Rome
1714
to...

Beneyento

Naples

N
A
P...

Balearic Is.

Minorca
1708/13–83
to Br.

Sardinia
1714 to Aust.
1720 to Savoy

Cagliari

Tangier
1662–84
to Eng.

Gibraltar
1704/13 to Br.

Ceuta

Melilla

MOROCCO

Oran
Until 1706
to Spain

Algiers

ALGIERS

1710

MEDITERRA...

Bona

TUNIS

Tunis

Palermo

Sicily
1713 to Sav.
1720 to Aust.

Malta
to Knights of
St. John

ATLANTIC OCEAN

SWEDEN
FINLAND
L. Onega
Olonets
L. Ladoga
Vyborg
Uppsala
Åland Is.
Helsingfors
G. of Finland
St. Petersburg
INGRIA
Vologda
Volga
Stockholm
Reval
ESTONIA
Narva
Novgorod
Kazan
Nizhniy Novgorod
1721 to Russia
LIVONIA
Rostov
Rzhev
Moscow
RUSSIA
Gotland
Riga
Nevel
Oka
Tambov
Saratov
COURLAND
Velizh
Oland
Calmer
Polotsk
Smolensk
Tauroggen
1688/90 to Prussia
Vilna
Desna
Don
Königsberg
K. OF PRUSSIA
From 1701
C. OF SERREY
1688/90 to Prussia
Minsk
Gomel
Danzig
Grodno
Bialystok
Pripet
Kharkov
Donets
Poznan
Vistula
Warsaw
LITHUANIA
Kiev
UKRAINE
Poltava
POLAND
Lublin
VOLHYNIA
Breslau
SILESIA
Krakow
Oder
GALICIA
Lvov
PODOLIA
1672–99 to Ottoman Emp.
Dnieper
Zaporogian Cossacks
Under Russian Sovereignty
from 1654/67
Azov
1696–1711
to Russia
MORAVIA
Kaschau
Dniester
BESSARABIA
JEDISAN
KHANATE OF CRIMEA
Sea of Azov
AUSTRIA
Vienna
Pressburg
Erlau
Jassy
MOLDAVIA
Crimea
Kerch
Circassians
Buda (Ofen)
Pest
Grosswardein
1699 to Austria
Kilia
BLACK SEA
HUNGARY
TRANSYLVANIA
Batumi
Mohacs
Temesvar
BANAT
1718 to Aust.
Galati
WALLACHIA
DOBRUJA
CROATIA
Jajce
Belgrade
Passarowitz
1718–39 to Aust.
Bucharest
1718–39 to Aust.
Danube
Sinope
Zara
BOSNIA
Sarajevo
SERBIA
1718–39 to Aust.
Nish
Varna
Trebizond
Spalato
HERZE-GOVINA
MONTENEGRO
Cattaro
OTTOMAN
BULGARIA
Sofia
Philippopolis
Amasia
RAGUSA
1718
ALBANIA
Üsküb
Adrianople
Sivas
Durazzo
Adriatic Sea
RUMELIA
Constantinople
Scutari
Nicomedia
ANATOLIA
Kayseri
Albistan
DARDANELLES
Austria
Taranto
Janina
Salonica
Brusa
Angora
Konia
KARAMAN
Euphrates
Messina
Reggio
MOREA
1685/99–1715/18
to Ven.
Athens
Napulia
Smyrna
Adalia
Aleppo
Modon
Monemvasia
(Malvasia)
Rhodes
Cyprus
Famagusta
SYRIA
Cerigo
Crete
Damascus
SEA
Ionian Is.
Aegean Sea
Sea of Marmara
EMPIRE

EUROPE, c.1812

Scale 1:15,000,000 (240 miles = 1 inch)

| 0 | 100 | 200 | 300 Miles |

Miles

| 0 | 100 | 200 | 300 | 400 |

Km.

- - - Boundary of Confederation of the Rhine

French Empire

States ruled by Napoleon's family

Other dependent states

Faroe Is.
to Den.

Shetland Is.

Orkney Is.

SCOTLAND

Hebrides

Glasgow
Edinburgh

UNITED KINGDOM OF
GREAT BRITAIN
AND IRELAND

IRELAND

Dublin
Liverpool Manchester
Hull

ISLE OF MAN

From 1801

WALES
Birmingham
Norwich
Bristol
London
ENGLAND

NORTH SEA

Bergen

NORWAY

United until 1814

Christiania

Göteborg

DENMARK

Aalborg
Copenhagen
Malmö
Bornholm

to Swede

Heligoland
1807/14 to Br.

Lübeck

Bremen
1807/10
to Fr.

Hamburg

Stettin

BRANDENBURG

Berlin

Hanover
Magdeburg

WESTPHALIA

BERG

Erfurt
to Fr.

Leipzig
Dresden

CONFEDERATION

Frankfurt

Main

OF THE

RHINE

Nuremberg

BOHE

Prague

ATLANTIC OCEAN

English Channel

Channel Is.

Calais Brussels

Amsterdam

Antwerp

1810 to Fr.

Cologne

Le Havre

Seine

Paris

Orléans

Strasbourg

Rhine

Stuttgart

STY

Munich

Salzburg

Innsbruck

Inn

CARI

Nantes

Loire

Tours

FRANCE

Saône

Neuchâtel

Basle

HELVETIA

Berne

Geneva
1798–1814
to Fr.

Lyons

Trent

ILLYRIAN

Danube

Bordeaux

Garonne

Bayonne

Toulouse

Rhône

Turin

Po

Milan

ITALY

Venice

Trieste

Adr

La Coruña

Oporto

Burgos

Valladolid

Duero

Ebro

Pamplona

Saragossa

Andorra

CATALONIA
1812–13 to Fr.

Barcelona

Marseilles

Genoa

Bologna

LUCCA

San Marino

Florence
TUSCANY

PAPAL STATES

Rome

NA

Corsica

Ajaccio

Pontecorvo

Benevento

Naples

PORTUGAL

SPAIN

Madrid

Toledo

Tagus

Guadiana
1801 to Spain

Lisbon

Lagos

Seville

Granada

Cartagena

Valencia

Balearic Is.

Minorca
1798–1802
to Br.

SARDINIA

Cagliari

Tangier

Gibraltar
to Br.

Ceuta
to Spain

Melilla
to Spain

Peñon de
la Gomera

Alhucemas
to Spain

MOROCCO

Oran

Algiers

ALGIERS

TUNIS

Bona

Tunis

MEDITERRANEAN

Palermo

SICILY

Malta
1798 to Fr.
1800 to Br.

EUROPE, c.1815

Scale 1:15,000,000 (240 miles=1 inch)

0   100   200   300 Miles

0   100   200   300   400   Km.

Boundary of German Confederation, 1815

United Kingdom and Hanover, united under the same ruler 1815-37

Austro-Hungarian military boundary zones, with date of duration

OL.   Oldenburg

20

Nikolaystad
(Vasa)

L. Onega

L. Ladoga
Olonets

Vologda

Helsingfors
Kronstadt
G. of Finland
St. Petersburg
Vyborg

Uppsala
Åland Is.
Revel
Narva
Novgorod
Volga
Nizhniy Novgorod
Kazan

Stockholm
Pskov
Tver
Moscow

Gotland
Riga

Jaroslavl

Oka
Tula
Tambov
Saratov

Polotsk
Smolensk
R U S S I A

Volga

Tauroggen
Vilna

Königsberg
Danzig
EAST PRUSSIA
Grodno
Minsk
Gomel
Belograd
Tsaritsyn

Thorn
Bialystok
Pripet
Don

Posen
Bug
P O L A N D
Warsaw
From 1815 united with Russia
1831 fully part of Russia
Kiev
Kharkov
Donets

Kalish
Breslau
Lublin
Poltava

SILESIA
Oder
Krakow
Vistula
Dnieper

MORAVIA
REP. OF KRAKOW
1815-46
Lemberg
(Lvov)
1815
to Austria
Rostov
Azov

A U S T R I A N
Tarnopol
Dniester
Kherson
Sea of Azov
Kerch
GREAT KABARDIA
From 1825 complete Russian Control

Vienna
Pressburg
Erlau
Jassy
Odessa
Crimea
Circassians

Buda
(Ofen)
Pest
MOLDAVIA
Trib.
Sevastopol

E M P I R E
Grosswardein
Galati
Poti

H U N G A R Y
Temesvar
1764-1851
WALLACHIA
Trib.
Bucharest
DOBRUJA
B L A C K   S E A
Batumi

Mohacs
1702-1878
1742-1872
Danube
Varna
Sinope
Trebizond

Sava
Belgrade
SERBIA
Trib.
Nish
BULGARIA
Sofia
Philippopolis
Amasia

BOSNIA
Sarajevo
Adrianople
Sivas

DALMATIA
HERZE-GOVINA
MONTENEGRO
Üsküb
THRACE
Constantinople
Scutari
Nicomedia

Ragusa
Cattaro
MACEDONIA
Salonica
Brusa
Angora
Kayseri
Albistan

Durazzo
ALBANIA
Sea of Marmara
E M P I R E
Euphrates

TWO SICILIES
Taranto
Aegean Sea
Konya
Adana
Aleppo

Messina
Reggio
Janina
Corfu
Ionian Is.
From 1815 Rep. under Br. Prot.
Smyrna
Adalia
Famagusta

Patras
Corinth
Athens
Cyprus
Damascus

MOREA
Cerigo
Crete
Rhodes

COPYRIGHT. GEORGE PHILIP & SON. LTD.

EUROPE, c.1914

Scale 1:15,000,000 (240 miles=1 inch)

0   100   200   300 Miles

0 100 200 300 400 Km.

1830 Date of independence

Faroe Is.
to Den.

Shetland Is.

Orkney Is.

NORWAY

Union 1815-1905

Bergen

Christiania

Stavanger

Göteborg

Hebr

SCOTLAND

Glasgow

Edinburgh

N O R T H
S E A

Aalborg

DENMARK

Copenhagen

Malmö

Bornholm

UNITED KINGDOM

IRELAND

I. of Man

Dublin

Liverpool

Hull

Manchester

SCHLESWIG

Heligoland
1890 to Germany

HOLSTEIN

Lübeck

Stettin

WALES

Birmingham

Norwich

Amsterdam

The Hague

Bremen

Hanover

Hamburg

G E R M A

ENGLAND

Bristol

London

NETHERLANDS

Berlin

EMPIRE

Leipzig

K. OF
SAXONY

A T L A N T I C   O C E A N

English   Channel

Channel Is.

Calais

BELGIUM

Brussels

1830

Cologne

HESSE-NASSAU

Frankfurt

BOHE

Prague

Seine

Sedan

PAL.
to Bav.

ALSACE-

Nuremberg

AU

Versailles

Paris

HESSE

Strassburg

LORRAINE
1871 to Ger.

WÜRTTEM-
BERG

Stuttgart

BAVARIA

Danube

Orléans

Tours

Nantes

Loire

Saône

Munich

Salzburg

Bad
Gastein

F R A N C E

Limoges

Lyons

Geneva

Basle

Zürich

LIECHTEN-
STEIN

Inn

Innsbruck

Berne

SWITZERLAND

Trent

Laibach

Bordeaux

Garonne

Rhône

Grenoble

1860
to Fr.

VENETIA
1866 to Italy

Trieste

La Coruña

Toulouse

Marseilles

1860 to Fr.

Milan

Turin

Po

Verona

Venice

Bologna

Broganza

Burgos

Pamplona

ANDORRA

Nice
1861 French Prot.

Genoa

Florence

SAN
MARINO

Oporto

Valladolid

Duero

Saragossa

Ebro

MONACO

Leghorn

Elba

From 1860

I T A L Y

PORTUGAL

Lisbon

SPAIN

Tagus

Madrid

Barcelona

Corsica

Ajaccio

From 1870
to Italy

Rome
From 1870 Capit

Guadiana

Toledo

Valencia

Naples

Seville

Cartagena

Granada

B a l e a r i c   I s.

Sardinia

Cagliari

Cadiz

Tangier

Gibraltar
to Br.

Ceuta

M E D I T E R R A

Palermo

Sicily

35

Melilla

Algiers

Bona

Tunis

Malta
to Br.

ERRIF
1912 Span Prot.

Alhucemas

Oran
1830 to Fr.

A L G E R I A

1830/48 to Fr.

TUNIS
1881 Fr. Prot.

MOROCCO
1912 Fr. Prot.

5   West from Greenwich   0   East from Greenwich   5   10

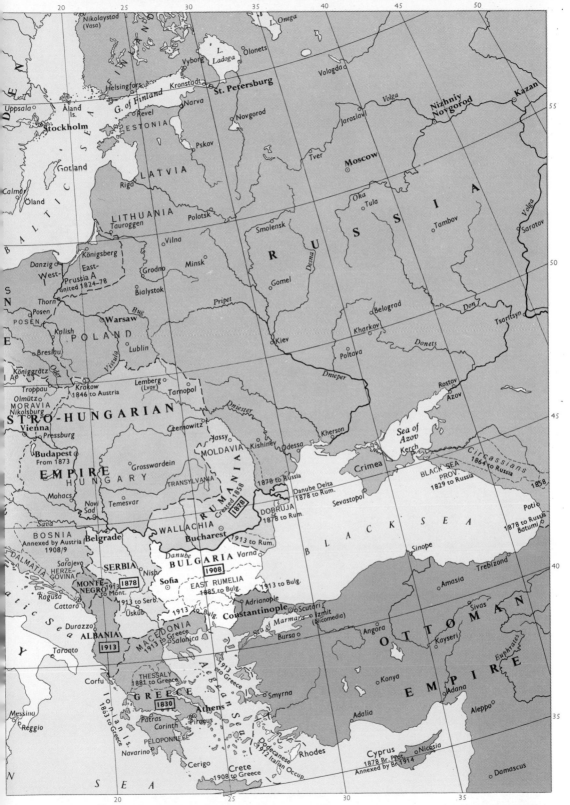

EUROPE, c. 1926

Scale 1:15,000,000 (240 miles = 1 inch)

0   100   200   300 Miles
0   100 200 300 400 Km.

1916 Date of independence

Demilitarized areas west and 50km. east of the Rhine and demilitarized "Zone of the Straits" in Turkey

S.A.   Sanjak of Alexandretta, 1920 autonomous within French Mandate of Syria

R.S.F.S.R. Russian Soviet Federal Socialist Republic

A.S.S.R. Autonomous Soviet Socialist Republic

S.S.R. Soviet Socialist Republic

A.R. Autonomous Region

84

EUROPE AFTER 1945

Scale 1:15,000,000 (240 miles = 1 inch)

0 100 200 300 Miles
0 100 200 300 400 Km.

| 1956 | Date of independence
| International boundaries 1945
| Functioning (de facto) boundary

Free State of Trieste, 1947–54:
Zone "A": Anglo-American administration from 1947; 1954 to Italy
Zone "B": Yugoslav military administration from 1947; 1954 to Yugoslavia

The "Iron Curtain" from 1955

EUROPE: RAILWAYS, 1870

Scale 1:15,000,000 (240 miles=1 inch)

Railways   Height of Land

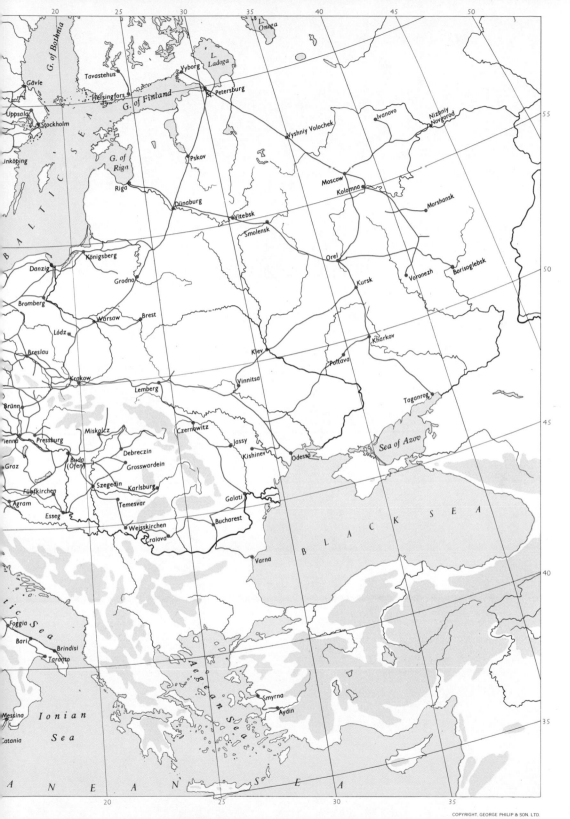

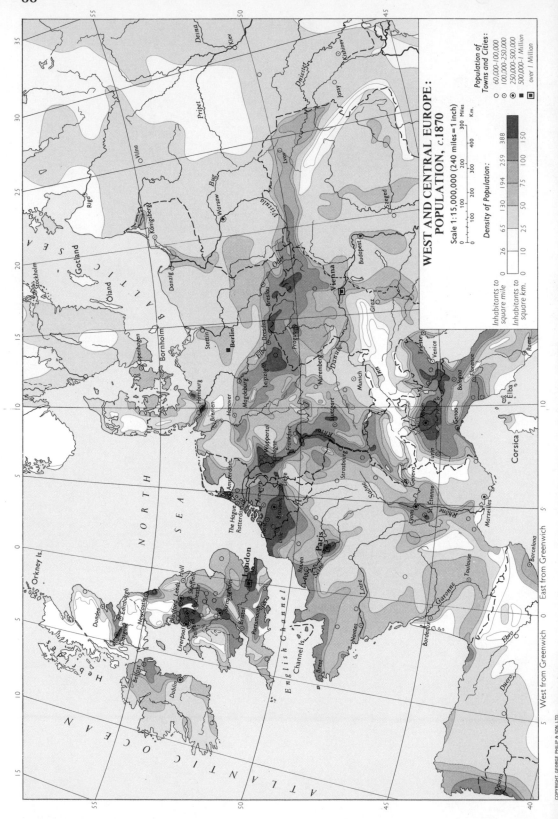

WEST AND CENTRAL EUROPE: POPULATION, c.1870

Scale 1:15,000,000 (240 miles=1 inch)

Density of Population:

Inhabitants to square mile

| 0 | 26 | 65 | 130 | 194 | 259 | 388 |

Inhabitants to square km.

| 0 | 10 | 25 | 50 | 75 | 100 | 150 |

Population of Towns and Cities:

○ 60,000–100,000
⊙ 100,000–250,000
◉ 250,000–500,000
■ 500,000–1 Million
▣ over 1 Million

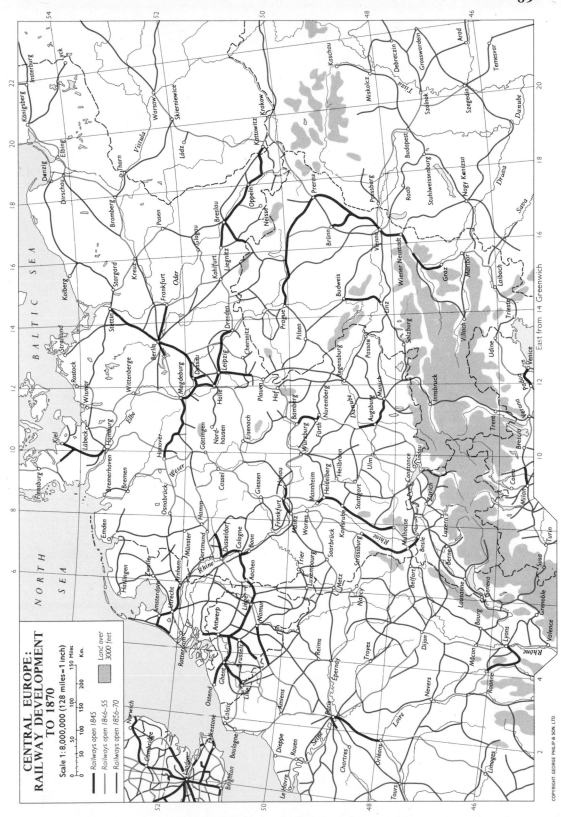

89

CENTRAL EUROPE:
RAILWAY DEVELOPMENT
TO 1870

Scale 1:8,000,000 (128 miles=1 inch)

0   50   100   150 Miles

0   50   100   150   200 Km.

Land over
3000 feet

Railways open 1845
Railways open 1846-55
Railways open 1856-70

East from 14 Greenwich

COPYRIGHT. GEORGE PHILIP & SON, LTD.

BALTIC SEA

NORTH SEA

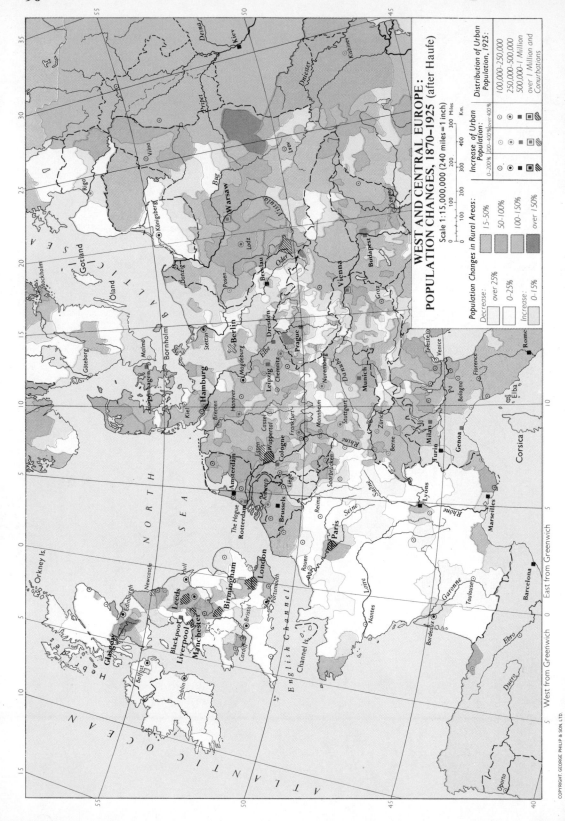

WEST AND CENTRAL EUROPE:
POPULATION CHANGES, 1870-1925 (after Haufe)

Scale 1:15,000,000 (240 miles = 1 inch)

Population Changes in Rural Areas:			
Decrease: over 25%	0-25%		
Increase: 0-15%	15-50%	50-100%	100-150%	over 150%

Increase of Urban Population:		
0-200%	200-400%	over 400%

Distribution of Urban Population, 1925:	
100,000-250,000	250,000-500,000
500,000-1 Million	over 1 Million and Conurbations

COPYRIGHT GEORGE PHILIP & SON, LTD.

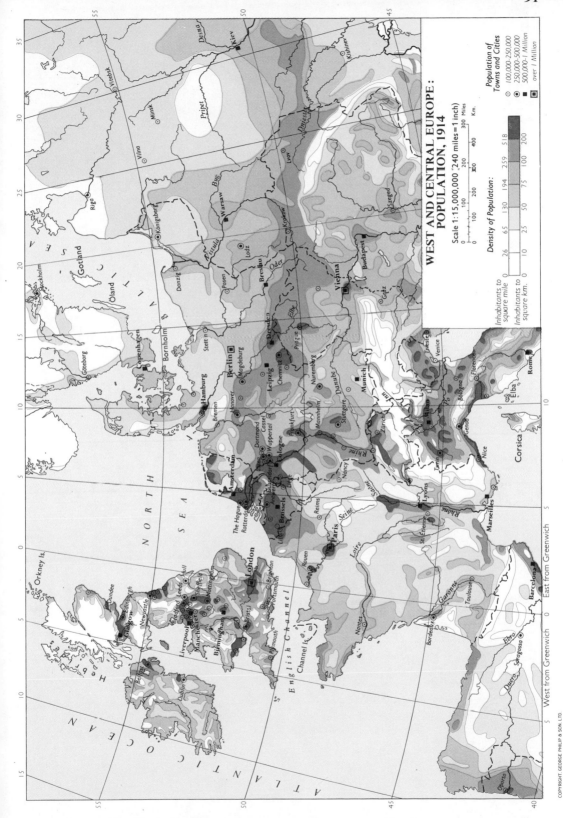

WEST AND CENTRAL EUROPE:
POPULATION, 1914

Scale 1:15,000,000 (240 miles=1 inch)

Density of Population:

Population of
Towns and Cities

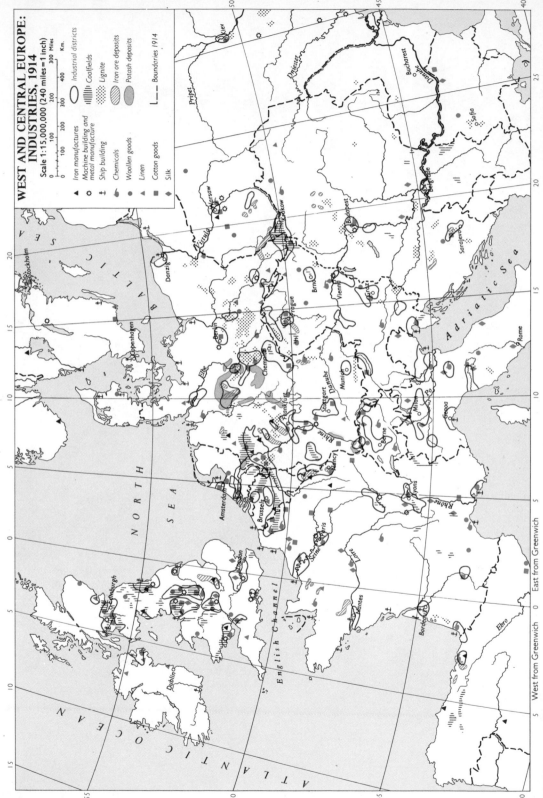

WEST AND CENTRAL EUROPE: INDUSTRIES, 1914

Scale 1:15,000,000 (240 miles = 1 inch)

Miles 0 100 200 300
Km. 0 100 200 300 400

Industrial districts
Coalfields
Lignite
Iron ore deposits
Potash deposits
Boundaries 1914

▲ Iron manufactures
✿ Machine building and metal manufacture
⊥ Ship building
✿ Chemicals
● Woollen goods
▲ Linen
■ Cotton goods
◆ Silk

COPYRIGHT. GEORGE PHILIP & SON, LTD.

EUROPE: INDUSTRIAL CHANGES, 1870-1965

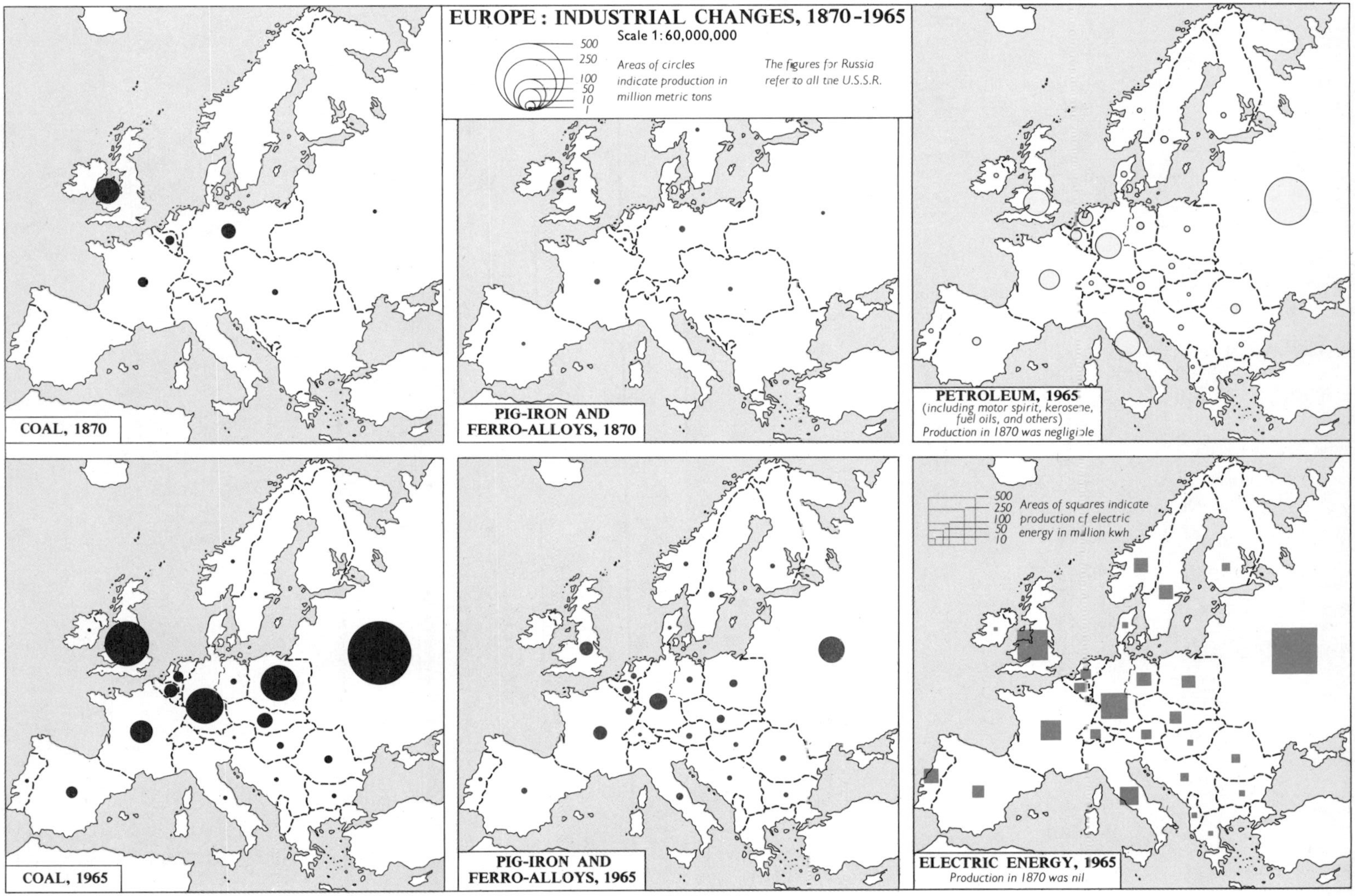
Scale 1:60,000,000
500
250
100
50
10
1
Areas of circles indicate production in million metric tons
The figures for Russia refer to all the U.S.S.R.
COAL, 1870
PIG-IRON AND FERRO-ALLOYS, 1870
PETROLEUM, 1965
(including motor spirit, kerosene, fuel oils, and others)
Production in 1870 was negligible
COAL, 1965
PIG-IRON AND FERRO-ALLOYS, 1965
500
250
100
50
10
Areas of squares indicate production of electric energy in million kwh
ELECTRIC ENERGY, 1965
Production in 1870 was nil

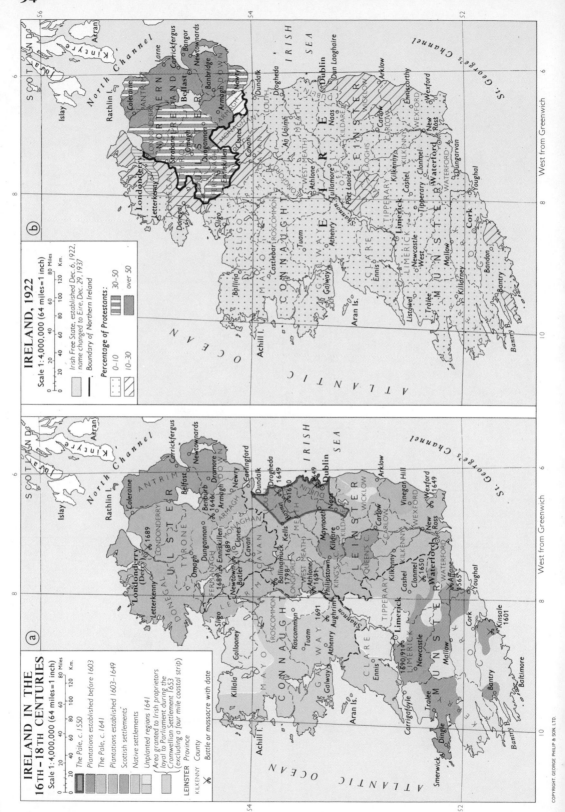

IRELAND IN THE 16TH–18TH CENTURIES

Scale 1:4,000,000 (64 miles=1 inch)

0 20 40 60 80 100 120 Km.
0 20 40 60 80 Miles

The Pale, c. 1550

Plantations established before 1603

The Pale, c. 1641

Plantations established 1603–1649

Scottish settlements

Native settlements

Unplanted regions 1641

Area granted to Irish proprietors loyal to Parliament during the Cromwellian Settlement 1653 (excluding a four mile coastal strip)

LEINSTER Province

KILKENNY County

✕ Battle or massacre with date

IRELAND, 1922

Scale 1:4,000,000 (64 miles=1 inch)

0 20 40 60 80 Miles
0 20 40 60 80 100 120 Km.

Irish Free State, established Dec. 6, 1922, name changed to Eire, Dec. 29, 1937

Boundary of Northern Ireland

Percentage of Protestants:

0–10

10–30

30–50

over 50

COPYRIGHT GEORGE PHILIP & SON LTD.

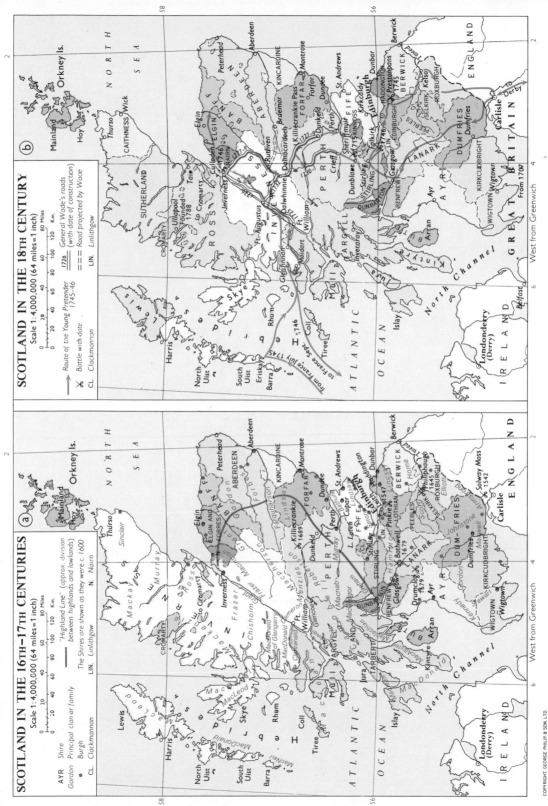

SCOTLAND IN THE 16TH–17TH CENTURIES

Scale 1:4,000,000 (64 miles=1 inch)

| 0 | 20 | 40 | 60 | 80 Miles |

| 0 | 20 | 40 | 60 | 80 | 100 | 120 Km. |

AYR Shire

Gordon Principal clan or family

• Burgh

CL. Clackmannan

"Highland Line" (approx. division between highlands and lowlands)
The Shires are shown as they were c. 1600

LIN. Linlithgow   N. Nairn

SCOTLAND IN THE 18TH CENTURY

Scale 1:4,000,000 (64 miles=1 inch)

| 0 | 20 | 40 | 60 | 80 Miles |

| 0 | 20 | 40 | 60 | 80 | 100 | 120 Km. |

→ Route of the Young Pretender 1745–46

✕ Battle with date

CL. Clackmannan

1726 General Wade's roads (with date of construction)

=== Road projected by Wace

LIN. Linlithgow

COPYRIGHT. GEORGE PHILIP & SON. LTD.

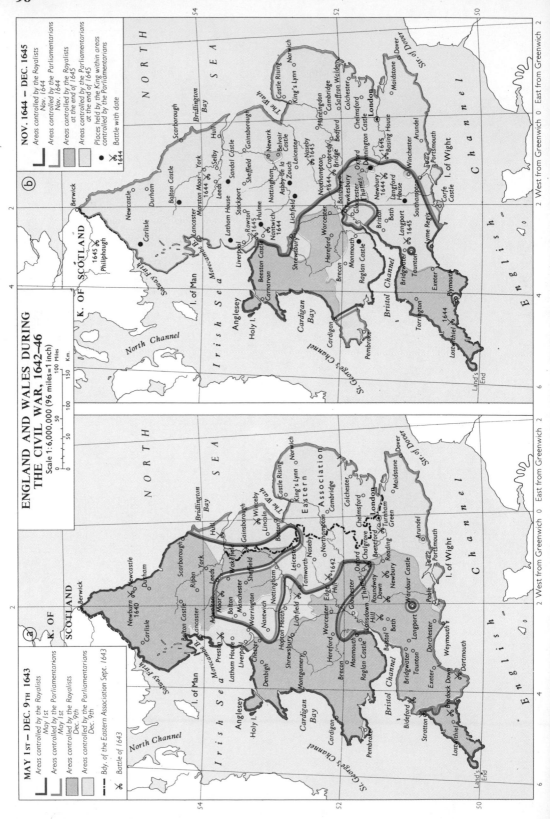

ENGLAND AND WALES DURING THE CIVIL WAR, 1642–46

Scale 1:6,000,000 (96 miles=1 inch)

(a) MAY 1ST – DEC. 9TH 1643

Areas controlled by the Royalists May 1st

Areas controlled by the Parliamentarians May 1st

Areas controlled by the Royalists Dec. 9th

Areas controlled by the Parliamentarians Dec. 9th

- - - Bdy. of the Eastern Association Sept. 1643

✕ Battle of 1643

(b) NOV. 1644 – DEC. 1645

Areas controlled by the Royalists Nov. 1644

Areas controlled by the Parliamentarians Nov. 1644

Areas controlled by the Royalists at the end of 1645

Areas controlled by the Parliamentarians at the end of 1645

● Places held by the King within areas controlled by the Parliamentarians

✕ 1644 Battle with date

COPYRIGHT GEORGE PHILIP & SON LTD

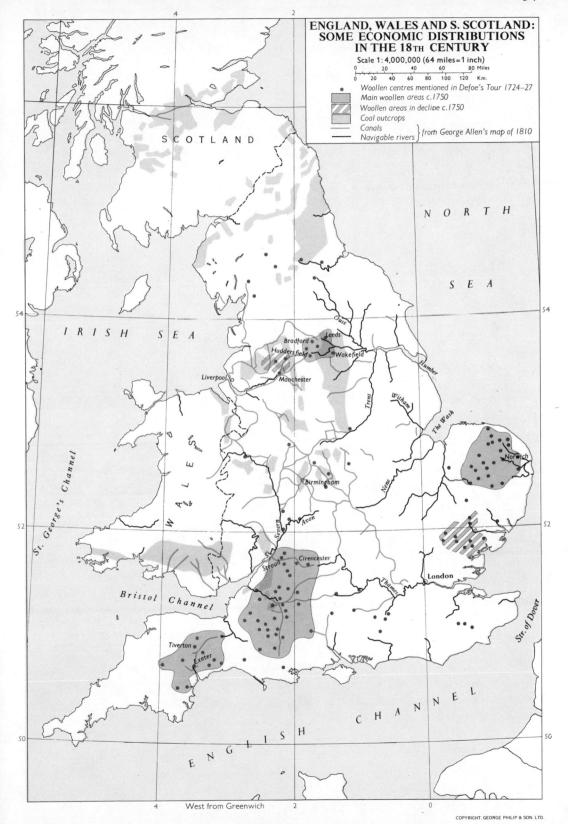

ENGLAND, WALES AND S. SCOTLAND:
SOME ECONOMIC DISTRIBUTIONS
IN THE 18TH CENTURY

Scale 1 : 4,000,000 (64 miles=1 inch)

0   20   40   60   80 Miles
0 20 40 60 80 100 120 Km.

- Woollen centres mentioned in Defoe's Tour 1724–27
- Main woollen areas c.1750
- Woollen areas in decline c.1750
- Coal outcrops
- Canals   } from George Allen's map of 1810
- Navigable rivers

SCOTLAND

NORTH SEA

IRISH SEA

Ouse

Bradford   Leeds
Huddersfield   Wakefield
Liverpool   Manchester

Humber

Trent   Witham

The Wash

Norwich

Birmingham

Nene

WALES

St. George's Channel

Severn   Avon

52

Cirencester
Stroud

London

Thames

Bristol Channel

Tiverton
Exeter

Str. of Dover

ENGLISH   CHANNEL

West from Greenwich

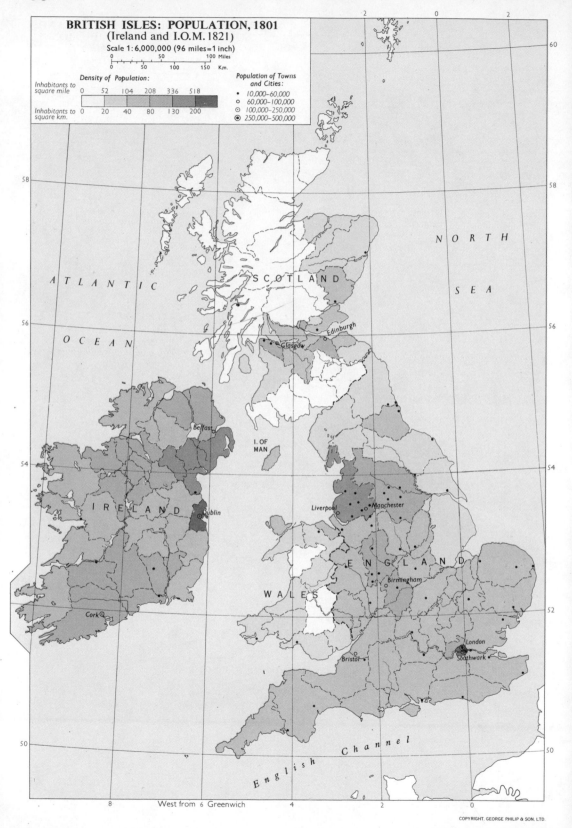

BRITISH ISLES: POPULATION, 1801
(Ireland and I.O.M. 1821)

Scale 1:6,000,000 (96 miles=1 inch)

Density of Population:

Inhabitants to square mile: 0 52 104 208 336 518

Inhabitants to square km.: 0 20 40 80 130 200

Population of Towns and Cities:
- 10,000–60,000
- 60,000–100,000
- 100,000–250,000
- 250,000–500,000

NORTH SEA

ATLANTIC

OCEAN

SCOTLAND

Edinburgh

Glasgow

Belfast

I. OF MAN

IRELAND

Dublin

Liverpool Manchester

ENGLAND

Birmingham

WALES

Cork

Bristol

London
Southwark

English Channel

West from 6 Greenwich

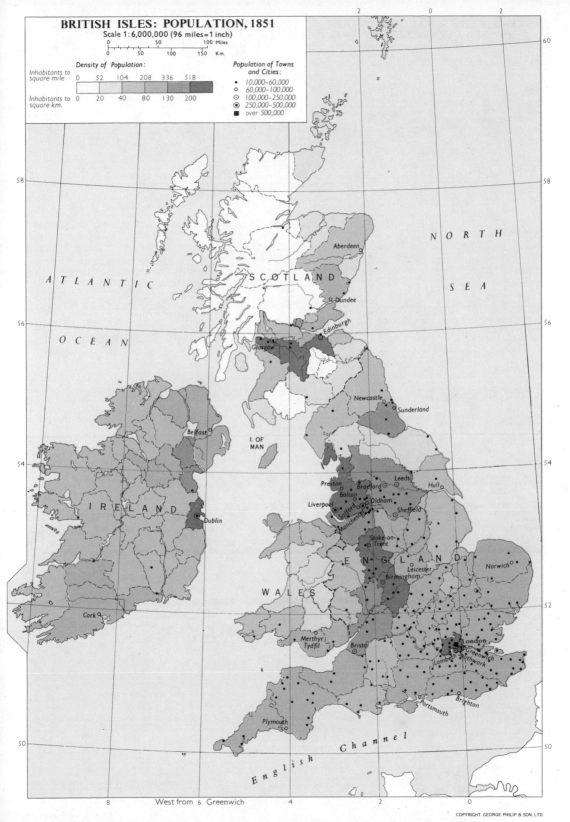

BRITISH ISLES: POPULATION, 1851

Scale 1 : 6,000,000 (96 miles = 1 inch)

| 0 | | 50 | | 100 Miles |

| 0 | 50 | 100 | 150 Km. |

Density of Population:

Inhabitants to square mile
0   52   104   208   336   518

Inhabitants to square km.
0   20   40   80   130   200

Population of Towns and Cities:
- •   10,000–60,000
- ○   60,000–100,000
- ◎   100,000–250,000
- ◉   250,000–500,000
- ■   over 500,000

ATLANTIC

OCEAN

NORTH

SEA

SCOTLAND

Aberdeen

Dundee

Edinburgh

Glasgow

Newcastle

Sunderland

I. OF MAN

IRELAND

Belfast

Dublin

Preston

Bradford

Leeds

Hull

Bolton

Liverpool

Oldham

Salford

Sheffield

Manchester

Stoke-on-Trent

ENGLAND

Leicester

Norwich

Birmingham

WALES

Cork

Merthyr Tydfil

Bristol

London

Greenwich

Lambeth Southwark

Portsmouth

Brighton

Plymouth

English Channel

West from 6 Greenwich

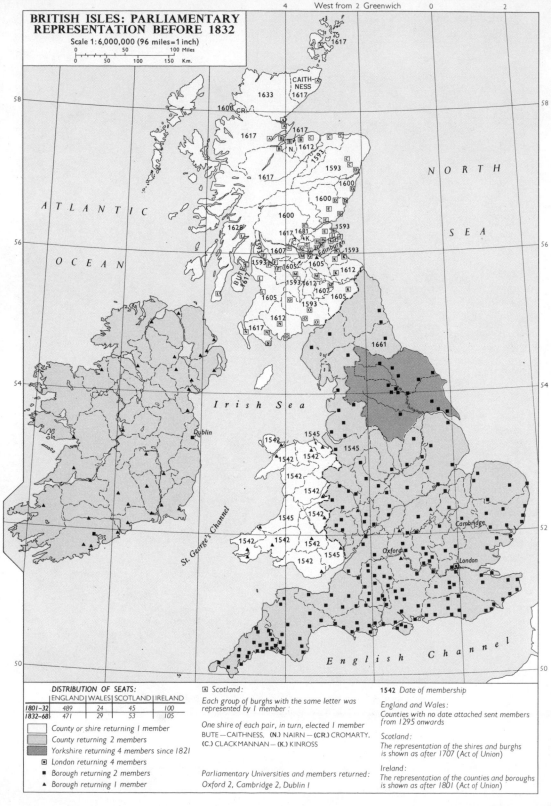

BRITISH ISLES: PARLIAMENTARY REPRESENTATION BEFORE 1832

Scale 1:6,000,000 (96 miles=1 inch)

0   50   100 Miles

0   50   100   150 Km.

West from 2 Greenwich

CAITH-NESS

N O R T H

S E A

A T L A N T I C

O C E A N

Edinburgh

BUTE

Irish Sea

Dublin

St. George's Channel

Cambridge

Oxford

London

English Channel

DISTRIBUTION OF SEATS:

	ENGLAND	WALES	SCOTLAND	IRELAND
1801–32	489	24	45	100
1832–68	471	29	53	105

County or shire returning 1 member

County returning 2 members

Yorkshire returning 4 members since 1821

⊡ London returning 4 members

■ Borough returning 2 members

▲ Borough returning 1 member

Ⓐ Scotland:
Each group of burghs with the same letter was represented by 1 member

One shire of each pair, in turn, elected 1 member
BUTE – CAITHNESS. (N.) NAIRN – (CR.) CROMARTY.
(C.) CLACKMANNAN – (K.) KINROSS

Parliamentary Universities and members returned:
Oxford 2, Cambridge 2, Dublin 1

1542 Date of membership

England and Wales:
Counties with no date attached sent members from 1295 onwards

Scotland:
The representation of the shires and burghs is shown as after 1707 (Act of Union)

Ireland:
The representation of the counties and boroughs is shown as after 1801 (Act of Union)

COPYRIGHT. GEORGE. PHILIP & SON. LTD

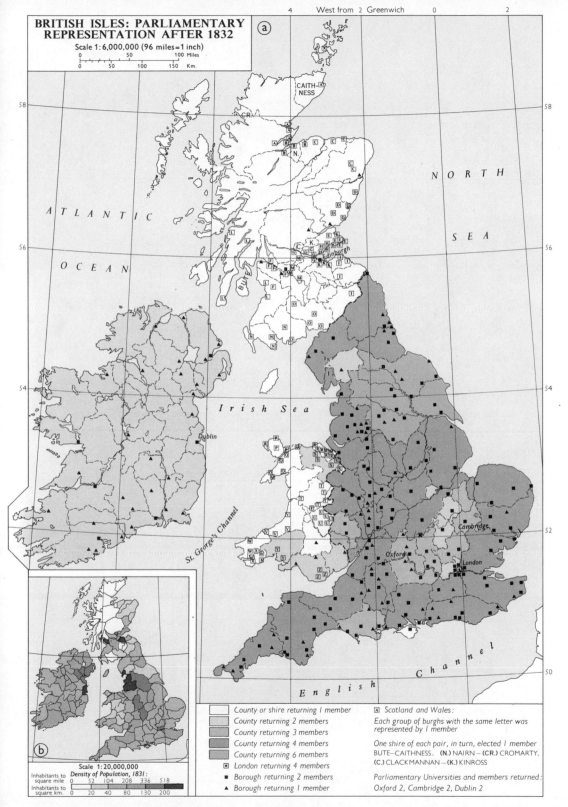

BRITISH ISLES: PARLIAMENTARY REPRESENTATION AFTER 1832

Scale 1:6,000,000 (96 miles=1 inch)

0   50   100 Miles

0   50   100   150 Km.

(a)

West from 2 Greenwich   0   2

4

58   58

CAITH-
NESS

CR.

N O R T H

S E A

56   56

A T L A N T I C

O C E A N

Bute

Edinburgh

54   54

Irish Sea

Dublin

Cambridge

52   52

St. George's Channel

Oxford

London

E n g l i s h   C h a n n e l

50   50

Density of Population, 1831:

Inhabitants to square mile 0   52   104   208   336   518

Inhabitants to square km.   0   20   40   80   130   200

Scale 1:20,000,000

(b)

☐ County or shire returning 1 member	Ⓐ **Scotland and Wales:**
County returning 2 members	*Each group of burghs with the same letter was represented by 1 member*
County returning 3 members	
County returning 4 members	*One shire of each pair, in turn, elected 1 member*
County returning 6 members	BUTE—CAITHNESS. **(N.)** NAIRN — **(CR.)** CROMARTY,
⊡ London returning 4 members	**(C.)** CLACKMANNAN — **(K.)** KINROSS
■ Borough returning 2 members	*Parliamentary Universities and members returned:*
▲ Borough returning 1 member	Oxford 2, Cambridge 2, Dublin 2

COPYRIGHT. GEORGE PHILIP & SON. LTD.

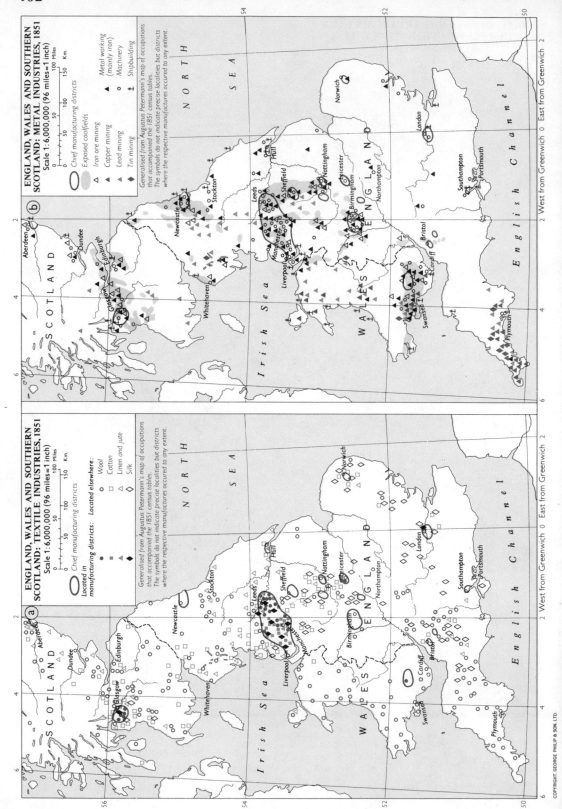

ENGLAND, WALES AND SOUTHERN SCOTLAND: METAL INDUSTRIES, 1851

Scale 1:6,000,000 (96 miles=1 inch)

Km. 0 50 100 150
Miles 0 50 100

○ Chief manufacturing districts
▨ Exposed coalfields

△ Iron ore mining
▲ Copper mining
▲ Lead mining
◆ Tin mining

▲ Metal working (mainly iron)
○ Machinery
✦ Shipbuilding

Generalised from Augustus Petermann's map of occupations that accompanied the 1851 census tables.
The symbols do not indicate precise localities but districts where the respective manufactures occurred to any extent.

ENGLAND, WALES AND SOUTHERN SCOTLAND: TEXTILE INDUSTRIES, 1851

Scale 1:6,000,000 (96 miles=1 inch)

Km. 0 50 100 150
Miles 0 50 100

○ Chief manufacturing districts

Located in manufacturing districts: Located elsewhere:

● ▨ ◆ Wool   ○ Wool
● ▨ ◆ Cotton   □ Cotton
● ▨ ◆ Linen and Jute   △ Linen and Jute
● ▨ ◆ Silk   ◇ Silk

Generalised from Augustus Petermann's map of occupations that accompanied the 1851 census tables.
The symbols do not indicate precise localities but districts where the respective manufactures occurred to any extent.

COPYRIGHT. GEORGE PHILIP & SON. LTD.

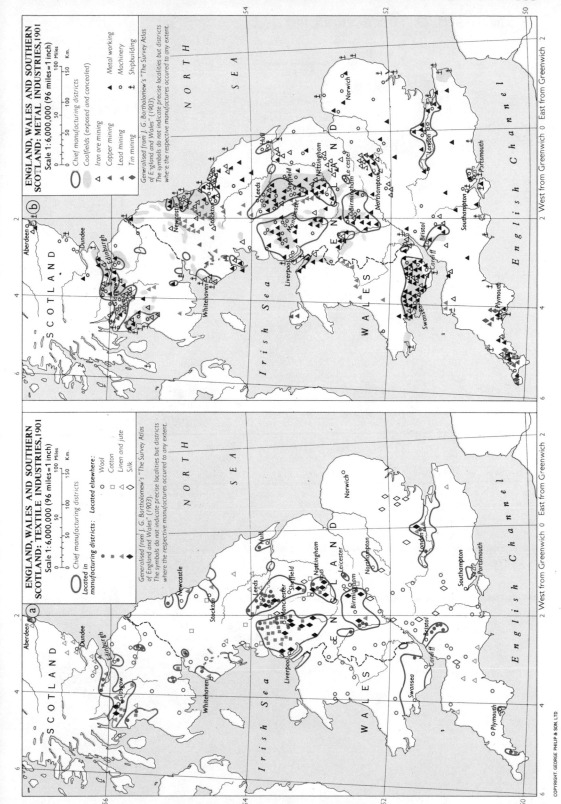

ENGLAND, WALES AND SOUTHERN SCOTLAND: METAL INDUSTRIES, 1901

Scale 1:6,000,000 (96 miles=1 inch)

Chief manufacturing districts
Coalfields (exposed and concealed)

- Iron ore mining
- Copper mining
- Lead mining
- Tin mining
- Metal working
- Machinery
- Shipbuilding

Generalised from J. G. Bartholomew's "The Survey Atlas of England and Wales" (1903). The symbols do not indicate precise localities but districts where the respective manufactures occured to any extent.

ENGLAND, WALES AND SOUTHERN SCOTLAND: TEXTILE INDUSTRIES, 1901

Scale 1:6,000,000 (96 miles=1 inch)

Chief manufacturing districts

Located in manufacturing districts:
- Wool
- Cotton
- Linen and jute
- Silk

Located elsewhere

Generalised from J. G. Bartholomew's "The Survey Atlas of England and Wales" (1903). The symbols do not indicate precise localities but districts where the respective manufactures occured to any extent.

COPYRIGHT. GEORGE PHILIP & SON, LTD.

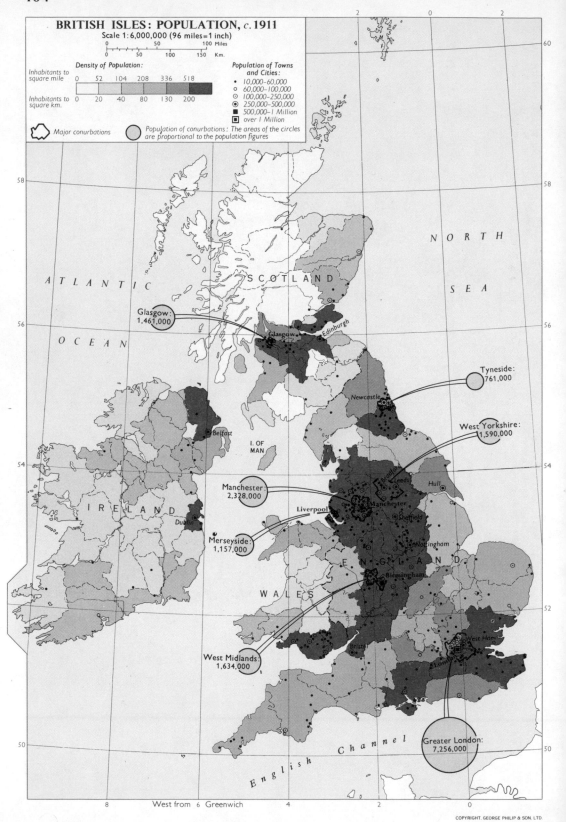

BRITISH ISLES: POPULATION, *c.* 1911

Scale 1:6,000,000 (96 miles=1 inch)

0   50   100 Miles
0   50   100   150 Km.

Density of Population:

Inhabitants to square mile   0   52   104   208   336   518

Inhabitants to square km.   0   20   40   80   130   200

Population of Towns and Cities:
- • 10,000–60,000
- ○ 60,000–100,000
- ⊙ 100,000–250,000
- ◉ 250,000–500,000
- ■ 500,000–1 Million
- ▣ over 1 Million

Major conurbations

Population of conurbations: The areas of the circles are proportional to the population figures

ATLANTIC OCEAN

SCOTLAND

NORTH SEA

Glasgow: 1,461,000

Glasgow   Edinburgh

Tyneside: 761,000

Newcastle

West Yorkshire: 1,590,000

Belfast

I. OF MAN

Manchester: 2,328,000

Bradford   Leeds   Hull

Liverpool   Manchester

IRELAND

Sheffield

Dublin

Merseyside: 1,157,000

Nottingham

ENGLAND

Birmingham

WALES

Bristol

West Midlands: 1,634,000

West Ham

London

Greater London: 7,256,000

English Channel

8   West from 6 Greenwich   4   2   0

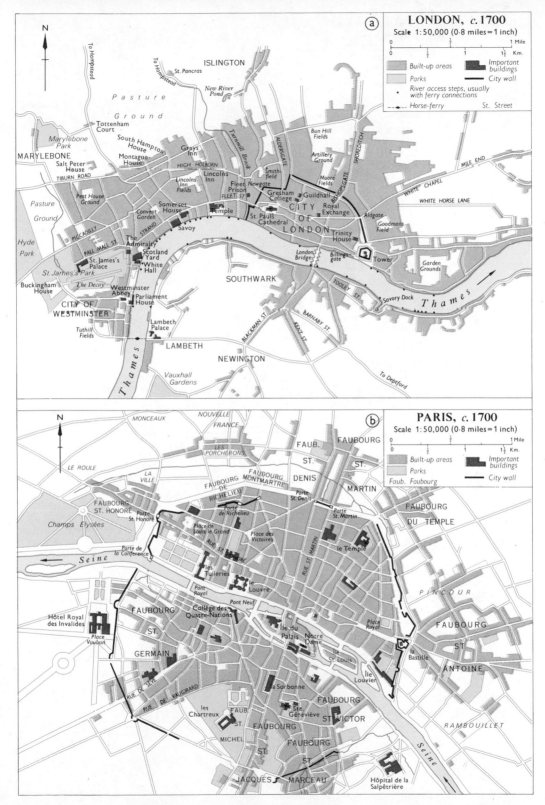

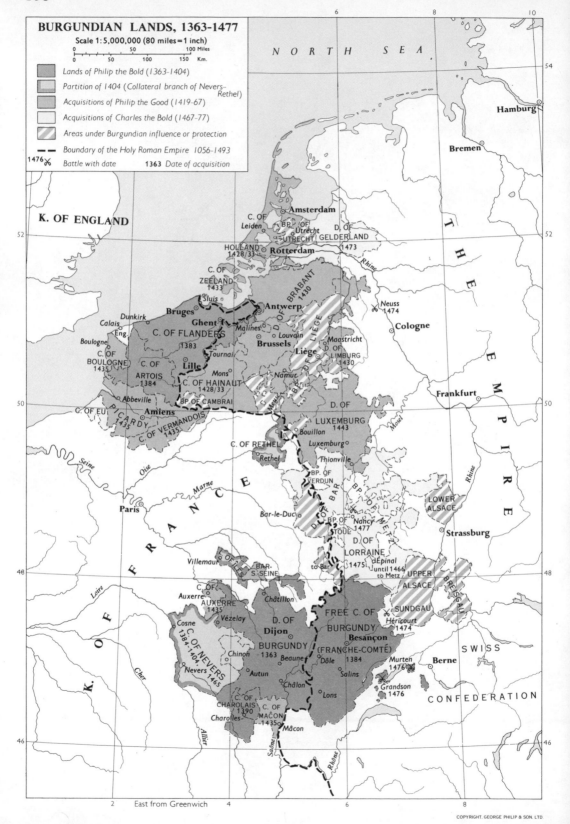

BURGUNDIAN LANDS, 1363–1477

Scale 1:5,000,000 (80 miles=1 inch)

Lands of Philip the Bold (1363–1404)

Partition of 1404 (Collateral branch of Nevers-Rethel)

Acquisitions of Philip the Good (1419–67)

Acquisitions of Charles the Bold (1467–77)

Areas under Burgundian influence or protection

Boundary of the Holy Roman Empire 1056–1493

1476 ⚔ Battle with date   **1363** Date of acquisition

NORTH SEA

THE

EMPIRE

Hamburg

Bremen

K. OF ENGLAND

Amsterdam
Leiden
C. OF
BP. OF
Utrecht UTRECHT
D. OF GELDERLAND 1473
HOLLAND 1428/33 **Rotterdam**
C. OF ZEELAND 1433
Sluis
Neuss 1474
Cologne

Bruges
Dunkirk
Calais
Eng.
Boulogne
C. OF BOULOGNE 1435
Ghent
C. OF FLANDERS 1383
Tournai
C. OF ARTOIS 1384
Lille
Mons
C. OF HAINAUT 1428/33
BP. OF CAMBRAI
Abbeville
C. OF EU 1475
PICARDY
Amiens
C. OF VERMANDOIS 1475

Antwerp
Malines
Louvain
Brussels
D. OF BRABANT 1430
Namur
Liège
BP. OF LIÈGE
Maastricht
D. OF LIMBURG 1430
Frankfurt

D. OF LUXEMBURG 1443
Bouillon
Luxemburg
C. OF RETHEL
Rethel
Thionville
BP. OF VERDUN

Paris

F R A N C E

Seine
Oise
Marne
Villemaur
BAR-S-SEINE
Bar-le-Duc
D. OF BAR
BP. OF METZ
BP. OF TOUL
Nancy 1477
D. OF LORRAINE 1475
to Bar
Épinal until 1466 to Metz
Mosel
LOWER ALSACE
Strassburg
Rhine

Loire
C. OF AUXERRE 1435
Auxerre
Vézelay
Châtillon
D. OF BURGUNDY
Dijon 1363
Beaune
FREE C. OF BURGUNDY (FRANCHE-COMTÉ) 1384
Besançon
Héricourt 1474
UPPER ALSACE
SUNDGAU
BREISGAU

K. OF FRANCE

Cosne
Chinon
C. OF NEVERS 1384–1404
Nevers 1465
Autun
Châlon
Dôle
Salins
Murten 1476
Grandson 1476
Lons
Berne
SWISS

C. OF CHAROLAIS 1390
Charolles
C. OF MÂCON 1435
Mâcon
Cher
Allier
Saône
Rhône

CONFEDERATION

2   East from Greenwich   4   6   8

COPYRIGHT. GEORGE PHILIP & SON. LTD.

FRANCE, c.1500

Scale 1:7,500,000 (120 miles = 1 inch)

0   50   100   150 Miles
0   50   100   150   200 Km.

French royal domain 1477 (including appanages)
Fiefs which fell to the French crown 1477-1527
Fiefs of Charles of Bourbon, taken in 1527 by
    the French crown
Other French fiefs
1498 Date of acquisition

NORTH SEA

Amsterdam

K. OF ENGLAND

London

Ghent

Brussels

THE

Frankfurt

EMPIRE

Rhine

English Channel

Calais 1347-1558
to Eng.
Boulogne
Occupied by England
1544-50
C. OF
ARTOIS
1477-93
Arras

C. OF
PICARDY
Amiens 1477/82
St. Quentin

C. OF
RETHEL

Reims

Nancy

Strassburg

Dieppe
C. OF
EU

Cherbourg

Channel Is.

Caen
Rouen
Seine
Clermont
Soissons

NORMANDY

ILE-DE-
FRANCE
Paris
D. OF VALOIS
1515

Vertus

CHAMPAGNE

BARROIS
MOUVANT
to Bar

Brest

D. OF BRITTANY
1491

Rennes
Vannes

ALENÇON
1525
C. OF
PERCHE
1474/83

C. OF
MAINE

Le Mans

Nemours
D. OF NEMOURS

Troyes

Rassigny
to Barrois
mouvant

Berne

Sens

Angers

ANJOU

D. OF
VENDOME
C. OF
DUNOIS
D. OF
Orléans
Blois
ORLÉANS
1498

Auxerre
Semur
D. OF
Dijon

Nantes

Tours
C. OF
BLOIS

TOURAINE

Sancerre

Saône

BURGUNDY
1477/82

Partheray

POITOU

Châtellerault

BERRY

Bourges

C. OF
NEVERS
Nevers

C. OF
CHAROLAIS
1477-93 to Fr.
1493 to Habsburgs

Mâcon

Poitiers

C. OF
Guéret
LA MARCHE

Moulins
D. OF BOURBON

C. OF

Bay of
Biscay

Rochefort

AUNIS
Niort

SAINTONGE

C. OF ANGOULÊME
1515
Angoulême

C. OF
Limoges
V.C. OF
LIMOGES

C. OF
Périgueux
PÉRIGORD
Turenne

Clermont

Thiers

D. OF
AUVERGNE
Murat

FOREZ

Montbrison

Vienne

LYONS

Le Puy

Grenoble

Valence

DAUPHINÉ

Bordeaux

Garonne

Castillon

GUYENNE

Cahors

Rodez

C. OF
RODEZ

Orange
C. OF
VENAISSIN
to the Papacy

Avignon

C. OF
PROVENCE
1481

Santander

Bilbao

Bayonne

S. OF
ALBRET
1520 Duchy

ASTARAC

Agen

Montauban

C. OF ARMAGNAC

Auch

Albi

Arles

Aix

Marseilles

V.C. OF
Pau
BÉARN

Tarbes
C. OF
BIGORRE

C. OF
COMINGES

Toulouse

LANGUEDOC

Montpellier

1507

Narbonne

Gulf of Lions

K. OF
NAVARRE

Pamplona

SOULE

C. OF
FOIX

ROUSSILLON

CERDAGNE
1462-93

Saragossa

K. OF SPAIN

Barcelona

MEDITERRANEAN

SEA

Tarragona

Rhône

4 West from Greenwich 2   0   2 East from Greenwich 4   6

COPYRIGHT. GEORGE PHILIP & SON. LTD.

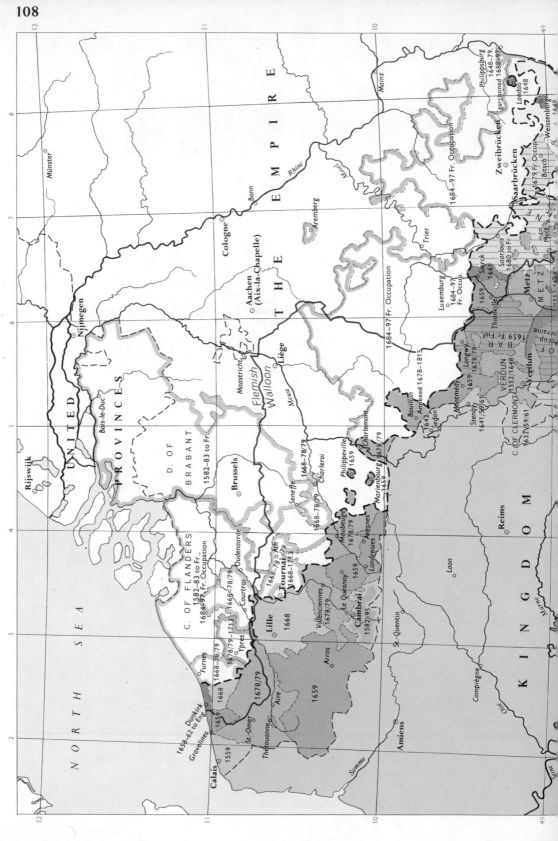

N O R T H   S E A

U N I T E D   P R O V I N C E S

T H E   E M P I R E

K I N G D O M

Münster

Rijswijk

Nijmegen

Bois-le-Duc

D. OF BRABANT
1582–83 to Fr.

Cologne

Bonn

Aachen
(Aix-la-Chapelle)

Aremberg

Mainz

Maastricht

Liège

Flemish
Walloon

Brussels

Meuse

Rhine

Mosel

Trier

1684–97 Fr. Occupation

Luxemburg
1684–97
Fr. Occup.

Philippsburg
1648–79,
garrisoned 1688–97

Landau 1648

Weissenburg
1648

Zweibrücken

Saarbrücken

1679 Fr. Occup.

Bitsch

Metz

Saarlouis
1680 to Fr.

Sierck
1661

Thionville
1659

B A R

VERDUN

1684–97 Fr. Occupation

Bouillon
Annexed 1678–1815

Sedan
1642

C. OF CLERMONT
1632/59–61

Montmédy
1659

Longwy
1678/79

Stenay
1641,59/61

Reims

Laon

Compiègne

C. OF FLANDERS
1582–83 to Fr.
1684–97 Fr. Occupation

Courtrai
1668–78/79

Oudenaarde

Seneffe

Charleroi

1668–78/79

1668–78/79

Philippeville
1659

Charlemont

Mariembourg
1659

1678/79

Ypres
1678/79–1713

Lille
1668

Ath
1668–78 o
Tournai
1668–1713

Maubeuge
1678/79

Avesnes
1659

Landrecies

Furnes
1668–78/79
1678/79

Valenciennes
1678/79

Le Quesnoy
1659

Cambrai
1582–95

St-Quentin

Dunkirk
1658–62 to Eng.

Gravelines
1659

1668

St-Omer

Thérouanne

Aire

Arras
1659

Amiens

Calais

1559

Somme

Oise

Reims

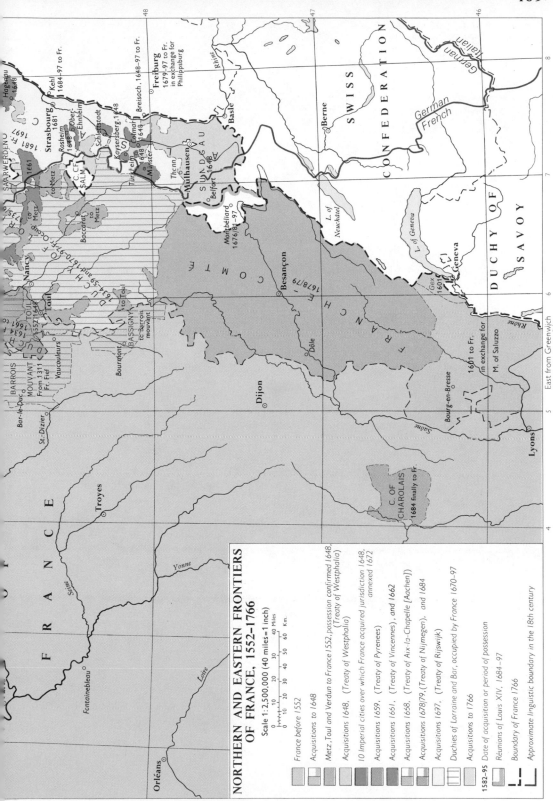

NORTHERN AND EASTERN FRONTIERS
OF FRANCE, 1552-1766

Scale 1:2,500,000 (40 miles=1 inch)

0 10 20 30 40 Miles
0 10 20 30 40 50 60 Km.

France before 1552

Acquisitions to 1648

Metz, Toul and Verdun to France 1552, possession confirmed 1648, (Treaty of Westphalia)

Acquisitions 1648. (Treaty of Westphalia)

10 Imperial cities over which France acquired jurisdiction 1648, annexed 1672

Acquisitions 1659. (Treaty of Pyrenees)

Acquisitions 1651. (Treaty of Vincennes), and 1662

Acquisitions 1668. (Treaty of Aix-la-Chapelle [Aachen])

Acquisitions 1678/79 (Treaty of Nijmegen), and 1684

Acquisitions 1697. (Treaty of Rijswijk)

Duchies of Lorraine and Bar, occupied by France 1670-97

Acquisitions to 1766

1582-95 Date of acquisition or period of possession

Réunions of Louis XIV, 1684-97

Boundary of France 1766

Approximate linguistic boundary in the 18th century

COPYRIGHT GEORGE PHILIP & SON LTD

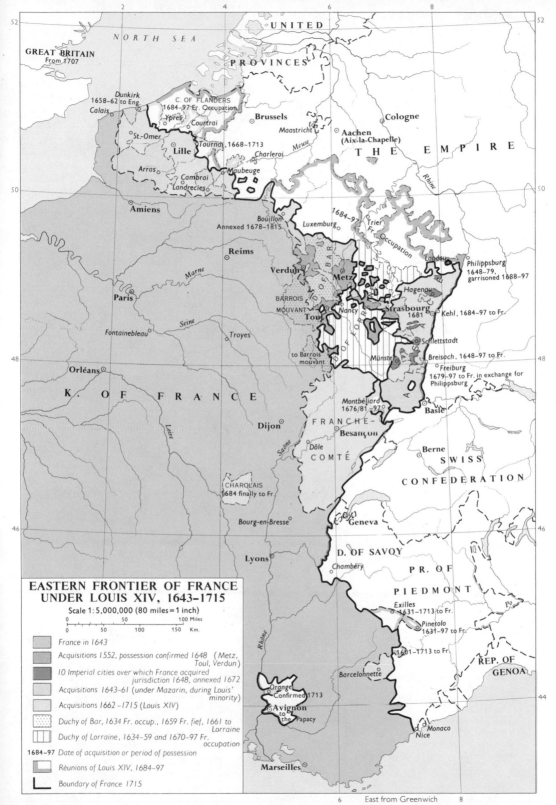

NORTH SEA

UNITED

P R O V I N C E S

GREAT BRITAIN
From 1707

Dunkirk
1658–62 to Eng.
Calais

Brussels

Cologne

Maastricht

Aachen
(Aix-la-Chapelle)

C. OF FLANDERS
1684–97 Fr. Occupation
Ypres
Courtrai
St.-Omer
Lille
Tournai, 1668–1713
Charleroi
Arras
Cambrai
Maubeuge
Landrecies

T H E   E M P I R E

Meuse

Amiens

Bouillon
Annexed 1678–1815

Luxemburg

1684–97
Trier
Fr. Occupation

Rhine

Reims

Verdun

Landau

Metz

Philippsburg
1648–79,
garrisoned 1688–97

Marne

BARROIS
MOUVANT

Hagenau

Paris

Toul

Nancy

Strasbourg
1681

Kehl, 1684–97 to Fr.

Seine

Fontainebleau

Troyes

to Barrois
mouvant

Schlettstadt

Münster

Breisach, 1648–97 to Fr.

Orléans

Freiburg
1679–97 to Fr. in exchange for
Philippsburg

K.   O F   F R A N C E

Montbéliard
1676/81–97

Basle

Loire

Dijon

F R A N C H E –

Berne

Besançon

SWISS

Dôle

C O M T É

CHAROLAIS
1684 finally to Fr.

CONFEDERATION

Bourg-en-Bresse

Geneva

Lyons

D. OF SAVOY

Chambéry

P R.   O F

P I E D M O N T

Exilles
1631–1713 to Fr.

Pinerolo
1631–97 to Fr.

Rhône

1601–1713 to Fr.

REP. OF

GENOA

Orange
Confirmed 1713

Barcelonnette

Avignon
to
the Papacy

Monaco
Nice

Marseilles

**EASTERN FRONTIER OF FRANCE
UNDER LOUIS XIV, 1643–1715**

Scale 1:5,000,000 (80 miles = 1 inch)

0   50   100 Miles
0   50   100   150 Km.

France in 1643

Acquisitions 1552, possession confirmed 1648 (Metz,
Toul, Verdun)

10 Imperial cities over which France acquired
jurisdiction 1648, annexed 1672

Acquisitions 1643–61 (under Mazarin, during Louis'
minority)

Acquisitions 1662–1715 (Louis XIV)

Duchy of Bar, 1634 Fr. occup., 1659 Fr. fief, 1661 to
Lorraine

Duchy of Lorraine, 1634–59 and 1670–97 Fr.
occupation

1684–97 Date of acquisition or period of possession

Réunions of Louis XIV, 1684–97

Boundary of France 1715

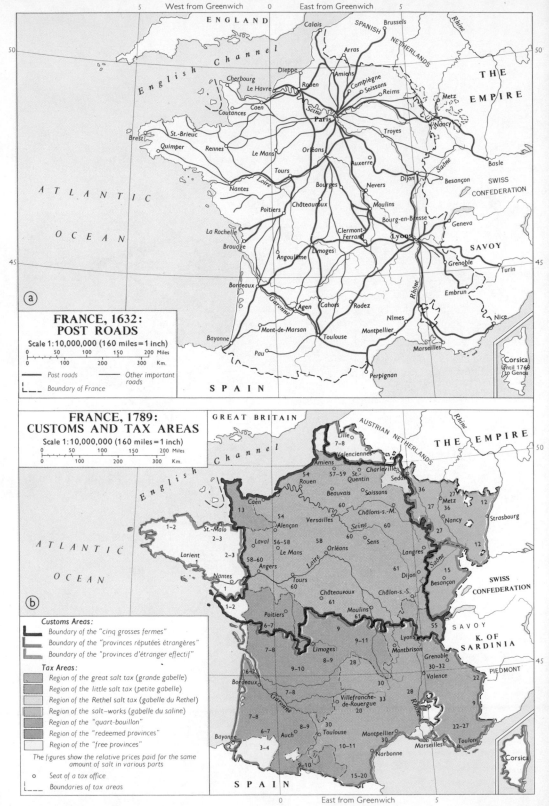

West from Greenwich 0 East from Greenwich 5

FRANCE, 1632: POST ROADS

Scale 1:10,000,000 (160 miles=1 inch)

| 0 | 50 | 100 | 150 | 200 Miles |
| 0 | 100 | 200 | 300 Km. |

—— Post roads
—— Other important roads
⌐⌐ Boundary of France

Corsica
Until 1768
to Genoa

FRANCE, 1789: CUSTOMS AND TAX AREAS

Scale 1:10,000,000 (160 miles=1 inch)

| 0 | 50 | 100 | 150 | 200 Miles |
| 0 | 100 | 200 | 300 Km. |

Customs Areas:
Boundary of the "cinq grosses fermes"
Boundary of the "provinces réputées étrangères"
Boundary of the "provinces d'étranger effectif"

Tax Areas:
Region of the great salt tax (grande gabelle)
Region of the little salt tax (petite gabelle)
Region of the Rethel salt tax (gabelle du Rethel)
Region of the salt-works (gabelle du saline)
Region of the "quart-bouillon"
Region of the "redeemed provinces"
Region of the "free provinces"

The figures show the relative prices paid for the same amount of salt in various parts

○ Seat of a tax office
⌐⌐ Boundaries of tax areas

0 East from Greenwich 5

COPYRIGHT. GEORGE PHILIP & SON, LTD.

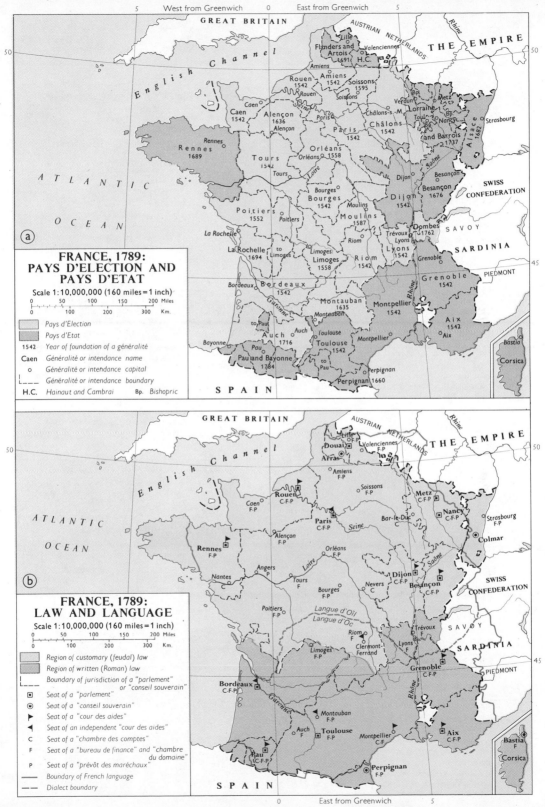

West from Greenwich 0 East from Greenwich

GREAT BRITAIN

THE EMPIRE

English Channel

AUSTRIAN NETHERLANDS

Lille
Flanders and Artois 1691
Valenciennes
H.C.

Amiens
Rouen 1542
Amiens 1542
Soissons 1595
Rouen
Soissons
Verdun
Metz
Lorraine
Nancy
Bp.
Strasbourg

Caen 1542
Caen
Alençon 1636
Alençon
Paris
Châlons-s-M.
Châlons 1542
Lorraine and Barrois 1737
Alsace 1682

Rennes 1689
Rennes
Tours 1542
Tours
Orléans 1542
Orléans 1558
Paris 1542
Dijon
Besançon 1676
Besançon

ATLANTIC
OCEAN

Bourges 1542
Bourges
Moulins
Moulins 1587
Dijon 1542
Saône
SWISS CONFEDERATION

Poitiers 1552
Poitiers
Riom
Trévoux 1762
Lyons 1542
Lyons
Dombes 1762
SAVOY

La Rochelle
La Rochelle 1694
to Limoges
Limoges 1558
Limoges
Riom 1542
Grenoble
SARDINIA

Bordeaux
Bordeaux 1542
Garonne
Montauban 1635
Montauban
Montpellier 1542
Grenoble 1542
PIEDMONT

Auch 1716
Auch
Toulouse 1542
Toulouse
Montpellier
Aix 1542
Aix

Bayonne
Pau
Pau and Bayonne 1784
to Pau
Perpignan 1660
Perpignan

SPAIN

Rhine

Bastia
Corsica

(a)

FRANCE, 1789:
PAYS D'ELECTION AND
PAYS D'ETAT

Scale 1:10,000,000 (160 miles = 1 inch)

0 50 100 150 200 Miles
0 100 200 300 Km.

▢ *Pays d'Election*
▨ *Pays d'Etat*
1542 *Year of foundation of a généralité*
Caen *Généralité or intendance name*
o *Généralité or intendance capital*
⌐ *Généralité or intendance boundary*
H.C. *Hainaut and Cambrai* **Bp.** *Bishopric*

GREAT BRITAIN

THE EMPIRE

English Channel

AUSTRIAN NETHERLANDS

Lille
O.F.P.
Douai
Valenciennes
F.P
Arras

Amiens
F.P
Soissons
F.P
Metz
C.F.P
Nancy
C.F.P
Strasbourg
F.P
Colmar

Rouen
C.F.P
Caen
F.P
Paris
C.F.P
Seine
Bar-le-Duc

ATLANTIC
OCEAN

Rennes
F.P
Alençon
F.P
Orléans
F.P
Dijon
C.F.P
Besançon
C.F.P

Nantes
Angers
Tours
F
Loire
Bourges
F.P
Nevers
F.P
SWISS CONFEDERATION

Poitiers
F.P
Langue d'Oïl
Langue d'Oc
Trévoux
F
SAVOY

Limoges
F
Clermont-Ferrand
Riom
F
Lyons
F
SARDINIA

Bordeaux
C.F.P
Garonne
Montauban
F
Grenoble
C.F.P
PIEDMONT

Auch
F
Toulouse
F.P
Montpellier
C.F
Aix
C.F.P

Pau
C.F.P
Perpignan
F.P
Rhine

SPAIN

Bastia
Corsica

(b)

FRANCE, 1789:
LAW AND LANGUAGE

Scale 1:10,000,000 (160 miles = 1 inch)

0 50 100 150 200 Miles
0 100 200 300 Km.

▢ *Region of customary (feudal) law*
▨ *Region of written (Roman) law*
⌐ *Boundary of jurisdiction of a "parlement"*
  or "conseil souverain"
▣ *Seat of a "parlement"*
◉ *Seat of a "conseil souverain"*
▶ *Seat of a "cour des aides"*
◀ *Seat of an independent "cour des aides"*
C *Seat of a "chambre des comptes"*
F *Seat of a "bureau de finance" and "chambre*
  du domaine"
P *Seat of a "prévôt des maréchaux"*
━━ *Boundary of French language*
┅┅ *Dialect boundary*

East from Greenwich 5

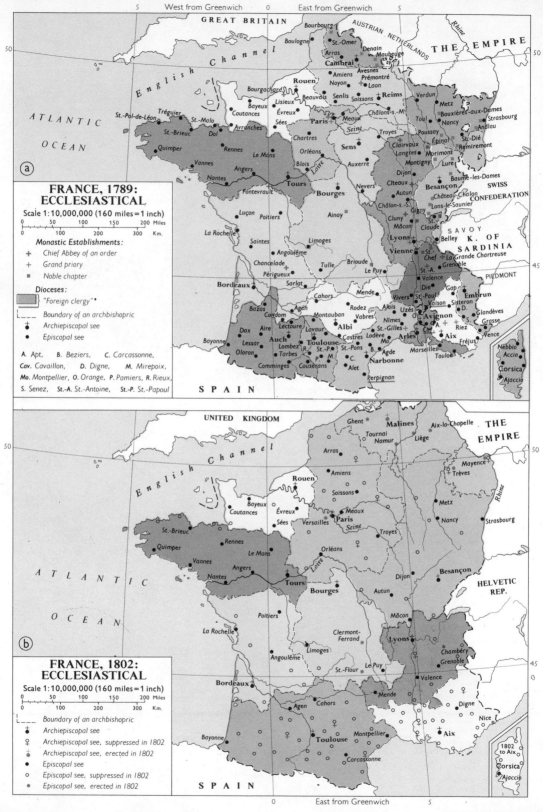

West from Greenwich 0 East from Greenwich

GREAT BRITAIN

AUSTRIAN NETHERLANDS

THE EMPIRE

English Channel

ATLANTIC OCEAN

FRANCE, 1789: ECCLESIASTICAL

Scale 1:10,000,000 (160 miles = 1 inch)

0   50   100   150   200 Miles
0   100   200   300 Km.

Monastic Establishments:

+ Chief Abbey of an order
+ Grand priory
■ Noble chapter

Dioceses:

"Foreign clergy" •

Boundary of an archbishopric

✝ Archiepiscopal see

• Episcopal see

A. Apt,   B. Beziers,   C. Carcassonne,
Cav. Cavaillon,   D. Digne,   M. Mirepoix,
Mo. Montpellier,   O. Orange,   P. Pamiers,   R. Rieux,
S. Senez,   St.-A. St.-Antoine,   St.-P. St.-Papoul

SWISS CONFEDERATION

SAVOY

K. OF SARDINIA

PIEDMONT

SPAIN

UNITED KINGDOM

THE EMPIRE

English Channel

ATLANTIC OCEAN

FRANCE, 1802: ECCLESIASTICAL

Scale 1:10,000,000 (160 miles = 1 inch)

0   50   100   150   200 Miles
0   100   200   300 Km.

Boundary of an archbishopric

✝ Archiepiscopal see
♀ Archiepiscopal see, suppressed in 1802
✝ Archiepiscopal see, erected in 1802
• Episcopal see
○ Episcopal see, suppressed in 1802
● Episcopal see, erected in 1802

HELVETIC REP.

1802 to Aix

Corsica
Ajaccio

SPAIN

East from Greenwich

COPYRIGHT. GEORGE PHILIP & SON. LTD.

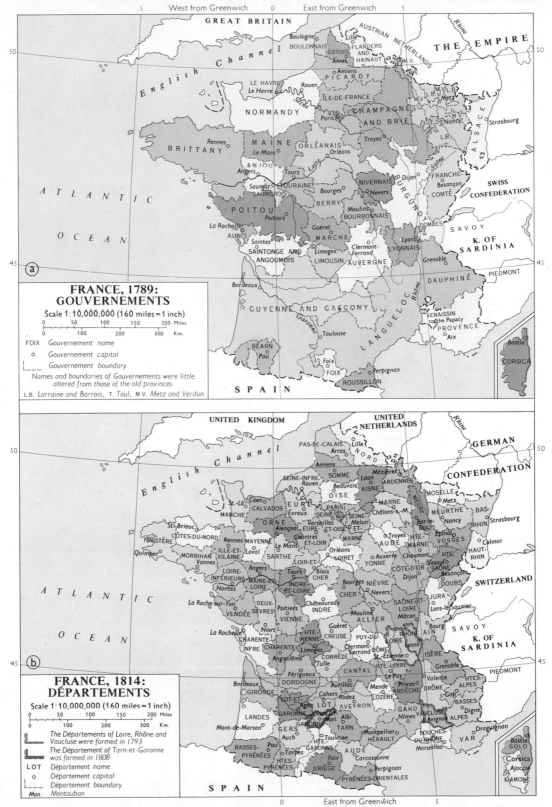

West from Greenwich 0 East from Greenwich 5

a

FRANCE, 1789: GOUVERNEMENTS

Scale 1:10,000,000 (160 miles=1 inch)

| 0 | 50 | 100 | 150 | 200 Miles |
| 0 | 100 | 200 | 300 Km. |

FOIX *Gouvernement name*

○ *Gouvernement capital*

| *Gouvernement boundary*

Names and boundaries of Gouvernements were little altered from those of the old provinces

L.B. Lorraine and Barrois, T. Toul, M.V. Metz and Verdun

b

FRANCE, 1814: DÉPARTEMENTS

Scale 1:10,000,000 (160 miles=1 inch)

| 0 | 50 | 100 | 150 | 200 Miles |
| 0 | 100 | 200 | 300 Km. |

The Départements of Loire, Rhône and Vaucluse were formed in 1793

The Département of Tarn-et-Garonne was formed in 1808

LOT *Département name*

○ *Département capital*

| *Département boundary*

Mon. Montauban

PARIS, 1789

Scale 1:25,000 (0·4 miles = 1 inch)

Built-up areas:
By 1700
by 1789

Important buildings

Parks

Gal. Galerie   Q. Quai   R. Rue   Churches

Extensions

N

la Bastille

Seine

le Temple

St. Martin des Champs

St. Nicolas des Champs

la Soubise

RUE   ST.   LOUIS

Porte St. Denis

RUE   SAINT   DENIS

RUE   SAINT   MARTIN

RUE   DU   TEMPLE

RUE   DE   LA   VERRERIE   DU   ROI   DE   SICILE

RUE   VIEILLE   DU   TEMPLE

CHEMIN   VERD

RUE   DE   LA   ROQUETTE

RUE   DU   FAUB.   ST.   ANTOINE

RUE   DE   CHARENTON

RUE   DE   BERCY

RUE   DE   LA   RAPÉE

DES   CHANTIERS

Place Royale

RUE   ST.   ANTOINE

les Célestins

Grand Arsenal

Île Louvier

FAUBOURG   ST.   VICTOR

St. Victor

RUE   DU   FAUB.   ST.   VICTOR

Q.   D'ANJOU

Île St. Louis

Q.   DE   BOURBON

Q.   D'ORLÉANS

Q.   DAUPHIN

St. Louis

les Bernardins

RUE   ST.   VICTOR

St. Étienne

Ste. Geneviève

RUE   DU   FAUB.   ST.   JACQUES

Hôtel de Ville

QUAI   DE   LA   GRÈVE

QUAI   DES   ORMES

GRANDS   DEGRÉS

Notre Dame

Île du Palais

la Conciergerie

la Sorbonne

RUE   ST.   JACQUES

RUE   DE   LA   HARPE

RUE   D'ENFER

les Halles

Cimetière des Innocents

R.   DU   FAUBOURG   MONTMARTRE

RUE   MONTMARTRE

RUE   DE   RICHELIEU

Bibliothèque Royale

Place des Victoires

Palais Royal

le Louvre

Pont Neuf

Q.   DE   LA   MÉGISSERIE

Q.   DES   MORFONDUS

Q.   DES   AUGUSTINS

RUE   DU   LOUVRE

RUE   ST.   HONORÉ

les Capucines

la Madeleine

FAUBOURG   ST.   HONORÉ

Place Vendôme

RUE   DE   LA   PAIX

RUE   SAINT   HONORÉ

les Tuileries

Jardin des Tuileries

Q.   DES   THÉATINS

Pont Royal

Q.   MALAQUIS

Collège des Quatre-Nations

la Charité

St. Germain des Prés

RUE   DU   FOUR

RUE   DE   VAUGIRARD

Jardin du Luxembourg

les Chartreux

Place de la Concorde

Louis XV

Q.   DE   LA   CONFÉRENCE

Pont de la Boule 1787-91

Q.   DE   LA   GRENOUILLÈRE

Q.   D'ORSAY

GAL.   DU   LOUVRE

RUE   DE   L'UNIVERSITÉ

RUE   DE   BOURBON

RUE   SAINT   DOMINIQUE

RUE   ST.   GERMAIN

RUE   DE   GRENELLE

RUE   DE   SÈVRES

les Incurables

Champs Élysées

Palais Colisée

COURS   LA   REINE

PORT   AUX   PIERRES

Seine

Pal. Bourbon

Hôtel Royal des Invalides

Place Vauban

NOUVEAU   COURS

École Royal Militaire

CHEMIN   DE   SÈVE   ET   DE   MEUDON

COPYRIGHT GEORGE PHILIP & SON LTD.

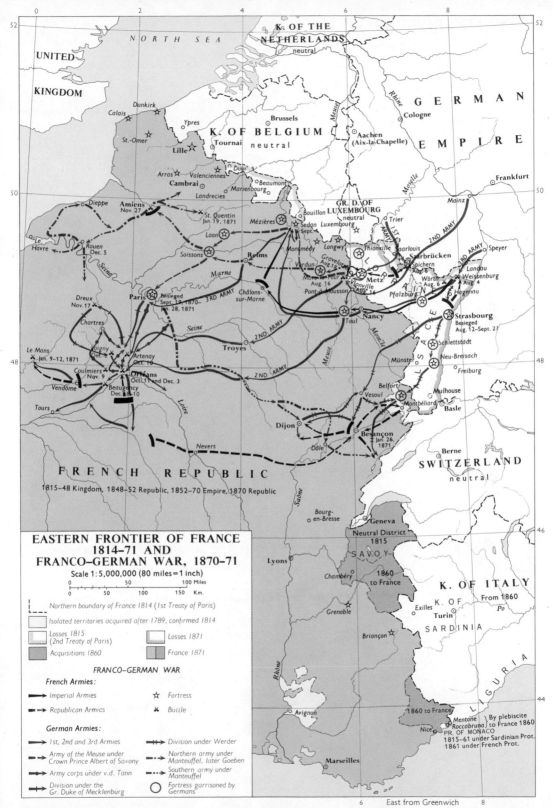

EASTERN FRONTIER OF FRANCE 1814–71 AND FRANCO–GERMAN WAR, 1870–71

Scale 1 : 5,000,000 (80 miles = 1 inch)

0   50   100 Miles
0   50   100   150 Km.

Northern boundary of France 1814 (1st Treaty of Paris)

Isolated territories acquired after 1789, confirmed 1814

Losses 1815 (2nd Treaty of Paris)   Losses 1871

Acquisitions 1860   France 1871

FRANCO–GERMAN WAR

French Armies:

→ Imperial Armies   ☆ Fortress

→ Republican Armies   ✕ Battle

German Armies:

→ 1st, 2nd and 3rd Armies   ⊩→ Division under Werder

→ Army of the Meuse under Crown Prince Albert of Saxony   ·–·→ Northern army under Manteuffel, later Goeben

→ Army corps under v.d. Tann   ·–·→ Southern army under Manteuffel

⊢→ Division under the Gr. Duke of Mecklenburg   ◯ Fortress garrisoned by Germans

East from Greenwich

COPYRIGHT. GEORGE PHILIP & SON. LTD.

118

HANSEATIC LEAGUE AND THE BALTIC
1370 – c.1500

Scale 1:10,000,000 (160 miles = 1 inch)

- **●** Principal towns ⎫ of the Hanseatic League
- **•** Other towns ⎭
- **■** Foreign Counting Houses (Faktoreien)
- **▪** Other Foreign Depots
- ⊙ ○ Towns not members of the Hanseatic League
- _Posen_ Trade Fair
- Principal Hanseatic trade routes by sea
- Principal competitive English and Dutch trade routes by sea
- Principal trade routes by land
- Seas and lakes frozen in winter

West from Greenwich 0 East from Greenwich

Kopperberget

Calmar

SWEDEN

Ume

Gulf of Bothnia

FINLAND

Uppsala

Stockholm

Åbo

Helsingfors

G. of Finland

Åland Is.

Reval

ESTONIA

Pernau

Dorpat

LIVONIA

Fellin

Narva

Novgorod
St. Peter's Court
Closed 1496

RUSSIA

Lake Onega

Lake Ladoga

Visby
Gotland

Calmar

Windau

G. of Riga

Wenden

Pskov

Moscow

Volga

BALTIC SEA

Riga

COURLAND

Polotsk

Vitebsk

55

Memel

Smolensk

Kovno

Vilna

Königsberg

Colberg

Stolpe

Danzig

Braunsberg

Elbing

PRUSSIA

Grodno

LITHUANIA

Gomel

Gollnow

Kulm

Thorn

Under the same ruler from 1386

Stargard

Posen

Warsaw

Vistula

Lublin

Kiev

50

auben

Breslau

POLAND

Oder

Krakow

Lvov

Dnieper

E

HUNGARY

COPYRIGHT. GEORGE PHILIP & SON. LTD.

SPREAD OF GERMAN SETTLEMENTS
EASTWARDS BY THE 15TH CENTURY

Scale 1:10,000,000 (160 miles=1 inch)

Boundary between Germans and Slavs, c.800	
Germans	Teutonic Group
Scandinavians	
Slavonic Group	
Romanic Group	
Letto–Lithuanian Group	
Finnish Group	
Magyars (Ugrian Group)	
1240	Date of foundation of German settlement

East from Greenwich

COPYRIGHT. GEORGE PHILIP & SON. LTD.

East from Greenwich

K. OF SWEDEN

NORTH SEA

K. OF DENMARK

BALTIC SEA

Danzig

K. OF ENGLAND

Amsterdam

Hamburg

Elbe

Stettin

K. OF POLAND

Bremen

Osnabrück

Braunschweig

Berlin

Jüterbog

Poznan

Münster

Magdeburg

Odor

Kottbus

Brussels

Halle

Leipzig

Breslau

Liège

Cologne

Cassel

Nordhausen

Erfurt

D. OF SILESIA

Aachen

Schmalkalden

Cambrai

Frankfurt

Prague

K. OF BOHEMIA

Luxemburg

Mainz

Bayreuth

MAR. OF MORAVIA

Verdun

Metz

Ansbach

Nuremberg

Brünn

Paris

Rhine

Eichstätt

Stuttgart

Regensburg

Danube

K. OF FRANCE

Offenburg

Ulm

Munich

Salzburg

Vienna

Buda (Ofen)

Montbéliard

Ravensburg

Constance

Graz

Boundary 1533/47

K. OF HUNGARY

Lyons

Berne

SWISS CONFEDERATION

D. OF SAVOY

Trieste

Turin

Milan

REP. OF VENICE

Venice

DALMATIA

IMPERIAL HUNGARY

Rhône

THE IMPERIAL CIRCLES, *c.1512*

Scale 1:10,000,000 (160 miles = 1 inch)

0   50   100   150   200 Miles

0   100   200   300 Km.

—— Boundary of the Holy Roman Empire

- - - - - Boundaries of the German Circles

Austrian Circle

Bavarian Circle

Upper Saxon Circle

Burgundian Circle

Swabian Circle

Lower Saxon Circle

Rhenish Palatinate Circle

Upper Rhine Circle

Districts not included in the Circles

Franconian Circle

Lower Rhine-Westphalian Circle

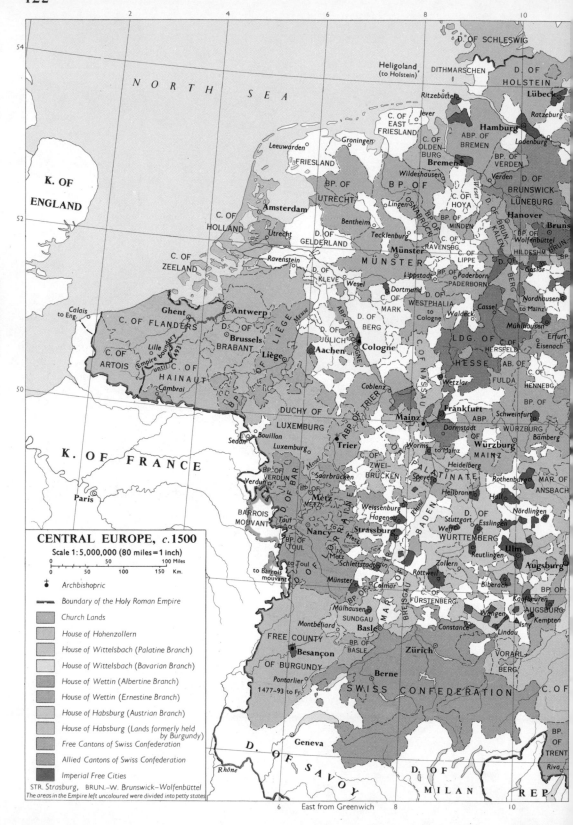

CENTRAL EUROPE, c.1500

Scale 1:5,000,000 (80 miles=1 inch)

0   50   100 Miles

0   50   100   150 Km.

Archbishopric

Boundary of the Holy Roman Empire

Church Lands

House of Hohenzollern

House of Wittelsbach (Palatine Branch)

House of Wittelsbach (Bavarian Branch)

House of Wettin (Albertine Branch)

House of Wettin (Ernestine Branch)

House of Habsburg (Austrian Branch)

House of Habsburg (Lands formerly held by Burgundy)

Free Cantons of Swiss Confederation

Allied Cantons of Swiss Confederation

Imperial Free Cities

STR. Strasburg,   BRUN.-W. Brunswick–Wolfenbüttel
The areas in the Empire left uncoloured were divided into petty states

East from Greenwich

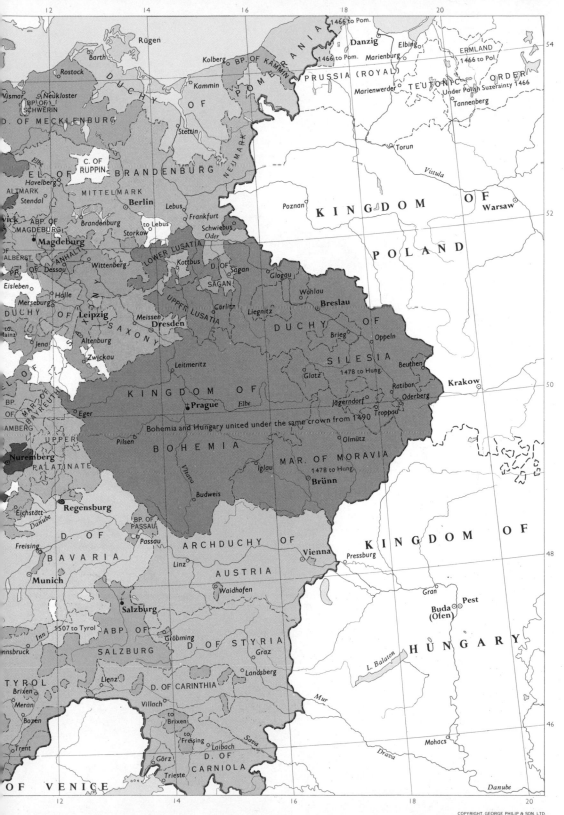

Rügen

Barth

Rostock

DUCHY OF POMERANIA

Kolberg

BP. OF KAMMIN

Kammin

1466 to Pom.

Danzig

Elbing

ERMLAND

1466 to Pol.

Marienburg

PRUSSIA (ROYAL)

Marienwerder

TEUTONIC ORDER

Under Polish Suzerainty 1466

Tannenberg

Wismar

Neukloster

BP. OF SCHWERIN

D. OF MECKLENBURG

Stettin

NEUMARK

EL. OF BRANDENBURG

C. OF RUPPIN

Havelberg

ALTMARK

Stendal

Berlin

MITTELMARK

Lebus

Frankfurt

Schwiebus

Poznan

Torun

Vistula

KINGDOM OF

Warsaw

POLAND

vick

ABP. OF MAGDEBURG

Magdeburg

Brandenburg

to Lebus

Storkow

Oder

ALBERT

OF ANHALT

PR.

Dessau

Wittenberg

LOWER LUSATIA

Kottbus

D. OF SAGAN

SAGAN

Glogau

Wohlau

Breslau

DUCHY OF SILESIA

Eisleben

Halle

Merseburg

DUCHY OF SAXONY

Leipzig

Meissen

UPPER LUSATIA

Görlitz

Liegnitz

Brieg

Oppeln

Beuthen

1478 to Hung.

Krakow

Dresden

Mainz

Jena

Altenburg

Zwickau

Leitmeritz

Glatz

Ratibor

Oderberg

EL. OF

BP. OF

MAR. OF BAIREUTH

OF

AMBERG

Eger

KINGDOM OF

Prague

Elbe

Jägerndorf

Troppau

UPPER

Pilsen

BOHEMIA

Vltava

Iglau

Budweis

Olmütz

MAR. OF MORAVIA

1478 to Hung.

Brünn

Nuremberg

PALATINATE

Bohemia and Hungary united under the same crown from 1490

Regensburg

Danube

D. OF BAVARIA

BP. OF PASSAU

Passau

Linz

ARCHDUCHY OF

AUSTRIA

Vienna

Pressburg

KINGDOM OF

Eichstätt

Freising

Munich

Waidhofen

Gran

Buda

(Ofen)

Pest

Salzburg

1507 to Tyrol

Inn

ABP. OF

SALZBURG

Glöbming

D. OF STYRIA

Graz

Landsberg

L. Balaton

HUNGARY

nnsbruck

TYROL

Brixen

Meran

Lenz

Villach

D. OF CARINTHIA

Mur

Bozen

to Brixen

Trent

to Freising

Laibach

Sava

Drava

Mohacs

Görz

D. OF

CARNIOLA

Trieste

OF VENICE

Danube

COPYRIGHT. GEORGE PHILIP & SON. LTD.

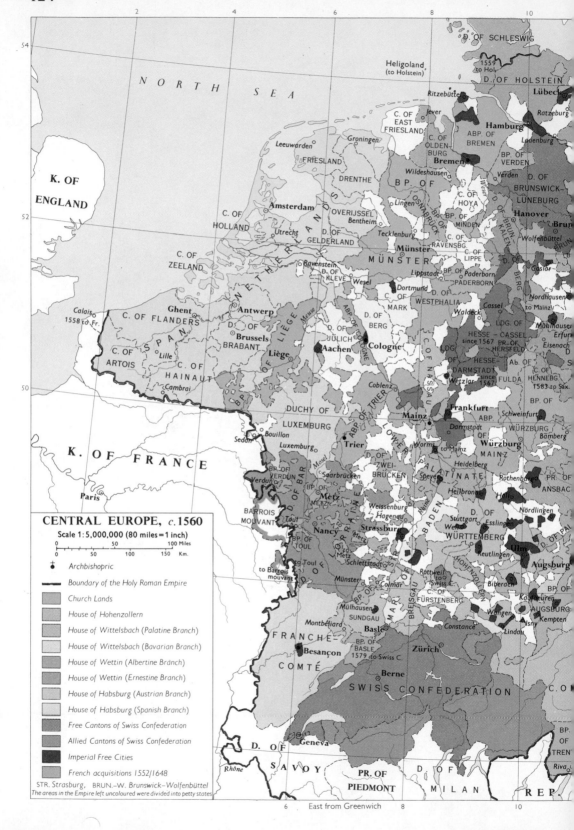

CENTRAL EUROPE, c.1560

Scale 1 : 5,000,000 (80 miles = 1 inch)

0   50   100 Miles
0   50   100   150 Km.

♱   Archbishopric

Boundary of the Holy Roman Empire

Church Lands

House of Hohenzollern

House of Wittelsbach (Palatine Branch)

House of Wittelsbach (Bavarian Branch)

House of Wettin (Albertine Branch)

House of Wettin (Ernestine Branch)

House of Habsburg (Austrian Branch)

House of Habsburg (Spanish Branch)

Free Cantons of Swiss Confederation

Allied Cantons of Swiss Confederation

Imperial Free Cities

French acquisitions 1552/1648

STR. Strasburg,   BRUN.–W. Brunswick–Wolfenbüttel
The areas in the Empire left uncoloured were divided into petty states

East from Greenwich

Rügen

Rostock

Neukloster

smar

BP. OF
SCHWERIN

OF MECKLENBURG

Stendal

1542
to Bran.

Havelberg

EL. OF BRANDENBURG

Berlin

Lebus

k ABP. OF
MAGDEBURG

Brandenburg

Magdeburg

1571/75
to Bran.

Frankfurt

Schwiebus

Oder

LBERST

ANHALT

Dessau

Wittenberg

LOWER LUSATIA

Kottbus

Sagan

Glogau

Wohlau

isleben

Halle

Merseburg

Naumburg

Leipzig

EL. OF SAXONY

Meissen

Altenburg

Zwickau

Jena

Dresden

1549 to Austria

Görlitz

Liegnitz

UPPER LUSATIA

Breslau

DUCHY OF

Brieg

Oppeln

SILESIA

Beuthen
1523–1617
to Bran.

Schweidnitz

nz

OF
XONY

1547 to Austria
1556/59 to Sax.

PR. OF
BAYREUTH

Eger

KINGDOM OF

Prague

Elbe

Schweidnitz

Glatz

Leitmeritz

Jägerndorf
1523–1621
to Bran.

Ratibor

Oderberg
1523–1617
to Bran.

Troppau

Krakow

MBERG

UPPER

Pilsen

BOHEMIA

Vltava

Iglau

Olmütz

MAR. OF MORAVIA

Brünn

Nuremberg

PALATINATE

NEUBURG

Eichstätt

Danube

Regensburg

Budweis

H
U
N
G
A
R
Y

Freising

D. OF

BAVARIA

Passau

BP. OF
PASSAU

ARCHDUCHY OF

Vienna

Pressburg

Munich

Linz

AUSTRIA

Gran

Buda
(Ofen)

Pest

Waidhofen

I
M
P
E
R
I
A
L

Inn

Salzburg

ABP. OF

Gröbming

D. OF STYRIA

Graz

Stuhlweissenburg

sbruck

SALZBURG

Landsberg

L. Balaton

TYROL

Brixen

Lienz

D. OF CARINTHIA

KINGDOM OF HUNGARY

Meran

Villach

to
Brixen

Mur

Bozen

to
Freising

Laibach

Sava

Mohacs

O T T O M A N

Trent

Görz

D. OF
CARNIOLA

Drava

Trieste

OF VENICE

Danube

E M P I R E

POMERANIA-WOLGAST

Kolberg

BP. OF KAMMIN

STETTIN

Danzig

Elbing

ERMLAND

Kammin

D. OF POMERANIA

PRUSSIA (ROYAL)
United with Poland 1569

Marienburg

Marienwerder

DUCHY

OF PRUSSIA
Under Polish Suzerainty

Stettin

Torun

Vistula

Poznan

KINGDOM OF

Warsaw

POLAND

126

CENTRAL EUROPE, *c.*1560:
RELIGIOUS SITUATION

Scale 1:10,000,000 (160 miles=1 inch)

0   50   100   150   200 Miles
0   100   200   300 Km.

- Lutherans
- Calvinists and Zwinglians
- Anglicans
- Waldensians and Moravians
- Anabaptists, Socinians etc.

- Roman Catholics
- Greek Orthodox
- Mohammedans
- – – Boundary of the Holy Roman Empire

K. OF SWEDEN

K. OF DENMARK

Copenhagen

BALTIC SEA

STETTIN

Danzig

ERMLAND

POM-WOLGAST

POM.

PRUSSIA

K. OF POLAND

Vistula

NORTH SEA

K. OF ENGLAND

Amsterdam

HOLSTEIN

Hamburg MECKLENBURG

Bremen

BREMEN

BRUNSWICK-LÜNEBURG

Hanover

Brunswick

BRANDENBURG

Berlin

Poznan

Stettin

Kottbus

Liegnitz

Breslau

Brieg

SILESIA

NETHERLANDS

SPAN.

Brussels

Münster

MÜNSTER

KLEVE

MARK

WEST-PHALIA

Minden

Magdeburg

Wittenberg

Halle

Leipzig

Erfurt EL. OF SAXONY

Dresden

Prague

Glatz

BOHEMIA

MORAVIA

Brünn

Cambrai

Liège

Cologne

Aachen

JULICH

BERG

HESSE

NASSAU

Cassel

FULDA

Schmalkalden

SAXONY

Elbe

HUNGARY

LUXEMBURG

Verdun

Metz

Mainz

Worms

Speyer

Frankfurt

WÜRZBURG

BAMBERG

Coburg

Bayreuth

Nuremberg

Ansbach

Eichstätt

Regensburg

Passau

Vienna

AUSTRIA

Buda (Ofen)

Rouen

Paris

Marne

Seine

Toul

LORRAINE

Strassburg

PAL.

BADEN

WÜRTTEMBERG

Stuttgart

Tübingen

Augsburg

BAVARIA

Munich

Salzburg

Danube

Graz

OTTOMAN

K. OF FRANCE

Loire

Montbéliard

FRANCHE-COMTÉ

Basle

Berne

Constance

Zürich

Innsbruck

SALZBURG

CARINTHIA

CARNIOLA

Trieste

EMPIRE

THE EMPIRE

SWISS CONFEDERATION

TYROL

Lyons

Geneva

SAVOY

PIEDMONT

Turin

MILAN

Milan

Po

Venice

REP. OF VENICE

Po

DALMATIA

Rhône

PARMA

Genoa

ADRIATIC SEA

Marseilles

Gulf of Lions

Florence

FLORENCE

Elba

PAPAL STATES

Rome

REP. OF RAGUSA

Barcelona

Corsica

NAPLES

Benevento

Naples

Sardinia

TYRRHENIAN SEA

East from Greenwich

COPYRIGHT. GEORGE PHILIP & SON. LTD.

**CENTRAL EUROPE, c.1618:
RELIGIOUS SITUATION**

Scale 1:10,000,000 (160 miles=1 inch)

0 50 100 150 200 Miles
0 100 200 300 Km.

Lutherans
Calvinists and Zwinglians
Anglicans
Waldensians and Moravians

Roman Catholics
Reclaimed to Roman Catholicism
Greek Orthodox
Mohammedans

– – – Boundary of the Holy Roman Empire

K. OF SWEDEN

BALTIC SEA

K. OF DENMARK

Copenhagen

55

NORTH SEA

K. OF ENGLAND

HOLSTEIN

BREMEN

Hamburg MECKLENBURG

POM. WOLGAST

POM.

STETTIN

Stettin

Danzig

ERMLAND

PRUSSIA

K. OF POLAND

Vistula

Amsterdam UNITED PROVINCES

Bremen

BRUNSWICK-LÜNEBURG

Hanover

BRANDENBURG

Berlin

Poznan

Minden

Brunswick

Magdeburg

Kottbus

SPAN. NETHERLANDS

Brussels

Liège

Münster

MÜNSTER

MARK

WEST-PHALIA

Cologne

BERG

Aachen

HESSE

Cambrai

KLEVE

JÜLICH

NASSAU

Halle

Wittenberg

Leipzig

Erfurt EL. OF SAXONY

Dresden

Liegnitz

Breslau

Brieg

SILESIA

Glatz

FULDA

Cassel

Schmalkalden

SAXONY

Frankfurt

Mainz

Coburg

Bayreuth

Prague

BOHEMIA

Brünn

MORAVIA

Rouen

Paris

Seine

Marne

Verdun

Metz

Toul

WÜRZ-BURG BAMBERG

WORMS

Speyer

PAL.

Nuremberg

Ansbach

Eichstätt

Regensburg

THE EMPIRE

50

K. OF FRANCE

Loire

LORRAINE

Strassburg

WÜRTTEMBERG

Stuttgart

Tübingen

BADEN

Augsburg

Passau

Danube

Vienna

Budo (Ofen)

R E M P I R E

 A U S T R I A

Salzburg

Graz

H U N G A R Y

Montbéliard

FRANCHE-COMTÉ

Basle

Constance

Zürich

Berne

SWISS CONFEDERATION

Geneva

SAVOY

Lyons

Rhône

Innsbruck

TYROL

SALZBURG

CARINTHIA

CARNIOLA

Trieste

OTTOMAN

EMPIRE

45

MILAN

PIEDMONT

Turin

Milan

Po

REP. OF VENICE

Venice

Po

DALMATIA

ADRIATIC SEA

REP. OF RAGUSA

PARMA

Genoa

Marseilles

Gulf of Lions

FLORENCE

Florence

Elba

PAPAL STATES

Rome

Benevento

NAPLES

Naples

Barcelona

Corsica

Sardinia

TYRRHENIAN SEA

40

East from Greenwich

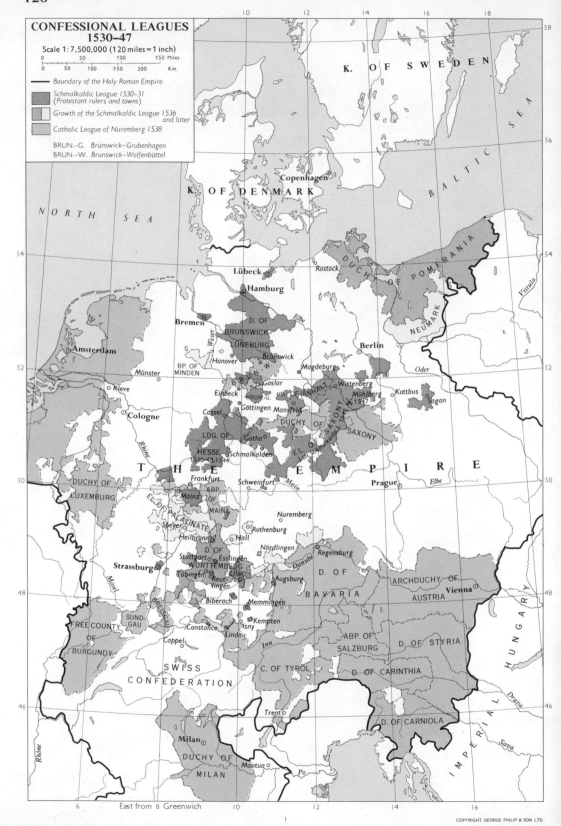

CONFESSIONAL LEAGUES 1530–47

Scale 1:7,500,000 (120 miles = 1 inch)

0   50   100   150 Miles
0   50   100   150   200 Km.

——— Boundary of the Holy Roman Empire

Schmalkaldic League 1530–31
(Protestant rulers and towns)

Growth of the Schmalkaldic League 1536
and later

Catholic League of Nuremberg 1538

BRUN.–G. Brünswick–Grubenhagen
BRUN.–W. Brünswick–Wolfenbüttel

K. OF SWEDEN

BALTIC SEA

NORTH SEA

K. OF DENMARK

Copenhagen

Lübeck

Hamburg

Rostock

DUCHY OF POMERANIA

NEUMARK

Bremen

Amsterdam

Münster

D. OF
BRUNSWICK
LÜNEBURG

Hanover

Brunswick

Berlin

Magdeburg

Oder

Kottbus

Sagan

BP. OF
MINDEN

Kleve

Cologne

BRUN.-W.

Goslar

Einbeck

BRUN.-G.

Göttingen

PR. OF ANHALT

Wittenberg

Mühlberg
× 1547

Cassel

Mansfeld

DUCHY OF
SAXONY

SAXONY

Rhine

LDG. OF

Gotha

HESSE
1530-49,1544

Schmalkalden

EL. OF
SAXONY

Left Schmalkald L.

T   H   E

Frankfurt

Schweinfurt

Main

Prague

Elbe

E   M   P   I   R   E

DUCHY OF
LUXEMBURG

EL. OF PALATINATE

Mainz

ABP.
OF
MAINZ

Speyer

Nuremberg

Heilbronn

Rothenburg

Hall

Nördlingen

Regensburg

Danube

D. OF
WÜRTTEMBERG

Stuttgart

Esslingen

Tübingen

Reutlingen

Ulm

Augsburg

D. OF
BAVARIA

ARCHDUCHY OF
AUSTRIA

Vienna

Strassburg

Morel

BREISGAU

Biberach

Memmingen

SUND-
GAU

Kempten

Isny

FREE COUNTY
OF
BURGUNDY

Constance

Lindau

ABP. OF
SALZBURG

D. OF STYRIA

Cappel

SWISS

CONFEDERATION

Inn

C. OF TYROL

D. OF CARINTHIA

H   U   N   G   A   R   Y

Drava

I   M   P   E   R   I   A   L

Rhône

Trent

D. OF CARNIOLA

Sava

Milan

Mantua

Po

DUCHY OF
MILAN

East from 8 Greenwich

COPYRIGHT. GEORGE PHILIP & SON. LTD.

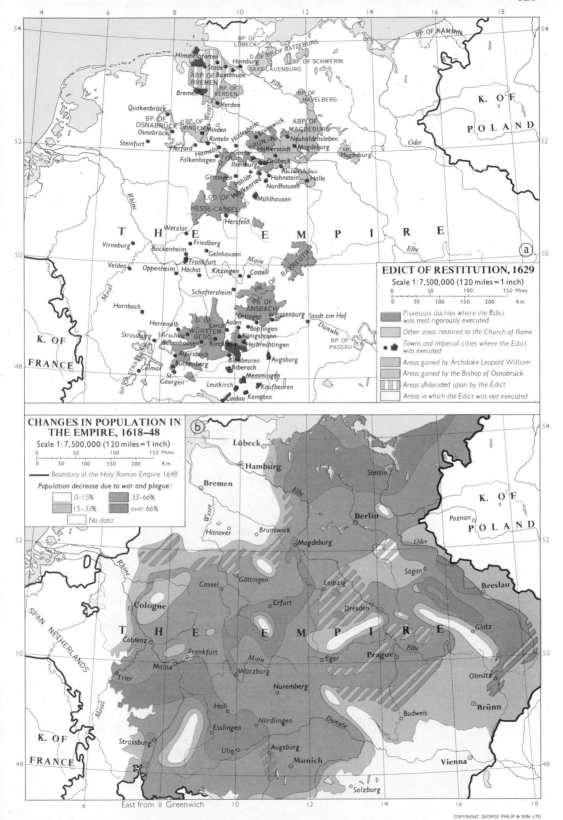

EDICT OF RESTITUTION, 1629
Scale 1:7,500,000 (120 miles = 1 inch)

0   50   100   150 Miles
0   50   100   150   200
Km.

Protestant duchies where the Edict was most rigorously executed

Other areas restored to the Church of Rome

Towns and imperial cities where the Edict was executed

Areas gained by Archduke Leopold William

Areas gained by the Bishop of Osnabrück

Areas undecided upon by the Edict

Areas in which the Edict was not executed

CHANGES IN POPULATION IN THE EMPIRE, 1618–48
Scale 1:7,500,000 (120 miles = 1 inch)

0   50   100   150 Miles
0   50   100   150   200
Km.

Boundary of the Holy Roman Empire 1648

Population decrease due to war and plague:

0–15%   33–66%
15–33%   over 66%
No data

East from 8 Greenwich

COPYRIGHT. GEORGE PHILIP & SON. LTD.

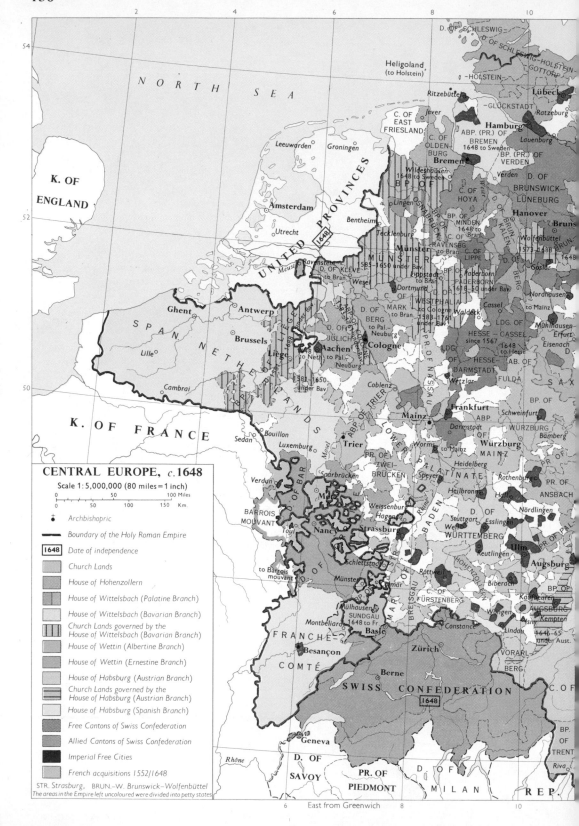

Rügen

HITHER POMERANIA
1648 to Sweden

Rostock

Wismar
Neukloster
1648 to Sweden
D. OF MECKLENBURG
Partition 1611/21
-SCHWERIN

GÜSTROW

Elbe

Huvelberg

Stendal

EL. OF BRANDENBURG

Spandau   Berlin

Brandenburg
Potsdam

wick   ABP. OF
MAGDEBURG

Magdeburg

Halberstadt
PR. OF   Dessau
Eisleben   Halle
Merseburg
Naumburg   Leipzig
EL. OF SAXONY
Meissen

BP. OF
Mainz
OF   Jena   Altenburg   Dresden
Jena
O N Y
1567/1660

BP.
OF   BAYREUTH
BAMBERG   UPPER
Eger

Nurem-   PR. OF PAL. SULZBACH
berg   PALATINATE
NEUBURG 1628/48
to Bav.

Eichstätt
Freising   Regensburg

EL. OF

BAVARIA

Munich

Kolberg

FARTHER POMERANIA

BP. (PR.) OF KAMMIN
1648 to Bran.

Kammin

Stettin

Boundary 1653

1637 to Pol.

LOWER LUSATIA

Lebus
Frankfurt
Schwiebus
Oder
Sagan
Kottbus
Glogau
1635/48 to Sax.
Wittenberg
1635/48 to Saxony
UPPER LUSATIA   Görlitz
Liegnitz

Leitmeritz

KINGDOM OF

Prague   Elbe

BOHEMIA

Pilsen

Vltava

Iglau

Budweis

Linz

BP. OF
PASSAU
1595-1664 under Aust.

Passau

ARCHDUCHY OF

AUSTRIA

Waidhofen

Salzburg

ABP. OF   Gröbming
SALZBURG   D. OF STYRIA
Graz

Innsbruck

TYROL

Brixen

Meran

Bozen

Lienz

Villach   D. OF CARINTHIA

to
Brixen

Trent

to
Freising   Laibach   Sava

Görz   D. OF
Trieste   CARNIOLA

OF VENICE

Danzig   Elbing   ERMLAND
1637 to Pol.
1637 to Pol.   Marienburg

Marienwerder

DUCHY
OF PRUSSIA
1618 to Brandenburg
under Polish Suzerainty
until 1657/60

Torun

Vistula

Poznan   KINGDOM   OF

Warsaw

POLAND

Wohlau   Öls
Breslau   DUCHY   OF
Brieg   Oppeln
Schweidnitz   SILESIA   Beuthen
Glatz   Ratibor   Krakow
Jägerndorf   Oderberg
Troppau

Olmütz

MAR. OF MORAVIA

Brünn

Vienna   Pressburg

IMPERIAL   HUNGARY

Gran

Buda
(Ofen)   Pest

Stuhlweissenburg

L. Balaton

KINGDOM OF HUNGARY

Mur

Landsberg

Drava

1630
to Austria   Mohacs

OTTOMAN

EMPIRE

Danube

COPYRIGHT. GEORGE PHILIP & SON. LTD.

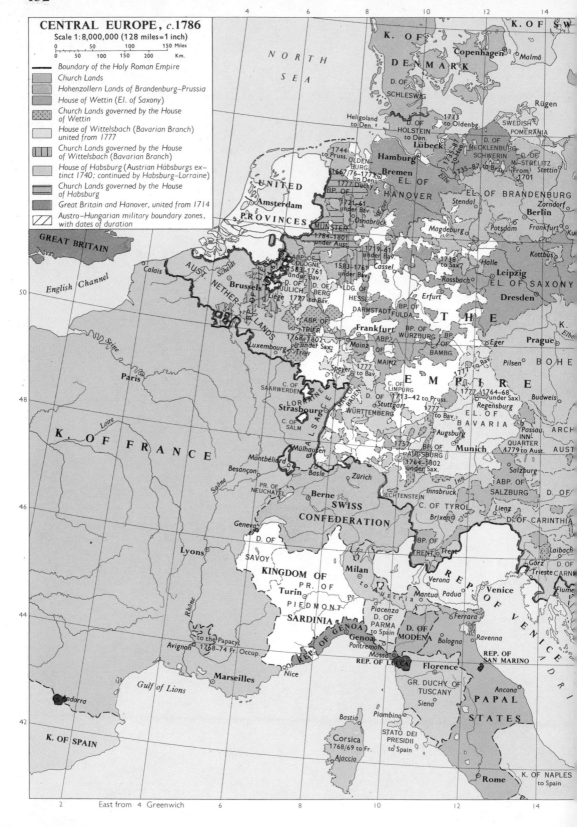

CENTRAL EUROPE, c.1786

Scale 1:8,000,000 (128 miles=1 inch)

0   50   100   150 Miles
0   50   100   150   200 Km.

— Boundary of the Holy Roman Empire
Church Lands
Hohenzollern Lands of Brandenburg-Prussia
House of Wettin (El. of Saxony)
Church Lands governed by the House of Wettin
House of Wittelsbach (Bavarian Branch) united from 1777
Church Lands governed by the House of Wittelsbach (Bavarian Branch)
House of Habsburg (Austrian Habsburgs extinct 1740; continued by Habsburg-Lorraine)
Church Lands governed by the House of Habsburg
Great Britain and Hanover, united from 1714
Austro-Hungarian military boundary zones, with dates of duration

NORTH SEA

K. OF SW

K. OF DENMARK

Copenhagen   Malmö

D. OF SCHLESWIG   Rügen   SWEDISH POMERANIA

Heligoland to Den.   1773 to Oldenbg.   D. OF HOLSTEIN to Den.

1744 to Pruss.   OLDEN-BURG   D. OF MECKLENBURG SCHWERIN   D. OF M-STRELITZ Stettin From 1701

Lübeck   Hamburg   Bremen   EL. OF HANOVER   EL. OF BRANDENBURG

1667/76-1771   1777 Duchy   BP. OF   Stendal   Zorndorf. Berlin

UNITED   1721-61 under Bav.   Osnabrück   Magdeburg   Potsdam   Frankfurt

Amsterdam   MÜNSTER   1719-41 under Bav.   Halle   Kottbus

PROVINCES   1784-1801 under Aust.   1583-1761 under Bav.   Cassel   1739 to Sax.   Leipzig   EL. OF SAXONY

GREAT BRITAIN   ABP. OF COLOGNE 1583-1761 under Bav.   Rossbach   Dresden

Calais   D. OF JÜLICH   Erfurt   THE   Prague   BOHE

Brussels   Liège   D. OF BERG 1777   HESSE DARMSTADT FULDA   BP. OF WÜRZBURG   Eger

AUST.   ABP. OF TRIER 1768-1802 under Sax.   Frankfurt   ABP. OF MAINZ   BP. OF BAMBG   Pilsen

NETHERLANDS   Luxembourg   Trier   Mainz   1777 to Bav.   EMPIRE   Budweis

Scheldt   C. OF SAARWERDEN   Speyer 1777 to Bav.   D. OF 1713-42 to Pruss.   1777 1764-68 under Sax.   Regensburg

Strasbourg   LORRAINE   BADEN   WÜRTTEMBERG Stuttgart   1777 to Bav.   EL. OF BAVARIA   Passau INN QUARTER 1779 to Aust. AUST

C. OF SALM   1757   BP. OF AUGSBURG 1764-1802 under Sax.   Augsburg   Munich   Salzburg

Montbéliard   Mülhausen   ABP. OF SALZBURG

Besançon   Basle   Zürich   Innsbruck   D. OF

Paris   Berne   SWISS CONFEDERATION   LIECHTENSTEIN   C. OF TYROL   Lienz   D. OF CARINTHIA

K. OF FRANCE   PR. OF NEUCHÂTEL   Geneva   Brixen   Laibach

Lyons   D. OF SAVOY   BP. OF TRENT   Trent   REP. OF VENICE   Görz   D. OF Trieste CARN

KINGDOM OF   Milan   Verona   Venice   Fiume

Turin   PR. OF   Po   Austria   Mantua   Padua   ADRI

PIEDMONT   Placenza   D. OF PARMA to Spain   Ferrara   REP. OF SAN MARINO

SARDINIA   to the Papacy 1768-74 Fr. Occup.   REP. OF GENOA   D. OF MODENA   Bologna   Ravenna

Avignon   Genoa   Pontremoli   Florence

Nice   Massa   REP. OF LUCCA   GR. DUCHY OF TUSCANY   Ancona

Marseilles   REP. OF GENOA   PAPAL

Gulf of Lions   Siena   STATES

K. OF SPAIN   Bastia   Piombino

Corsica 1768/69 to Fr.   STATO DEI PRESIDII to Spain

Ajaccio   Rome   K. OF NAPLES to Spain

Andorra

English Channel

EDEN

SAMOGITIA

Polotsk

Smolensk

BALTIC SEA

Bornholm

Tauroggen
1688/90–1795 to Prussia

Vilna

RUSSIAN

Königsberg

EAST PRUSSIA

C. OF
SERREY
1688/90–1793 to Prussia

Minsk

WHITE RUTHENIA

Kolberg

Danzig

Elbing
ERMLAND

EMPIRE

POMERANIA

LITHUANIA

WEST PRUSSIA
1772 to Pruss.

Białystok

BLACK RUSSIA

Gomel

K. OF PRUSSIA

NETZE DISTRICT

Torun

MAZOVIA

K. OF POLAND

Pripet

ersdorf

GREAT POLAND

Poznan

Vistula

Warsaw

Liegnitz

Breslau

Piotrków

Lublin

PODLESIA

LITTLE RUSSIA

Kiev

Leuthen

Landshut

DUCHY OF
SILESIA
1742 to Pruss.

LITTLE
POLAND

VOLHYNIA

UKRAINE

Neisse

OF

Ratibor

Kraków

Kolin

Neustadt

AUSTRIAN SILESIA

Teschen

K. OF GALICIA

RED RUSSIA

Lemberg
(Lvov)

Bar

PODOLIA

MIA

Olmütz

MAR. OF MORAVIA

AND LODOMERIA
1772 to Austria

Kolomea

Czernowitz

BESSARABIA

Iglau

Brünn

Z I P S
1770/72 to Hung.

Jassy

Kishinev

DUCHY OF
RIA

Vienna

Pressburg

D. OF
BUKOVINA
1775 to Aust.

Danube

Gran

Erlau

Debreczin

MOLDAVIA

STYRIA

St. Gotthard

Buda
(Ofen)

Pest

K. OF HUNGARY

Grosswardein

GR. PR. OF

L. Balaton

Hereditary Monarchy from 1684,
1699 to Austria

TRANSYLVANIA

1699 to Austria,
1765 Gr. Pr.

Galati

Ismail

Drava

Mures

Szegedin

Temesvar

BANAT
1718 to Austria

Kronstadt

CIVIL-
CROATIA
1701

Mohacs

OA

(K. OF)
SLAVONIA
CIVIL-SLAVONIA 1743

1702–1878

1538/1717–1878

1764–1881

1742–1871

WALLACHIA

Bucharest

Constanta

Peterwardein

Belgrade

CROATIA

Sava

Sobac

Passarowitz

Craiova

Danube

Varna

Zara

DALMATIA

Sarajevo

SERBIA

Nish

BULGARIA

BLACK
SEA

Spalato

HERZEGOVINA

Burgas

BOSNIA

OTTOMAN

Sofia

REP. OF
RAGUSA

Ragusa

Cattaro

MONTENEGRO

Scutari

Üsküb
(Skoplje)

Philippopolis

EMPIRE

Adrianople

RUMELIA

Constantinople

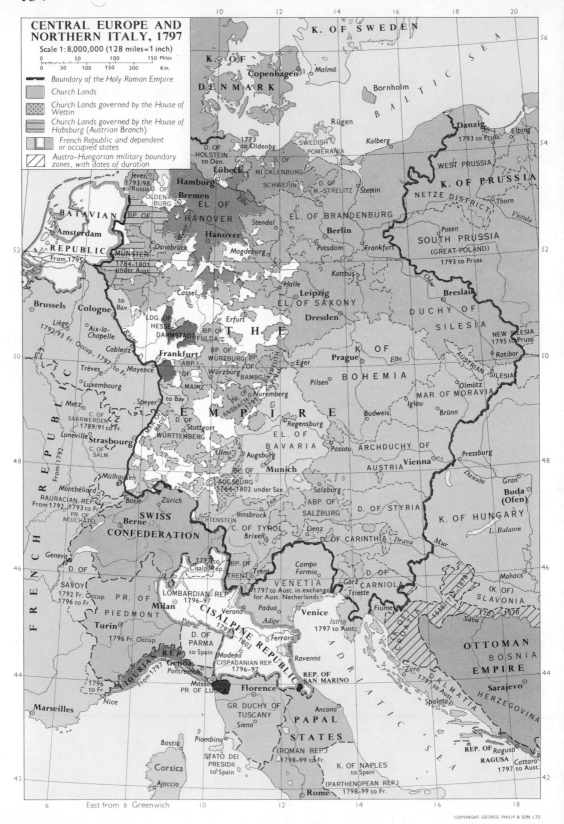

CENTRAL EUROPE AND
NORTHERN ITALY, 1797

Scale 1:8,000,000 (128 miles=1 inch)

0   50   100   150 Miles
0   50 100 150 200 Km.

- - - Boundary of the Holy Roman Empire
Church Lands
Church Lands governed by the House of Wettin
Church Lands governed by the House of Habsburg (Austrian Branch)
French Republic and dependent or occupied states
Austro–Hungarian military boundary zones, with dates of duration

K. OF SWEDEN

K. OF DENMARK

Copenhagen   Malmö

Bornholm

BALTIC SEA

Rügen

SWEDISH POMERANIA

Kolberg

Danzig
1793 to Pruss.   Elbing

WEST PRUSSIA

K. OF PRUSSIA

NETZE DISTRICT   Thorn

Vistula

1773 to Oldenbg
D. OF HOLSTEIN to Den.

Lübeck

MECKLENBURG

D. OF M-STRELITZ   Stettin

SOUTH PRUSSIA
(GREAT-POLAND)
1793 to Pruss.

BATAVIAN

Jever
1793/98
to Russia
OLDENBURG

Hamburg

Bremen

EL. OF HANOVER

SCHWERIN

BP. OF

Hanover

Amsterdam

REPUBLIC
From 1795

MÜNSTER
1784-1801
under Aust.

Osnabrück

Magdeburg

EL. OF BRANDENBURG

Berlin

Potsdam   Frankfurt

Posen

Breslau

DUCHY OF SILESIA

NEW SILESIA
1795 to Pruss.

Brussels

Liège
1792/93 Fr. Occup. 1797 to Fr.

Cologne   to Bav.

Aix-la-Chapelle

Stendal

Halle

Leipzig

EL. OF SAXONY

Dresden

Kottbus

Oder

Ratibor

AUSTRIAN SILESIA

Cassel

LDG. OF HESSEL
DARMSTADT

Erfurt

BP. OF FULDA

Rhine

Coblenz

Frankfurt

ABP.

OF

MAINZ

BP. OF WÜRZBURG

BP. OF BAMBG.

BAYREUTH

Eger

Prague

Pilsen

K. OF

BOHEMIA

Elbe

MAR. OF MORAVIA

Olmütz

THE

Trèves

Luxembourg

Metz

C. OF SAARWERDEN
1789/91 to Fr.

Speyer   to Bav.

BADEN

Würzburg

Nuremberg

PR. OF ANSBACH
1791

EMPIRE

Regensburg

Budweis

Brünn

Iglau

Luneville

C. OF SALM

Strasbourg

D. OF WÜRTTEMBERG

Stuttgart

Ulm

EL. OF BAVARIA

Passau

ARCHDUCHY OF

Vienna

Pressburg

Gran

Buda
(Ofen)

From 1792

RAURACIAN REP.
From 1792, 1793 to Fr.

Montbéliard

Mülhausen

Basle

Zürich

Augsburg

BP. OF
AUGSBURG
1764-1802 under Sax.

Munich

Salzburg

AUSTRIA

Danube

L. Balaton

PR. OF NEUCHÂTEL

Berne

SWISS

CONFEDERATION

LIECHTENSTEIN

Innsbruck

C. OF TYROL

Brixen

ABP. OF
SALZBURG

D. OF STYRIA

K. OF HUNGARY

Geneva

D. OF

BP. OF
TRENT

Trent

Lienz

D. OF CARINTHIA

Drava

Mur

Mohács

1797 to
Cisalp. Rep.

Campo Formio

D. OF

CARNIOLA

(K. OF)

SLAVONIA

SAVOY
1792 Fr. Occup.
1796 to Fr.

PR. OF

PIEDMONT

LOMBARDIAN REP.
1796-97

Milan

VENETIA
1797 to Aust. in exchange for Aust. Netherlands

Görz

Trieste

Fiume

Istria

Sava

Zara

CROATIA

1578 to 1878

OTTOMAN

BOSNIA

EMPIRE

FRENCH REPUBLIC

Turin
1796 Fr. Occup.

CISALPINE
REPUBLIC
1797-1802

Verona

Padua

Adige

Venice
1797 to Aust.

ADRIATIC

Spalato

DALMATIA
1797 to Aust.

1797 to Aust.

Sarajevo

HERZEGOVINA

LIGURIAN REP.
From 1797

Genoa

Pontremoli

D. OF PARMA
to Spain

Modena

Ferrara

Ravenna

SEA

1796
to Fr.

Nice

Massa
PR. OF LUCCA

Florence

REP. OF
SAN MARINO

Ancona

REP. OF Ragusa

RAGUSA
1797 to Aust.

Cattaro

Marseilles

Bastia

Corsica

Ajaccio

Piombino

STATO DEI
PRESIDII
to Spain

GR. DUCHY OF
TUSCANY

Siena

PAPAL

STATES

(ROMAN REP.)
1798-99 to Fr.

Rome

K. OF NAPLES
to Spain

(PARTHENOPEAN REP.)
1798-99 to Fr.

East from 8 Greenwich

CENTRAL EUROPE AND NORTHERN ITALY, 1803

Scale 1:8,000,000 (128 miles=1 inch)

0   50   100   150 Miles
0   50   100   150   200 Km.

—— Boundary of the Holy Roman Empire

Brandenburg-Prussia

House of Wittelsbach (Bavarian Branch)

House of Habsburg (Austrian Branch) and Secundogeniture

French Republic and dependent states

Austro–Hungarian military boundary zones, with dates of duration

K. OF SWEDEN

BALTIC SEA

K. OF DENMARK
Copenhagen
Malmö
Bornholm
Rügen
Kolberg
Danzig
Elbing
SWEDISH POMERANIA

to Oldenbg.
D. OF HOLSTEIN to Den.
Lübeck
Jeven to Russia
D. OF OLDEN-BURG
Hamburg
Bremen
MECKLENBURG
SCHWERIN
D. OF M-STRELITZ
Stettin
WEST PRUSSIA
NETZE DISTRICT
Thorn
Vistula
K. OF PRUSSIA

BATAVIAN REPUBLIC
Amsterdam
Münster
EL. OF HANOVER
Hanover
Osnabrück
Stendal
Magdeburg
EL. OF BRANDENBURG
Berlin
Potsdam
Frankfurt
Posen
SOUTH PRUSSIA

Brussels
Liège
Cologne
Aix-la-Chapelle
Coblenz
BERG to Bav.
1803 to Pruss.
LDG. OF Cassel
1803 to Pruss.
HESSE
HESSE From 1803
DARMSTADT
Halle
Leipzig
Erfurt
1803 to Pruss.
EL. OF SAXONY
Dresden
Elbe
Breslau
Glatz
DUCHY OF SILESIA
NEW SILESIA
Ratibor
AUSTRIAN SILESIA

Frankfurt
THURINGIAN STATES
T H E
BAYREUTH
PR. OF ANSBACH
Eger
Prague
K. OF
BOHEMIA
Pilsen
Elbe
Budweis
MAR. OF MORAVIA
Olmütz
Brünn
Iglau

Trèves
Luxembourg
Moselle
Speyer
Mayence
to Bavaria
E M P I R E
Nuremberg
Regensburg
Salzburg
Salzburg
Passau
ARCHDUCHY OF

Strasbourg
BADEN
EL. OF Stuttgart
WÜRTTEMBERG From 1803
Ulm
Augsburg
Munich
Hohenlinden
BAVARIA
EL. OF
AUSTRIA
Vienna
Pressburg
Gran
Buda (Ofen)

Mülhouse 1798 to Fr.
Montbéliard
Basle
Zürich
Helv.
LIECHTENSTEIN
Innsbruck
Salzburg
EL. OF SALZBURG
D. OF STYRIA
K. OF HUNGARY
L. Balaton

PR. OF NEUCHÂTEL
HELVETIC REPUBLIC 1798–1803
Berne
C. OF TYROL
Brixen
Lienz
D. OF CARINTHIA
Drava
Mur

Geneva 1798 to Fr.
REP. OF VALAIS 1802–10
D. OF SAVOY
Trent
Campo Formio
D. OF
Laibach
Görz
Trieste
CARNIOLA
Mohacs
(K. OF) SLAVONIA

1792–1804
FRENCH REPUBLIC
1802 to Ital. Rep.
Milan
PR. OF PIEDMONT
Turin
1798/1802 to Fr.
Marengo
VENETIA
Verona
Padua
Adige
Venice
Fiume
Zara
OTTOMAN
BOSNIA
EMPIRE

LIGURIAN REP. 1797–1805
Genoa
Pontremoli
PARMA 1802–05 to Spain
Modena
Bologna
Ferrara
Ravenna
REP. OF SAN MARINO
DALMATIA
Spalato
Sarajevo
HERZEGOVINA

Marseilles
Nice
Masa
REP. OF LUCCA 1799–1805
Florence
Ancona 1803 to Fr.
PAPAL STATES
REP. OF Ragusa
RAGUSA
Cattaro

K. OF ETRURIA
Siena Kingdom 1801 to Spain
Piombino 1801 to Fr.
Corsica
Bastia
Ajaccio
Elba
Orbetello 1801 to Etruria
Rome to Spain
K. OF NAPLES

ADRIATIC SEA

CENTRAL EUROPE AND NORTHERN ITALY, 1806
Scale 1:8,000,000 (128 miles = 1 inch)

0 50 100 150 Miles
0 50 100 150 200 Km.

- – – Boundary of the Confederation of the Rhine at its foundation, 12th July 1806
French Empire
States ruled by Napoleon's family
Other dependent states
Austro–Hungarian military boundary zones, with dates of duration

K. OF SWEDEN

K. OF DENMARK

Copenhagen Malmö

Heligoland to Den.

Lübeck Bornholm

BALTIC SEA

Rügen

Kolberg Danzig

Hamburg D. OF MECKLENBURG-SCHWERIN Stettin WEST PRUSSIA

Jever to Russia until 1807 D. OF OLDEN-BURG Bremen D. OF M.-STRELITZ

to Oldenbg.

K. OF HOLLAND 1806–10 Amsterdam

HANOVER 1805/06 to Prussia KINGDOM OF PRUSSIA

Hanover BRANDENBURG Berlin

Osnabrück Magdeburg Potsdam Frankfurt Posen

Branswick Stendal SOUTH PRUSSIA

Münster Halle Kottbus Glogau Breslau

GR. D. OF BERG From 1806 CASSEL EL. OF HESSE Leipzig K. OF SAXONY From 1806 SILESIA

Brussels Cologne GR. D. OF HESSE From 1806 Auerstedt Dresden NEW SILESIA

Liège Aix-la-Chapelle Erfurt Jena Ratibor

Trèves Fulda THURINGIAN STATES Eger Prague AUSTRIAN SILESIA

Frankfurt BOHEMIA Olmütz

GR. D. OF WÜRZBURG 1805–14 Elbe MORAVIA Austerlitz

Luxembourg PR. OF BAYREUTH Pilsen Iglau Brünn

Mayence Budweis

Speyer 1806 to Bav. CONFEDERATION

Strasbourg K. OF WÜRTTEMB. From 1805 1806 to Bav. 1805 to Bav. Regensburg 1805 to Bav. AUSTRIAN

OF THE RHINE Ulm Augsburg Passau EMPIRE

GR. D. OF BADEN From 1806 1805 to Würt. K. OF Munich Schönbrunn Pressburg

FRENCH EMPIRE From 1804 Basle 1805 to Baden BAVARIA From 1805 Salzburg Berchtesgaden AUSTRIA Vienna Buda (Ofen)

PR. OF NEUCHATEL 1806 to Fr. Zürich Constance 1805 to Baden LIECHTENSTEIN Innsbruck SALZBURG 1805 to Aust. STYRIA K. OF HUNGARY

Berne HELVETIA From 1803 TYROL Lienz CARINTHIA Drava Mur L. Balaton

Geneva Brixen 1805 to Bav. Laibach

REP. OF VALAIS 1802–10 Trent VENETIA 1805 to Italy CARNIOLA Trieste Mohacs

Milan Verona Fiume (K. OF) SLAVONIA 1699 1737 1878

KINGDOM OF ITALY Padua Venice 1805 to Italy CROATIA 1702 1578

Turin Po Guastalla 1805 1806 to Fr. to Italy Ferrara Zara DALMATIA 1805 to It. OTTOMAN BOSNIA EMPIRE

LIGURIAN REP. 1805 to Fr. PARMA 1805 to Fr. Modena Bologna Ravenna Spalato Sarajevo

Genoa Pontremoli REP. OF SAN MARINO HERZEGOVINA

Marseilles Nice Massa 1806 to Lucca Florence Ancona Ragusa 1806–08 to Russia

Bastia PR. OF LUCCA From 1805 PAPAL Cattaro 1805 to Italy 1806–07 to Russia

Corsica Piombino 1805 Pr. Elba K. OF ETRURIA to Spain Siena STATES

Ajaccio K. OF NAPLES 1806 Rome

COPYRIGHT. GEORGE PHILIP & SON. LTD.

East from Greenwich

CENTRAL EUROPE AND NORTHERN ITALY, 1810

Scale 1:8,000,000 (128 miles=1 inch)

0   50   100   150 Miles
0 50 100 150 200 Km.

- - - Boundary of the Confederation of the Rhine
French Empire
States ruled by Napoleon's family
Other dependent states

K. OF SWEDEN

BALTIC SEA

K. OF DENMARK
Copenhagen
Malmö
Bornholm
Rügen
Kolberg
REP. OF DANZIG
1807-14
Danzig

K. OF PRUSSIA
Graudenz
Thorn

Heligoland
1807/14 to Br.
Lübeck
SWEDISH POMERANIA
D. OF MECKLENBURG-SCHWERIN
D. OF M-STRELITZ
Stettin
GR. D. OF WARSAW
From 1807 to Sax.,
1809 Gr. Duchy
Vistula

Jever
1807
to Holland
Hamburg
Bremen
HANOVER
1807 to Fr.,
1810 to Westphalia
K. OF BRANDENBURG
Berlin
Potsdam
Frankfurt
Posen
Oder

K. OF HOLLAND
Amsterdam
1810 to Fr.
Osnabrück
1807
to Westphalia
1807
to Berg
Münster
Hanover
Stendal
1807 to Fr.,
1810 to Westphalia
Brunswick
Magdeburg
Graudenz

Brussels
Liège
Aix-la-Chapelle
Cologne
GR. D. OF BERG
WESTPHALIA
From 1807
GR. D. OF HESSE
Cassel
Halle
Kottbus
1807
to Sax.
SILESIA
Breslau
1809
to Warsaw
Ratibor
AUSTRIAN SILESIA

Trèves
Luxembourg
Mayence
1807 to Fr.
Erfurt
1807-14
to Fr.
THURINGIAN STATES
GR. D. OF FRANKFURT
From 1810
GR. D. OF WÜRZBURG
Würzburg
K. OF SAXONY
Leipzig
Dresden
Eger
Prague
BOHEMIA
Pilsen
Olmütz
MORAVIA
Brünn

FRENCH EMPIRE
Moselle
Rhine
GR. D. OF BADEN
Frankfurt
1810 to Hesse
PR. OF BAYREUTH
1810 to Bav.
Nuremberg
K. OF BAVARIA
1810 to Bav.
Regensburg
Budweis
Iglau

Strasbourg
Stuttgart
K. OF WÜRTTEMBG.
1810 to Württ.
Ulm
Augsburg
Munich
Passau
1810 to Bav.
AUSTRIAN
Schönbrunn
Wagram
Aspern
Pressburg
AUSTRIA
Vienna
EMPIRE
Buda
(Ofen)

Basle
Zürich
LIECHTENSTEIN
Innsbruck
Salzburg
SALZBURG
1810 to Bav.
STYRIA
K. OF HUNGARY
L. Balaton

Neuchâtel
Berne
HELVETIA
Geneva
1810 to Baden
1810 to Württ.
TYROL
Brixen
1810 to Fr.
Lienz
CARINTHIA
Drava
Mur
Mohacs
(K. OF) SLAVONIA

REP. OF VALAIS
1810 to Fr.
Trent
1810 to Italy
VENETIA
Verona
Padua
Laibach
Trieste
Fiume
1809 to Fr.
ILLYRIAN PROVINCES
Sava
Zara

Milan
KINGDOM OF ITALY
Po
Venice
ADRIATIC SEA
OTTOMAN
BOSNIA
EMPIRE
Sarajevo
HERZEGOVINA

Turin
Genoa
Parma
Modena
Bologna
Ferrara
Ravenna
REP. OF SAN MARINO
Ancona
1808
to Italy
Ragusa
1808 to Fr.
Cattaro
1807 to Fr.

Marseilles
Nice
Pontremoli
Massa
PR. OF LUGCA
Florence
GR. DUCHY OF TUSCANY
1807 to Fr.
PAPAL STATES
1809 to Fr.

Bastia
Corsica
Ajaccio
PR. OF PIOMBINO
Elba
K. OF NAPLES
Rome

East from 8 Greenwich

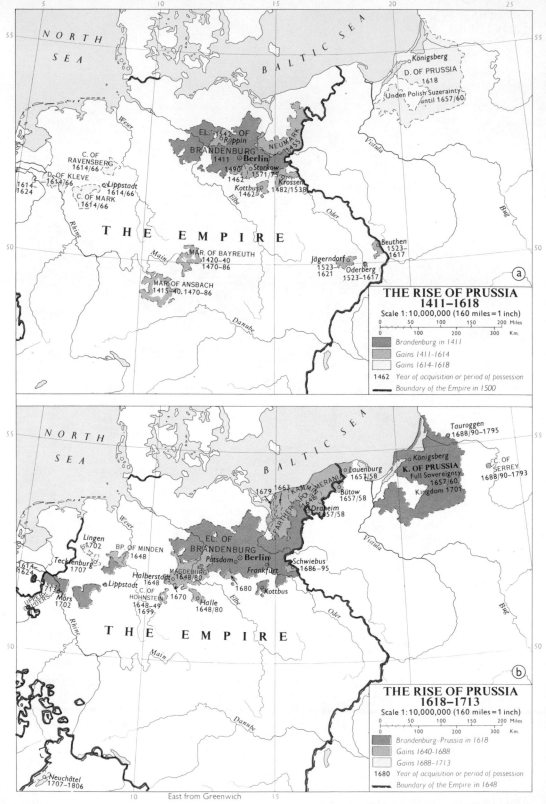

a

NORTH SEA

BALTIC SEA

Königsberg
D. OF PRUSSIA
1618
Under Polish Suzerainty
until 1657/60

EL. 1542 OF
Ruppin
BRANDENBURG
1411   **Berlin**   NEUMARK
1490   Storkow
1462   1571/75
Kottbus   Krossen
1462   1482/1538

C. OF
RAVENSBERG
1614/66
Ds OF KLEVE
1614/766
1614-   Lippstadt
1624   1614/66
C. OF MARK
1614/66

Weser

Vistula

Bug

Rhine

THE   EMPIRE

Elbe

Oder

Beuthen
1523–
1617

Main   MAR. OF BAYREUTH
1420–40
1470–86

Jägerndorf
1523–   Oderberg
1621   1523–1617

MAR. OF ANSBACH
1415–40, 1470–86

Danube

THE RISE OF PRUSSIA
1411–1618
Scale 1:10,000,000 (160 miles=1 inch)

0 50 100 150 200	Miles
0 100 200 300	Km.

    Brandenburg in 1411
    Gains 1411–1614
    Gains 1614–1618
1462   *Year of acquisition or period of possession*
    Boundary of the Empire in 1500

b

NORTH SEA

BALTIC SEA

Tauroggen
1688/90–1795

Lauenburg   Königsberg   C. OF
1657/58   **K. OF PRUSSIA**   SERREY
Full Sovereignty   1688/90–1793
1657/60
Bütow   Kingdom 1701
1657/58

1679   1663   KAMMIN
Draheim
1657/58

EL. OF
BRANDENBURG
Potsdam   **Berlin**
Frankfurt
Schwiebus
1686–95

Lingen
1702
BP. OF MINDEN
Tecklenburg   1648
1707
1614-   Halberstadt   MAGDEBURG
1624   1648   1648/80   1680
UPPER   1713   Lippstadt   C. OF   Kottbus
GELDERS.   Mörs   HOHNSTEIN   1670
1702   1648–49   Halle
1699   1648/80

Weser

FARTHER POMERANIA

Vistula

Bug

Rhine

THE   EMPIRE

Main

Elbe

Oder

Danube

Neuchâtel
1707–1806

THE RISE OF PRUSSIA
1618–1713
Scale 1:10,000,000 (160 miles=1 inch)

0 50 100 150 200	Miles
0 100 200 300	Km.

    Brandenburg-Prussia in 1618
    Gains 1640–1688
    Gains 1688–1713
1680   *Year of acquisition or period of possession*
    Boundary of the Empire in 1648

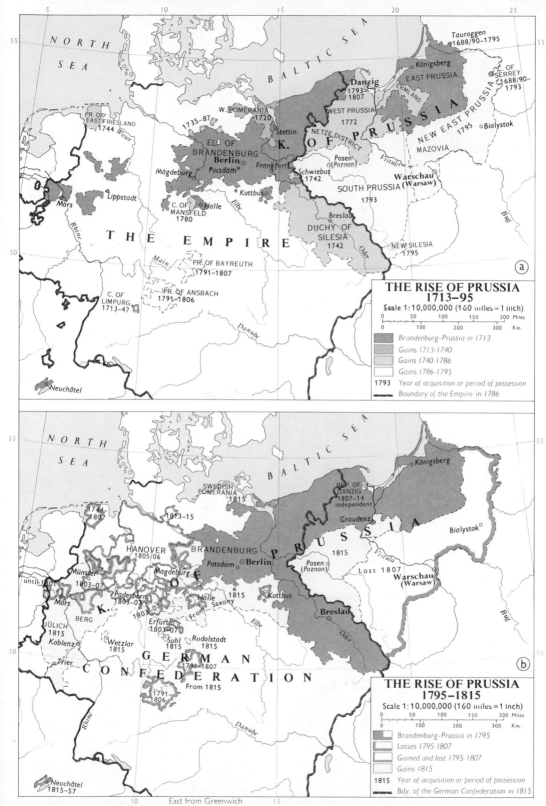

THE RISE OF PRUSSIA 1713–95

Scale 1:10,000,000 (160 miles = 1 inch)

| 0 | 50 | 100 | 150 | 200 Miles |

| 0 | 100 | 200 | 300 Km. |

Brandenburg-Prussia in 1713
Gains 1713-1740
Gains 1740-1786
Gains 1786-1795
1793 Year of acquisition or period of possession
—— Boundary of the Empire in 1786

THE RISE OF PRUSSIA 1795–1815

Scale 1:10,000,000 (160 miles = 1 inch)

| 0 | 50 | 100 | 150 | 200 Miles |

| 0 | 100 | 200 | 300 Km. |

Brandenburg-Prussia in 1795
Losses 1795-1807
Gained and lost 1795-1807
Gains 1815
1815 Year of acquisition or period of possession
—— Bdy. of the German Confederation in 1815

East from Greenwich

COPYRIGHT GEORGE PHILIP & SON LTD

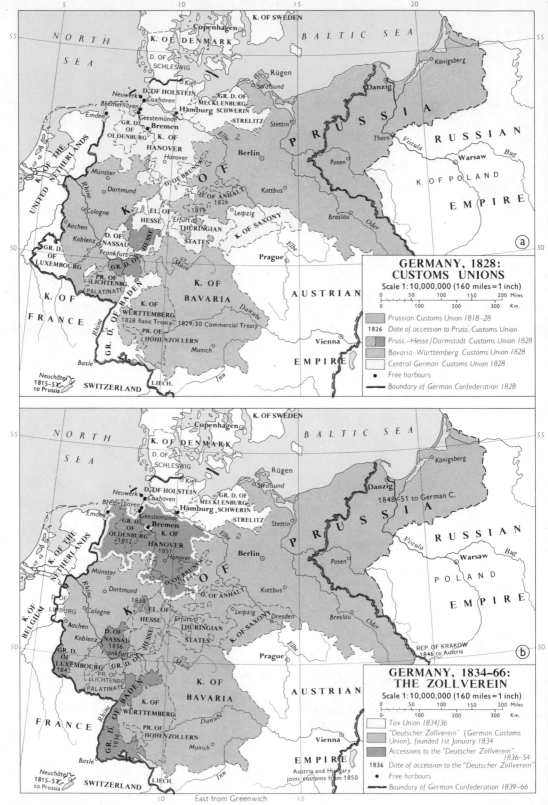

GERMANY, 1828:
CUSTOMS UNIONS
Scale 1:10,000,000 (160 miles = 1 inch)

Prussian Customs Union 1818–28
1826 Date of accession to Pruss. Customs Union
Pruss.–Hesse/Darmstadt Customs Union 1828
Bavaria–Württemberg Customs Union 1828
Central German Customs Union 1828
• Free harbours
Boundary of German Confederation 1828

GERMANY, 1834–66:
THE ZOLLVEREIN
Scale 1:10,000,000 (160 miles = 1 inch)

Tax Union 1834/36
"Deutscher Zollverein" (German Customs Union), founded 1st January 1834
Accessions to the "Deutscher Zollverein" 1836–54
1836 Date of accession to the "Deutscher Zollverein"
• Free harbours
Boundary of German Confederation 1839–66

East from Greenwich

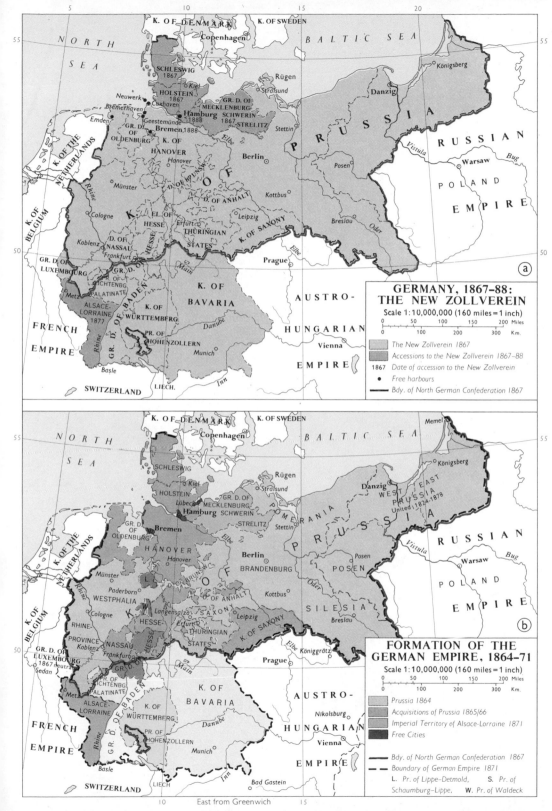

GERMANY, 1867–88:
THE NEW ZOLLVEREIN

Scale 1:10,000,000 (160 miles = 1 inch)

| 0 | 50 | 100 | 150 | 200 Miles |

| 0 | 100 | 200 | 300 | Km. |

The New Zollverein 1867

Accessions to the New Zollverein 1867–88

1867   Date of accession to the New Zollverein

•   Free harbours

Bdy. of North German Confederation 1867

FORMATION OF THE
GERMAN EMPIRE, 1864–71

Scale 1:10,000,000 (160 miles = 1 inch)

| 0 | 50 | 100 | 150 | 200 Miles |

| 0 | 100 | 200 | 300 | Km. |

Prussia 1864

Acquisitions of Prussia 1865/66

Imperial Territory of Alsace-Lorraine 1871

Free Cities

Bdy. of North German Confederation 1867

Boundary of German Empire 1871

L. Pr. of Lippe-Detmold,   S. Pr. of
Schaumburg-Lippe,   W. Pr. of Waldeck

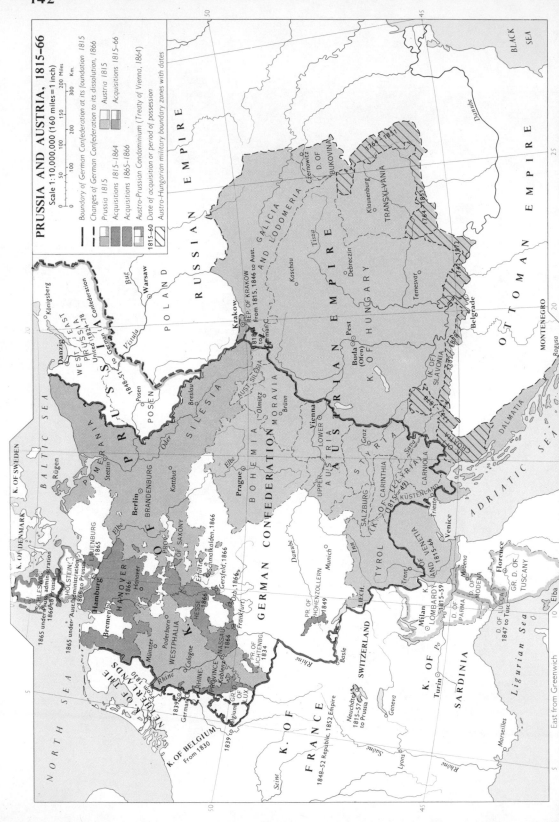

PRUSSIA AND AUSTRIA, 1815–66

Scale 1:10,000,000 (160 miles=1 inch)

0 100 200 300 Miles	
0 100 200 300 Km.	

Boundary of German Confederation at its foundation 1815

Changes of German Confederation to its dissolution, 1866

Prussia 1815   Austria 1815

Acquisitions 1815–1864

Acquisitions 1865–1866   Acquisitions 1815–66

Austro-Prussian Condominium (Treaty of Vienna, 1864)

Date of acquisition or period of possession

Austro-Hungarian military boundary zones with dates

1815-60

BLACK SEA

RUSSIAN EMPIRE

OTTOMAN EMPIRE

AUSTRIAN EMPIRE

GERMAN CONFEDERATION

K. OF PRUSSIA

K. OF SWEDEN

K. OF DENMARK

BALTIC SEA

NORTH SEA

Königsberg

Danzig

EAST PRUSSIA
United 1824–78

WEST PRUSSIA

German Confederation

Warsaw

Bug

Vistula

POLAND

POMERANIA

Rügen

Stettin

Posen

POSEN
1848–51

SILESIA

AUST. SILESIA

Breslau

Oder

Berlin

BRANDENBURG

Kottbus

Elbe

PROV. OF SAXONY

Erfurt

Schmalkalden, 1866

Gersfeld, 1866

Orb, 1866

Frankfurt

Prague

BOHEMIA

MORAVIA

Olmütz

Brünn

Krakow

REP. OF KRAKOW
From 1815, 1846 to Aust.

GALICIA AND LODOMERIA

Czernowitz

D. OF BUKOVINA

Tissa

Kaschau

Debreczin

Klausenburg

TRANSYLVANIA

Temesvar

K. OF HUNGARY

Pest

Buda (Ofen)

Vienna

LOWER AUSTRIA

UPPER AUSTRIA

SALZBURG

STYRIA

Graz

CARINTHIA

CARNIOLA

KÜSTENLAND

Trieste

TYROL

Trent

Inn

Munich

PR. OF HOHENZOLLERN
1849

SWITZERLAND

Basle

Rhine

Neuchâtel
1815–57 to Prussia

Geneva

K. OF FRANCE
1848–52 Republic. 1852 Empire

Seine

Saône

Rhône

Lyons

Marseilles

Ligurian Sea

K. OF SARDINIA

Turin

Po

MILAN

K. OF LOMBARDY
1815–59

D. OF PARMA
1847 to Tusc.

D. OF MODENA

Modena

GR. D. OF TUSCANY

Florence

D. OF LUCCA
1847 to Tusc.

Elba

VENETIA
1815–66

Venice

ADRIATIC SEA

DALMATIA

Ragusa

MONTENEGRO

Belgrade

K. OF CROATIA

K. OF SLAVONIA

Danube

MECKLENBURG
1865

Hamburg

Bremen

HANOVER
1866

Hanover

K. OF HANOVER
1866

WESTPHALIA

Münster

Paderborn

HESSE
1866

NASSAU
1866

Cologne

Koblenz

RHINE PROVINCE

GRD. OF LICHTENBG.
1834

GR. D. OF LUX.

K. OF NETHERLANDS
from 1830

K. OF BELGIUM
From 1830

1839

1865 under Pruss. administration
1866 to Prussia

HOLSTEIN
1865 under Austr. administration
1866 to Prussia

SCHLESWIG

1815 under Prussia

East from Greenwich

COPYRIGHT GEORGE PHILIP & SON LTD

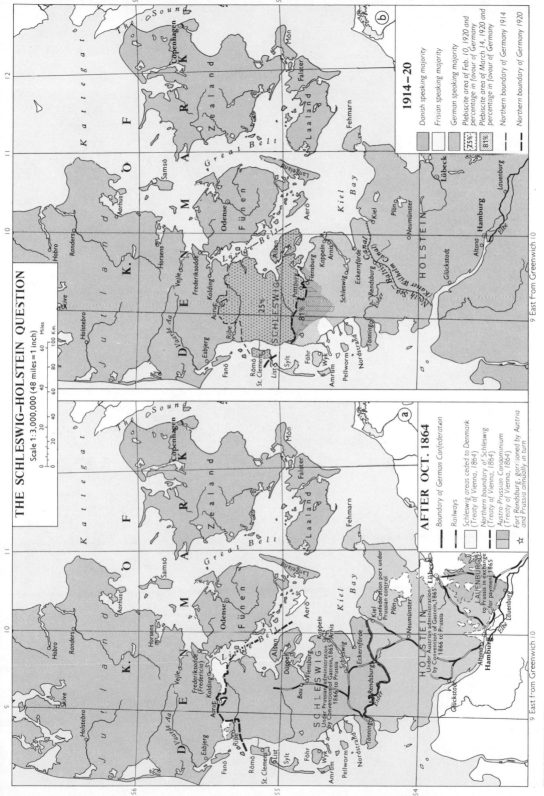

THE SCHLESWIG-HOLSTEIN QUESTION

Scale 1 : 3,000,000 (48 miles=1 inch)

AFTER OCT. 1864 (a)

Boundary of German Confederation

Railways

Schleswig areas ceded to Denmark (Treaty of Vienna, 1864)

Northern boundary of Schleswig (Treaty of Vienna, 1864)

Austro-Prussian Condominium (Treaty of Vienna, 1864)

☆ Fort Rendsburg, garrisoned by Austria and Prussia annually in turn

HOLSTEIN Under Austrian administration by Convention of Gastein, 1865 1866 to Prussia

SCHLESWIG Under Prussian administration by Convention of Gastein, 1865 1866 to Prussia

Kiel Confederation port under Prussian control

LAUENBURG to Prussia in exchange for payment 1865

9 East From Greenwich 10

1914-20 (b)

Danish speaking majority

Frisian speaking majority

German speaking majority

25% Plebiscite area of Feb. 10, 1920 and percentage in favour of Germany

81% Plebiscite area of March 14, 1920 and percentage in favour of Germany

Northern boundary of Germany 1914

Northern boundary of Germany 1920

9 East From Greenwich 10

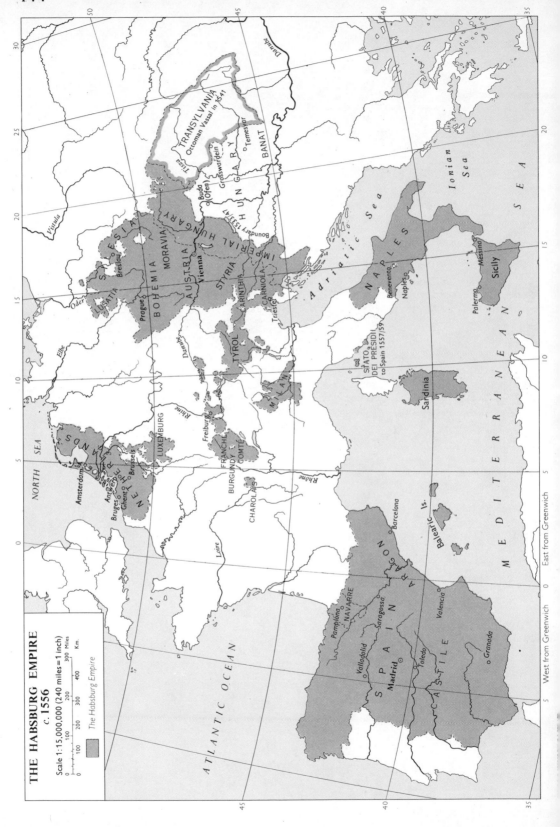

THE HABSBURG EMPIRE
c. 1556

Scale 1:15,000,000 (240 miles = 1 inch)

The Habsburg Empire

0 100 200 300 400 Miles
0 100 200 300 Km.

NORTH SEA

ATLANTIC OCEAN

West from Greenwich *East from Greenwich*

MEDITERRANEAN SEA

NETHERLANDS
Amsterdam
Antwerp
Bruges
Ghent
Brussels
LUXEMBURG
FRANCHE COMTÉ
BURGUNDY
CHAROLAIS
Freiburg
Rhine
Loire
Rhône

SPAIN
Madrid
Valladolid
Pamplona
NAVARRE
Saragossa
ARAGON
Barcelona
Balearic Is.
Toledo
Valencia
CASTILE
Granada

SILESIA
Breslau
LUSATIA
Oder
Prague
BOHEMIA
MORAVIA
Elbe
AUSTRIA
Vienna
STYRIA
TYROL
CARINTHIA
CARNIOLA
Trieste
Danube
MILAN
IMPERIAL HUNGARY
Boundary 1533/41
HUNGARY
Buda (Ofen)
Grosswardein
Tisza
BANAT
Temesvar
TRANSYLVANIA
Ottoman Vassal in 1541
Vistula
Danube

Adriatic Sea
Ionian Sea

NAPLES
Benevento
Naples
STATO DEI PRESIDII to Spain 1557/59
Sardinia
Sicily
Palermo
Messina

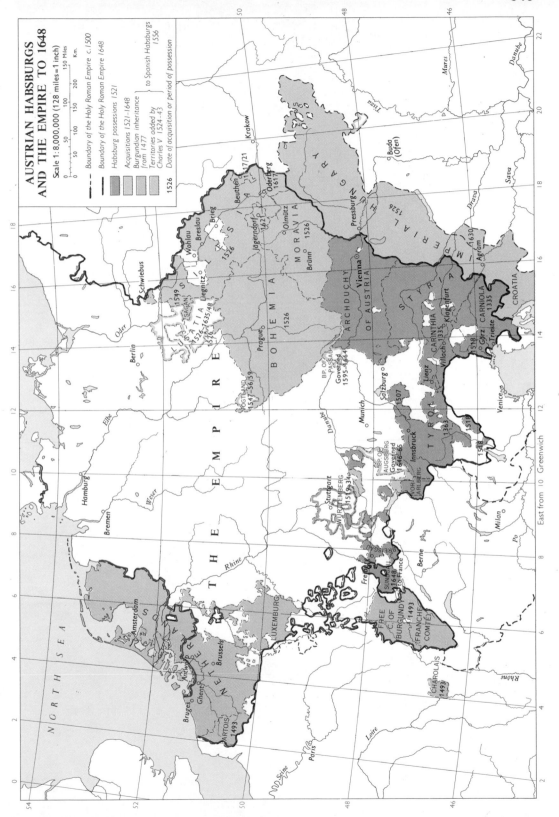

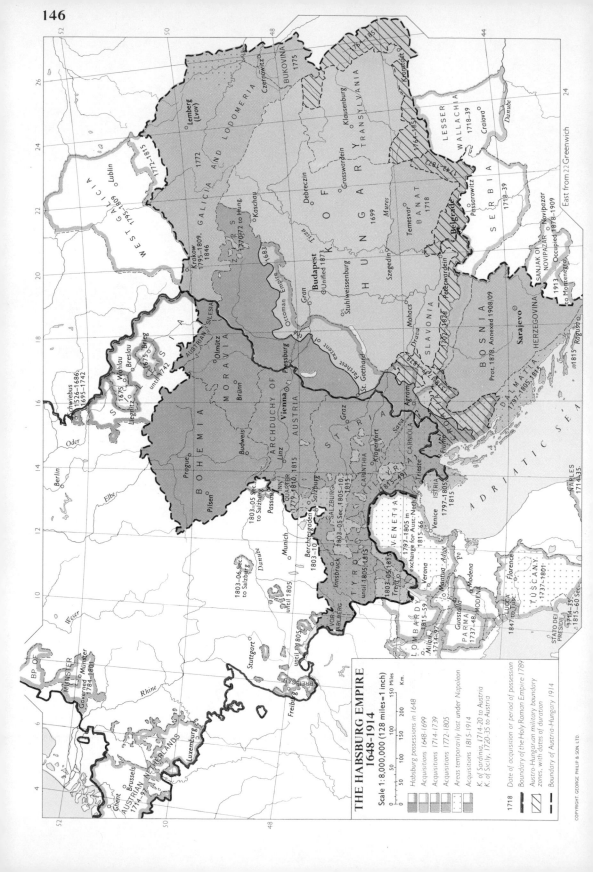

THE HABSBURG EMPIRE
1648–1914

Scale 1:8,000,000 (128 miles=1 inch)

| | 0 | 50 | 100 | 150 Miles |
| | 0 | 50 | 100 | 150 | 200 | Km. |

Habsburg possessions in 1648
Acquisitions 1648–1699
Acquisitions 1714–1739
Acquisitions 1772–1805
Areas temporarily lost under Napoleon
Acquisitions 1815–1914

K. of Sardinia, 1714–20 to Austria
K. of Sicily, 1720–35 to Austria

1718 — Date of acquisition or period of possession

Boundary of the Holy Roman Empire 1789

Austro-Hungarian military boundary
zones, with dates of duration

Boundary of Austria-Hungary 1914

COPYRIGHT GEORGE PHILIP & SON LTD.

East from 22 Greenwich

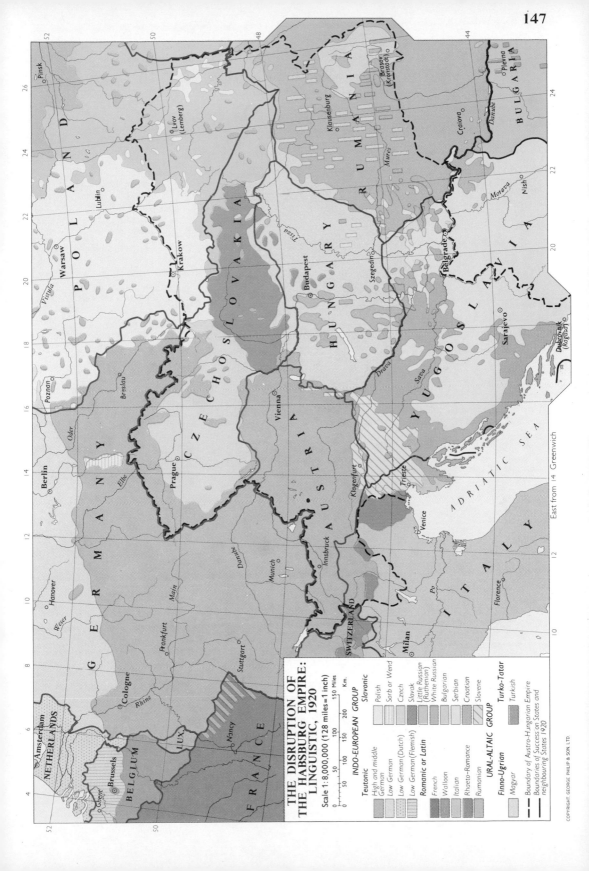

THE DISRUPTION OF
THE HABSBURG EMPIRE:
LINGUISTIC, 1920
Scale 1:8,000,000 (128 miles=1 inch)

0   50   100   150   200   150 Miles
0 50 100 150 200 250 Km.

INDO-EUROPEAN GROUP

Teutonic
High and middle German
Low German
Low German (Dutch)
Low German (Flemish)

Romanic or Latin
French
Walloon
Italian
Rhaeto-Romance
Rumanian

URAL-ALTAIC GROUP

Finno-Ugrian
Magyar

Slavonic
Polish
Sorb or Wend
Czech
Slovak
Little Russian (Ruthenian)
White Russian
Bulgarian
Serbian
Croatian
Slovene

Turko-Tatar
Turkish

Boundary of Austro-Hungarian Empire

Boundaries of Success on States and neighbouring States 1920

COPYRIGHT GEORGE PHILIP & SON LTD.

East from 14 Greenwich

NETHERLANDS
BELGIUM
LUX.
FRANCE
GERMANY
POLAND
CZECHO-SLOVAKIA
AUSTRIA
SWITZERLAND
HUNGARY
RUMANIA
YUGOSLAVIA
BULGARIA
ITALY
ADRIATIC SEA

Amsterdam
Brussels
Ghent
Hanover
Berlin
Cologne
Frankfurt
Stuttgart
Nancy
Munich
Innsbruck
Vienna
Prague
Breslau
Poznan
Warsaw
Lublin
Lvov (Lemberg)
Pinsk
Krakow
Budapest
Szegedin
Klausenburg
Brasov (Kronstadt)
Plevna
Craiova
Belgrade
Nish
Sarajevo
Dubrovnik (Ragusa)
Klagenfurt
Trieste
Venice
Milan
Florence

Vistula
Oder
Elbe
Weser
Rhine
Main
Danube
Tisza
Drava
Sava
Mures
Morava
Danube
Po

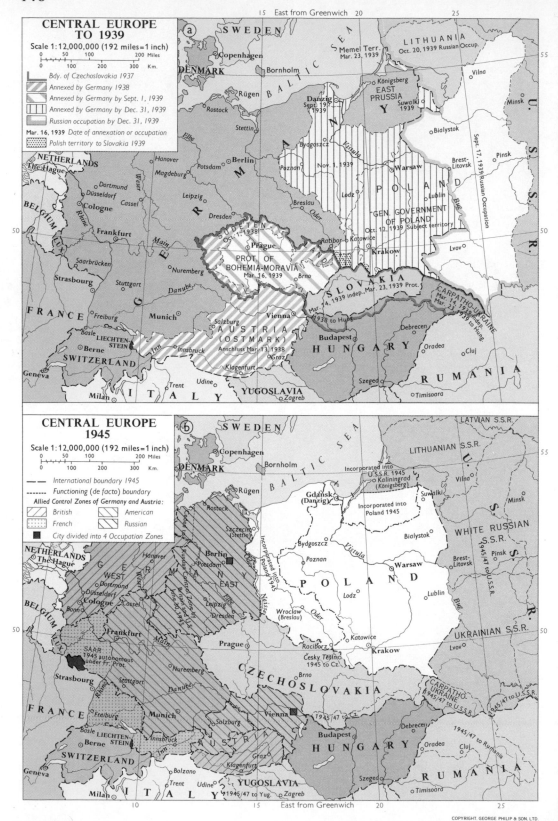

CENTRAL EUROPE TO 1939

Scale 1:12,000,000 (192 miles=1 inch)

0   50   100   200 Miles

0   Km.

Bdy. of Czechoslovakia 1937

Annexed by Germany 1938

Annexed by Germany by Sept. 1, 1939

Annexed by Germany by Dec. 31, 1939

Russian occupation by Dec. 31, 1939

Mar. 16, 1939 Date of annexation or occupation

Polish territory to Slovakia 1939

CENTRAL EUROPE 1945

Scale 1:12,000,000 (192 miles=1 inch)

0   50   100   200 Miles

0   200   300 Km.

International boundary 1945

Functioning (de facto) boundary

Allied Control Zones of Germany and Austria:

British

French

American

Russian

City divided into 4 Occupation Zones

COPYRIGHT. GEORGE PHILIP & SON. LTD.

SCANDINAVIA AND THE BALTIC, 1523—1660

Scale 1:12,000,000 (192 miles=1 inch)

| | | Sweden 1523-60 (Gustavus Vasa) |
| Acquisitions of Sweden 1560-92 (Eric XIV 1560-68, John III 1568-92) |
| Acquisitions of Sweden 1611-54 (Gustavus Adolphus 1611-32, Queen Christina, Chancellor A. Oxenstierna 1632-54) |
| Acquisitions of Sweden 1654-60 (Charles X) |
| Extent of Swedish colonization in Finland |

1645 Date of acquisition or period of possession

▲ Iron   ▲ Copper
● Gold   ○ Silver

Land over 500m

Seas and lakes frozen in winter

NORWEGIAN

SEA

Arctic Circle

Lapland

RUSSIAN

Torne

Norrbotten

Torneå

White Sea

Luleå

EMPIRE

Umeå

Gamlakarleby (Kokkola)

Trondheim

JÄMTLAND   ÅNGERMAN-LAND

1645

HÄRJEDALEN

Vasa

CARELIA 1617

TRONDHELM 1658-60 to Sweden

Särna   DALECARLIA

Björneborg (Pori)

Lake Ladoga

Bergen

Klar   Falun   Gävle

Åbo   Northern limit of oak

Vyborg

Christiania (Oslo)

Åland Is.

Helsingfors

Kymmene (Kymi)

INGRIA 1583-95 1617

Stolbova

G. of Finland

Area of Swedish Occup. at the beginning of

Karlstad   Uppsala

Västerås

Reval   Narva   Ivangorod

Novgorod 1610-17

Stavanger

Vänern

Stockholm

1561   ESTONIA   Jangorod

1613

Tönsberg

Stångebro

1582   1582   1581

L. Pskov

Porkhov

BOHUS-LÄN 1658

Linköping

Norrköping

Dagö 1582

Dorpat

Vättern

Gotland

Windau

LIVONIA 1621/29-1721

Göteborg   Jönköping

1645   Visby

Öland

Ösel 1645

NORTH SEA

Jutland

HALLAND 1658

SMÅLAND

Calmar

Riga 1621/29 to Sweden

COURLAND

1561 to Pol.

Adlborg

Knared

Halmstad

1658 BLEKINGE Brömsebro

Libau

Frederiksodde (Fredericia)

Odense

Copenhagen

SKANE

Landskrona

Lund   Malmö

Bornholm 1658-60 to Sweden

Memel

Niemen

Funen

Zeeland

Skanör

K. OF DENMARK

Schleswig

Bornholm 1658-60 to Sweden

Labiau

GR. PR. OF

Rügen 1648

Swedish Occup. 1629-35

Königsberg

LITHUANIA

1648-1715/19

Hamburg

Wismar 1648-1803 Neukloster

HITHER POMERANIA

Oliva

Danzig

Pillau

Elbing

PRUSSIA

Bremen (ABP.) OF BREMEN-VERDEN

Stettin

K. OF POLAND

Wildeshausen 1648-79

Berlin

Vistula

BALTIC SEA

KINGDOM OF SWEDEN

KINGDOM OF NORWAY

United 1380-1814

10   East from Greenwich   15   20   25   30

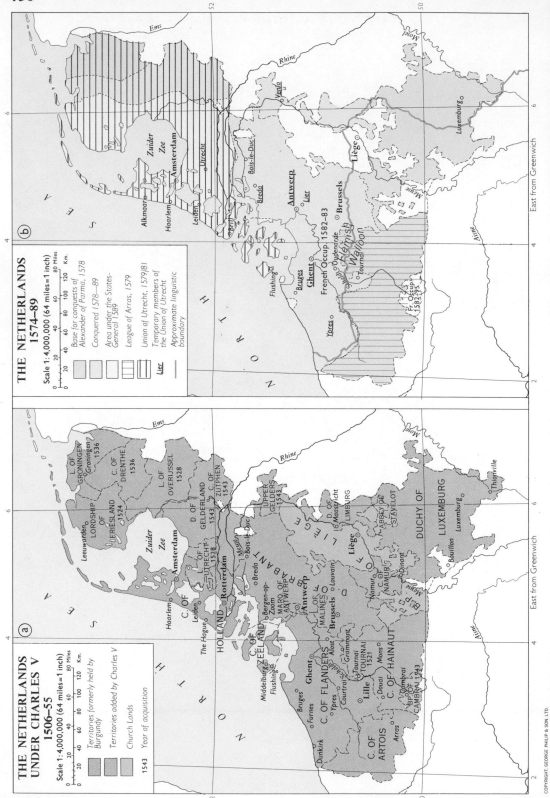

THE NETHERLANDS UNDER CHARLES V
1506–55

Scale 1:4,000,000 (64 miles=1 inch)

0 20 40 60 80 Miles
0 20 40 60 80 100 120 Km.

Territories formerly held by Burgundy

Territories added by Charles V

Church Lands

1543 Year of acquisition

(a)

L. OF GRONINGEN Groningen 1536
C. OF DRENTHE 1536
L. OF OVERIJSSEL 1528
C. OF ZUTPHEN 1543
LORDSHIP OF FRIESLAND 1524
Leeuwarden
Zuider Zee
Amsterdam
D. OF GELDERLAND 1543
UPPER GELDERS 1543
Haarlem
C. OF HOLLAND
Leiden
L. OF UTRECHT 1528
The Hague
Rotterdam
Breda
Bois-le-Duc
Meuse
D. OF BRABANT
D. OF LIMBURG
Maastricht
ABBEY OF STAVELOT
Middelburg
C. OF ZEELAND
Flushing
Bergen-op-Zoom
MARQ. OF ANTWERP
Antwerp
MALINES
Brussels
Louvain
Liège
L. OF LIÈGE
Namur
C. OF NAMUR
Dinant
Bouillon
DUCHY OF LUXEMBURG
Luxemburg
Furnes
Dunkirk
Bruges
Ypres
C. OF FLANDERS
Ghent
Alost
Grammont
Audenarde
Courtrai
Lille
Tournai
TOURNAI 1521
Mons
C. OF HAINAUT
Douai
Cambrai
B. OF CAMBRAI 1543
Arras
C. OF ARTOIS
Thionville
Moselle
Rhine
Ems
NORTH SEA
East from Greenwich

THE NETHERLANDS
1574–89

Scale 1:4,000,000 (64 miles=1 inch)

0 20 40 60 80 Miles
0 20 40 60 80 100 120 Km.

Base for conquests of Alexander of Parma, 1578

Conquered 1578–89

Area under the States-General 1589

League of Arras, 1579

Union of Utrecht, 1579/81

Temporary members of the Union of Utrecht

Lier Approximate linguistic boundary

(b)

Ems
Rhine
Zuider Zee
Amsterdam
Alkmaar
Haarlem
Leiden
Utrecht
Brill
Venlo
Bois-le-Duc
Breda
Antwerp
Lier
Brussels
Flushing
Bruges
Ghent
French Occup. 1582–83
Oudenarde
Flemish
Walloon
Tournai
Ypres
Liège
Luxemburg
Meuse
Moselle
French Occup. 1582–83
Aisne
NORTH SEA
East from Greenwich

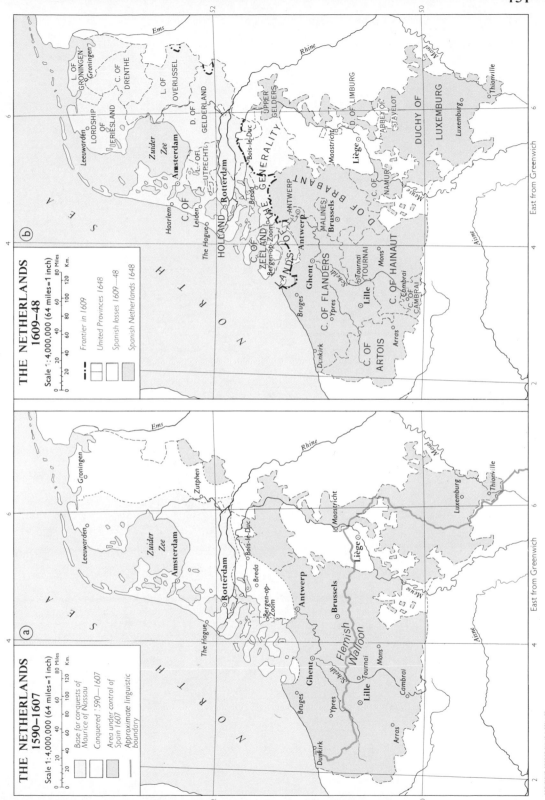

THE NETHERLANDS 1609–48

Scale 1 : 4,000,000 (64 miles=1 inch)

Km.
0   20   40   60   80   100   120
0   20   40   60   80 Miles

- - - Frontier in 1609

United Provinces 1648

Spanish losses 1609–48

Spanish Netherlands 1648

Ems
Rhine
Meuse
L. OF GRONINGEN   Groningen
C. OF DRENTHE
L. OF FRIESLAND
LORDSHIP OF FRIESLAND
Leeuwarden
L. OF OVERIJSSEL
D. OF GELDERLAND
UPPER GELDERS
D. OF LIMBURG
ABBEY OF STAVELOT
DUCHY OF LUXEMBURG
Luxemburg
Thionville
Zuider Zee
Amsterdam
Haarlem
Leiden
C. OF HOLLAND
UTRECHT
D. OF
Bois-le-Duc
Breda
Bergen-op-Zoom
THE GENERALITY
D. OF BRABANT
ANTWERP
Antwerp
MALINES
Brussels
Maastricht
Liège
C. OF NAMUR
The Hague
Rotterdam
HOLLAND
C. OF ZEELAND
LANDS OF
Ghent
C. OF FLANDERS
Bruges
Ypres
Dunkirk
Lille
Tournai
TOURNAI
Mons
C. OF HAINAUT
Cambrai
C. OF CAMBRAI
Arras
C. OF ARTOIS
NORTH SEA
East from Greenwich
Aisne

THE NETHERLANDS 1590–1607

Scale 1 : 4,000,000 (64 miles=1 inch)

Km.
0   20   40   60   80   100   120
0   20   40   60   80 Miles

Base for conquests of Maurice of Nassau

Conquered 1590–1607

Area under control of Spain 1607

—— Approximate linguistic boundary

Ems
Rhine
Meuse
Groningen
Zutphen
Leeuwarden
Zuider Zee
Amsterdam
Rotterdam
The Hague
Bergen-op-Zoom
Breda
Bois-le-Duc
Maastricht
Liège
Luxemburg
Thionville
Antwerp
Brussels
Ghent
Bruges
Ypres
Dunkirk
Lille
Tournai
Mons
Cambrai
Arras
Flemish
Walloon
Scheldt
NORTH SEA
East from Greenwich
Aisne

THE NETHERLANDS AND BELGIUM
1814—39

Scale 1:3,000,000 (48 miles = 1 inch)

Losses of the United Netherlands to Prussia 1815/19

Acquisitions of the United Netherlands 1815
(2nd Treaty of Paris)

Kingdom of the United Netherlands 1815-30

Areas under same crown as Netherlands 1839

Kingdom of the Netherlands 1839

Kingdom of Belgium 1839

1830 Date of independence

Northern boundary of France 1814 (1st Treaty of Paris)

Boundary of German Confederation 1815

Boundary changes of German Confederation 1839

Approximate linguistic boundary

☆ Fortresses

N O R T H   S E A

Schiermonnikoog
Ameland
Terschelling
Vlieland
Texel
Delfzijl
Emden
GRONINGEN
Groningen
Dollart
Leeuwarden
FRIESLAND
Assen
DRENTHE
Meppen
Coevorden
Ems
Zwolle
OVERIJSSEL
Almelo
Enschede
Deventer
Münster

Zuider Zee
NORTH HOLLAND
Amsterdam
Harderwijk
Haarlem
Het Loo
Apeldoorn
The Hague
SOUTH HOLLAND
UTRECHT
Utrecht
GELDERLAND
Rotterdam
Lek
Arnhem
Waal
Nijmegen
Hellevoetsluis
Dordrecht
's-Hertogenbosch
Kleve
Wesel
ZEELAND
NORTH BRABANT
Middelburg
Bergen-op-Zoom
Breda
Flushing (Vlissingen)
Eindhoven
D. OF LIMBURG
GERMAN
Ostend
Turnhout
Antwerp
1832 to Belgium
ANTWERP
Bruges
Mechelen (Malines)
LIMBURG
Dunkirk
Calais
WEST
EAST
Ghent
Scheldt
Hasselt
CONFEDERATION
Cologne
Ypres
FLANDERS
Kortrijk
1830
Brussels
SOUTH
BRABANT
Louvain
Maastrich
Flemish
Aachen
St.-Omer
Lille
Altenberg
Eupen
HAINAUT
Walloon
Liège
LIÈGE
Mons
Namur
Seraing
Malmedy
Valenciennes
Dour
Charleroi
St. Vith
Arras
NAMUR
Cambrai
Beaumont
Philippeville
Landrecies
Marienbourg
Givet
Wiltz
St.-Hubert
LUXEMBOURG
Assigned 1831,
confirmed 1839
to Belgium
GR. D. OF
LUXEMBOURG
Trier
Bouillon
Sedan
Arlon
Luxembourg
Compiègne
Aisne
Montmédy
Longwy
Merzig
Saarlouis
Amiens
Somme
Saarbrücken
Reims
German
French
K.   O F   F R A N C E
Seine
Marne
Mosel
Rhine
Ruhr
Meuse
Paris

East from Greenwich

COPYRIGHT. GEORGE. PHILIP & SON. LTD.

153

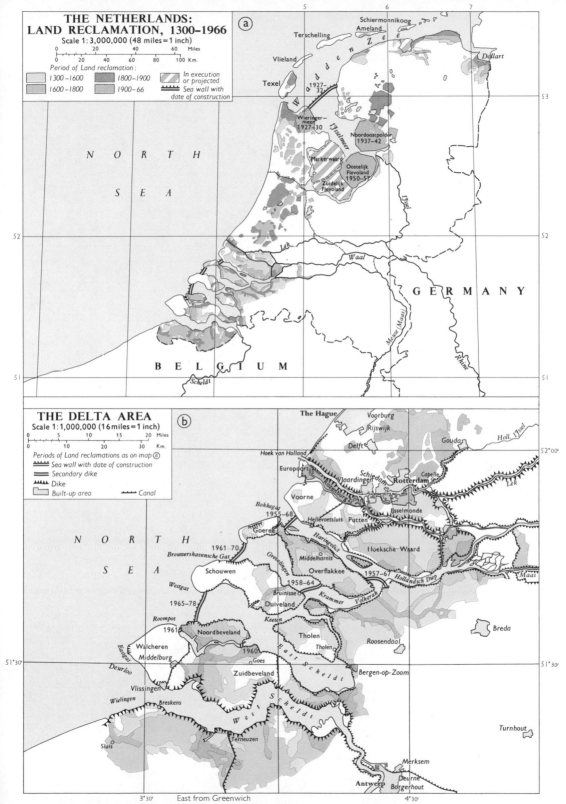

THE NETHERLANDS:
LAND RECLAMATION, 1300–1966

THE DELTA AREA

COPYRIGHT. GEORGE PHILIP & SON. LTD.

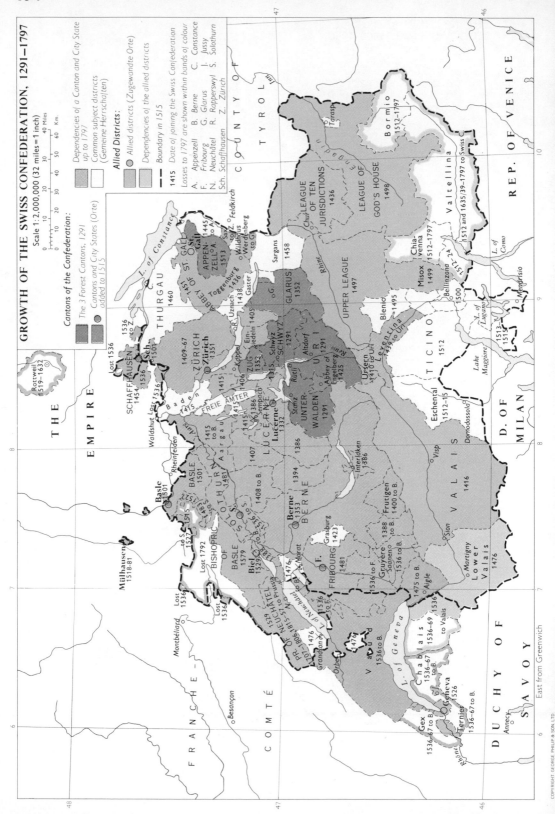

GROWTH OF THE SWISS CONFEDERATION, 1291–1797

Scale 1:2,000,000 (32 miles=1 inch)

0 10 20 30 40 Miles
0 10 20 30 40 50 60 Km.

Cantons of the Confederation:

The 3 Forest Cantons, 1291

Cantons and City States (Orte) added to 1515

Dependencies of a Canton and City State up to 1797

Common subject districts (Gemeine Herrschaften)

Allied Districts:

Allied districts (Zugewandte Orte)

Dependencies of the allied districts

Boundary in 1515

1415 Date of joining the Swiss Confederation

Losses to 1797 are shown within bands of colour

A. Appenzell B. Berne C. Constance
F. Fribourg G. Glarus J. Jussy
N. Neuchâtel R. Rapperswyl S. Solothurn
Sch. Schaffhausen Z. Zürich

Rottweil 1519–1632

THE EMPIRE

COUNTY OF TYROL

REP. OF VENICE

Müllhausen 1518–81

SCHAFFHAUSEN 1454
Lost 1536
1536 to Z.
1501
Sch.

THURGAU 1460

L. of Constance

St. Gall
ST. O. 1454 to A.
ABBEY OF ST. GALL 1451
APPEN-ZELL A. 1513
Saxo Z. Feldkirch
Sax 1445 to A.
Wildhaus to G.
Werdenberg to G.

Tarasp

Bormio 1512–1797

LEAGUE OF TEN JURISDICTIONS 1436
Chur
LEAGUE OF GOD'S HOUSE 1498

Toggenburg 1436
R. Uznach 1438
Gaster 1438

Sargans

UPPER LEAGUE 1497

Valtellina
1512 and 1635/39–1797 to Swiss

Waldshut Lost 1536
Baden 1415
Rheinfelden
1415 to B.
FREIE ÄMTER
Kappel 1405
Einsiedeln 1405
Ein-siedeln 1350

ZÜRICH 1351
1409–67
Sch.

GLARUS 1352

ZUG 1352
Schwyz 1291
SCHWYZ
Rüti 1415
Abbey of Engelberg 1425

Blenio 1495
Misox 1499
Chia-venna 1512–1797

ZÜRICH 1351

Altdorf 1291
URI

Ursern 1410 to Uri

Leventina 1439 to Uri

Eschental 1512–15
Domodossola

Bellinzona 1512
1500

Mendrisio
1512
1513–1515

TICINO

L. of Lugano
Lake Maggiore

L. of Como

BASLE 1501

SOLOTHURN 1481

Aargau 1415 to B.

LUCERNE 1332
Sempach 1386
1407

Stans 1291
UNTER-WALDEN 1291
Interlaken 1386

1408 to B.
BERNE 1353
Berne 1353

VALAIS 1416

D. OF MILAN

Basle 1501

BASLE 1529
BISHOPRIC OF
Biel 1529

BERNE 1353
1394
1386

Grasburg 1423

Gruyère 1388
Saanen to F.
1536 to B.

Visp
Sion

Martigny 1476
Lower Valais

Besançon

Lost 1792
Lost 1536

PR. OF NEUCHÂTEL 1707–1805/1815–57 to Prussia
Lost 1536
Lost 1536

1529
1536 to B.

F. Morat 1476
FRIBOURG 1481

Frutigen 1400 to B.
1536 to F.
1536 to B.

1475 to B.
Aigle

1536–69 to Valais

Montbéliard

Grandson 1476
Orbe

Vaud
1536 to B.

1476

Chablais 1536–67 to B.

Lower Valais 1476

Martigny 1476

FRANCHE-COMTÉ

COUNTY OF
PR. OF NEUCHÂTEL

L. of Geneva

Gex 1536–67 to B.
Geneva 1526
Ternier 1536–67 to B.
Anneçy

DUCHY OF SAVOY

East from Greenwich

COPYRIGHT GEORGE PHILIP & SON LTD.

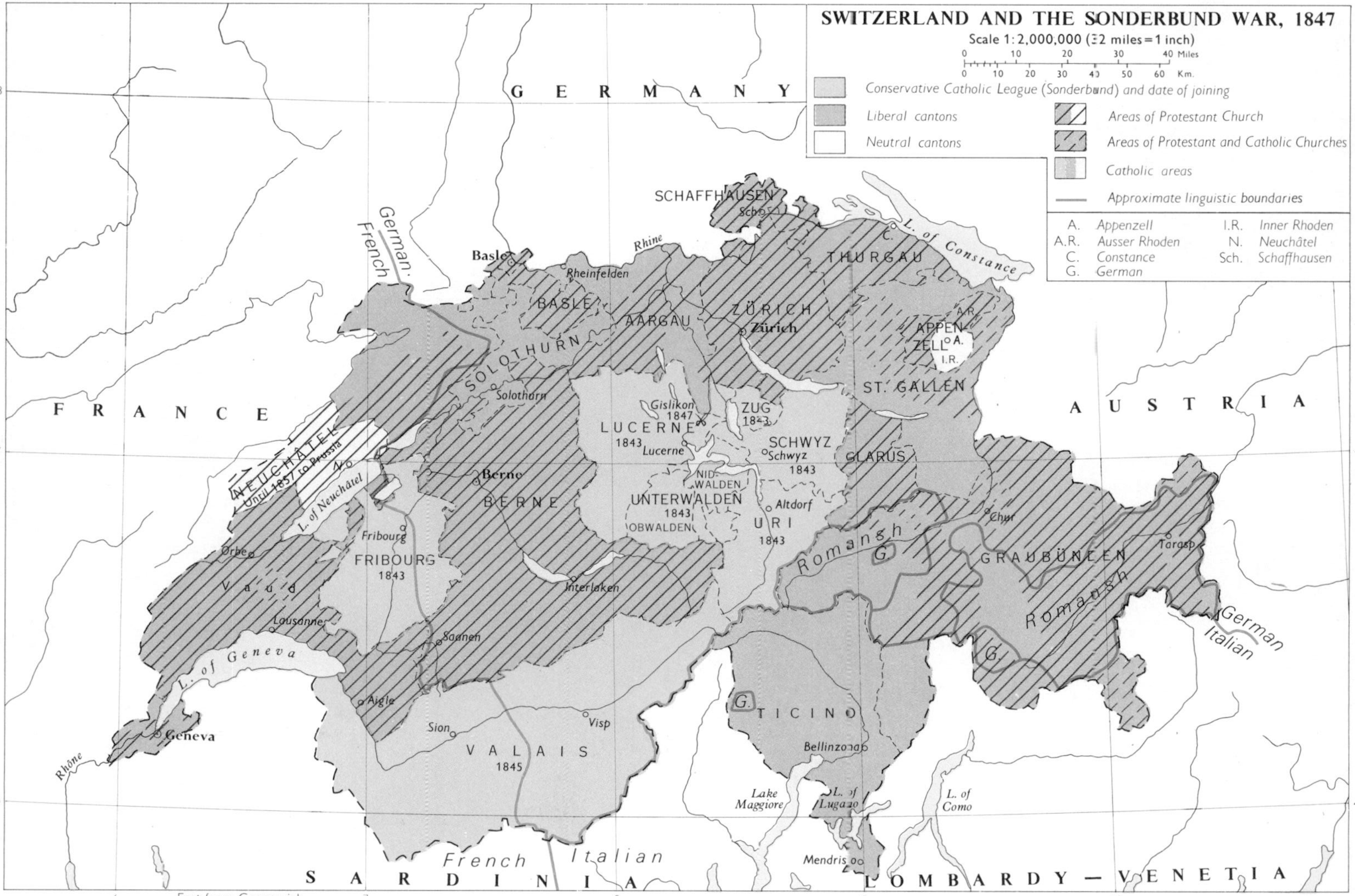
SWITZERLAND AND THE SONDERBUND WAR, 1847
Scale 1: 2,000,000 (32 miles = 1 inch)
Miles
Km.
Conservative Catholic League (Sonderbund) and date of joining
Liberal cantons
Neutral cantons
Areas of Protestant Church
Areas of Protestant and Catholic Churches
Catholic areas
Approximate linguistic boundaries
A. Appenzell
A.R. Ausser Rhoden
C. Constance
G. German
I.R. Inner Rhoden
N. Neuchâtel
Sch. Schaffhausen
GERMANY
FRANCE
AUSTRIA
SARDINIA
LOMBARDY — VENETIA
SCHAFFHAUSEN
Sch.
THURGAU
L. of Constance
Rhine
Basle
Rheinfelden
BASLE
AARGAU
ZÜRICH
Zürich
APPENZELL
A.R.
I.R.
ST. GALLEN
SOLOTHURN
Solothurn
NEUCHÂTEL
Until 1857 to Prussia
L. of Neuchâtel
LUCERNE
Gislikon
1847
1843
Lucerne
ZUG
1843
SCHWYZ
Schwyz
1843
GLARUS
Berne
BERNE
NIDWALDEN
UNTERWALDEN
1843
OBWALDEN
Altdorf
URI
1843
Chur
GRAUBÜNDEN
Tarasp
Romangh
Romangh
G.
Fribourg
FRIBOURG
1843
Orbe
Vaud
Lausanne
Interlaken
Saanen
L. of Geneva
Geneva
Rhône
Aigle
Sion
Visp
VALAIS
1845
TICINO
Bellinzona
Lake Maggiore
L. of Lugano
L. of Como
Mendris
German
French
German
Italian
French
Italian
48
47
46
6
7
8
9
10
East from Greenwich

COPYRIGHT GEORGE PHILIP & SON LTD

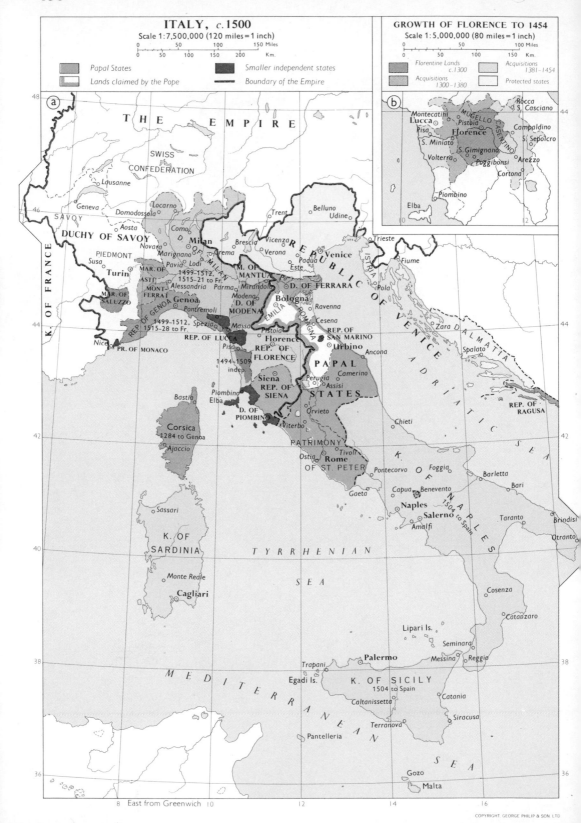

ITALY, c.1500

Scale 1:7,500,000 (120 miles=1 inch)

```
0        50       100      150 Miles
0    50   100   150   200
                            Km.
```

Papal States	Smaller independent states
Lands claimed by the Pope	Boundary of the Empire

GROWTH OF FLORENCE TO 1454

Scale 1:5,000,000 (80 miles=1 inch)

```
0        50       100 Miles
0    50   100   150
                    Km.
```

Florentine Lands c.1300	Acquisitions 1381–1454
Acquisitions 1300–1380	Protected states

(a)

THE EMPIRE

SWISS CONFEDERATION

Lausanne

Geneva   Domodossola   Locarno   Trent   Belluno   Udine

SAVOY   Aosta   Como   Trieste

DUCHY OF SAVOY   Novara   D. OF MILAN   Brescia   Vicenza   Fiume

PIEDMONT   Marignano   Crema   Verona   REPUBLIC OF VENICE   ISTRIA

Susa   Turin   MAR. OF   Pavia Lodi   M. OF MANTUA   Padua   Este   Pola

MAR. OF ASTI   1499–1512, 1515–21 to Fr.   Parma   Mirandola   D. OF FERRARA

MAR. OF SALUZZO   MONT-FERRAT   Alessandria   Modena   Bologna   Ravenna

Nice   REP. OF GENOA   Genoa   Pontremoli   D. OF MODENA   EMILIA   ROMAGNA   Cesena   Zara   DALMATIA

PR. OF MONACO   1499–1512, 1515–28 to Fr.   Spezia   Massa   REP. OF SAN MARINO   REP. OF URBINO   Ancona   Spalato

REP. OF LUCCA   Pisa   Florence   Urbino   ADRIATIC

1494–1509 indep.   REP. OF FLORENCE   PAPAL   Camerino   REP. OF RAGUSA

Siena   REP. OF SIENA   Perugia   Assisi   STATES   Chieti   SEA

Bastia   Piombino   Elba   D. OF PIOMBINO   Orvieto

Corsica 1284 to Genoa   Viterbo   PATRIMONY   Tivoli

Ajaccio   OF ST. PETER   Ostia   Rome   Pontecorvo   K. OF NAPLES   Foggia   Barletta

Sassari   Capua   Benevento   Bari

K. OF SARDINIA   Gaeta   Naples   1504 to Spain   Taranto   Brindisi

TYRRHENIAN   Salerno   Otranto

Monte Reale   Amalfi

Cagliari   SEA   Cosenza

Catanzaro

Lipari Is.   Seminara

MEDITERRANEAN   Palermo   Messina   Reggio

Trapani   K. OF SICILY   Catania

Egadi Is.   1504 to Spain

Caltanissetta   Siracusa

Terranova   SEA

Pantelleria

Gozo   Malta

(b)

Rocca S. Casciano

Montecatini   MUGELLO   Compaldino

Lucca   Pistoia   S. Sepolcro

Pisa   Florence   CASENTINO

S. Miniato   S. Gimignano   Arezzo

Volterra   Poggibonsi   Cortona

Piombino

Elba

East from Greenwich   8   10   12   14   16

COPYRIGHT GEORGE PHILIP & SON LTD

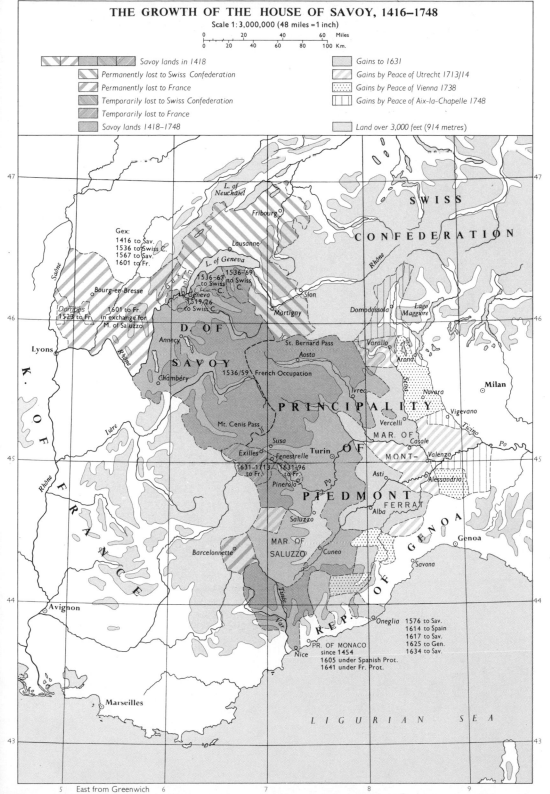

THE GROWTH OF THE HOUSE OF SAVOY, 1416–1748

Scale 1:3,000,000 (48 miles = 1 inch)

0   20   40   60   Miles

0   20   40   60   80   100 Km.

Savoy lands in 1418

Permanently lost to Swiss Confederation

Permanently lost to France

Temporarily lost to Swiss Confederation

Temporarily lost to France

Savoy lands 1418–1748

Gains to 1631

Gains by Peace of Utrecht 1713/14

Gains by Peace of Vienna 1738

Gains by Peace of Aix-la-Chapelle 1748

Land over 3,000 feet (914 metres)

SWISS CONFEDERATION

L. of Neuchâtel

Fribourg

Lausanne

L. of Geneva

Gex:
1416 to Sav.
1536 to Swiss C.
1567 to Sav.
1601 to Fr.

Bourg-en-Bresse

Dombes
1523 to Fr.

1601 to Fr.
in exchange for
M. of Saluzzo

1536–69
to Swiss C.

1536–67
to Swiss
C.

Geneva
1519, 26
to Swiss C.

Sion

Martigny

Domodossola

Lago Maggiore

Lyons

D OF

SAVOY

Annecy

St. Bernard Pass

Aosta

1536/59
French Occupation

Varallo

Arona

Novara

Milan

Chambéry

Ivrea

Vigevano

PRINCIPALITY

Mt. Cenis Pass

Susa

Exilles

Fenestrelle

Turin

Vercelli

MAR. OF
MONT-

Casale

Ticino

Po

Valenzo

OF

Asti

Alessandria

PIEDMONT

1631–1713
to Fr.

1631–96
to Fr.

Pinerolo

Po

FERRAT

Alba

REP. OF GENOA

Saluzzo

MAR. OF
SALUZZO

Cuneo

Genoa

Barcelonnette

Savona

K. OF FRANCE

Isère

Rhône

Avignon

Oneglia   1576 to Sav.
1614 to Spain
1617 to Sav.
1625 to Gen.
1634 to Sav.

PR. OF MONACO
since 1454
1605 under Spanish Prot.
1641 under Fr. Prot.

Nice

Tinée

Var

Marseilles

LIGURIAN   SEA

5   East from Greenwich   6   7   8   9

COPYRIGHT. GEORGE PHILIP & SON. LTD.

158

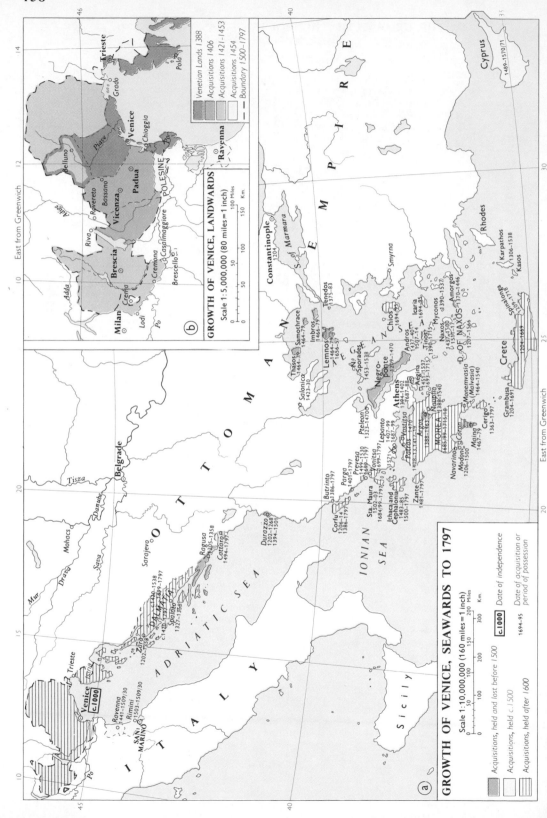

GROWTH OF VENICE, LANDWARDS (b)

Scale 1 : 5,000,000 (80 miles = 1 inch)

Venetian Lands 1388
Acquisitions 1406
Acquisitions 1421–1453
Acquisitions 1454
Boundary 1500–1797

GROWTH OF VENICE, SEAWARDS TO 1797 (a)

Scale 1 : 10,000,000 (160 miles = 1 inch)

Acquisitions, held and lost before 1500
Acquisitions, held c.1500
Acquisitions, held after 1600

c.1000 Date of independence
1694–95 Date of acquisition or period of possession

COPYRIGHT GEORGE PHILIP & SON LTD

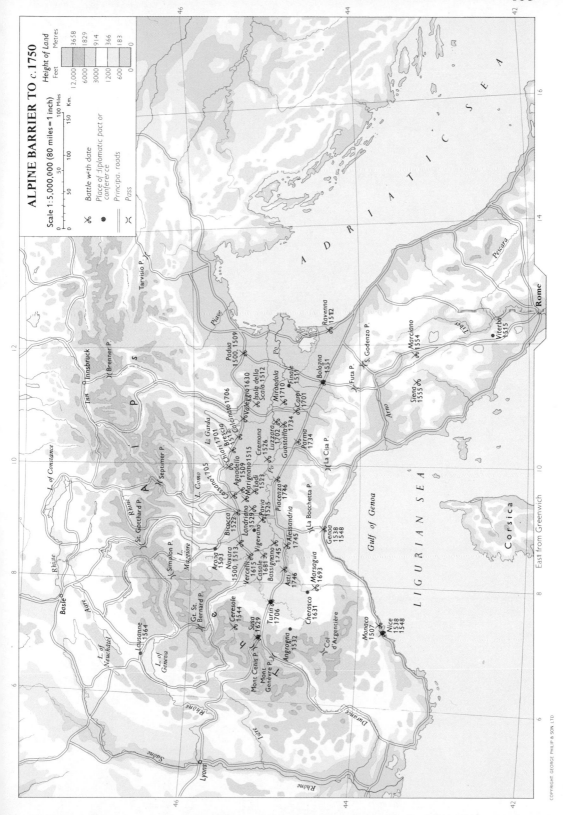

ALPINE BARRIER TO c. 1750

Scale 1:5,000,000 (80 miles = 1 inch)

Height of Land

Feet	Metres
12,000	3658
6000	1829
3000	914
1200	366
600	183
0	0

✕ Battle with date

● Place of diplomatic pact or conference

═ Principal roads

)(Pass

Km. 100 150

Miles 50 100

A D R I A T I C   S E A

L I G U R I A N   S E A

Gulf of Genoa

Corsica

East from Greenwich

COPYRIGHT GEORGE PHILIP & SON LTD.

Tarvisio P.

Innsbruck

Brenner P.

Inn

A L P S

Piave

Padua 1500, 1509

Valeggio 1630

Isola della Scala 1512

Miradola 1710

Carpi 1701

Finale 1511

Bologna 1551

Ravenna 1512

Futa P.

S. Godenzo P.

Marciano 1554

Siena 1555

Arno

Viterbo 1515

Tiber

Rome

Pescara

L. of Constance

Septimer P.

L. of Como

La Garda

Chiari 1701

Brescia

Calcinato 1706

Cassano 1705

Agnadello 1509

Cremona

Rhine

St. Gotthard P.

Rhine

Simplon P.

L. Maggiore

Mezzano

Bicocca 1522

Landriano 1529

Lodi

Marignano 1515

Pavia 1525

Vigevano 1523

Alessandria 1745

La Bocchetta P.

Lazzara 1702

Guastalla 1734

Parma 1734

La Cisa P.

Po

Novara 1500, 1513

Vercelli 1615

Casale 1681

Bassignano 1745

Piacenza 1746

Genoa 1538 1548

Basle

Aar

Gt. St. Bernard P.

J U R A

Ceresole 1544

Susa 1629

Turin 1706

Cherasco 1631

Asti 1746

Marsaglia 1693

Lausanne 1564

L. of Neuchâtel

L. of Geneva

Rhône

Arola 1503

Angrogna 1532

Col d'Argentière

Mont Cenis P.

Mont-Genèvre P.

Monaco 1507

Nice 1538 1548

Rhône

Isère

Durance

Saône

Lyons

ITALY, 1713–48
Scale 1:7,500,000 (120 miles=1 inch)

Habsburg Lands
(Austrian Habsburgs extinct 1740;
continued by Habsburg–Lorraine)
Spanish Bourbon Lands

Boundary of the Empire

THE EMPIRE

SWISS CONFEDERATION

K. OF FRANCE

Geneva
D. OF SAVOY

K. OF SARDINIA
PR. OF PIEDMONT
Turin
Susa
Vigevano
Po
Pavia
1714 Aust.

1713 to France

REP. OF GENOA
Pontremoli
Finale
Spezia
Oneglia
Nice
PR. OF MONACO

Como
D. OF MILAN
Bergamo
Brescia
MILAN
D. OF MANTUA
D. OF PARMA
1731 to Sp.
1735 to Aust.
1748 to Sp.
Guastalla
1748 to Parma
D. OF MODENA
Massa
REP. OF LUCCA
Pisa
Leghorn
Piombino
Elba
STATO DEI PRESIDII
Orbetello
1714 to Aust.
1735 to Spain

Trent
Belluno
Udine
Rovereto
Vicenza
Padua
Bergamo
Brescia

Görz
Trieste
Fiume

REPUBLIC OF VENICE

Venice
ISTRIA
Pola

Ferrara
Bologna
Ravenna
EMILIA
ROMAGNA

Florence
GR. DUCHY OF TUSCANY
1737 to Habsburg–Lorraine
Siena

REP. OF SAN MARINO
Urbino
Ancona

PAPAL STATES
Perugia
Assisi
Spoleto
Orvieto
Viterbo
Chieti

Zara
DALMATIA
Spalato

REP. OF RAGUSA
1718 independent

ADRIATIC SEA

Bastia
Corsica
to Genoa
Ajaccio

PATRIMONY OF ST. PETER
Rome
Velletri
Pontecorvo
1512 to Papal States
Gaeta
Capua
Benevento

K. OF NAPLES
1714 to Austria, 1735 to Spain
Foggia
Barletta
Bari

Sassari

K. OF SARDINIA
1714 to Austria, 1717 Spanish Occup.,
1720 to Savoy

Monte Reale
Cagliari

Naples
Salerno
Amalfi

Taranto
Brindisi
Lecce
Otranto

TYRRHENIAN SEA

Cosenza

Catanzaro

Lipari Is.

Seminara

MEDITERRANEAN SEA

Trapani
Egadi Is.
Palermo
Messina
Reggio

K. OF SICILY
1713 to Savoy, 1718 Spanish Occup.,
1720 to Austria, 1735 to Spain
Catania

Siracusa

Terranova

Pantelleria

Gozo
Malta
1530–1798 to Knights of St. John

East from Greenwich

COPYRIGHT GEORGE PHILIP & SON LTD.

ITALY, 1815–1924
Scale 1:7,500,000 (120 miles = 1 inch)

K. of Sardinia 1815
Northern boundary of Italy 1914
1860 Dates are those of annexation, first to the K. of Sardinia, and after 1860, to the K. of Italy
Acquisitions 1919/20
☆ Austrian quadrilateral fortresses (Peschiera, Verona, Legnago, Mantua)

SWITZERLAND

SOUTH TYROL
Bolzano (Bozen)
1919/20
Trento

Belluno
Udine
1866

Geneva
1815
Neutral District

1859

1815-59 to Aust.

1815-66 to Aust.

K. OF LOMBARDY AND VENETIA

Trieste

1860 to Fr.

Novara
Magenta
Milan
Peschiera
Vicenza

1919/20 Fiume 1920 Free City
1920 Ital. Occup.
1924 to Italy

Grenoble

K. OF
PIEDMONT
Turin
Alessandria

☆ Verona
Solferino Custozza
Goito ☆ Legnago
Mantua

Venice

Pola
Cherso

Briançon

FRANCE

SARDINIA

Po

Genoa

Guastalla
1847 to Mod.
D. OF
D. OF PARMA MODENA

Ferrara

1860 to Fr.

LIGURIA

1860

1860

Bologna

Zara
1919/20

Nice

Pontremoli Tusc.
1847 to Parma
1829 to Mod. Massa
Pietrasanta

Fivizzano Tusc.
1847 to Mod.
D. OF
LUCCA

REP. OF SAN MARINO
from 1861 under Italian Prot.

Spalato

PR. OF MONACO
1815-61 under Sardinian Prot.
1861 under French Prot.

1847 to
Tusc.

Florence

Urbino

Ancona

Castelfidardo

Lagosta
1919/20

Bastia

Elba

Leghorn

GR. DUCHY OF
TUSCANY

1860

Assisi

Corsica
1768 to Fr.

Ajaccio

Siena
1860

Perugia

PAPAL
STATES

Chieti

Sassari

1870

Mentana
Rome
Velletri Pontecorvo

Foggia

Bari

Sardinia

Gaeta

Capua Benevento

Naples Nola

1860

Taranto

Brindisi
Otranto

Cagliari

TYRRHENIAN

SEA

K. OF THE

Salerno

Cosenza

TWO SICILIES

Lipari Is.

Palermo

Milazzo 1862
Messina Aspromonte
Reggio

Trapani

Egadi Is.

Calatafimi
Sicily
1860

Catania

MEDITERRANEAN

Pantelleria
to Sicily

Siracusa

SEA

Gozo

Malta
1814 to Br.

East from Greenwich

COPYRIGHT. GEORGE PHILIP & SON. LTD.

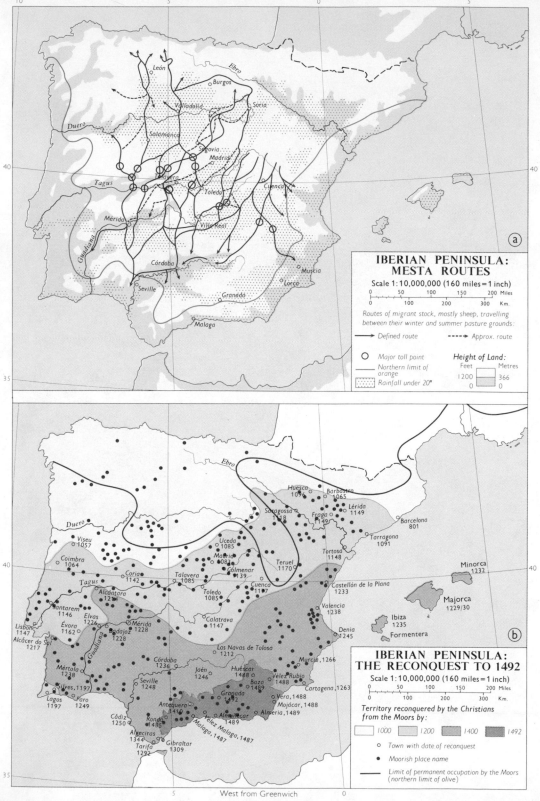

IBERIAN PENINSULA: MESTA ROUTES

Scale 1:10,000,000 (160 miles=1 inch)

0   50   100   150   200 Miles
0   100   200   300   Km.

Routes of migrant stock, mostly sheep, travelling between their winter and summer pasture grounds:

——▶ Defined route   - - -▶ Approx. route

◯ Major toll point

—— Northern limit of orange

Rainfall under 20"

Height of Land:

Feet	Metres
1200	366
0	0

(a)

IBERIAN PENINSULA: THE RECONQUEST TO 1492

Scale 1:10,000,000 (160 miles=1 inch)

0   50   100   150   200 Miles
0   100   200   300   Km.

Territory reconquered by the Christians from the Moors by:

1000	1200	1400	1492

○ Town with date of reconquest

● Moorish place name

—— Limit of permanent occupation by the Moors (northern limit of olive)

(b)

West from Greenwich

COPYRIGHT. GEORGE PHILIP & SON. LTD

Map (a) labels: León, Burgos, Ebro, Valladolid, Soria, Salamanca, Duero, Segovia, Madrid, Tagus, Toledo, Cuenca, Mérida, Villa Real, Guadiana, Córdoba, Seville, Murcia, Lorca, Granada, Malaga

Map (b) labels: Ebro, Huesca 1096, Barbastro 1065, Saragossa 1118, Lérida 1149, Fraga 1149, Barcelona 801, Tarragona 1091, Viseu 1057, Duero, Uceda 1085, Madrid 1083, Teruel 1170, Tortosa 1148, Coimbra 1064, Coria 1142, Talavera 1085, Colmenar 1139, Cuenca 1177, Castellón de la Plana 1233, Minorca 1232, Tagus, Alcántara 1214, Toledo 1085, Valencia 1238, Majorca 1229/30, Santarem 1146, Elvas 1226, Mérida 1228, Calatrava 1147, Denia 1245, Ibiza 1235, Lisbon 1147, Évora 1162, Badajoz 1228, Guadiana, Formentera, Alcácer do Sal 1217, Las Navas de Tolosa 1212, Murcia 1266, Mértola 1238, Córdoba 1236, Jaén 1246, Huéscar 1488, Vélez Rubio 1488, Cartagena 1263, Elvas 1197, Seville 1248, Baza 1489, Vera 1488, Lagos 1197, Faro 1249, Antequera 1410, Granada 1492, Mojácar 1488, Almería 1489, Cádiz 1250, Ronda 1485, Almuñecar 1489, Algeciras 1344, Vélez Malaga 1487, Málaga 1487, Tarifa 1292, Gibraltar 1309

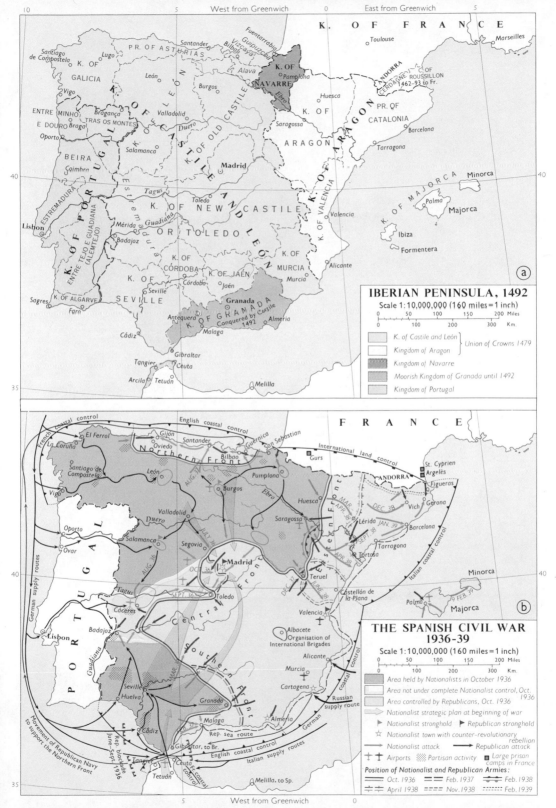

IBERIAN PENINSULA, 1492

Scale 1:10,000,000 (160 miles = 1 inch)

0   50   100   150   200 Miles
0   100   200   300 Km.

K. of Castile and León ⎫
⎬ Union of Crowns 1479
Kingdom of Aragon ⎭

Kingdom of Navarre

Moorish Kingdom of Granada until 1492

Kingdom of Portugal

THE SPANISH CIVIL WAR 1936–39

Scale 1:10,000,000 (160 miles = 1 inch)

0   50   100   150   200 Miles
0   100   200   300 Km.

Area held by Nationalists in October 1936

Area not under complete Nationalist control, Oct. 1936

Area controlled by Republicans, Oct. 1936

Nationalist strategic plan at beginning of war

▶ Nationalist stronghold   ▶ Republican stronghold

☆ Nationalist town with counter-revolutionary rebellion

→ Nationalist attack   → Republican attack

✛ Airports   ▒ Partisan activity   ◼ Large prison camps in France

Position of Nationalist and Republican Armies:
Oct. 1936   Feb. 1937   Feb. 1938
April 1938   Nov. 1938   Feb. 1939

THE EMPIRE

POLA

FRANCE

Berlin

Warsaw

Paris

Frankfurt

Prague

Krakow

Elbe

Oder

Vistula

Rhine

Danube

GALICIA

Lvov
(Lemberg)

Vienna
1683

Komárom
Győr

Nove Zamky
Gran

Erlau

Kolomea

Kamenec

Chotin

STYRIA
St. Gotthard

Buda Pest
(Ofen)

HUNGARY

Grosswardein
1664

TRANSYLVANIA
1541

Suceava

Villach

1541

Szegedin

Gyula

MOLDA

Milan

Venice

to Austria 1630

Szigetvar

Mohacs

Temesvar

1504

Trieste

1664

1526

Peterwardein

Rhône

CROATIA

1528

Jajce

Sabac

Belgrade

WALLACHIA
1393

Barcelona

DALMATIA

BOSNIA
1463

Semendria

Bucharest

Sebenico

Spalato

HERZE-
GOVINA

SERBIA
1459

Nicopolis

Rome

RAGUSA
1526

Ottoman
Vassal

Cattaro

1389

Kosovo
Polje

BULGARIA
1393

Durazzo

MONTENEGRO

Üsküb

Sofia

Philippopolis
1364

ALBANIA

RUMELIA

Adrianople
1361

MEDITE

Otranto
Ottoman Occup.
1480–81

Salonica

Gallipoli 1356

Algiers
1510–29 to Spain

Bugia
1510–55 to Spain

Bona
1535–74 to Spain

Prevesa

Lemnos
1656/57 to Ven.

Chanak
(Çanakkale)

Lesbos
1462

ALGIERS
1518

Tunis
1535–74 to Spain

Lepanto
1499

1571

Negroponte
1470

Chios
1566

Smyrna

Athens

MOREA
1458/60

Nauplia

Samos
1550

Djerba

Navarino

Naxos

Modon
1500

Coron

1540

1566

Tripoli

Cerigo

Monemvasia
(Malvasia)

Crete
1669

TUNIS
1574

Benghazi

TRIPOLI
1551

CYRENAICA
1521

EG

Adriatic Sea

Ionian Sea

Ionian Is.

RANEAN

MEDITERRANEAN

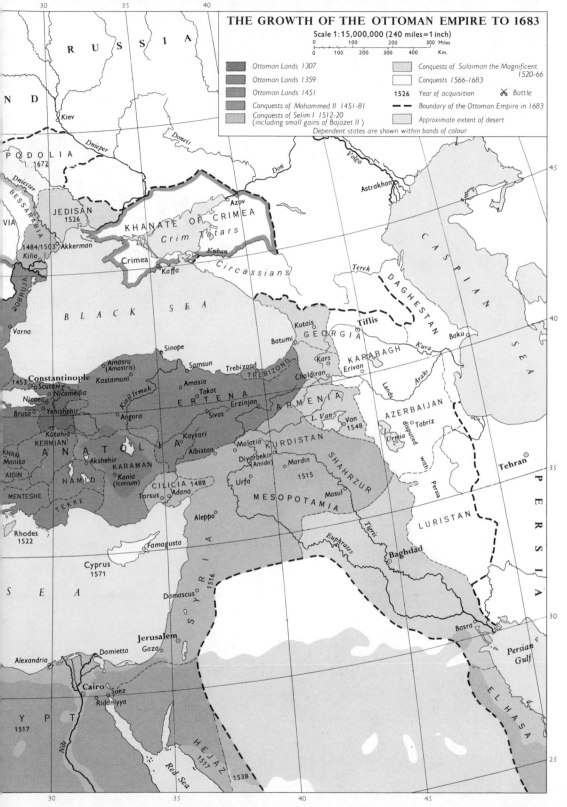

THE GROWTH OF THE OTTOMAN EMPIRE TO 1683

Scale 1:15,000,000 (240 miles = 1 inch)

0 100 200 300 Miles

0 100 200 300 400 Km.

Ottoman Lands 1307

Ottoman Lands 1359

Ottoman Lands 1451

Conquests of Mohammed II 1451-81

Conquests of Selim I 1512-20
(including small gains of Bajazet II)

Conquests of Sulaiman the Magnificent 1520-66

Conquests 1566-1683

1526 Year of acquisition   ✕ Battle

- - - Boundary of the Ottoman Empire in 1683

Approximate extent of desert

Dependent states are shown within bands of colour

RUSSIA

Kiev

PODOLIA
1672

BESSARABIA
VIA

JEDISAN
1526

Dnieper

Donets

Don

Volga

Astrakhan

KHANATE OF CRIMEA

Crim Tatars

Azov

Kuban

Circassians

DOBRUJA

1484/1503 Akkerman
Kilia

Crimea

Kaffa

Terek

DAGHESTAN

CASPIAN SEA

Baku

Varna

BLACK SEA

Sinope

Samsun

Trebizond

Batumi

Kutais

GEORGIA

Tiflis

Kars

Erivan

KARABAGH

Kura

Araks

Amasru
(Amastris)

Kastamuni

TREBIZOND

Chaldiran

1453 Constantinople
Scutari
Nicaea Nicomedia
Brusa Yenishehir

Kizil Irmak

Amasia

Tokat

Sivas

Erzinjan

ERTENA

ARMENIA

AZERBAIJAN

Tabriz

Urmia

Lands
disputed

with

Persia

Tehran

Angora

L. Van

Van
1548

KHAM
KERMIAN
Kütahia
Manisa
AIDIN

ANATOLIA

Akshehir

Kaysari

Malatia

Albistan

KURDISTAN

Diyarbekin
(Amida)

Mardin
1515

SHAHRZUR

PERSIA

MENTESHE
HAMID
TEKKE
KARAMAN

Konia
(Iconium)

CILICIA 1488

Tarsus

Adana

Urfa

MESOPOTAMIA

Mosul

LURISTAN

Rhodes
1522

Famagusta

Aleppo

Euphrates

Tigris

Cyprus
1571

SEA

Damascus
1516

SYRIA

Baghdad

Basra

Persian
Gulf

Jerusalem

Gaza

Alexandria

Damietta

Cairo

Suez

Riddniyya

YPT
1517

Nile

HEJAZ
1517

1538

EL HASA

Red Sea

45

40

35

30

25

30 35 40

35 40 45

COPYRIGHT. GEORGE PHILIP & SON, LTD.

GERMANY

Berlin

Warsaw

POLAND

Paris

Frankfurt

Prague

Krakow

FRANCE

Rhine

Danube

Elbe

Oder

Vistula

Cherno

SWITZERLAND

AUSTRIA

Vienna

1683

Boundary 1683

Budapest

BUKOVINA
to Austria
1775

HUNGARY
to Austria 1699

Grosswardein

TRANSYLVANIA
to Austria 1699

MOLDAVIA

1829

Milan

Venice

Rhine

Trieste

Mohacs

Temesvar

Carlowitz

BANAT
to Austria
1718

WALLACHIA

1829

R O M A N I A
Created 1858

1878

Barcelona

I T A L Y

CROATIA

DALMATIA
to Venice 1699–1797
to Austria 1797
to Italy 1805–9
to France 1809–16

BOSNIA
to Austria-Hung.
1878

Belgrade

Passarowitz

to Austria
1718–39

SERBIA
to Austria 1718–39

1817

1878

Craiova

Danube

Bucharest

1878

Rome

RAGUSA

1718

Cuttaro

Sarajevo

Nish

Plevna

BULGARIA

1878

1908

MONTENEGRO

1878
renewed

Scutari
(Shkodra)

Skoplje
(Üsküb)

to Serbia
1913

Sofia

EAST RUMELIA

1878

Philippopolis

to Bulg. 1885

Adr
to Gr
1920

ALBANIA

1913

M A C E D O N I A

to Bulg.
1913

Salonica

Gallipoli

Algiers

EPIRUS

Ionian Is.
to Ven. until 1797
Fr. 1797–99 and 1807–15
Br. Prot. 1815–63
to Greece 1863

THESSALY
to Greece 1881

Larisa

Negroponte (Euboea)

Chios

to Gr
1920

M E D I T E R R A N E A N

Tunis

Missolonghi

G R E E C E

1830

MOREA
to Ven.
1685/99–
1715/18

Argos

Athens

Samos

Smyrna

Dodecanese
to Italy 1912

ALGIERS

1710
to France 1830/48

TUNIS

Nominally Subject
until 1881
Fr. Prot. 1881

Navarino

Suda

Spinalonga

Turk. 1718

Crete

Turk. 1718

1898
to Greece 1908

Tripoli

T R I P O L I

Ottoman Vassal until 1835,
Ottoman Province 1835–1912,
to Italy 1912

Benghazi

C Y R E N A I C A

Ottoman Vassal until 1835,
Ottoman Province 1835–1912

E G

Br. Occup.

F E Z Z A N

Ottoman Province 1842–1912

THE DECLINE OF THE OTTOMAN EMPIRE
1683–1924

Scale 1:15,000,000 (240 miles = 1 inch)

Losses 1683-99 (T. of Carlowitz)	Losses 1916-23 (T. of Lausanne)
Losses 1700-18 (T. of Passarowitz)	Turkey in 1923
Losses 1719-74 (T. of Kutchuk-Kainarji)	1878 Date or period of autonomy
Losses 1775-1812 (T. of Bucharest)	1878 Date of independence
Losses 1813-29/30 (T. of Adrianople)	Boundaries of spheres of influence in Anatolia after the 1914-18 War
Losses 1830-78 (T. of Berlin)	Boundary after T. of Sèvres 1920
Losses 1879-1915 (Ts. of London & Bucharest)	Boundary after T. of Lausanne 1923
	Approximate extent of desert

COPYRIGHT. GEORGE PHILIP & SON. LTD.

BALKAN PENINSULA
c. **1830**

Scale 1:8,000,000 (128 miles=1 inch)

0   50   100   150 Miles
0   50   100   150   200
Km.

Ottoman Lands in 1830

1830 Date of independence

1817 Date of autonomy

Austro–Hungarian military boundary zones, with dates of duration

K. OF GALICIA 1809–15
AND to Russia
LODOMERIA

RUSSIAN EMPIRE

Czernowitz
D. OF
BUKOVINA

Debreczin

BESSARABIA
1812 to Russia

Jassy

Kishinev

AUSTRO–HUNGARIAN EMPIRE

K. OF HUNGARY

GR. PR.
OF
TRANSYLANIA

MOLDAVIA
1829

Szegedin

(K. OF) SLAVONIA
1538 1777-1876
1702-1618

BANAT

Kronstadt

1764-1851

Galati
1856 to Moldavia
1829 to Russ.
Izmail
1856 to Ottom.
Emp.

Sava

1742-1872

Belgrade

PRINCIPALITY
OF
SERBIA
1817

WALLACHIA
1829

Bucharest

Craiova

Constanta

BOSNIA

K. OF DALMATIA
From 1916

Sarajevo

HERZEGOVINA

1833 to Serbia

Morava

Danube

Plevna

Varna

BULGARIA

BLACK
SEA

Ragusa

Novipazar

Nish

Leskovac

Sofia

MONTENEGRO
Cattara 1852 Principality
Scutari

ADRIATIC

SEA

Üsküb
(Skoplje)

Ochrida
Bitola

Philippopolis

Martisa

Burgas

Adrianople

RUMELIA

Constantinople

Str. of Otranto

ALBANIA

MACEDONIA

Salonica

Mt. Athos

Thasos

Gallipoli

Sea of Marmara

EMPIRE

OTTOMAN

Corfu

EPIRUS

Janina

Arta

THESSALY

Larisa

Lemnos

Mitilini
(Lesbos)

IONIAN

Ionian Is.
Brit. Prot. 1815-1863

CARNANIA

LIVADIA

Missolonghi

K. OF
Euboea

AEGEAN SEA

Chios
1832

Smyrna

GREECE
1830

Corinth

Athens

Samos 1832

Tripolis
Nauplia
Epidaurus

MOREA
(PELEPONNESE)
Hydra
Spezzia

Cyclades

Dodecanese

Navarino

IONIAN

SEA

Cerigo

Rhodes

Crete
1824–1840 to Egypt

Candia

COPYRIGHT. GEORGE PHILIP & SON. LTD.

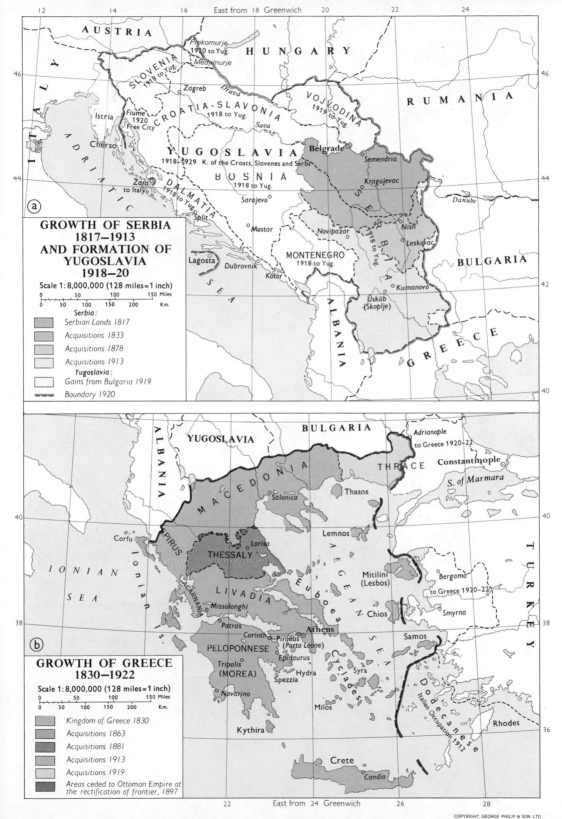

GROWTH OF SERBIA 1817–1913 AND FORMATION OF YUGOSLAVIA 1918–20

Scale 1:8,000,000 (128 miles=1 inch)

0   50   100   150 Miles
0   50 100 150 200 Km.

Serbia:
Serbian Lands 1817
Acquisitions 1833
Acquisitions 1878
Acquisitions 1913
Yugoslavia:
Gains from Bulgaria 1919
Boundary 1920

GROWTH OF GREECE 1830–1922

Scale 1:8,000,000 (128 miles=1 inch)

0   50   100   150 Miles
0   50 100 150 200 Km.

Kingdom of Greece 1830
Acquisitions 1863
Acquisitions 1881
Acquisitions 1913
Acquisitions 1919
Areas ceded to Ottoman Empire at the rectification of frontier, 1897

COPYRIGHT. GEORGE PHILIP & SON, LTD.

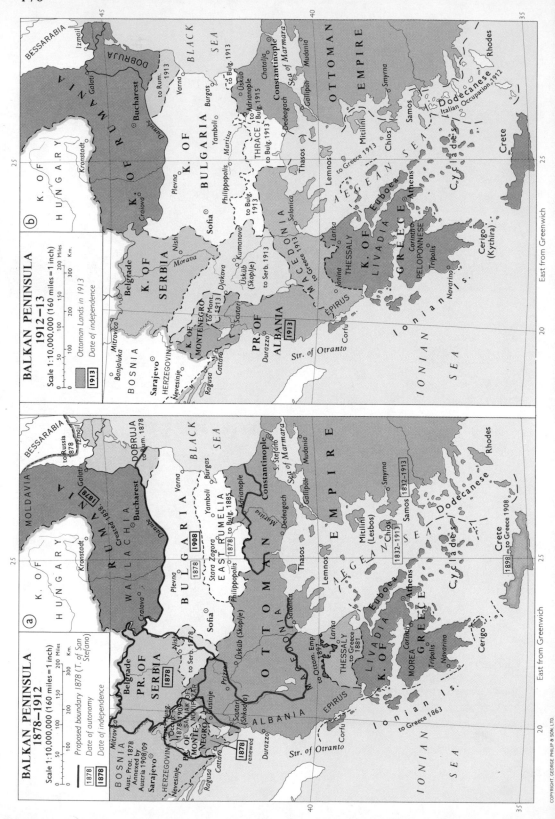

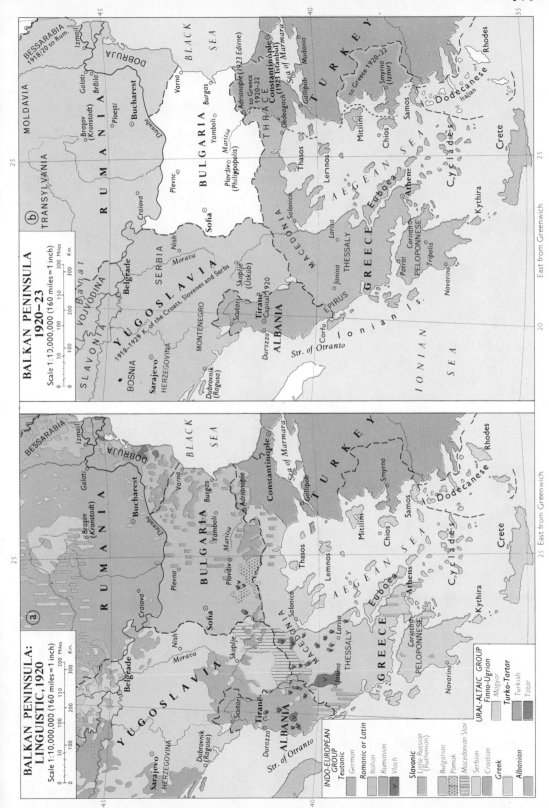

BALKAN PENINSULA 1920–23

Scale 1:13,000,000 (160 miles=1 inch)

0   100   150   200 Miles
0   100   200   300 Km

(b)

BALTIC SEA · BLACK SEA

MOLDAVIA

BESSARABIA 1918/20 to Rum.

Izmail

DOBRUJA

Galati
Brăila

RUMANIA

Braşov (Kronstadt)
Ploesti
Bucharest

Danube

Varna

Burgas

BULGARIA

Yamboli
Plevna

Plovdiv (Philippopolis)

Sofia

TRANSYLVANIA

Craiova

SERBIA

Nish

Morava

Belgrade

VOJVODINA

Ban̄at

SLAVONIA

BOSNIA

Sarajevo
HERZEGOVINA

Dubrovnik (Ragusa)

MONTENEGRO

YUGOSLAVIA
1918–1929 K. of the Croats, Slovenes and Serbs

Scutari

Skopje (Üsküb)

Tiranë
Capital 1920

ALBANIA

Durazzo

Str. of Otranto

Ionian Is.

IONIAN SEA

THRACE

Adrianople (1923 Edirne)
to Greece 1920–22

Constantinople (1923 Istanbul)

Sea of Marmara

Gallipoli

Mudania

TURKEY

to Greece 1920–22

Smyrna (Izmir)

Dedeagatch

MACEDONIA

Salonica

Thasos

Lemnos

Mitilini

Chios

Samos

AEGEAN SEA

EPIRUS

Janina

THESSALY

Larisa

GREECE

Euboea

Athens

Corinth
PELOPONNESE
Tripolis
Patrai

Navarino

Kythira

Cyclades

Crete

Dodecanese
Italian

Rhodes

East from Greenwich

BALKAN PENINSULA: LINGUISTIC, 1920

Scale 1:10,000,000 (160 miles=1 inch)

0   100   150   200 Miles
0   100   200   300 Km

(a)

BESSARABIA

Izmail

DOBRUJA

Galati

Braşov (Kronstadt)

Bucharest

RUMANIA

Danube

BLACK SEA

Varna

Burgas

BULGARIA

Yamboli

Adrianople

Plevna

Plovdiv

Martsa

Sofia

Craiova

Nish

Morava

Belgrade

YUGOSLAVIA

Sarajevo

HERZEGOVINA

Dubrovnik (Ragusa)

Scutari

Skopje

Tiranë
ALBANIA

Durazzo

Str. of Otranto

Constantinople

Sea of Marmara

Gallipoli

TURKEY

Smyrna

MACEDONIA

Salonica

Thasos

Lemnos

Mitilini

Chios

Samos

AEGEAN SEA

Janina

THESSALY

Larisa

GREECE

Euboea

Athens

Corinth
PELOPONNESE

Navarino

Kythira

Cyclades

Crete

Dodecanese

Rhodes

25 East from Greenwich

INDO-EUROPEAN GROUP

Teutonic
  German

Romanic or Latin
  Italian
  Rumanian
  Vlach

Slavonic
  Little Russian (Ruthenian)
  Bulgarian
  Pomak
  Macedonian Slav
  Serbian
  Croatian

Greek

Albanian

URAL-ALTAIC GROUP
  Finno-Ugrian
  Magyar

Turko-Tartar
  Turkish
  Tatar

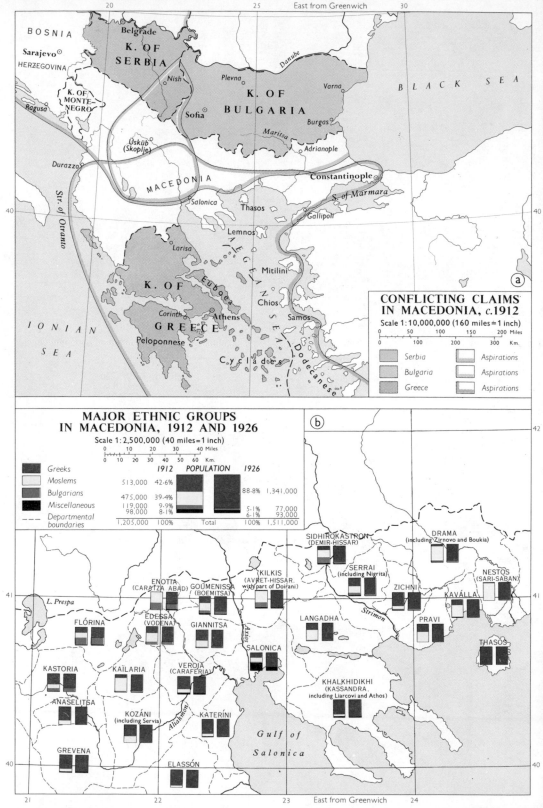

East from Greenwich

**CONFLICTING CLAIMS
IN MACEDONIA, c.1912**

Scale 1:10,000,000 (160 miles ≈ 1 inch)

| 0 | 50 | 100 | 150 | 200 Miles |

| 0 | 100 | 200 | 300 Km. |

- Serbia
- Bulgaria
- Greece
- Aspirations
- Aspirations
- Aspirations

**MAJOR ETHNIC GROUPS
IN MACEDONIA, 1912 AND 1926**

Scale 1:2,500,000 (40 miles=1 inch)

| 0 | 10 | 20 | 30 | 40 Miles |

| 0 | 10 | 20 | 30 | 40 | 50 | 60 Km. |

	Greeks
	Moslems
	Bulgarians
	Miscellaneous
---	Departmental boundaries

	1912	POPULATION	1926	
Greeks	513,000	42·6%	88·8%	1,341,000
Moslems	475,000	39·4%		
Bulgarians	119,000	9·9%	5·1%	77,000
Miscellaneous	98,000	8·1%	6·1%	93,000
Total	1,205,000	100%	100%	1,511,000

COPYRIGHT. GEORGE PHILIP & SON. LTD.

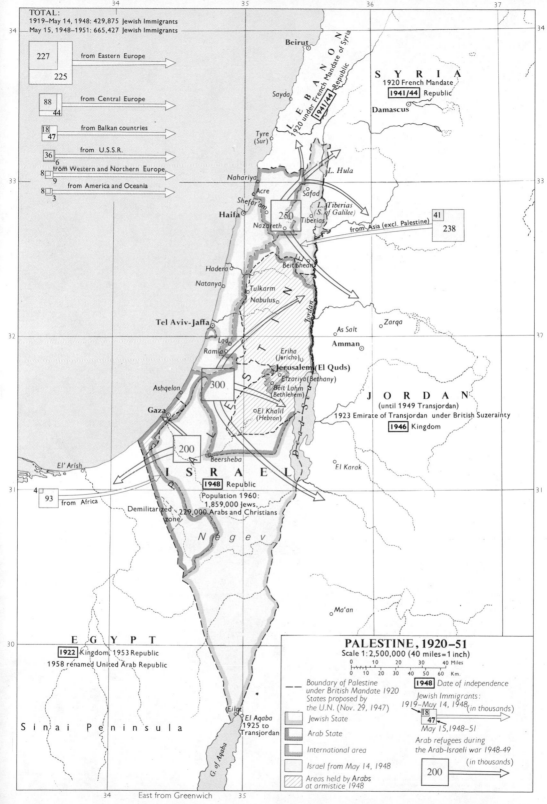

TOTAL:
1919–May 14, 1948: 429,875 Jewish Immigrants
May 15, 1948–1951: 665,427 Jewish Immigrants

227 / 225   from Eastern Europe

88 / 44   from Central Europe

18 / 47   from Balkan countries

36 / 6   from U.S.S.R.

8 / 9   from Western and Northern Europe

8 / 3   from America and Oceania

41 / 238   from Asia (excl. Palestine)

4 / 93   from Africa

Beirut

S Y R I A
1920 French Mandate
1941/44 Republic
Damascus

L E B A N O N
1920 under French Mandate of Syria
1941/44 Republic

Sayda

Tyre
(Sur)

Nahariya
Acre
Shefar'am
Haifa
Nazareth
Hadera
Natanya
Tulkarm
Nabulus
Tel Aviv-Jaffa
Lod
Ramla
Ashqelon
Gaza
El'Arish

Safad
L. Hula
L. Tiberias
(S. of Galilee)
Tiberias
Beit Shean

P A L E S T I N E

Jordan

As Salt
Zarqa

Amman

Eriha
(Jericho)
Jerusalem (El Quds)
Etzariya (Bethany)
Beit Lahm
(Bethlehem)
El Khalil
(Hebron)

J O R D A N
(until 1949 Transjordan)
1923 Emirate of Transjordan under British Suzerainty
1946 Kingdom

Beersheba
El Karak

I S R A E L
1948 Republic
Population 1960:
1,859,000 Jews,
229,000 Arabs and Christians

Demilitarized zone

N e g e v

Ma'an

E G Y P T
1922 Kingdom, 1953 Republic
1958 renamed United Arab Republic

Eilat
El Aqaba
1925 to
Transjordan

S i n a i   P e n i n s u l a

G. of Aqaba

PALESTINE, 1920–51
Scale 1:2,500,000 (40 miles=1 inch)
0   10   20   30   40 Miles
0 10 20 30 40 50 60 Km.

Boundary of Palestine
under British Mandate 1920
States proposed by
the U.N. (Nov. 29, 1947)
Jewish State
Arab State
International area
Israel from May 14, 1948
Areas held by Arabs
at armistice 1948

1948 Date of independence

Jewish Immigrants:
1919–May 14, 1948 (in thousands)
18
May 15,1948–51   47

Arab refugees during
the Arab-Israeli war 1948-49
(in thousands)
200

East from Greenwich

COPYRIGHT. GEORGE PHILIP & SON. LTD.

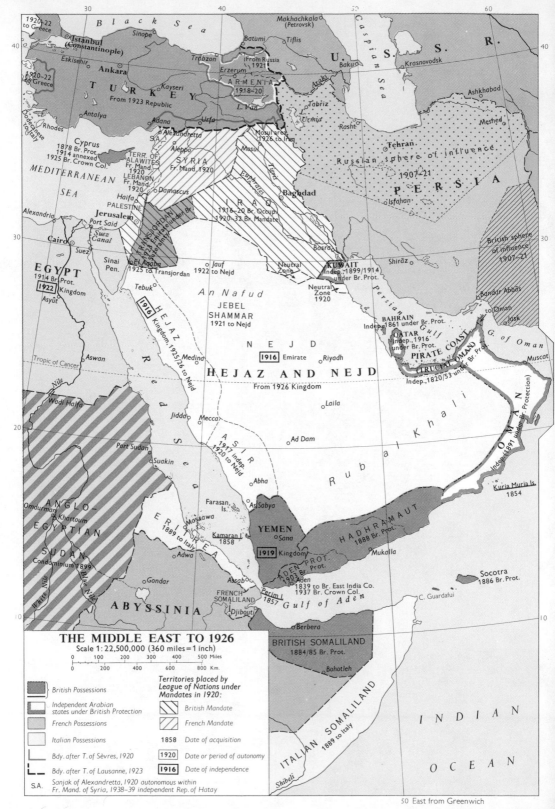

THE MIDDLE EAST TO 1926
Scale 1:22,500,000 (360 miles=1 inch)

| 0 | 100 | 200 | 300 | 400 | 500 Miles |
| 0 | 200 | 400 | 600 | 800 Km. |

British Possessions

Independent Arabian states under British Protection

French Possessions

Italian Possessions

⌐ Bdy. after T. of Sèvres, 1920

⌐ Bdy. after T. of Lausanne, 1923

S.A. Sanjak of Alexandretta, 1920 autonomous within Fr. Mand. of Syria, 1938–39 independent Rep. of Hatay

Territories placed by League of Nations under Mandates in 1920:

British Mandate

French Mandate

1858 Date of acquisition

1920 Date or period of autonomy

1916 Date of independence

50 East from Greenwich

COPYRIGHT. GEORGE PHILIP & SON. LTD.

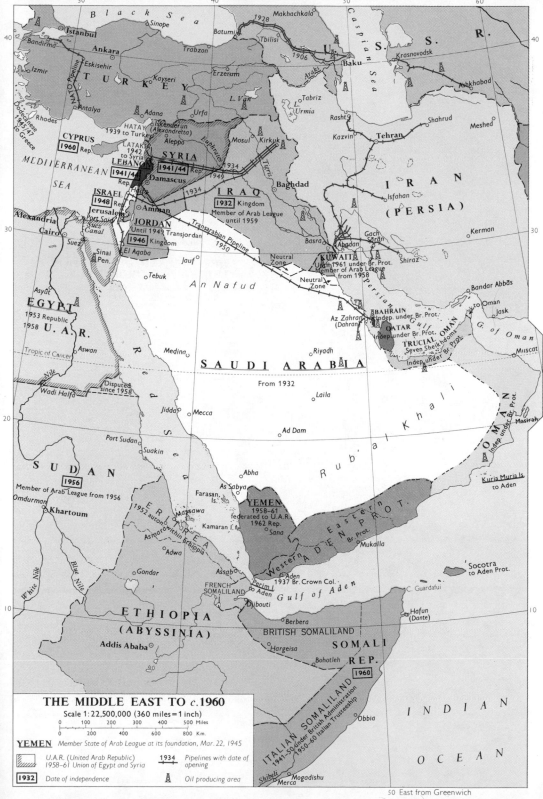

THE MIDDLE EAST TO *c.*1960

Scale 1:22,500,000 (360 miles=1 inch)

0   100   200   300   400   500 Miles
0   200   400   600   800 Km.

YEMEN   *Member State of Arab League at its foundation, Mar. 22, 1945*

U.A.R. (United Arab Republic)
1958–61 Union of Egypt and Syria

1934   Pipelines with date of opening

1932   Date of independence

⚒   Oil producing area

50 East from Greenwich

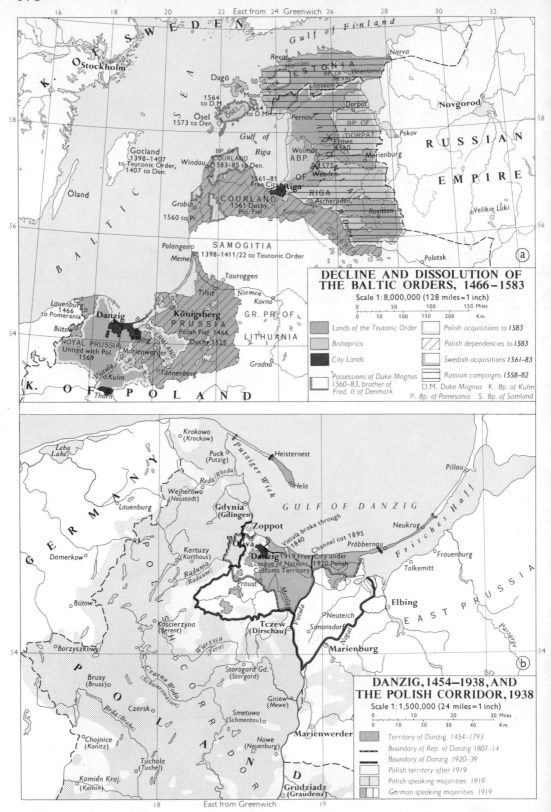

DECLINE AND DISSOLUTION OF THE BALTIC ORDERS, 1466–1583

Scale 1:8,000,000 (128 miles=1 inch)

0   50   100   150 Miles
0   50   100   200 Km.

	Lands of the Teutonic Order		Polish acquisitions to 1583
	Bishoprics		Polish dependencies to 1583
	City Lands		Swedish acquisitions 1561–83
	Possessions of Duke Magnus 1560–83, brother of Fred. II of Denmark		Russian campaigns 1558–82

D.M. Duke Magnus   K. Bp. of Kulm
P. Bp. of Pomesania   S. Bp. of Samland

DANZIG, 1454–1938, AND THE POLISH CORRIDOR, 1938

Scale 1:1,500,000 (24 miles=1 inch)

0   10   20   30 Miles
0   10   20   30 40   Km.

	Territory of Danzig 1454–1793
	Boundary of Rep. of Danzig 1807–14
	Boundary of Danzig 1920–39
	Polish territory after 1919
	Polish speaking majorities 1919
	German speaking majorities 1919

COPYRIGHT. GEORGE PHILIP & SON. LTD.

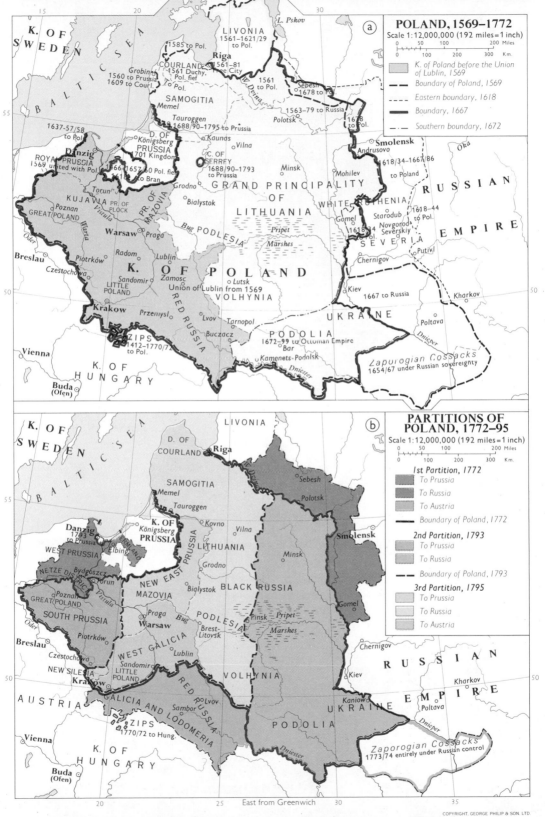

POLAND, 1569–1772

Scale 1:12,000,000 (192 miles = 1 inch)

| 0 | 50 | 100 | 200 Miles |

| 0 | 100 | 200 | 300 Km. |

K. of Poland before the Union of Lublin, 1569
Boundary of Poland, 1569
Eastern boundary, 1618
Boundary, 1667
Southern boundary, 1672

K. OF SWEDEN

BALTIC SEA

L. Pskov

LIVONIA 1561–1621/29 to Pol.
1585 to Pol.
Riga 1561–81 Free City
COURLAND 1561 Duchy, Pol. fief
Grobin 1560 to Prussia 1609 to Courl.
SAMOGITIA
Memel
Tauroggen 1688/90–1795 to Prussia
1637–57/58 to Pol.
Danzig
D. OF Königsberg PRUSSIA 1701 Kingdom
ROYAL PRUSSIA 1569 united with Pol.
1466–1657/60 Pol. fief 1618 to Bran
C. OF SERREY 1688/90–1793 to Prussia
Kaunas
Vilna
1561 to Pol.
W. Dwina
Polotsk
1563–79 to Russia
Sebesh 1678 to Pol.
1678
Smolensk
Andrusovo
1618/34–1667/86 to Poland
Oka
RUSSIAN
PR. OF PLOCK
KUJAVIA PR. OF MAZOVIA
Poznan
GREAT POLAND
Torun
Vistula
Warta
Oder
Breslau
Piotrków
Czestochowa
LITTLE POLAND
Krakow
ZIPS 1412–1770/72 to Pol.
Vienna
K. OF HUNGARY
Buda (Ofen)

GRAND PRINCIPALITY OF LITHUANIA
Grodno
Bialystok
Minsk
Mohilev
WHITE RUTHENIA
Gomel
Starodub 1618–44 to Pol.
Novgorod Severskiy
1618/34
SEVERIA
Putivl
EMPIRE
Bug PODLESIA
Pripet
Marshes
Chernigov
Radom
Lublin
Sandomir
Zamosc
Lutsk
Union of Lublin from 1569
VOLHYNIA
Przemysl
RED RUSSIA
Lvov
Tarnopol
Buczacz
Bar
PODOLIA 1672–99 to Ottoman Empire
Kamenets-Podolsk
Dniester
Kiev
1667 to Russia
UKRAINE
Poltava
Kharkov
Dnieper
Zaporogian Cossacks 1654/67 under Russian sovereignty

K. OF SWEDEN

BALTIC SEA

PARTITIONS OF POLAND, 1772–95

Scale 1:12,000,000 (192 miles = 1 inch)

| 0 | 50 | 100 | 200 Miles |

| 0 | 100 | 200 | 300 Km. |

1st Partition, 1772
To Prussia
To Russia
To Austria
Boundary of Poland, 1772

2nd Partition, 1793
To Prussia
To Russia
Boundary of Poland, 1793

3rd Partition, 1795
To Prussia
To Russia
To Austria

LIVONIA
D. OF COURLAND
Riga
Dwina
Sebesh
Polotsk
SAMOGITIA
Memel
Tauroggen
K. OF PRUSSIA
Danzig 1793 to Prussia
Königsberg PRUSSIA
Elbing
WEST PRUSSIA
NETZE DISTRICT
Bydgoszcz
Torun
GREAT POLAND
SOUTH PRUSSIA
Poznan
Kovno
Vilna
LITHUANIA
Grodno
NEW EAST MAZOVIA
Bialystok
BLACK RUSSIA
Minsk
Smolensk
Gomel
Oder
Breslau
Piotrków
Czestochowa
NEW SILESIA
LITTLE POLAND
Sandomir
Krakow
WEST GALICIA
Praga Bug
Warsaw
Brest-Litovsk
PODLESIA
Pinsk
Pripet
Marshes
Lublin
RED RUSSIA
VOLHYNIA
A U S T R I A
GALICIA AND LODOMERIA
Sambor
Lvov
ZIPS 1770/72 to Hung.
Vienna
K. OF HUNGARY
Buda (Ofen)
PODOLIA
Chernigov
Kiev
Kaniow
UKRAINE
Poltava
Kharkov
Dnieper
Dniester
Zaporogian Cossacks 1773/74 entirely under Russian control

R U S S I A N   E M P I R E

East from Greenwich

COPYRIGHT. GEORGE PHILIP & SON. LTD.

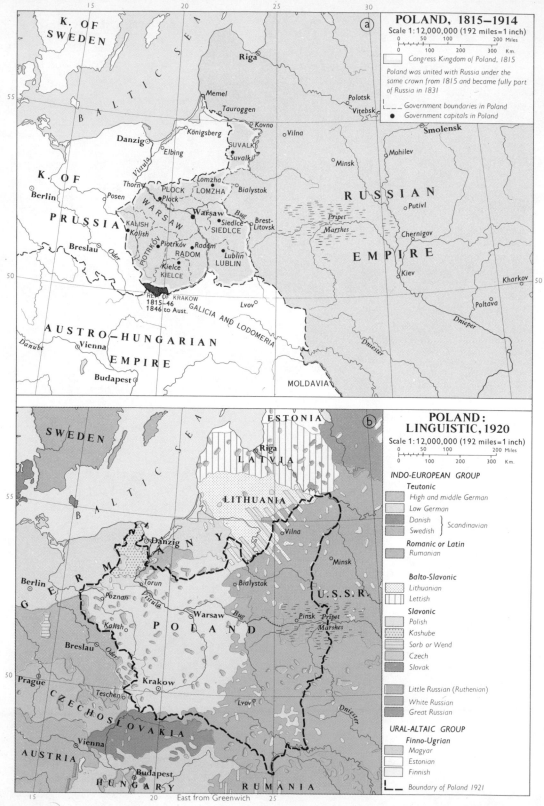

POLAND, 1815–1914

Scale 1:12,000,000 (192 miles=1 inch)

0   50   100   200 Miles
0   100   200   300 Km.

Congress Kingdom of Poland, 1815

Poland was united with Russia under the
same crown from 1815 and became fully part
of Russia in 1831

Government boundaries in Poland
Government capitals in Poland

POLAND:
LINGUISTIC, 1920

Scale 1:12,000,000 (192 miles=1 inch)

0   50   100   200 Miles
0   100   200   300 Km.

INDO-EUROPEAN GROUP

Teutonic
High and middle German
Low German
Danish
Swedish   } Scandinavian

Romanic or Latin
Rumanian

Balto-Slavonic
Lithuanian
Lettish

Slavonic
Polish
Kashube
Sorb or Wend
Czech
Slovak

Little Russian (Ruthenian)
White Russian
Great Russian

URAL-ALTAIC GROUP

Finno-Ugrian
Magyar
Estonian
Finnish

Boundary of Poland 1921

East from Greenwich

COPYRIGHT. GEORGE PHILIP & SON LTD

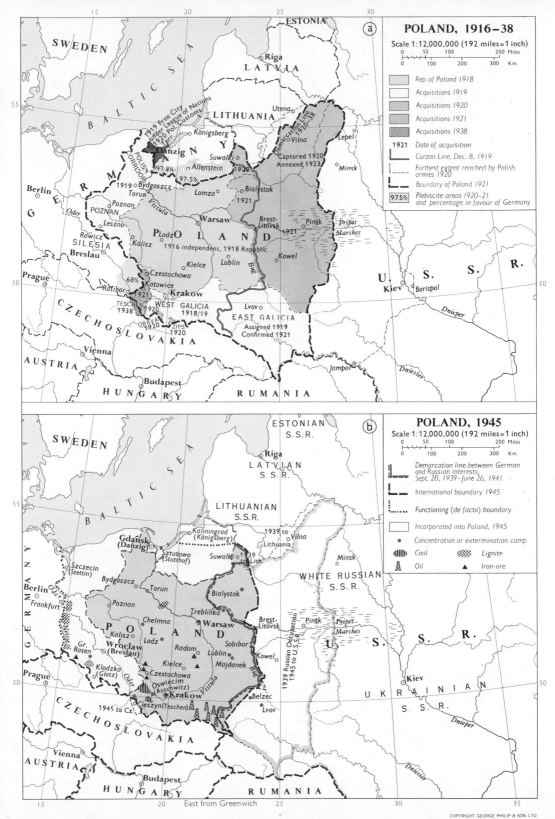

POLAND, 1916–38

Scale 1:12,000,000 (192 miles=1 inch)

0	50	100		200 Miles
0	100	200	300	Km.

- Rep. of Poland 1918
- Acquisitions 1919
- Acquisitions 1920
- Acquisitions 1921
- Acquisitions 1938

1921 Date of acquisition

Curzon Line, Dec. 8, 1919

Furthest extent reached by Polish armies 1920

Boundary of Poland 1921

97.5% Plebiscite areas 1920–21 and percentage in favour of Germany

SWEDEN
ESTONIA
LATVIA
Riga
LITHUANIA
BALTIC SEA
Utena
Vilna
Lepel
Königsberg
Danzig
1919 Free City under League of Nations
1920 Pol. Customs Terr.
POLISH CORRIDOR
Suwalki
97.8%
Allenstein
Captured 1920
Annexed, 1923
Minsk
97.5%
1920
1919 Bydgoszcz
Torun
Lomza
Bialystok
1921
Berlin
GERMANY
Oder
POZNAN
Vistula
Warsaw
Brest-Litovsk
1921
Pinsk
Pripet Marshes
Leszno
P Lodz OLAND
1916 independent, 1918 Republic
Rawicz
Kalisz
Kielce
Lublin
Kowel
U. S. S. R.
SILESIA
Breslau
Czestochowa
68%
Katowice
1921
Krakow
Kiev
Borispol
Prague
Ratibor
WEST GALICIA
1918/19
Lvov
EAST GALICIA
Assigned 1919
Confirmed 1921
Dnieper
TESCHEN 1938
1920
ORAVA 1920
ZIPS 1920
CZECHOSLOVAKIA
Vienna
AUSTRIA
Budapest
HUNGARY
RUMANIA
Jampol
Dniester

POLAND, 1945

Scale 1:12,000,000 (192 miles=1 inch)

0	50	100		200 Miles
0	100	200	300	Km.

Demarcation line between German and Russian interests, Sept. 28, 1939–June 26, 1941

International boundary 1945

Functioning (de facto) boundary

Incorporated into Poland, 1945

- Concentration or extermination camp

Coal   Lignite

Oil   Iron-ore

SWEDEN
ESTONIAN S.S.R.
Riga
LATVIAN S.S.R.
BALTIC SEA
LITHUANIAN S.S.R.
1939 to Vilna
1939 to Lithuania
Kaliningrad (Königsberg)
Gdansk (Danzig)
Sztutowo (Stutthof)
Suwalki
1939 to Lith.
Minsk
Szczecin (Stettin)
Bydgoszcz
Torun
Bialystok
WHITE RUSSIAN S.S.R.
Berlin
Frankfurt
GERMANY
Oder
Poznan
Treblinka
Chelmna
Warsaw
Brest-Litovsk
Pinsk
Pripet Marshes
Gr. Rosen
Kalisz
Lodz
Radom
Lublin
Sobibor
Kowel
U. S. S. R.
Wroclaw (Breslau)
Kielce
Majdanek
1939 Russian Occupation 1945 to U.S.S.R.
Klodzko (Glatz)
Czestochowa
Oswiecim (Auschwitz)
Kiev
Prague
Krakow
Belzec
Lvov
UKRAINIAN S.S.R.
1945 to Cz.
Cieszyn (Teschen)
Vistula
Dnieper
CZECHOSLOVAKIA
Vienna
AUSTRIA
Budapest
HUNGARY
RUMANIA
Dniester

East from Greenwich

COPYRIGHT. GEORGE PHILIP & SON. LTD.

Ob

Pelym
F.1592

Rising of the Bashkirs 1662-67/1675-83

U r a l   M o u n t a i n s

B a s h k i r s

Ufa o 1586

Solikamsk

Yegoshikho

N e n e t s

Pechora

Kama

Vyatka
1485

Kazan
O 1552

Samara
F.1586

V o l g a

Ustyug

Southern limit of coniferous forest

Nizhniy
Novgorod Tatars

Simbirsk
F.1648

M o r d v i n i a n s

Penza
F.1663

Northern limit
of grassland

N. Dvina

Kazan

Barents Sea

Kolguyev I.

S a m o y e d s

N O V G O R O D

G
U
G 1465 - 1488

Kargopol

Galich

Kostroma
1364

Suzdal

Vladimir

Murom

Danko

Arkhangelsk
F.1583

Sea

Solovetski
Is.

White Sea

Kola Pen.

L a p p s

K a r e l i a n s

L. Onega

Onubruej

Belozersk F.862
1362/89 to Muscovy
Vologda

Yaroslavl
1463

Rostov
1474

Tver
1485

MUSCOVY

Moscow
1500

Kashino

Ugra

Kaluga

Ryazan

Kozelsk

Oka

P.1564 o Orel

PRINCIPALITY   OF

Olonets

Stalbova

L.
Ladoga

Staraya Russa
1478

Novgorod
1478

Velikie
Luki

Rzhev

Vyazma

Nevel

Belyi

Yelizh

Smolensk

Desna

CARELIA
1617
to Sweden

INGRIA
1583-95,
1617 to Sweden

Narva

Pskov
1510

Sebezh

Polotsk
1563-79 to Russia

Minsk

Mohilev

Helsingfors

G. of Finland

Reval

Dorpat

ESTONIA

LIVONIA

Riga

W. Dvina

Dünaburg

Vilna

Bialystok

L I T H U A N I A

1561-81
Free City

N O R W A Y

L a p l a n d

S W E D E N

Gulf of Bothnia

Stockholm

F I N L A N D

B A L T I C   S E A

Danzig

Vistula

Warsaw

Arctic Circle

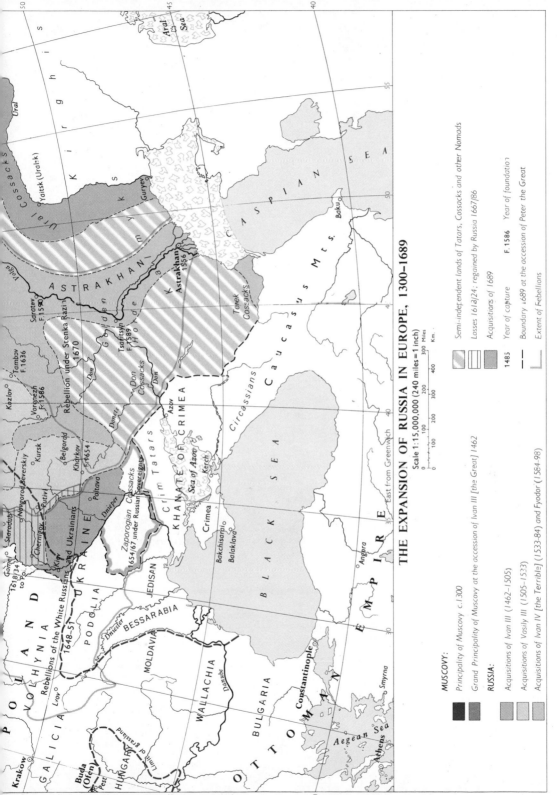

THE EXPANSION OF RUSSIA IN EUROPE, 1300–1689

Scale 1:15,000,000 (240 miles = 1 inch)

MUSCOVY:

Principality of Muscovy c.1300

Grand Principality of Muscovy at the accession of Ivan III [the Great] 1462

RUSSIA:

Acquisitions of Ivan III (1462–1505)

Acquisitions of Vasily III (1505–1533)

Acquisitions of Ivan IV [the Terrible] (1533–84) and Fyodor (1584–98)

Semi-independent lands of Tatars, Cossacks and other Nomads

Losses 1612/24: regained by Russia 1667/86

Acquisitions of 1689

1485   Year of capture   F.1586   Year of foundation

Boundary 1689 at the accession of Peter the Great

Extent of Rebellions

182

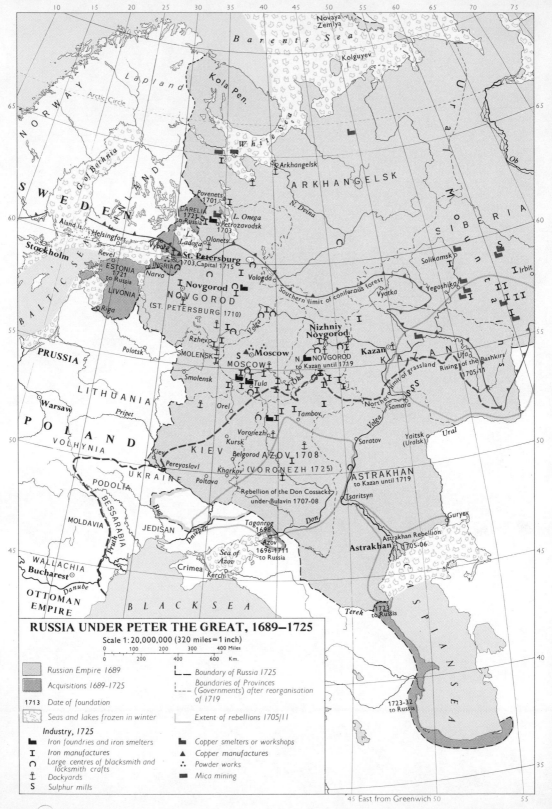

RUSSIA UNDER PETER THE GREAT, 1689–1725

Scale 1:20,000,000 (320 miles = 1 inch)

0	100 200 300	400 Miles
0	200 400	600 Km.

Russian Empire 1689

Acquisitions 1689–1725

1713   Date of foundation

Seas and lakes frozen in winter

Boundary of Russia 1725

Boundaries of Provinces (Governments) after reorganisation of 1719

Extent of rebellions 1705/11

Industry, 1725

⌐ Iron foundries and iron smelters
I   Iron manufactures
⊃ Large centres of blacksmith and locksmith crafts
⚓ Dockyards
S   Sulphur mills

◗ Copper smelters or workshops
▲ Copper manufactures
∴ Powder works
▬ Mica mining

45 East from Greenwich 50

COPYRIGHT. GEORGE PHILIP & SON. LTD.

THE EXPANSION OF RUSSIA IN EUROPE
1725–1855

Scale 1 : 20,000,000 (320 miles=1 inch)

| 0 | 100 | 200 | 300 | 400 Miles |

| 0 | 200 | 400 | 600 | Km. |

	Russian Empire 1725		Acquisitions 1825-1855 (Nicholas I)
	Acquisitions 1730-1740 (Anna Ivanovna)	**1795**	Date of acquisition
	Acquisitions 1740-1762 (Elisabeth Petrovna)		Boundary of Russia 1855
	Acquisitions 1762-1796 (Catherine II)		Bdies. of Provinces (Governments) after reorganisation of 1775
	Acquisitions 1796-1801 (Paul I)		Extent of rebellions 1735-74
	Acquisitions 1801-1825 (Alexander I)		Seas and lakes frozen in winter

45 East from Greenwich 50   55

COPYRIGHT. GEORGE PHILIP & SON. LTD.

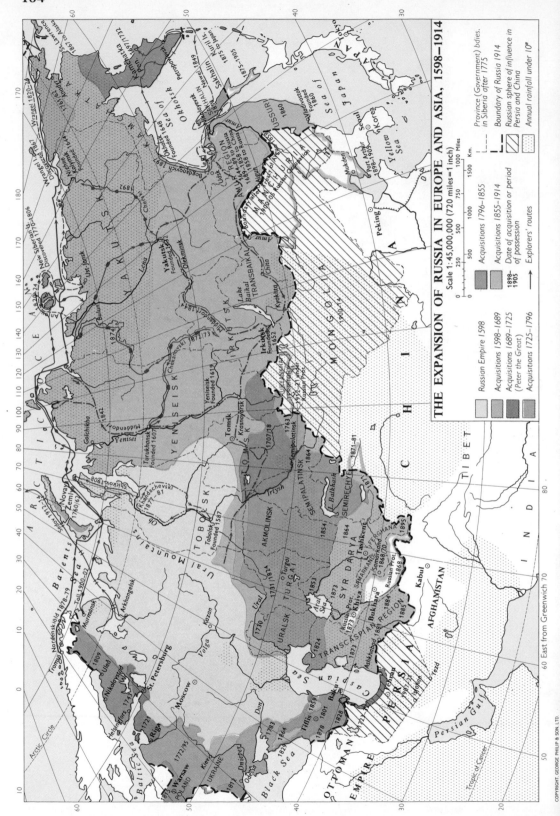

THE EXPANSION OF RUSSIA IN EUROPE AND ASIA, 1598–1914

Scale 1:45,000,000 (720 miles=1 inch)

	Russian Empire 1598
	Acquisitions 1598–1689
	Acquisitions 1689–1725 (Peter the Great)
	Acquisitions 1725–1796

	Acquisitions 1796–1855
	Acquisitions 1855–1914
1898–1905	Date of acquisition or period of possession
→	Explorers' routes

Province (Government) bdies. in Siberia after 1775
Boundary of Russia 1914
Russian sphere of influence in Persia and China
Annual rainfall under 10"

60 East from Greenwich 70

COPYRIGHT. GEORGE PHILIP & SON, LTD.

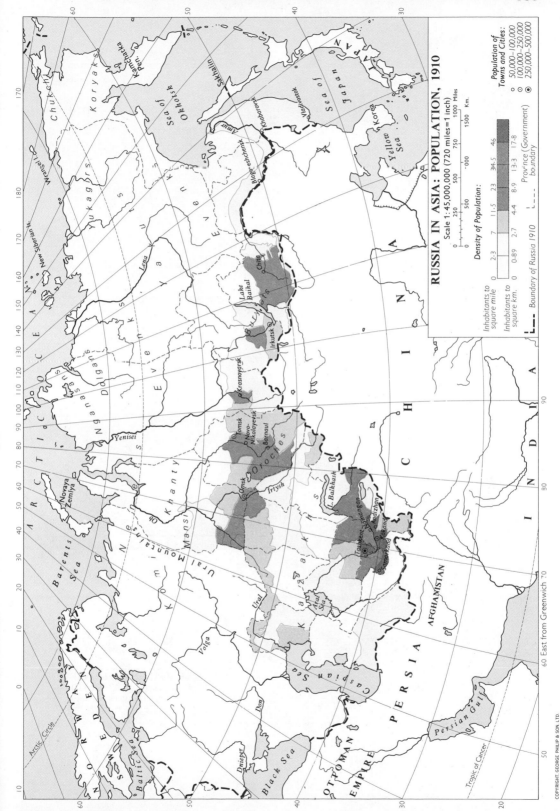

RUSSIA IN ASIA: POPULATION, 1910

Scale 1:45,000,000 (720 miles=1 inch)

| 0 | 250 | 500 | 750 | 1000 Miles |
| 0 | 500 | 1000 | 1500 Km. |

Density of Population:

Inhabitants to square mile

| 0 | 2.3 | 7 | 11.5 | 23 | 34.5 | 46 |

Inhabitants to square km.

| 0 | 0.89 | 2.7 | 4.4 | 8.9 | 13.3 | 17.8 |

Province (Government) boundary

Boundary of Russia 1910

Population of Towns and Cities:
- 50,000–100,000
- 100,000–250,000
- 250,000–500,000

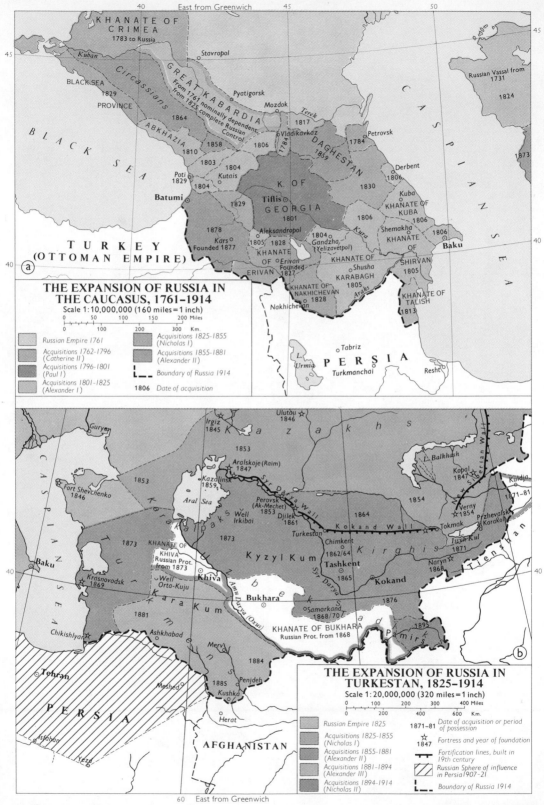

East from Greenwich

THE EXPANSION OF RUSSIA IN THE CAUCASUS, 1761–1914

Scale 1:10,000,000 (160 miles=1 inch)

0 50 100 150 200 Miles
0 100 200 300 Km.

- Russian Empire 1761
- Acquisitions 1762-1796 (Catherine II)
- Acquisitions 1796-1801 (Paul I)
- Acquisitions 1801-1825 (Alexander I)
- Acquisitions 1825-1855 (Nicholas I)
- Acquisitions 1855-1881 (Alexander II)
- - - Boundary of Russia 1914
- **1806** Date of acquisition

KHANATE OF CRIMEA
1783 to Russia
Kuban
BLACK SEA
1829
PROVINCE
Stavropol
Pyatigorsk
Mozdok
GREAT KABARDIA
From 1761 nominally dependent
from 1825 complete Russian Control
Circassians
1864
ABKHAZIA
1858
1810
1803
1804
Poti 1829
Kutais
1804
1829
Batumi
1878
Kars Founded 1877
1805 1828
KHANATE OF ERIVAN
Founded 1827
Aleksandropol
Erivan
KHANATE OF NAKHICHEVAN
1828
Nakhichevan
Terek
1817
Vladikavkaz
1806 1784
DAGHESTAN
1859
1784
Petrovsk
Derbent
1806
1830
K. OF GEORGIA
Tiflis
1801
Kura
1806
1806
Shemakha
KHANATE OF KUBA
Kuba
KHANATE OF SHIRVAN
1805
1806
Baku
1804
Gandzha (Yelizavetpol)
1804
Shusha
KHANATE OF KARABAGH
1805
Araks
KHANATE OF TALISH
1813

BLACK SEA

TURKEY (OTTOMAN EMPIRE)

CASPIAN SEA

Russian Vassal from 1731
1824
1873

PERSIA
Tabriz
Urmia
Turkmanchai
Resht

THE EXPANSION OF RUSSIA IN TURKESTAN, 1825–1914

Scale 1:20,000,000 (320 miles=1 inch)

0 100 200 300 400 Miles
0 200 400 600 Km.

- Russian Empire 1825
- Acquisitions 1825-1855 (Nicholas I)
- Acquisitions 1855-1881 (Alexander II)
- Acquisitions 1881-1894 (Alexander III)
- Acquisitions 1894-1914 (Nicholas II)
- **1871-81** Date of acquisition or period of possession
- ☆ **1847** Fortress and year of foundation
- Fortification lines, built in 19th century
- Russian Sphere of influence in Persia 1907-21
- - - Boundary of Russia 1914

Guryev
Irgiz 1845
Ulutou 1846
Kazakhs
1853
Aralskoje (Raim) 1847
Kazalinsk 1859
Fort Shevchenko 1846
1853
Aral Sea
Karakalpaks
Perovsk (Ak-Mechet) 1853
Well Irkibai
Djilek 1861
Syr Darya Wall
1873
1873
KHANATE OF
KHIVA Russian Prot. from 1873
Well Orta-Kuju
Khiva
Amu Darya (Oxus)
Kara Kum
1881
Chikishlyar
Krasnovodsk 1869
Baku
Ashkhabad
Merv
1884
Kushka
Penjdeh 1885
L. Balkhash
Kopal 1847
Verny 1854
Kuldja 1871-81
Przhevalsk Karakol
1854
Tokmak
Issyk Kul
1871
Kokand Wall
Turkestan
Chimkent 1862/64
Tashkent 1865
Kokand
Naryn 1868
Kyzyl Kum
Kirghiz
1864
Samarkand 1868/70
1876
KHANATE OF BUKHARA
Russian Prot. from 1868
Bukhara
Pamirs 1895
Tien-shan

PERSIA
Tehran
Meshed
Isfahan
Yezd
AFGHANISTAN
Herat

60 East from Greenwich

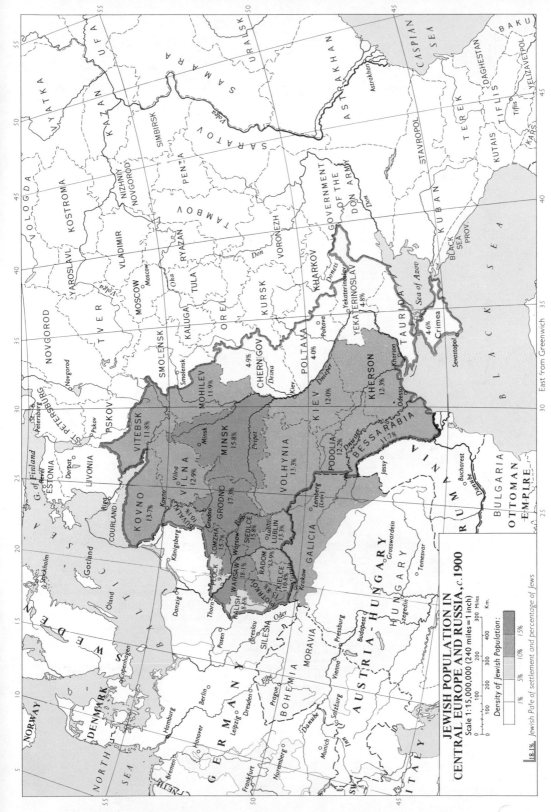

JEWISH POPULATION IN
CENTRAL EUROPE AND RUSSIA, c.1900

Scale 1:15,000,000 (240 miles=1 inch)

Density of Jewish Population:

1%   5%   10%   15%

8.1%   Jewish Pale of settlement and percentage of Jews

COPYRIGHT GEORGE PHILIP & SON LTD.

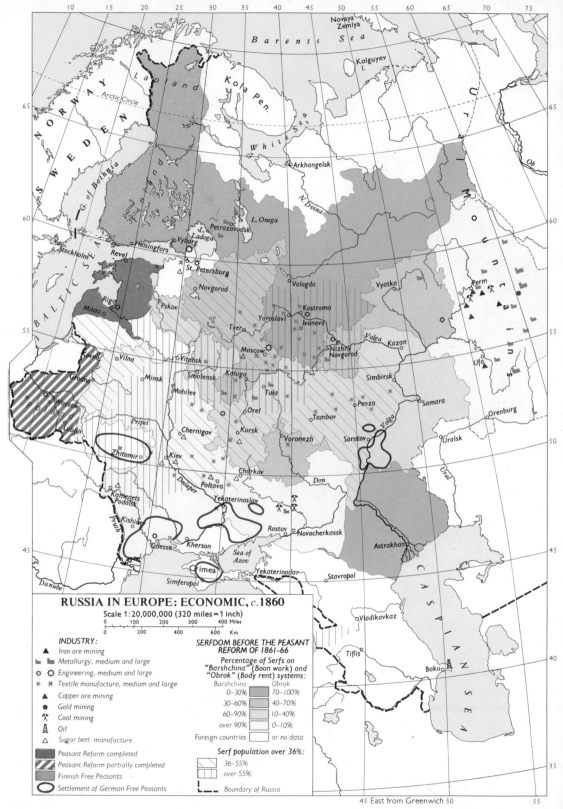

RUSSIA IN EUROPE: ECONOMIC, c.1860

Scale 1:20,000,000 (320 miles=1 inch)

0   100   200   300   400 Miles

0   200   400   600 Km.

INDUSTRY:

▲ Iron ore mining

🔨 Metallurgy, medium and large

⚙ Engineering, medium and large

✳ Textile manufacture, medium and large

▲ Copper ore mining

● Gold mining

⚒ Coal mining

⛏ Oil

△ Sugar beet manufacture

Peasant Reform completed

Peasant Reform partially completed

Finnish Free Peasants

◯ Settlement of German Free Peasants

SERFDOM BEFORE THE PEASANT REFORM OF 1861-66

Percentage of Serfs on "Barshchina" (Boon work) and "Obrok" (Body rent) systems:

Barshchina	Obrok
0-30%	70-100%
30-60%	40-70%
60-90%	10-40%
over 90%	0-10%

Foreign countries   or no data

Serf population over 36%:

36-55%

over 55%

▬ ▬ Boundary of Russia

45 East from Greenwich 50

COPYRIGHT. GEORGE PHILIP & SON, LTD.

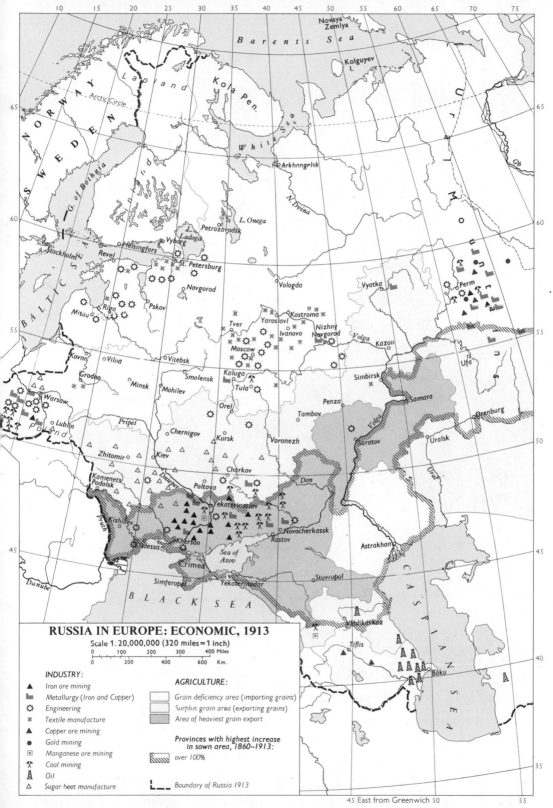

RUSSIA IN EUROPE: ECONOMIC, 1913

Scale 1:20,000,000 (320 miles = 1 inch)

0   100   200   300   400 Miles

0   200   400   600 Km.

INDUSTRY:

▲ Iron ore mining

▬ Metallurgy (Iron and Copper)

✿ Engineering

✳ Textile manufacture

▲ Copper ore mining

● Gold mining

▣ Manganese ore mining

⚒ Coal mining

⛽ Oil

△ Sugar beet manufacture

AGRICULTURE:

☐ Grain deficiency area (importing grains)

☐ Surplus grain area (exporting grains)

▨ Area of heaviest grain export

Provinces with highest increase in sown area, 1860–1913:

▨ over 100%

▟ Boundary of Russia 1913

45 East from Greenwich 50

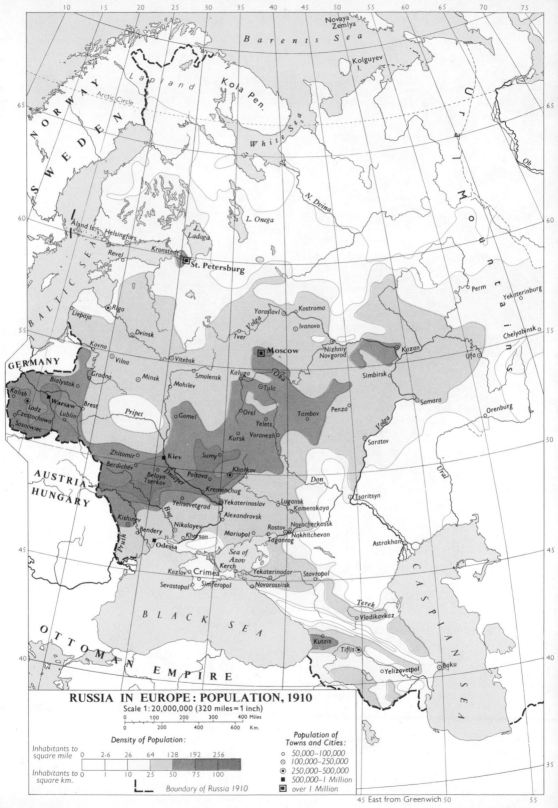

RUSSIA IN EUROPE: POPULATION, 1910

Scale 1:20,000,000 (320 miles=1 inch)

0   100   200   300   400 Miles

0   200   400   600 Km.

Density of Population:

Inhabitants to square mile	0	2·6	26	64	128	192	256
Inhabitants to square km.	0	1	10	25	50	75	100

Boundary of Russia 1910

Population of Towns and Cities:

∘   50,000–100,000
⊙   100,000–250,000
◉   250,000–500,000
■   500,000–1 Million
▣   over 1 Million

45 East from Greenwich 50

COPYRIGHT. GEORGE PHILIP & SON. LTD.

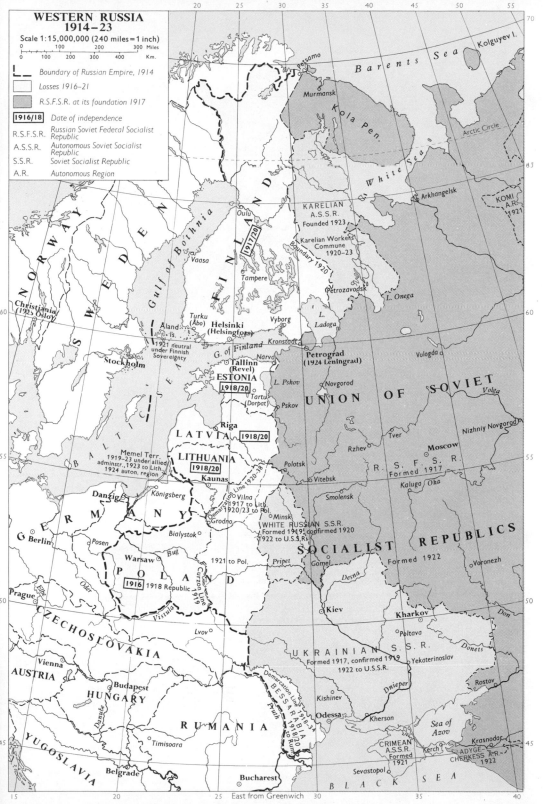

**WESTERN RUSSIA
1914–23**

Scale 1:15,000,000 (240 miles = 1 inch)

0   100   200   300 Miles
0   100   200   300   400   500
Km.

Boundary of Russian Empire, 1914

Losses 1916–21

R.S.F.S.R. at its foundation 1917

1916/18   Date of independence

R.S.F.S.R.   Russian Soviet Federal Socialist Republic

A.S.S.R.   Autonomous Soviet Socialist Republic

S.S.R.   Soviet Socialist Republic

A.R.   Autonomous Region

Barents   Sea   Kolguyev I.

Petsamo

Murmansk

Kola Pen.

Arctic Circle

KOMI
A.R.
1921

White Sea

Arkhangelsk

KARELIAN
A.S.S.R.
Founded 1923

Karelian Workers'
Commune
1920–23

Boundary 1920

N O R W A Y

S W E D E N

Oulu

1917/20

F I N L A N D

Vaasa

Tampere

Petrozavodsk

L. Onega

Gulf   of   Bothnia

Christiania
(1923) Oslo

Turku
(Åbo)

Helsinki
(Helsingfors)

Vyborg

L.
Ladoga

Åland
Is.
1921 neutral
under Finnish
Sovereignty

Stockholm

G. of Finland

Kronstadt

Vologda

Tallinn
(Revel)

Narva

Petrograd
(1924 Leningrad)

ESTONIA

1918/20

L. Pskov

Novgorod

U N I O N   O F   S O V I E T

Tartu
(Dorpat)

Pskov

Volga

B A L T I C   S E A

Riga

1918/20

Tver

Moscow

Nizhniy Novgorod

L A T V I A

Rzhev

R . S . F . S . R .
Formed 1917

LITHUANIA

1918/20

Polotsk

Kaluga   Oka

Memel Terr.
1919–23 under allied
adminstr., 1923 to Lith.
1924 auton. region

Kaunas

Vitebsk

Danzig

Königsberg

Demarcation Line 1920–38

Smolensk

G E R M A N Y

Vilna
1917 to Lith.
1920/23 to Pol.

Grodno

Minsk

WHITE RUSSIAN S.S.R.
Formed 1919, confirmed 1920
1922 to U.S.S.R.

S O C I A L I S T   R E P U B L I C S

Voronezh

G. Berlin

Posen

Bialystok

Pripet

Gomel

Formed 1922

Prague

Oder

Warsaw

Bug

1921 to Pol.

Desna

Curzon Line 1919

1916   1918 Republic

P O L A N D

C Z E C H O S L O V A K I A

Vistula

Lvov

Kiev

Kharkov

Poltava

Don

Donets

Vienna

AUSTRIA

Budapest

H U N G A R Y

U K R A I N I A N   S . S . R .
Formed 1917, confirmed 1919
1922 to U.S.S.R.

Yekaterinoslav

Rostov

Danube

Pruth

Demarcation Line 1918–34

BESSARABIA 1918/20

Kishinev

Dnieper

R U M A N I A

Timisoara

1918 to Rum.

Odessa

Kherson

Sea of
Azov

Krasnodar

Y U G O S L A V I A

Belgrade

Bucharest

CRIMEAN
A.S.S.R.
Formed
1921

Kerch

ADYGE
CHERKESS A.R.
1922

Sevastopol

B L A C K   S E A

East from Greenwich

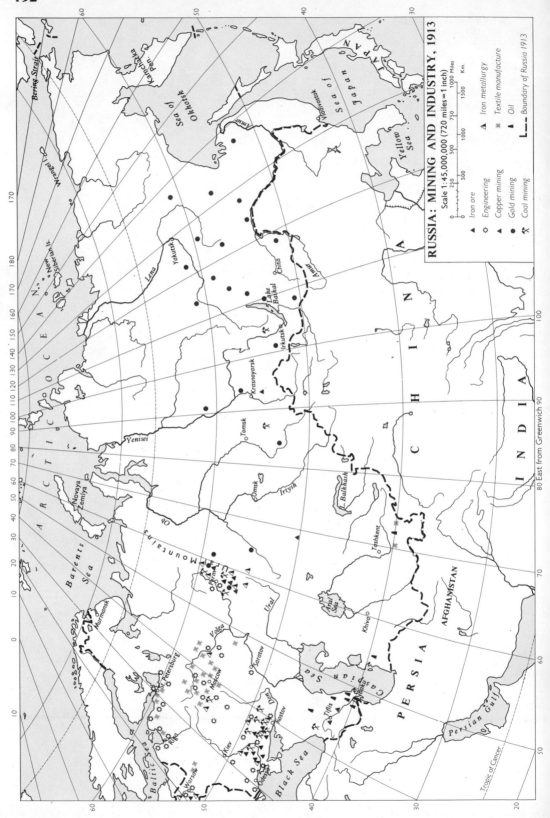

RUSSIA: MINING AND INDUSTRY, 1913

Scale 1:45,000,000 (720 miles=1 inch)

▲ Iron ore   ▲ Iron metallurgy

✿ Engineering   ✳ Textile manufacture

▲ Copper mining   ▲ Oil

● Gold mining   ▬ ▬ Boundary of Russia 1913

✖ Coal mining

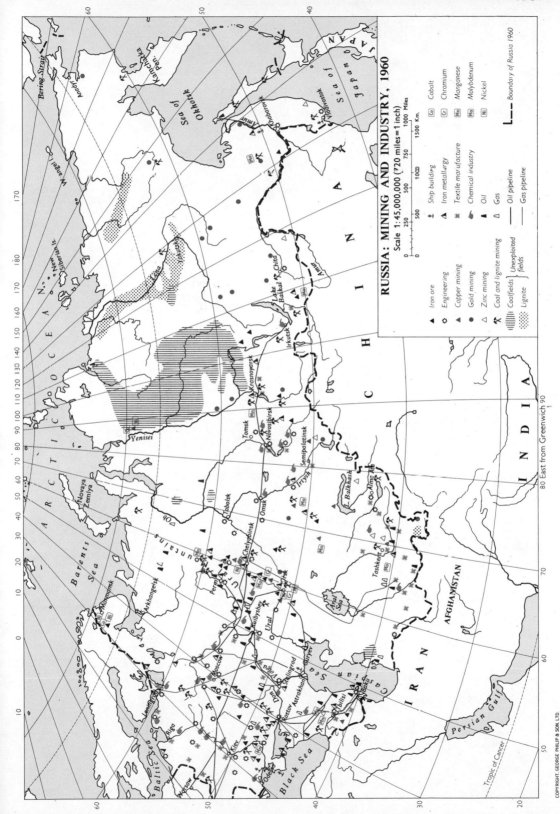

RUSSIA: MINING AND INDUSTRY, 1960

Scale 1:45,000,000 (720 miles=1 inch)

▲	Iron ore	
✿	Engineering	
▲	Copper mining	
●	Gold mining	
△	Zinc mining	
〴	Coal and lignite mining	
▥	Coalfields	Unexploited fields
⠿	Lignite	

⚓	Ship building	
▲	Iron metallurgy	
✳	Textile manufacture	
✳	Chemical industry	
▲	Oil	
△	Gas	
——	Oil pipeline	
——	Gas pipeline	

Co	Cobalt	
Cr	Chromium	
Mn	Manganese	
Mo	Molybdenum	
Ni	Nickel	
▄▄	Boundary of Russia 1960	

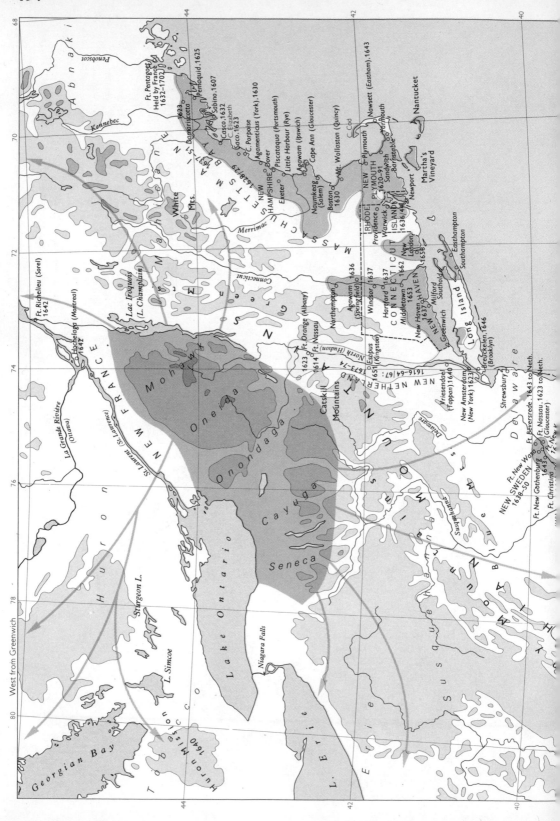

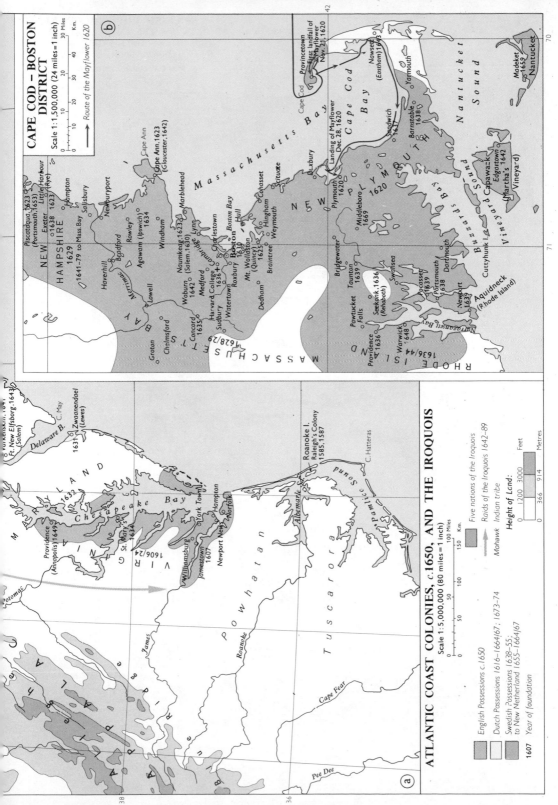

CAPE COD – BOSTON DISTRICT

Scale 1:1,500,000 (24 miles=1 inch)

0 10 20 30 Miles
0 10 20 30 40 Km.

→ Route of the Mayflower 1620

ⓑ

NEW HAMPSHIRE 1629

Piscataqua, 1623 (Portsmouth, 1653)
Little Harbour (Rye)
Exeter 1638
1623
Hampton
Salisbury
1641–79 to Mass. Bay
Haverhill
Bradford
Rowley
Agawam (Ipswich) 1634
Newburyport
Cape Ann, 1623 (Gloucester, 1642)
Windham
Marblehead
Naumkeag, 1623 (Salem, 1630)
Lynn
Charlestown
Harvard College 1636/38
Watertown
Cambridge
Boston 1630
Mt. Wollaston (Quincy) 1625
Roxbury
Hull
Boston Bay
Hingham 1633
Weymouth
Scituate
Cohasset
Duxbury
Plymouth 1620
Middleboro 1669
Bridgewater 1639
Taunton 1639
Swansea
Dorchester
Sandwich 1637
Barnstable 1638
Yarmouth
Nowsett (Eastham) 1644
Landing of Mayflower Dec. 28, 1620
First landfall of Mayflower Nov. 21, 1620
Provincetown
Cape Cod
Cape Cod Bay

MASSACHUSETTS BAY

Medford
Woburn 1642
Dedham
Sudbury
Concord 1635
Chelmsford
Groton
Lowell
Merrimac
Massachusetts Bay

Bay
1628/29

NEW PLYMOUTH

Nantucket Sound

Buzzards Bay
Cuttyhunk I.
Capawack
Vineyard Sound
Edgartown 1642
Martha's Vineya'd
Madeket 1659
Nantucket

RHODE ISLAND 1636/44

Providence 1636
Pawtucket Falls
Seekonk, 1636 (Rehoboth)
Warwick 1648
Pocasset 1639
Portsmouth 1638
Newport 1639
Aquidneck (Rhode Island)
Dartmouth
Narragansett Bay

42

70

71

ATLANTIC COAST COLONIES, c.1650, AND THE IROQUOIS

Scale 1:5,000,000 (80 miles=1 inch)

0 50 100 150 Miles
0 50 100 150 Km.

ⓐ

MARYLAND

Providence (Annapolis) 1649
St. Mary's 1634
Potomac
Chesapeake Bay
Williamsburg
Jamestown 1607
York Town
1606/24
Newport News
Hampton
Norfolk
Albemarle Sd.

Ft. Kreiskill, 1631
Zwaanendael (Lewes)
Delaware B.
C. May
New Elfsborg, 1643

VIRGINIA

Roanoke
James
Powhatan

Tuscarora

Roanoke I. Raleigh's Colony 1585, 1587
Pamlico Sd.
C. Hatteras

Sound

Cape Fear
Pee Dee

Legend:

English Possessions c.1650

Dutch Possessions 1616–1664/67; 1673–74

Swedish Possessions 1638–55; to New Netherland 1655–1664/67

1607 Year of foundation

Five nations of the Iroquois

→ Raids of the Iroquois 1642–89

Mohawk Indian tribe

Height of Land:

| 0 | 1200 | 3000 | Feet |
| 0 | 366 | 914 | Metres |

38

36

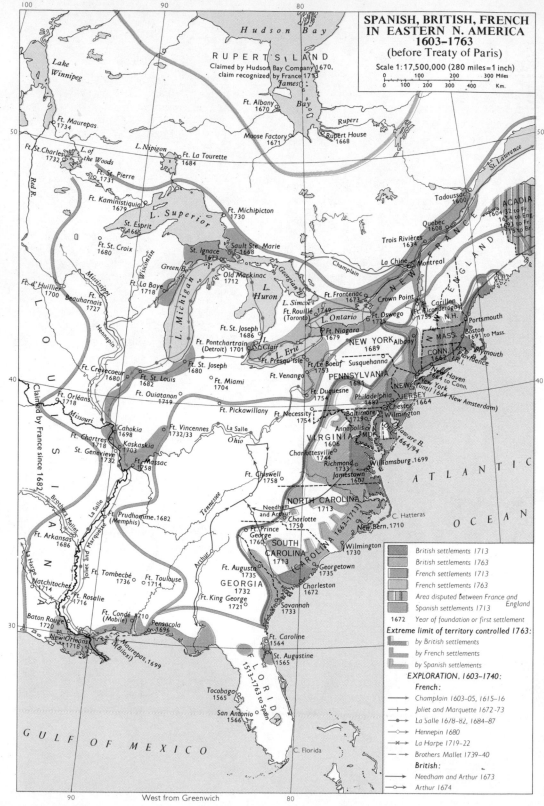

**SPANISH, BRITISH, FRENCH
IN EASTERN N. AMERICA
1603-1763**
(before Treaty of Paris)

Scale 1:17,500,000 (280 miles=1 inch)

| | | | |
0   100   200   300 Miles
0   100   200   300   400 Km.

Hudson Bay

RUPERT'S LAND
Claimed by Hudson Bay Company 1670,
claim recognized by France 1713

James
Bay

Ft. Albany
1670

Moose Factory
1671

Rupert

Rupert House
1668

Lake
Winnipeg

Ft. Maurepas
1734

L. Nipigon

Ft. La Tourette
1684

Ft. St Charles
1732

L. of
the Woods

Ft. St. Pierre
1731

Red R.

Ft. Kaministiquia
1679

Ft. Michipicton
1730

L. Superior

St. Esprit
1665

Tadoussac
1600

ACADIA
1604 to Eng.
1654 to Eng.
1667 to Fr.
1691 to Fr.
1713 to Br.

Quebec
1608

Ft. St. Croix
1680

Sault Ste. Marie
1668

Trois Rivières
1634

St. Ignace
1673

Ft. d'Huillier
1700

Wisconsin

Green B.

La Baye
1718

Old Mackinac
1712

Georgian B.

Champlain

La Chine

Montreal

Ft.
Beauharnais
1727

Hennepin

L. Michigan

*L.
Huron*

L. Simcoe

Ft. Frontenac
1673

Crown Point

Ft. Carillon
(Ticonderoga)
1755

N.H.

Mississippi

Ft. St. Joseph
1686

Ft. Rouillé
(Toronto) 1749

L. Ontario

Ft. Oswego
1722

Portsmouth

Ft. Crevecoeur
1680

Ft. Pontchartrain
(Detroit) 1701

St. Clair

Ft. Niagara
1679

NEW YORK
1689

Albany

N. MASS.
Boston
1691 to Mass.

Ft. St. Joseph
1680

Ft. St. Louis
1682

L. Erie

Ft. Presqu'Isle

PENNSYLVANIA
1681

CONN.
1662

Plymouth

New Haven
1664 until 1664 to Conn.

R.I.

Providence

Ft. Miami
1704

Ft. Ouiatanon
1719

Ft. Le Boeuf
1753

Susquehanna

**NEW
JERSEY**
1664

New York
1664 (New Amsterdam)
until 1664

L O U I S I A N A

Ft. Orléans
1718

Missouri

Ft. Venango

Ft. Duquesne
1754

Philadelphia
1682

Ft. Pickawillany

Ft. Necessity
1754

Chester
1720

Wilmington

Baltimore
1729

Cahokia
1698

Ft. Chartres
1718

Ft. Vincennes
1732/33

La Salle

Ohio

Delaware B.
1664/94

Kaskaskia
1703

Ft. St. Louis

VIRGINIA
1606

Annapolis
MD.

St. Genevieve
1732

Ft. Massac
1758

Charlottesville
1744

Williamsburg 1699

A T L A N T I C

Richmond
1733

Jamestown
1607

Ft. Chiswell
1758

Claimed by France since 1682

Brothers Mallet

Tennessee

Arthur

NORTH CAROLINA
1713

O C E A N

La Salle

Needham
and Arthur

Charlotte
1750

C. Hatteras

Ft. Prudhomme 1682
(Memphis)

Ft. Prince
George
1760

New Bern 1710

Ft. Arkansas
1686

**SOUTH
CAROLINA**
1713

Wilmington
1730

(CAROLINA 1663-1713)

Georgetown
1735

Natchitoches
1714

La Harpe

Ft. Rosalie
1716

Joliet and Marquette

Ft. Tombecbé
1736

Ft. Augusta
1735

Ft. Toulouse
1714

GEORGIA
1732

Charleston
1672

Baton Rouge
1720

Ft. Condé
(Mobile) 1710

Ft. King George
1721

Savannah
1733

New Orleans
1718

Pensacola
1696

R. Maurepas
(Biloxi), 1699

Ft. Caroline
1564

F L O R I D A
1513-1763 to Spain

St. Augustine
1565

G U L F   O F   M E X I C O

Tocobaga
1565

San Antonio
1566

C. Florida

	British settlements 1713
	British settlements 1763
	French settlements 1713
	French settlements 1763
	Area disputed between France and England
	Spanish settlements 1713
1672	Year of foundation or first settlement

Extreme limit of territory controlled 1763:
by British settlements
by French settlements
by Spanish settlements

EXPLORATION, 1603-1740:
French:
Champlain 1603-05, 1615-16
Joliet and Marquette 1672-73
La Salle 1678-82, 1684-87
Hennepin 1680
La Harpe 1719-22
Brothers Mallet 1739-40
British:
Needham and Arthur 1673
Arthur 1674

100   90   80

50   50

40   40

30   30

90   West from Greenwich   80

Quebec
1759 to Br.

Trois Rivières

N E W   F R A N C E

Montreal
1760 to Br.

Chambly

Ottawa
La
Chine

Ft. St. John's
1713 to Br.

L.
Champlain

St. Lawrence

La Présentation

Ft. Frontenac
1758 to Br.

Crown Point
1759 to Br.

Ft. Independence

Ipswich

Portland

Ft. Rouillé
(Toronto)

L. Ontario

Ft. Oswego
1726/27 to Br.

Ft. Ontario
1755 to Br.

Ft. Ticonderoga
1759 to Br.

Ft. William Henry

Ft. Anne

Concord

Portsmouth

Ft. Niagara
1759 to Br.

Ft. Stanwix

Ft. George

Ft. Edward
1755 to Br.

Londonderry

Ft. Herkimer

Mohawk

Ft. Dummer

Salem

Boston

C. Cod

L. Erie

Ft. Hunter

Hudson

Albany

MASSACHUSETTS

Worcester

Ft. Presqu'Isle

N E W   Y O R K

Northampton

Springfield

RHODE

Plymouth

Ft. Le Boeuf

Kingston

Hartford

Providence

Warwick   ISLAND

Newport

Ft. Venango

Susquehanna

Newburgh

CONNECTICUT

New
Haven

Ft. Augusta

Wilkes Barre

Ft.
Montgomery

Long I.

Ohio

P E N N S Y L V A N I A

Sunbury

Delaware

New York

Brooklyn

Ft. Duquesne
(Ft. Pitt)

Ft. Ligonier

Carlisle

N E W

Ft. Necessity

Germantown

Trenton

J E R S E Y

Ft. Bedford

York

Philadelphia

Burlington

A T L A N T I C

Ft. Cumberland

Hagerstown

Wilmington

Winchester

Baltimore

M A R Y L A N D

DELAWARE

Potomac

Shenandoah

Mount Vernon

Delaware Bay

O C E A N

Staunton

Charlottesville

V I R G I N I A

James

Chesapeake Bay

Richmond

Williamsburg

Jamestown

Yorktown

Norfolk

Warrenton

Roanoke

Hillsboro

Salem

N O R T H   C A R O L I N A

C. Hatteras

New Bern

Cheraw
SOUTH
CAROLINA

Elizabethtown

Wilmington

Simcoe

Georgian Bay

Blue Ridge Mts

Alleghany Mts

NORTH-EAST AMERICA TO 1763: BRITISH AND FRENCH RIVALRY
(before Treaty of Paris)

Scale 1: 7,500,000 (120 miles = 1 inch)

| 0 | 50 | 100 | 150 Miles |

| 0 | 50 | 100 | 150 | 200 Km. |

☐ *British settlements*

☐ *French settlements*

☐ *Extreme limit of territory controlled in 1763 by British settlements*

☐ *Extreme limit of territory controlled in 1763 by French settlements*

☆ *British fort*

☆ *French fort*

★ *French fort to Britain in Seven Years' War*

═ *Main colonial road*

── *Secondary road or trail*

Height of Land:

| 0 | 1200 | 3000 | Feet |

| 0 | 366 | 914 | Metres |

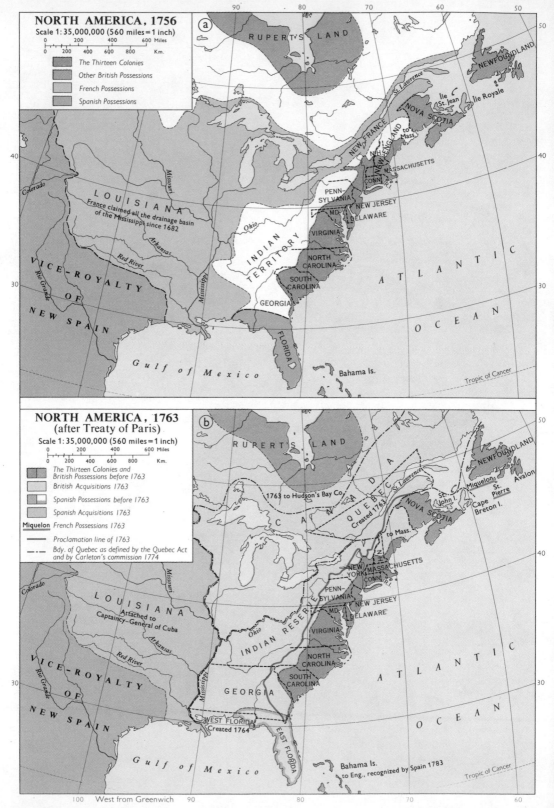

NORTH AMERICA, 1756

Scale 1:35,000,000 (560 miles=1 inch)

- The Thirteen Colonies
- Other British Possessions
- French Possessions
- Spanish Possessions

RUPERT'S LAND

NEWFOUNDLAND

St. Lawrence

Ile St. Jean · Ile Royale

NEW FRANCE

NOVA SCOTIA

to Mass.

NEW ENGLAND

N.H.

CONN.

MASSACHUSETTS

PENN-SYLVANIA

NEW JERSEY

MD. DELAWARE

Ohio

INDIAN TERRITORY

VIRGINIA

NORTH CAROLINA

SOUTH CAROLINA

GEORGIA

ATLANTIC OCEAN

Colorado

Missouri

L O U I S I A N A

France claimed all the drainage basin of the Mississippi since 1682

Arkansas

Red River

V I C E - R O Y A L T Y

O F

N E W S P A I N

Rio Grande

Mississippi

FLORIDA

Gulf of Mexico

Bahama Is.

Tropic of Cancer

a

NORTH AMERICA, 1763
(after Treaty of Paris)

Scale 1:35,000,000 (560 miles=1 inch)

- The Thirteen Colonies and British Possessions before 1763
- British Acquisitions 1763
- Spanish Possessions before 1763
- Spanish Acquisitions 1763
- Miquelon French Possessions 1763
- —— Proclamation line of 1763
- -·-·- Bdy. of Quebec as defined by the Quebec Act and by Carleton's commission 1774

RUPERT'S LAND

1763 to Hudson's Bay Co.

C A N A D A

QUEBEC Created 1763

St. Lawrence

St. John I.

Miquelon, St. Pierre

NEWFOUNDLAND

Avalon

NOVA SCOTIA

Cape Breton I.

to Mass.

NEW YORK

CONN.

MASSACHUSETTS

N.J.

R.I.

PENN-SYLVANIA

NEW JERSEY

MD. DELAWARE

Ohio

INDIAN RESERVE

VIRGINIA

NORTH CAROLINA

SOUTH CAROLINA

GEORGIA

Colorado

Missouri

L O U I S I A N A

Attached to Captaincy-General of Cuba

Arkansas

Red River

V I C E - R O Y A L T Y

O F

N E W S P A I N

Rio Grande

Mississippi

WEST FLORIDA Created 1764

EAST FLORIDA

ATLANTIC OCEAN

Gulf of Mexico

Bahama Is.
to Eng., recognized by Spain 1783

Tropic of Cancer

b

100   West from Greenwich   90

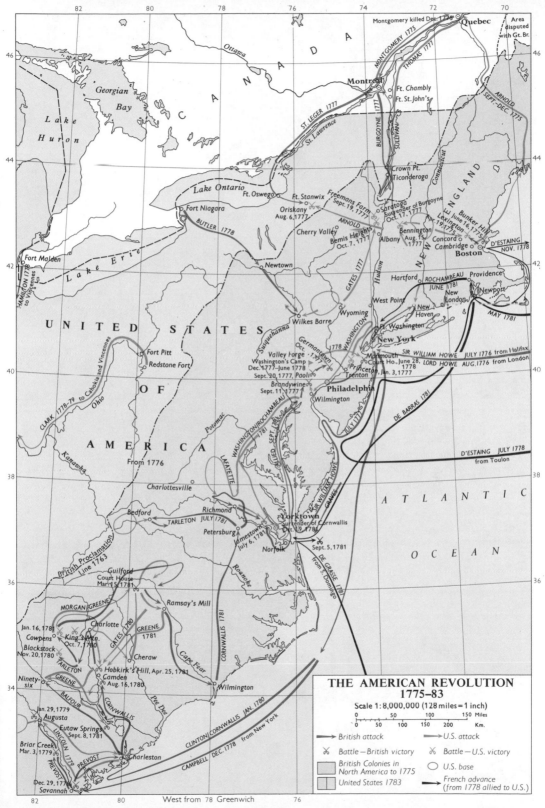

Montgomery killed Dec. 1775 — **Quebec**
Ft. Chambly
Ft. St. John's

Georgian Bay

Area disputed with Gt. Br.

ARNOLD SEPT.-DEC. 1775

Lake Huron

C A N A D A

Ottawa

St. Lawrence

Montreal

ST. LEGER 1777

MONTGOMERY 1777

THOMAS 1777

BURGOYNE 1777

SULLIVAN

Crown Pt.
Ticonderoga

Connecticut

Lake Ontario

Ft. Oswego

Fort Niagara

Ft. Stanwix

Freemans Farm
Sept. 19, 1777

Oriskany
Aug. 6, 1777

BUTLER 1778

Cherry Valley

Bemis Heights
Oct. 7, 1777

ARNOLD

Saratoga
Surrender of Burgoyne
Oct. 17, 1777

Albany

Bennington
Aug. 15, 1777

N E W

E N G L A N D

Bunker Hill
June 16, 1775

Concord
Cambridge
Lexington Apr. 19, 1775

Boston

D'ESTAING
NOV. 1778

Fort Malden

HAMILTON 1778
to Vincennes

Lake Erie

Newtown

GATES 1777

Hudson

Hartford

Susquehanna

Wyoming

Wilkes Barre

West Point

New Haven

ROCHAMBEAU

JUNE 1781

New London

Providence

Newport

U N I T E D   S T A T E S

Fort Pitt

Redstone Fort

CLARK 1778-79 to Cahokia and Vincennes

Ohio

O F

Kanawha

A M E R I C A
From 1776

Charlottesville

Potomac

Germantown
Oct. 4, 1777

1778 WASHINGTON

New York

Ft. Washington

Valley Forge
Washington's Camp
Dec. 1777-June 1778
Sept. 20, 1777, Paoli

Brandywine
Sept. 11, 1777

Philadelphia

Wilmington

Monmouth
Court Ho., June 28, 1778
Princeton, Jan. 3, 1777
Trenton, Jan. 3, 1777

SIR WILLIAM HOWE   JULY 1776 from Halifax
LORD HOWE   AUG.1776 from London

JULY 1777

DE BARRAS 1781

D'ESTAING   JULY 1778
from Toulon

WASHINGTON/ROCHAMBEAU 1781
ALLIED-SEPT. 1781

LAFAYETTE

Bedford

Richmond

TARLETON JULY 1781

Petersburg

Jamestown
July 6, 1781

Norfolk

Yorktown
Surrender of Cornwallis
Oct. 19, 1781

SIR WILLIAM HOWE

GAINES

DE GRASSE 1781
from S. Domingo

Sept. 5, 1781

A T L A N T I C

O C E A N

British Proclamation Line 1763

Guilford
Court House
Mar. 15, 1781

Ramsay's Mill

Roanoke

CORNWALLIS 1781

MORGAN GREENE

Charlotte

GREENE
1781

GATES 1780

King's Mtn.
Oct. 7, 1780

Jan. 16, 1781
Cowpens
Blackstock
Nov. 20, 1780

TARLETON

Cheraw

Cape Fear

Hobkirk's Hill, Apr. 25, 1781
Camden
Aug. 16, 1780

GREENE

Ninety-six

BALFOUR

Wilmington

Pee Dee

Jan. 29, 1779
Augusta

CORNWALLIS

Eutaw Springs
Sept. 8, 1781

LINCOLN 1779

CLINTON/CORNWALLIS JAN. 1780

CAMPBELL DEC. 1778 from New York

Briar Creek
Mar. 3, 1779

PREVOST

Dec. 29, 1778
Savannah

Charleston

THE AMERICAN REVOLUTION
1775–83

Scale 1: 8,000,000 (128 miles = 1 inch)

0   50   100   150 Miles

0   50   100   150   200 Km.

→ British attack   → U.S. attack

✗ Battle—British victory   ✗ Battle—U.S. victory

British Colonies in North America to 1775   ○ U.S. base

United States 1783   → French advance (from 1778 allied to U.S.)

West from 78 Greenwich

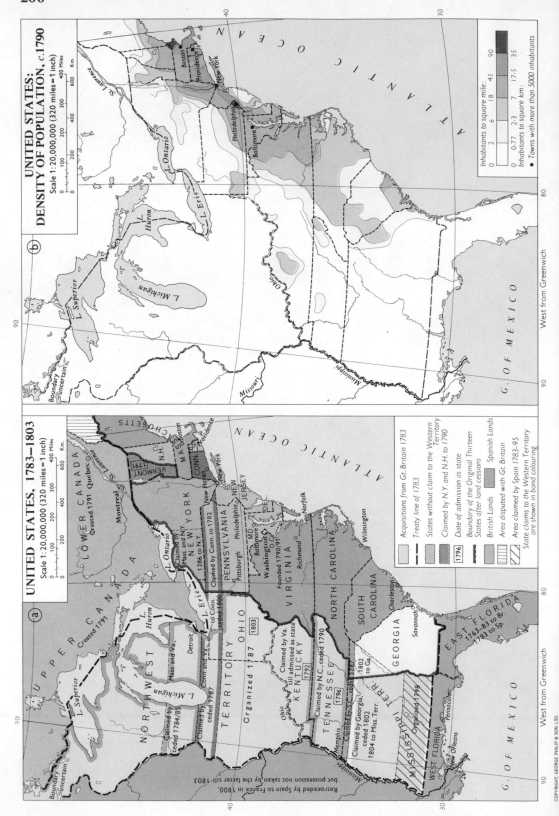

UNITED STATES:
DENSITY OF POPULATION, c.1790

Scale 1:20,000,000 (320 miles = 1 inch)

0   200   400   600   Km.
0   200   400 Miles

Inhabitants to square mile:
0   0.77   2.3   7   17.5   35
0   2   6   18   45   90
Inhabitants to square km:
● Towns with more than 5000 inhabitants

UNITED STATES, 1783–1803

Scale 1:20,000,000 (320 miles = 1 inch)

0   200   400   600   Km.
0   200   400 Miles

Acquisitions from Gt. Britain 1783
Treaty line of 1783
States without claim to the Western Territory
Claimed by N.Y. and N.H. to 1790
Date of admission as state
Boundary of the Original Thirteen States after land cessions
British Lands   Spanish Lands
Area disputed with Gt. Britain
State claims to the Western Territory are shown in band colouring

1796

COPYRIGHT GEORGE PHILIP & SON, LTD.

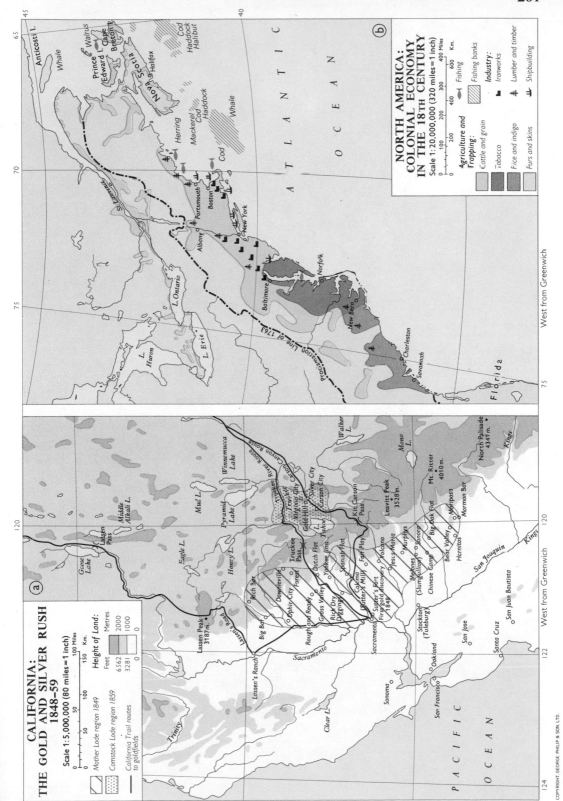

CALIFORNIA: THE GOLD AND SILVER RUSH 1848–59

Scale 1:5,000,000 (80 miles = 1 inch)

Mother Lode region 1849
Comstock Lode region 1859
California Trail routes to goldfields

Height of Land:
Feet Metres
6562 2000
3281 1000
0   0

NORTH AMERICA: COLONIAL ECONOMY IN THE 18TH CENTURY

Scale 1:20,000,000 (320 miles = 1 inch)

Agriculture and Trapping:
Cattle and grain
Tobacco
Rice and indigo
Furs and skins

Fishing
Fishing banks

Industry:
Ironworks
Lumber and timber
Shipbuilding

West from Greenwich

COPYRIGHT GEORGE PHILIP & SON LTD.

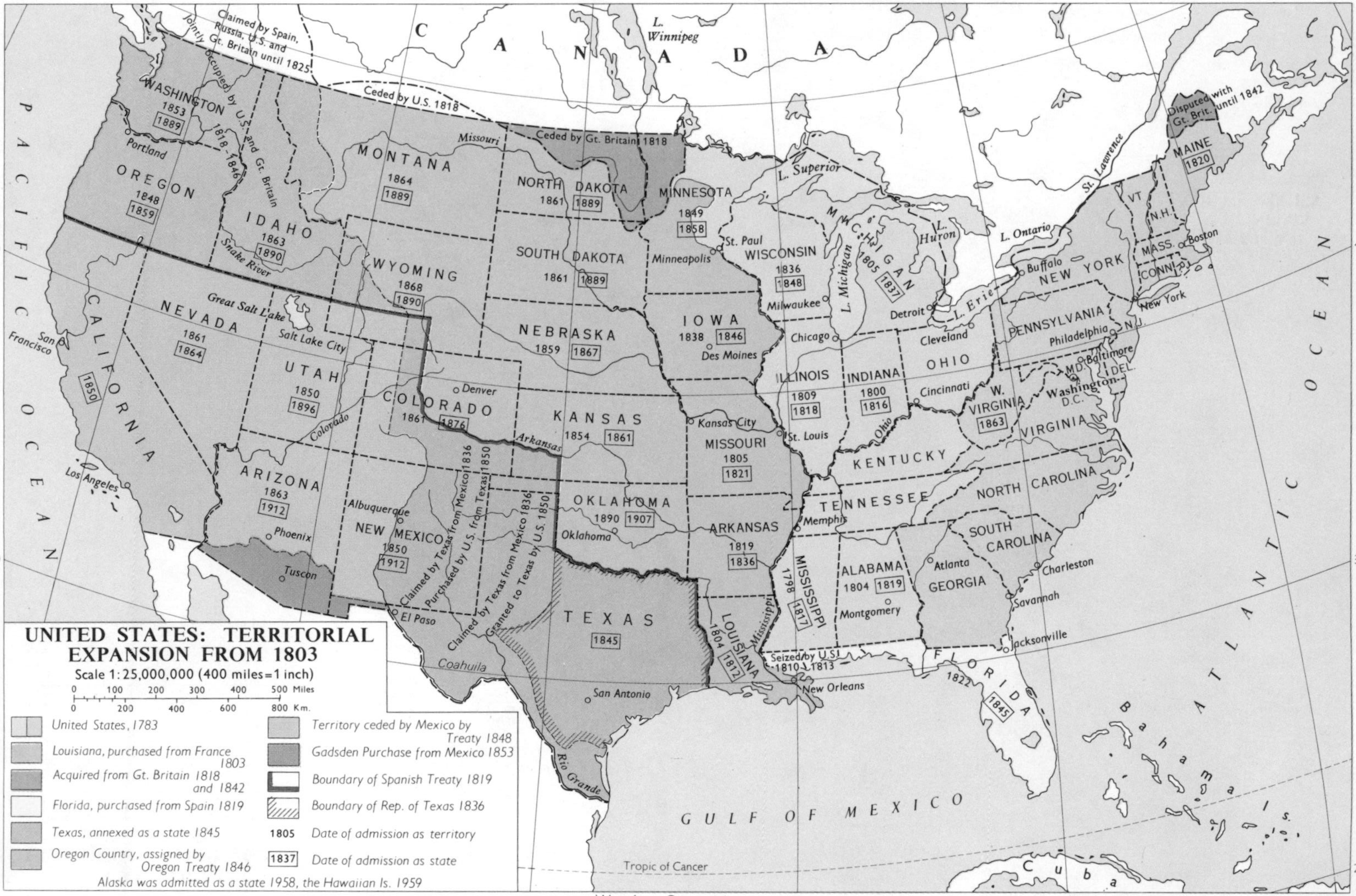

UNITED STATES: TERRITORIAL
EXPANSION FROM 1803
Scale 1:25,000,000 (400 miles=1 inch)

| 0 | 100 | 200 | 300 | 400 | 500 Miles |

| 0 | 100 | 200 | 300 | 400 | 500 | 600 | 700 | 800 Km. |

United States, 1783

Louisiana, purchased from France 1803

Acquired from Gt. Britain 1818 and 1842

Florida, purchased from Spain 1819

Texas, annexed as a state 1845

Oregon Country, assigned by
Oregon Treaty 1846

Alaska was admitted as a state 1958, the Hawaiian Is. 1959

Territory ceded by Mexico by
Treaty 1848

Gadsden Purchase from Mexico 1853

Boundary of Spanish Treaty 1819

Boundary of Rep. of Texas 1836

1805 Date of admission as territory

1837 Date of admission as state

COPYRIGHT GEORGE PHILIP & SON, LTD.

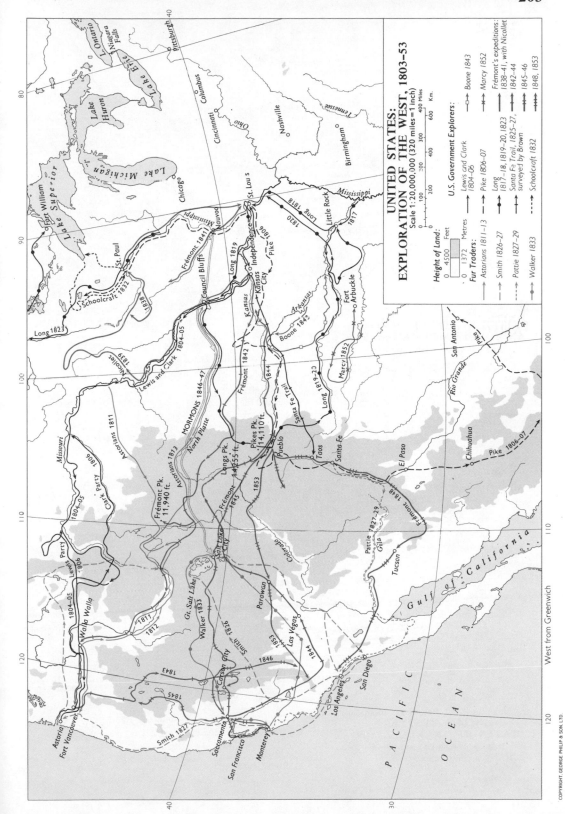

UNITED STATES:
EXPLORATION OF THE WEST, 1803–53
Scale 1:20,000,000 (320 miles=1 inch)

Height of Land:
Feet Metres
4500 1372
0   0

U.S. Government Explorers:
Lewis and Clark 1804–06
Pike 1806–07
Long 1817–18, 1819–20, 1823
Santa Fe Trail, 1825–27, surveyed by Brown
Schoolcraft 1832

Fur Traders:
Smith 1826–27
Pattie 1827–29
Walker 1833

Explorers:
Boone 1843
Marcy 1852

Frémont's expeditions:
1838–41, with Nicollet
1842–44
1845–46
1848, 1853

0 100 200 300 400 Miles
0 200 400 600 Km.

West from Greenwich

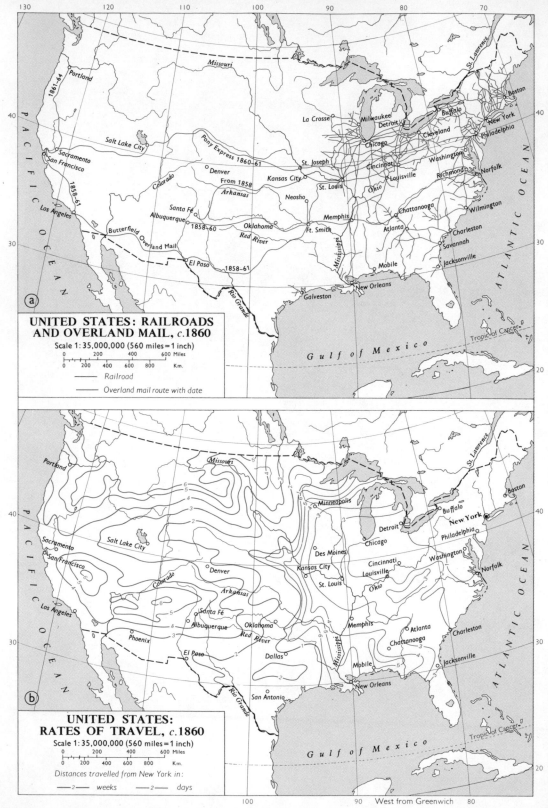

(a)

UNITED STATES: RAILROADS AND OVERLAND MAIL, *c.*1860

Scale 1:35,000,000 (560 miles = 1 inch)

0 200 400 600 Miles
0 200 400 600 800 Km.

—— Railroad

—— Overland mail route with date

(b)

UNITED STATES: RATES OF TRAVEL, *c.*1860

Scale 1:35,000,000 (560 miles = 1 inch)

0 200 400 600 Miles
0 200 400 600 800 Km.

Distances travelled from New York in:

—2— weeks   —2— days

West from Greenwich

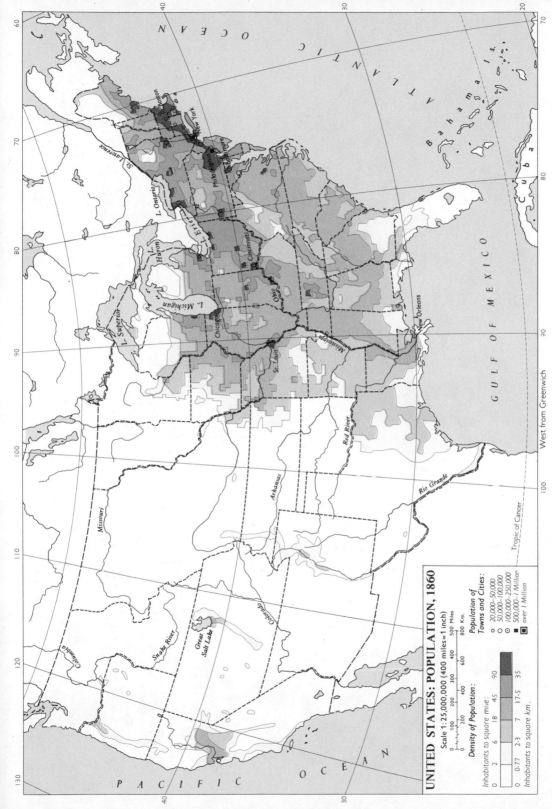

UNITED STATES: POPULATION, 1860

Scale 1:25,000,000 (400 miles=1 inch)

Population of Towns and Cities:
- ○ 20,000–50,000
- ○ 50,000–100,000
- ◉ 100,000–250,000
- ■ 500,000–1 Million
- ▣ over 1 Million

Density of Population:

Inhabitants to square mile:
0   2   6   18   45   90
0   0.77   2·3   7   17·5   35
Inhabitants to square km.

0   100   200   300   400   500 Miles
0   200   400   600   800 Km.

West from Greenwich

COPYRIGHT. GEORGE PHILIP & SON, LTD.

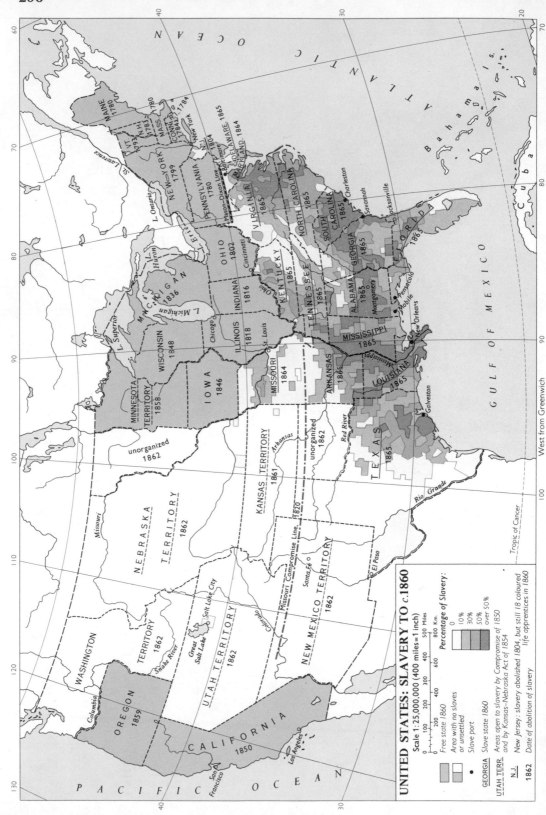

UNITED STATES: SLAVERY TO c.1860

Scale 1:25,000,000 (400 miles=1 inch)

0 100 200 300 400 500 Miles

0 200 400 600 800 Km.

Percentage of Slavery:

0
10%
30%
50%
over 50%

Free state 1860

Area with no slaves or unsettled

● Slave port

GEORGIA   Slave state 1860

Areas open to slavery by Compromise of 1850 and by Kansas–Nebraska Act of 1854

N.J.   New Jersey: slavery abolished 1804, but still 18 coloured
1862   life apprentices in 1860

UTAH TERR.   Date of abolition of slavery

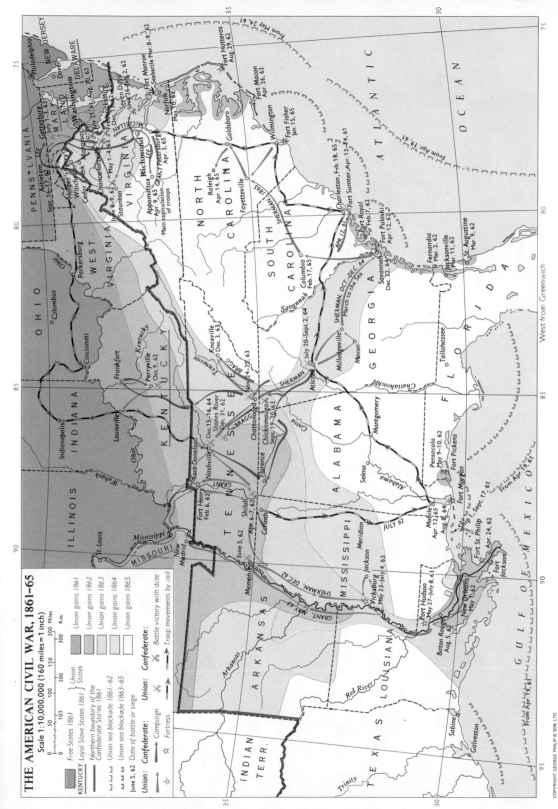

THE AMERICAN CIVIL WAR, 1861-65
Scale 1:10,000,000 (160 miles = 1 inch)

Free States 1861

KENTUCKY Loyal Slave States 1861 } Union States

Northern boundary of the Confederate States 1861

Union sea blockade 1861–62

Union sea blockade 1863–65

June 5, 62 Date of battle or siege

	Confederate:	Union:
Campaign		
Fortress		
Battle victory with date		
Troop movements by rail		

Union gains 1861
Union gains 1862
Union gains 1863
Union gains 1864
Union gains 1865

0 50 100 150 200 Miles
0 100 200 300 Km.

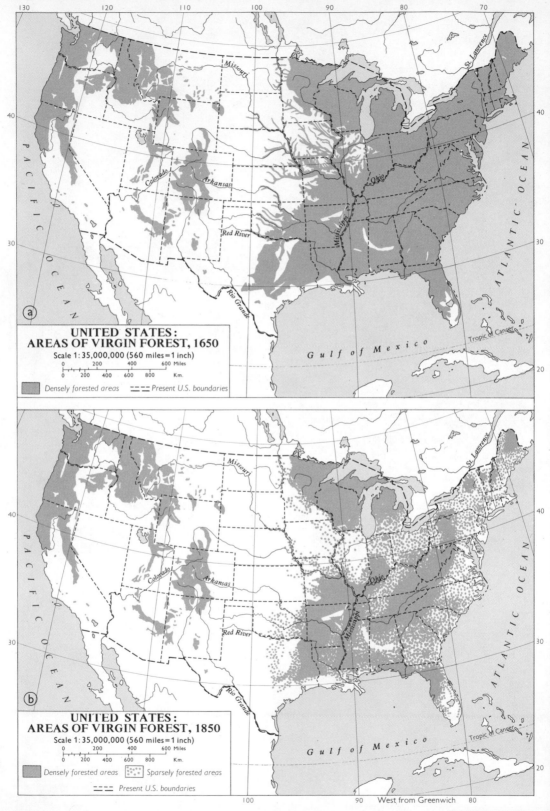

UNITED STATES:
AREAS OF VIRGIN FOREST, 1650

Scale 1:35,000,000 (560 miles=1 inch)

0   200   400   600 Miles

0   200   400   600   800   Km.

■ Densely forested areas   ‒‒‒ Present U.S. boundaries

UNITED STATES:
AREAS OF VIRGIN FOREST, 1850

Scale 1:35,000,000 (560 miles=1 inch)

0   200   400   600 Miles

0   200   400   600   800   Km.

■ Densely forested areas   ░ Sparsely forested areas

‒‒‒ Present U.S. boundaries

West from Greenwich   80

COPYRIGHT. GEORGE PHILIP & SON. LTD.

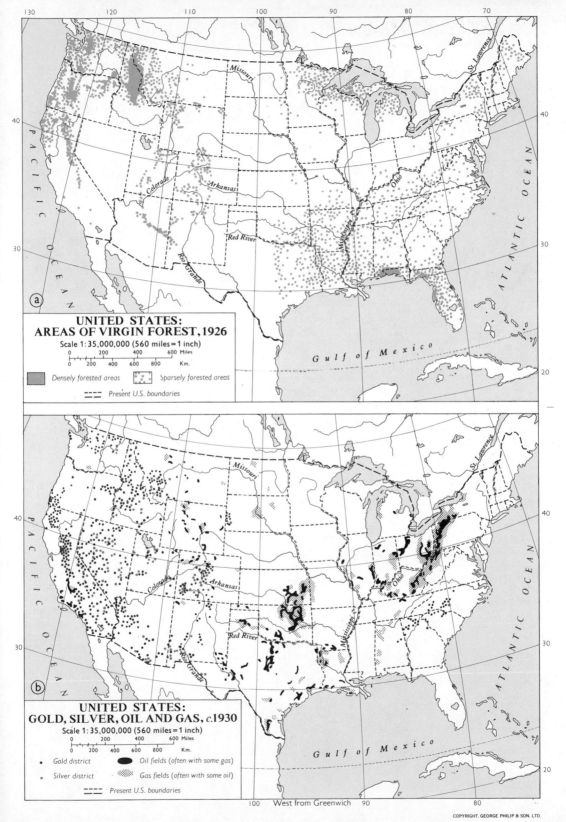

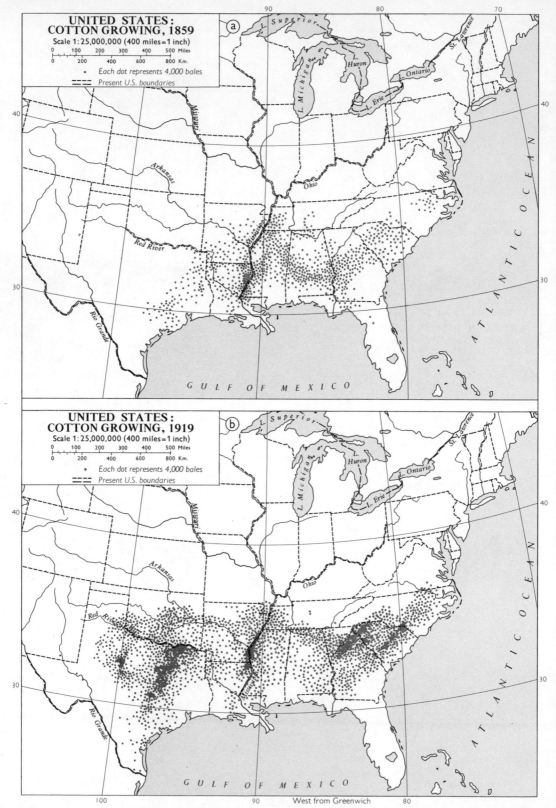

**UNITED STATES:
COTTON GROWING, 1859**

Scale 1:25,000,000 (400 miles=1 inch)

0   100 200,000,000 300 400 500 Miles
0   200   400   600   800 Km.

· Each dot represents 4,000 bales
--- Present U.S. boundaries

ⓐ

L. Superior
L. Michigan
L. Huron
L. Ontario
L. Erie
St. Lawrence

Missouri
Arkansas
Ohio
Red River
Mississippi
Rio Grande

ATLANTIC OCEAN

GULF OF MEXICO

**UNITED STATES:
COTTON GROWING, 1919**

Scale 1:25,000,000 (400 miles=1 inch)

0   100 200 300 400 500 Miles
0   200   400   600   800 Km.

· Each dot represents 4,000 bales
--- Present U.S. boundaries

ⓑ

L. Superior
L. Michigan
Huron
L. Ontario
L. Erie
St. Lawrence

Missouri
Arkansas
Ohio
Red River
Mississippi
Rio Grande

ATLANTIC OCEAN

GULF OF MEXICO

West from Greenwich

COPYRIGHT. GEORGE PHILIP & SON. LTD.

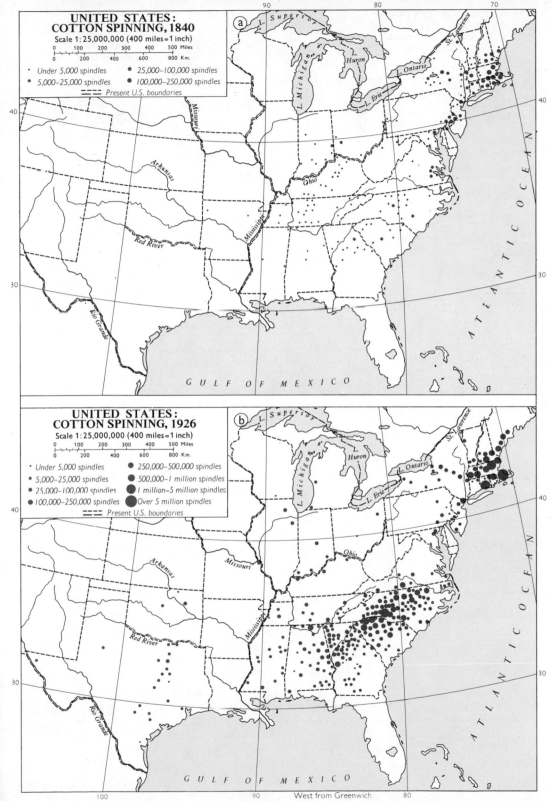

UNITED STATES:
COTTON SPINNING, 1840
Scale 1:25,000,000 (400 miles=1 inch)

0   100   200   300   400   500 Miles
0   200   400   600   800 Km.

· Under 5,000 spindles   · 25,000–100,000 spindles
· 5,000–25,000 spindles ● 100,000–250,000 spindles
--- Present U.S. boundaries

UNITED STATES:
COTTON SPINNING, 1926
Scale 1:25,000,000 (400 miles=1 inch)

0   100   200   300   400   500 Miles
0   200   400   600   800 Km.

· Under 5,000 spindles   ● 250,000–500,000 spindles
· 5,000–25,000 spindles   ● 500,000–1 million spindles
· 25,000–100,000 spindles   ● 1 million–5 million spindles
● 100,000–250,000 spindles   ● Over 5 million spindles
--- Present U.S. boundaries

West from Greenwich

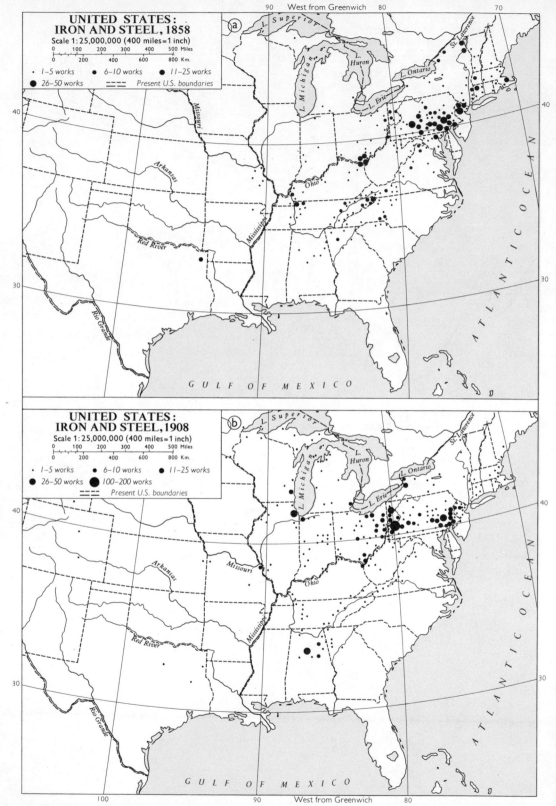

UNITED STATES:
IRON AND STEEL, 1858
Scale 1:25,000,000 (400 miles=1 inch)
0   100   200   300   400   500 Miles
0   200   400   600   800 Km.

· 1–5 works   ● 6–10 works   ● 11–25 works
● 26–50 works   === Present U.S. boundaries

UNITED STATES:
IRON AND STEEL, 1908
Scale 1:25,000,000 (400 miles=1 inch)
0   100   200   300   400   500 Miles
0   200   400   600   800 Km.

· 1–5 works   ● 6–10 works   ● 11–25 works
● 26–50 works   ● 100–200 works   === Present U.S. boundaries

COPYRIGHT. GEORGE PHILIP & SON. LTD.

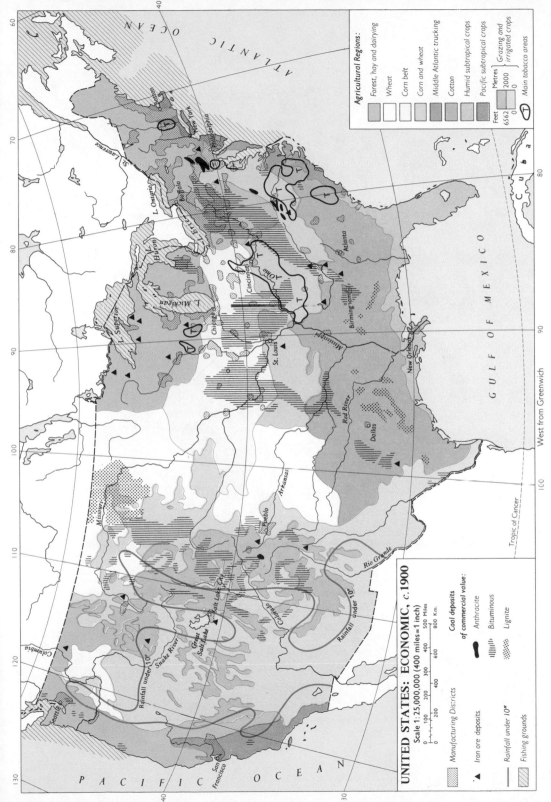

UNITED STATES: ECONOMIC, c.1900

Scale 1:25,000,000 (400 miles=1 inch)

Agricultural Regions:

Forest, hay and dairying
Wheat
Corn belt
Corn and wheat
Middle Atlantic trucking
Cotton
Humid subtropical crops
Pacific subtropical crops
Grazing and irrigated crops
Main tobacco areas

Feet 6562
Metres 2000
0

Coal deposits of commercial value:

Anthracite
Bituminous
Lignite

Manufacturing Districts

Iron ore deposits

Rainfall under 10"

Fishing grounds

ATLANTIC OCEAN

PACIFIC OCEAN

GULF OF MEXICO

Cuba

West from Greenwich

Tropic of Cancer

St. Lawrence

L. Ontario
L. Erie
L. Huron
L. Michigan
L. Superior

Boston
New York
Philadelphia
Buffalo
Chicago
Cincinnati
Atlanta
Birmingham
St. Louis
New Orleans
Dallas
Pueblo
Salt Lake City
Great Salt Lake
San Francisco
Seattle

Ohio
Mississippi
Red River
Arkansas
Rio Grande
Columbia
Snake River
Colorado
Missouri

Rainfall under 10"

0 100 200 300 400 500 Miles
0 200 400 600 800 Km.

COPYRIGHT GEORGE PHILIP & SON LTD.

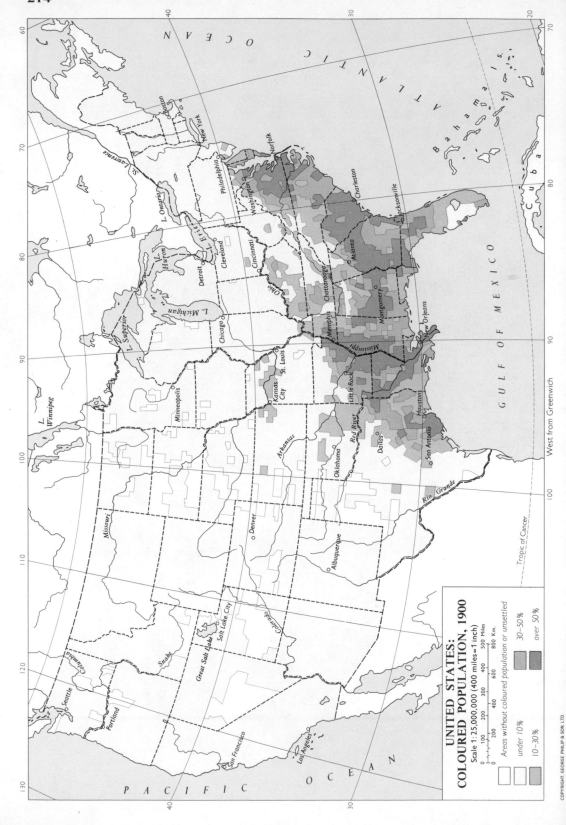

UNITED STATES:
COLOURED POPULATION, 1900

Scale 1:25,000,000 (400 miles = 1 inch)

Areas without coloured population or unsettled

under 10%

10–30%

30–50%

over 50%

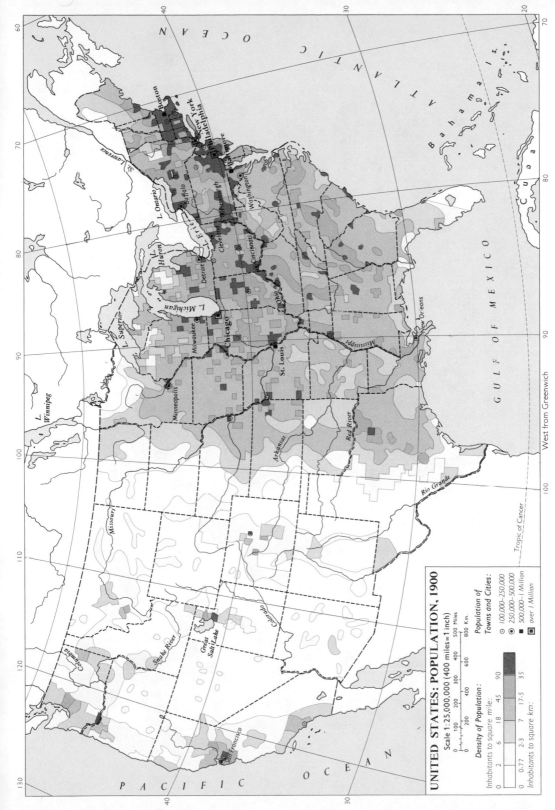

UNITED STATES: POPULATION, 1900

Scale 1:25,000,000 (400 miles=1 inch)

0   100   200   300   400   500 Miles

0   100 200 300 400 500 600 700 800 Km.

Density of Population:

Inhabitants to square mile:

| 0 | 2 | 6 | 18 | 45 | 90 |
| 0 | 0.77 | 2.3 | 7 | 17.5 | 35 |

Inhabitants to square km:

Population of Towns and Cities:

⊙ 100,000–250,000

⊚ 250,000–500,000

■ 500,000–1 Million

▣ over 1 Million

West from Greenwich

EUROPEAN EMIGRATION TO U.S., 1851-1910

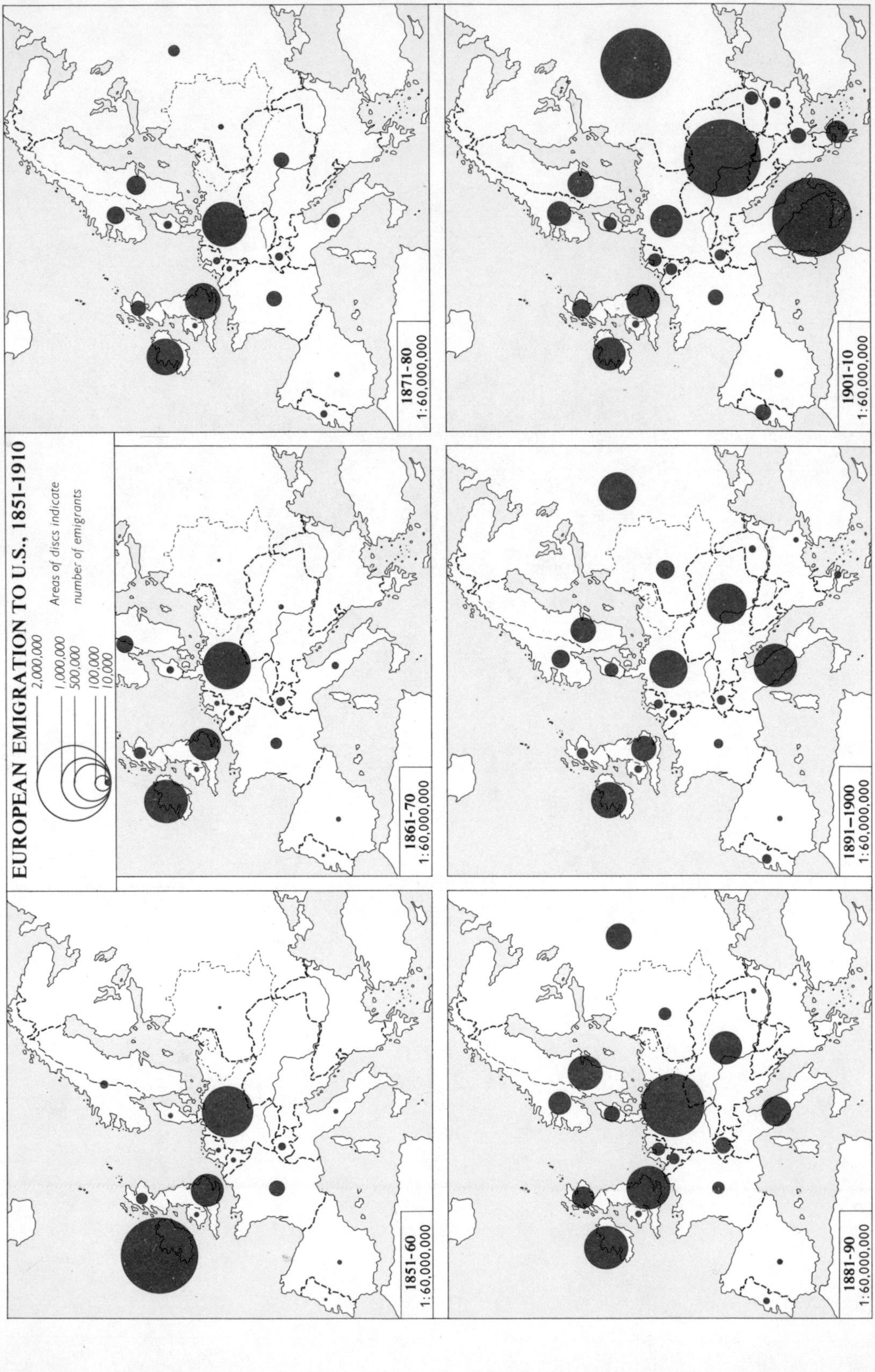

Areas of discs indicate
number of emigrants

2,000,000
1,000,000
500,000
100,000
10,000

1851-60
1:60,000,000

1861-70
1:60,000,000

1871-80
1:60,000,000

1881-90
1:60,000,000

1891-1900
1:60,000,000

1901-10
1:60,000,000

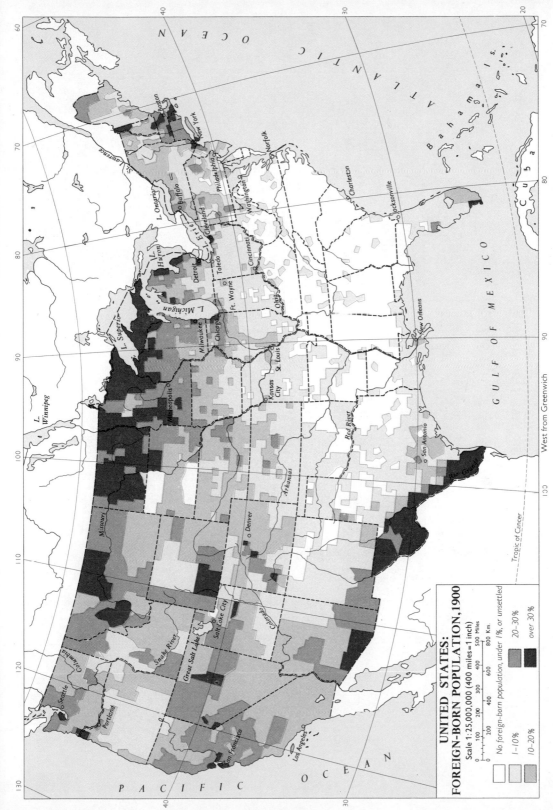

UNITED STATES:
FOREIGN-BORN POPULATION, 1900

Scale 1:25,000,000 (400 miles=1 inch)

0 100 200 300 400 500 Miles

0 100 200 300 400 500 600 700 800 Km.

No foreign-born population, under 1%, or unsettled

1–10%

10–20%

20–30%

over 30%

UNITED STATES: PRESIDENTIAL ELECTIONS

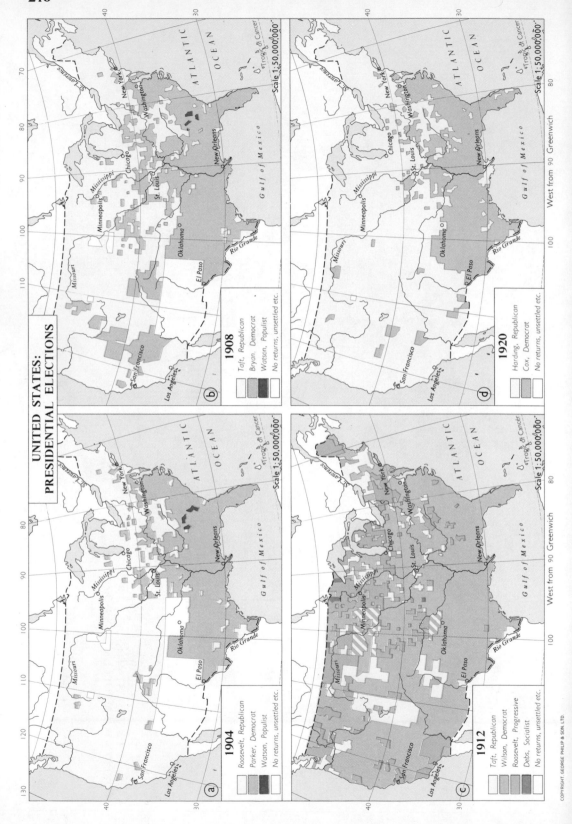

1904
- Roosevelt, Republican
- Parker, Democrat
- Watson, Populist
- No returns, unsettled etc.

Scale 1:50,000,000

1908
- Taft, Republican
- Bryan, Democrat
- Watson, Populist
- No returns, unsettled etc.

Scale 1:50,000,000

1912
- Taft, Republican
- Wilson, Democrat
- Roosevelt, Progressive
- Debs, Socialist
- No returns, unsettled etc.

Scale 1:50,000,000

1920
- Harding, Republican
- Cox, Democrat
- No returns, unsettled etc.

Scale 1:50,000,000

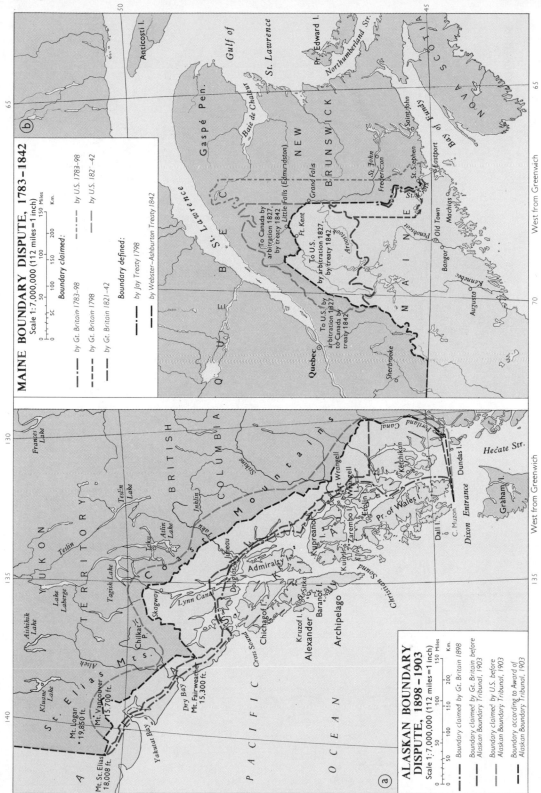

MAINE BOUNDARY DISPUTE, 1783–1842

Scale 1:7,000,000 (112 miles=1 inch)

Boundary claimed:

——·— by Gt. Britain 1783-98
----- by Gt. Britain 1798
——— by Gt. Britain 1821-42

——— by U.S. 1783-98
——— by U.S. 182 -42

Boundary defined:

——·— by Jay Treaty 1798
——— by Webster–Ashburton Treaty 1842

ALASKAN BOUNDARY
DISPUTE, 1898–1903

Scale 1:7,000,000 (112 miles=1 inch)

——·— Boundary claimed by Gt. Britain 1898
——— Boundary claimed by Gt. Britain before Alaskan Boundary Tribunal, 1903
——— Boundary claimed by U.S. before Alaskan Boundary Tribunal, 1903
——— Boundary according to Award of Alaskan Boundary Tribunal, 1903

West from Greenwich

West from Greenwich

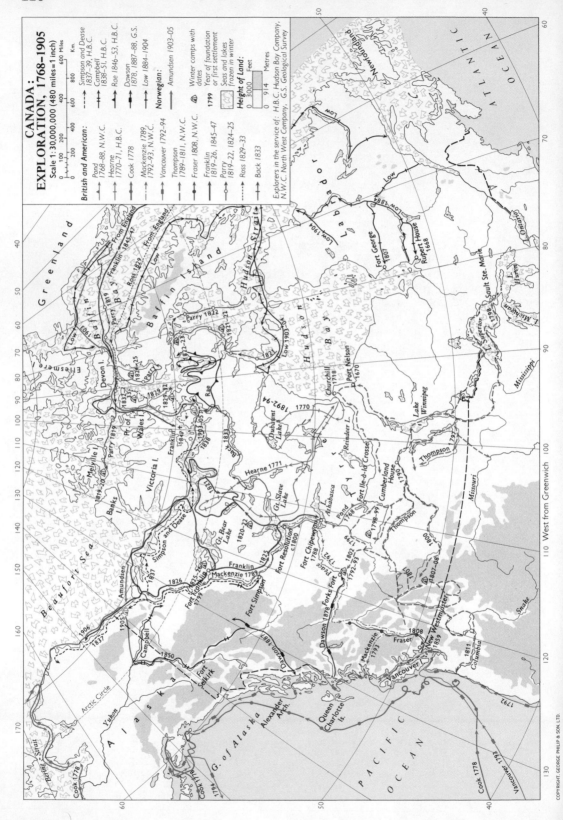

CANADA:
EXPLORATION, 1768–1905

Scale 1:30,000,000 (480 miles=1 inch)

Km.
0 200 400 600 800
Miles
0 100 200 300 400 500 600

British and American:

Pond 1768–88, N.W.C.		Simpson and Deese 1837–39, H.B.C.
Hearne 1770–71, H.B.C.		Campbell 1838–51, H.B.C.
Cook 1778		Rae 1846–53, H.B.C.
Mackenzie 1789 1792–93, N.W.C.		Dawson 1878, 1887–88, G.S.
Vancouver 1792–94		Low 1884–1904

Norwegian:

Thompson 1789–1811, N.W.C.
Fraser 1808, N.W.C.   Amundsen 1903–05
Franklin 1819–26, 1845–47
Parry 1819–22, 1824–25
Ross 1829–33
Back 1833

Winter camps with dates

1799 Year of foundation or first settlement

Seas and lakes frozen in winter

Height of Land:

Metres
0   914
Feet
0   3000

Explorers in the service of: H.B.C. Hudson Bay Company,
N.W.C. North West Company, G.S. Geological Survey

COPYRIGHT GEORGE PHILIP & SON LTD.

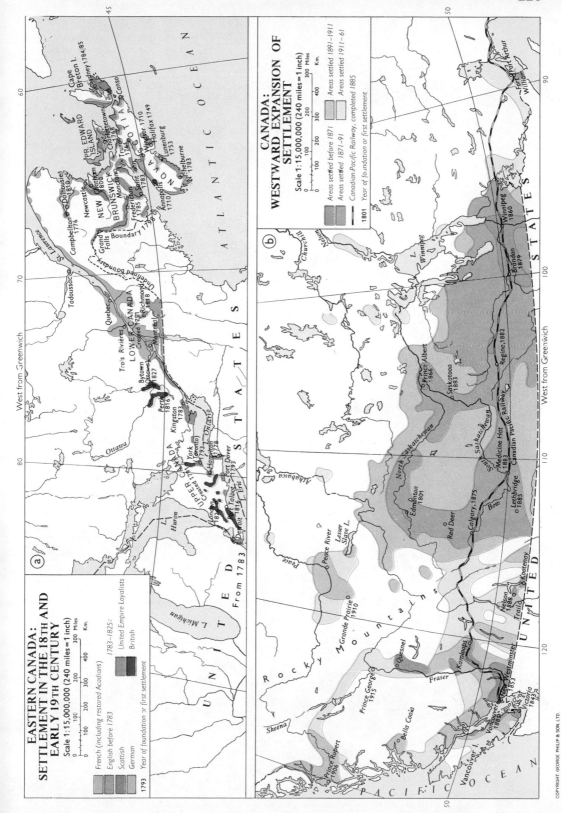

EASTERN CANADA:
SETTLEMENT IN THE 18TH AND
EARLY 19TH CENTURY

Scale 1:15,000,000 (240 miles=1 inch)

0   100   200   300   400   Km.
0   100   200   300 Miles

French (including restored Acadians)	1783–1825:
English before 1783	United Empire Loyalists
Scottish	British
German	

1793 Year of foundation or first settlement

(a)

West from Greenwich

A T L A N T I C   O C E A N

Cape I.
Breton I.
Sydney 1784/85
Canso

PR. EDWARD
ISLAND
Charlottetown 1768

NOVA SCOTIA

Windsor 1710
Halifax 1749
Lunenburg 1753
Shelburne 1783

NEW
BRUNSWICK
Newcastle
Chatham 1800
Moncton
Truro 1759
Saint John 1783
Annapolis 1710
Fredericton 1785

Campbellton 1776
Grand Falls
Undefined boundary

Dalhousie 1810

St. Lawrence

Tadoussac

Quebec

Tro's Rivières

LOWER CANADA

Montreal
Richmond 1818

Brown
Ottawa
1827
Perth 1816

Kingston

UPPER CANADA
York (Toronto) 1793
Hamilton 1778
Talbot 1816
Port Dover 1793
Long Pt 1837
Detroit 1837 Port Erie

Ottawa

Huron

L. Michigan

U N I T E D   S T A T E S

From 1783

CANADA:
WESTWARD EXPANSION OF
SETTLEMENT

Scale 1:15,000,000 (240 miles=1 inch)

0   100   200   300   400   Km.
0   100   200   300 Miles

Areas settled before 1871	Areas settled 1891–1911
Areas settled 1871–91	Areas settled 1911–61

Canadian Pacific Railway, completed 1885

1801 Year of foundation or first settlement

(b)

West from Greenwich

Fort
Port Arthur
Fort
William

Churchill

Nelson

L. Winnipeg

Winnipeg 1860
Brandon 1879

Regina, 1882

Prince Albert 1866

Saskatoon 1883

North Saskatchewan

South Saskatchewan

Medicine Hat 1883

Canadian Pacific Railway

Lethbridge 1885

Edmonton 1801

Red Deer

Calgary, 1875

Bow

Athabasca

Peace River

Lesser
Slave L.

Peace

Grande Prairie 1910

Rocky Mountains

Quesnel

Prince George 1915

Prince Rupert 1906

Skeena

Bella Coola

Fraser

Kamloops

Nelson 1886
Trail 1886

Kootenay

Vancouver 1886
Westminster 1853
New Westminster
Victoria 1843

Vancouver I.

U N I T E D   S T A T E S

P A C I F I C   O C E A N

COPYRIGHT. GEORGE PHILIP & SON LTD.

222

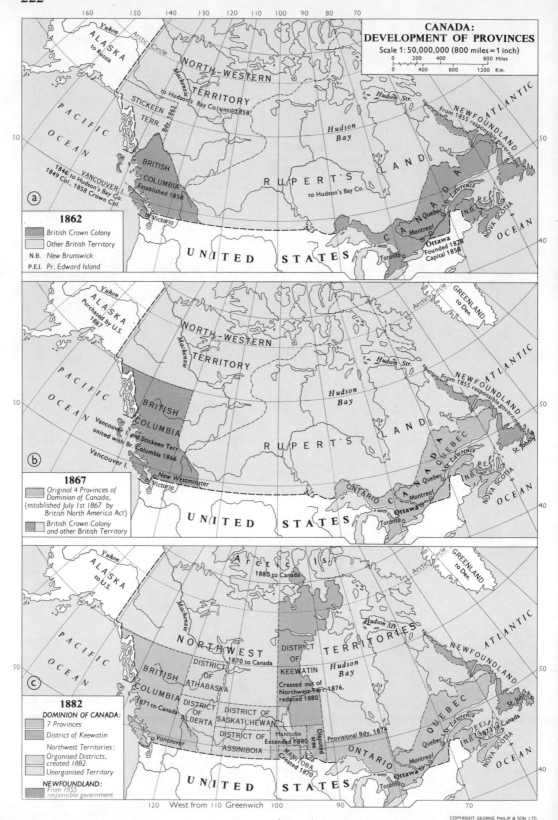

CANADA:
DEVELOPMENT OF PROVINCES

Scale 1:50,000,000 (800 miles=1 inch)

0   200   400   800 Miles
0   400   800   1200 Km.

(a)

1862

British Crown Colony
Other British Territory

N.B.   New Brunswick
P.E.I. Pr. Edward Island

(b)

1867

Original 4 Provinces of
Dominion of Canada,
(established July 1st 1867 by
British North America Act)

British Crown Colony
and other British Territory

(c)

1882

DOMINION OF CANADA:
7 Provinces
District of Keewatin

Northwest Territories:
Organised Districts,
created 1882
Unorganised Territory

NEWFOUNDLAND:
From 1855
responsible government

West from 110 Greenwich

COPYRIGHT. GEORGE PHILIP & SON. LTD.

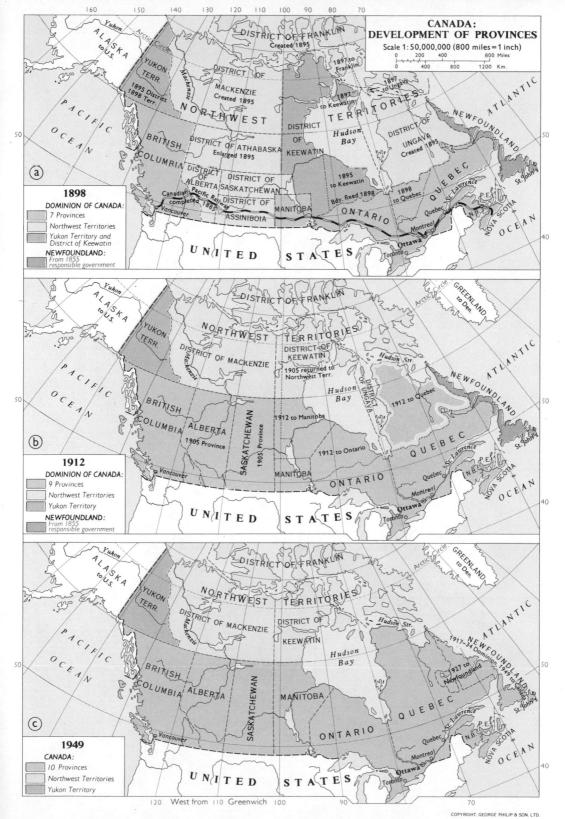

CANADA: DEVELOPMENT OF PROVINCES

Scale 1:50,000,000 (800 miles = 1 inch)

0   200   400   800 Miles

0   400   800   1200 Km.

(a) 1898

DOMINION OF CANADA:
- 7 Provinces
- Northwest Territories
- Yukon Territory and District of Keewatin

NEWFOUNDLAND:
- From 1855 responsible government

(b) 1912

DOMINION OF CANADA:
- 9 Provinces
- Northwest Territories
- Yukon Territory

NEWFOUNDLAND:
- From 1855 responsible government

(c) 1949

CANADA:
- 10 Provinces
- Northwest Territories
- Yukon Territory

COPYRIGHT. GEORGE PHILIP & SON. LTD.

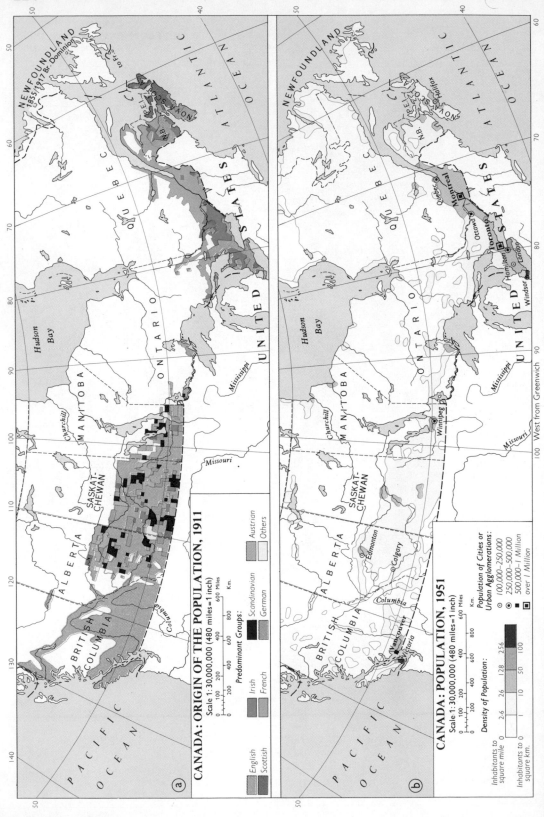

CANADA: ORIGIN OF THE POPULATION, 1911
Scale 1: 30,000,000 (480 miles = 1 inch)

0 100 200 300 400 600 Miles
0 200 400 600 800 Km.

Predominant Groups:

English
Scottish
Irish
French
Scandinavian
German
Austrian
Others

CANADA: POPULATION, 1951
Scale 1: 30,000,000 (480 miles = 1 inch)

0 100 200 300 400 600 Miles
0 200 400 600 800 Km.

Population of Cities or
Urban Agglomerations:

100,000–250,000
250,000–500,000
500,000–1 Million
over 1 Million

Density of Population:

Inhabitants to
square mile 0   1   10   26   50   100 256

Inhabitants to
square km.   0   2.6   10   26   50   128 256

West from Greenwich

COPYRIGHT GEORGE PHILIP & SON LTD.

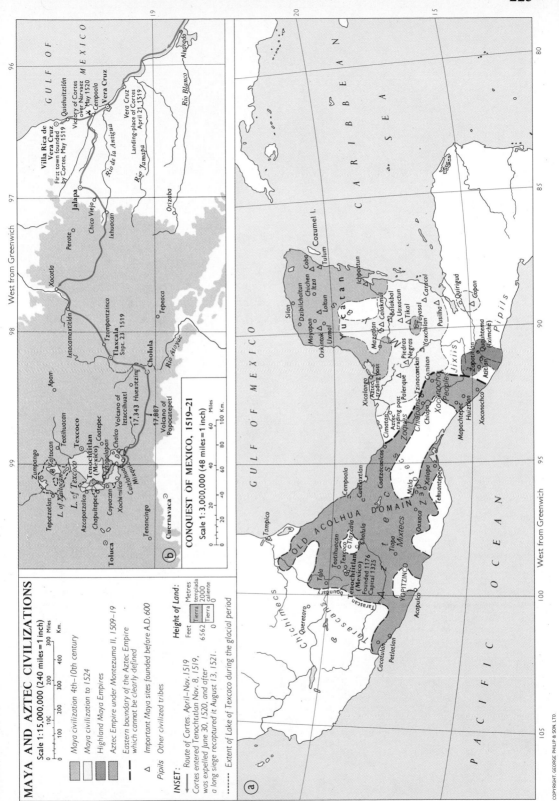

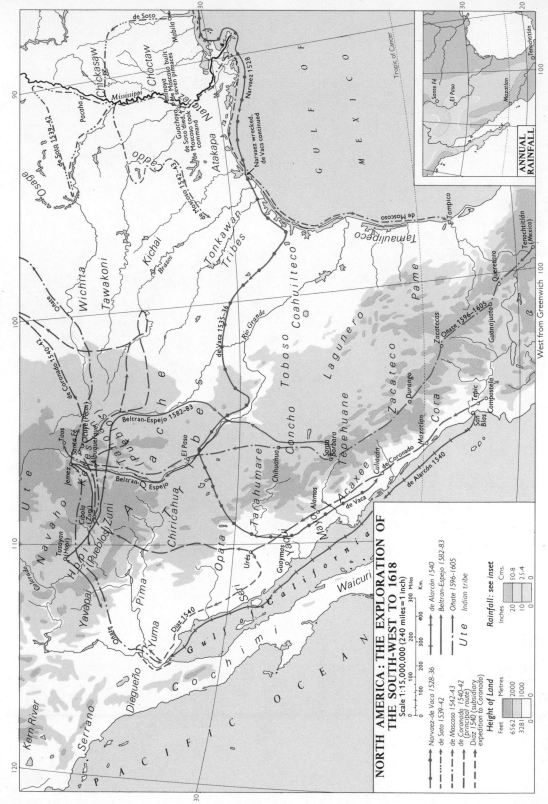

NORTH AMERICA: THE EXPLORATION OF THE SOUTH-WEST TO 1618

Scale 1:15,000,000 (240 miles=1 inch)

0	100	200	300	400	Miles
0	100	200	300	400	Km.

Narvaez–de Vaca 1528-36 → de Alarcón 1540
de Soto 1539-42 → Beltran-Espejo 1582-83
de Moscoso 1542-43 → Oñate 1596-1605
de Coronado 1540-42 (principal route)
Diaz 1540 (subsidiary *Ute* Indian tribe
expedition to Coronado)

Rainfall: see inset

Inches	Cms.
20	50.8
10	25.4

Height of Land

Feet	Metres
6562	2000
3281	1000
0	0

ANNUAL RAINFALL

West from Greenwich

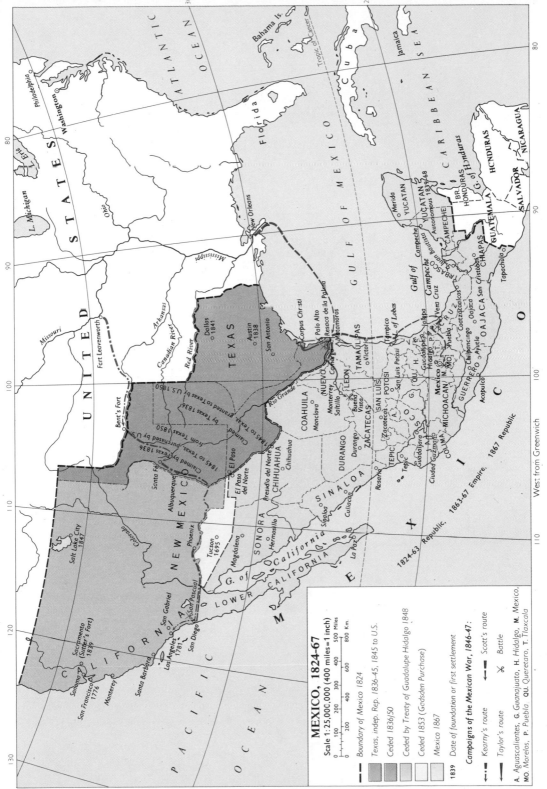

MEXICO, 1824-67

Scale 1:25,000,000 (400 miles=1 inch)

		Boundary of Mexico 1824
		Texas, indep. Rep. 1836-45, 1845 to U.S.
		Ceded 1836/50
		Ceded by Treaty of Guadalupe Hidalgo 1848
		Ceded 1853 (Gadsden Purchase)
		Mexico 1867

1839 Date of foundation or first settlement

Campaigns of the Mexican War, 1846-47:

Kearny's route   Scott's route

Taylor's route   ✕ Battle

A. Aguascalientes, G. Guanajuato, H. Hidalgo, M. Mexico,
MO. Morelos, P. Puebla, QU. Queretaro, T. Tlaxcala

Scale bar: 0 100 200 300 400 500 Miles
0 200 400 600 800 Km.

West from Greenwich

COPYRIGHT GEORGE PHILIP & SON, LTD

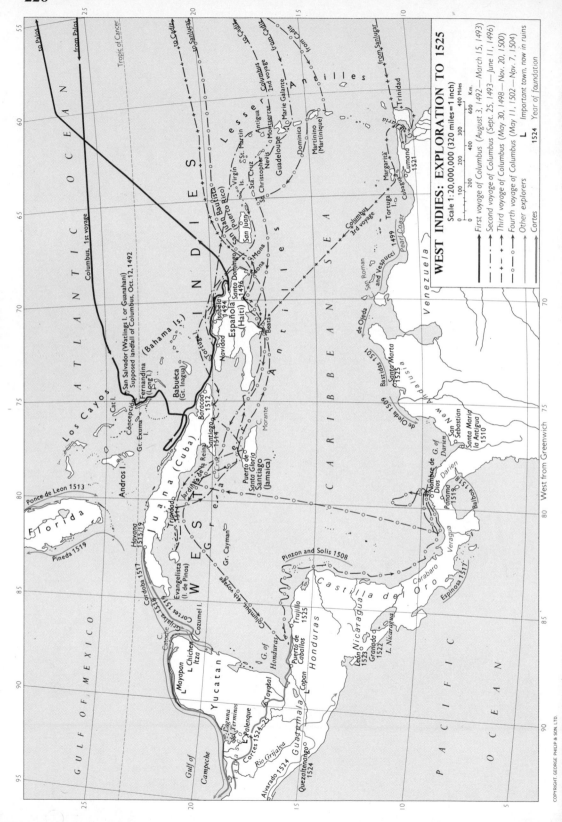

228

WEST INDIES: EXPLORATION TO 1525

Scale 1:20,000,000 (320 miles = 1 inch)

Miles		
0 100 200 300 400		
Km.		
0 200 400 600		

→ First voyage of Columbus (August 3, 1492 — March 15, 1493)
–·–·– Second voyage of Columbus (Sept. 25, 1493 — June 11, 1496)
+ + + Third voyage of Columbus (May 30, 1498 — Nov. 20, 1500)
o o o Fourth voyage of Columbus (May 11, 1502 — Nov. 7, 1504)
→ Other explorers
→ Cortes
L Important town, now in ruins
1524 Year of foundation

West from Greenwich

A T L A N T I C   O C E A N

Columbus, 1st voyage

to Palos
from Palos

Tropic of Cancer

to Cadiz
to Sanlucar
from Cadiz
from Cadiz
from Cadiz
from Sanlucar

Columbus 2nd voyage

L e s s e r   A n t i l l e s

Antigua
St. Martin
Virgin Is.
Sta. Cruz
St. Christopher
Nevis
Montserrat
Guadeloupe
Marie Galante
Dominica
Martinique (Martinique)

Margarita
Cubagua
Cumana 1521
Toruga
Columbus 3rd voyage
Pearl Coast
Columbus and Vespucci 1499

Trinidad
Pana

Venezuela

San Roman
de Ojeda 1501

Bastidas 1501

Santa Marta 1525

Andalusia

C A R I B B E A N   S E A

G r e a t e r   A n t i l l e s

San Salvador (Watlings I. or Guanahani)
Supposed landfall of Columbus, Oct. 12, 1492

(Bahama Is.)

W E S T   I N D I E S

Fernandina (Long I.)
Cat I.
Concepcion
Gt. Exuma
Babueca (Gt. Inagua)
Tortuga
Baracoa 1512

Navidad
Isabela 1494
Española (Haiti)
Santo Domingo 1496
Beata
C. Morante

Mona
Bona
Mona

San Juan
Boriquen (Puerto Rico)
San Juan

Los Cayos

Andros I.

Juana (Cuba)
Havana 1515,19
Trinidad
Jard. de la Reina
Concepcion
Santiago 1514
Puerto de Santa Gloria
Santiago (Jamaica)

Gr. Cayman

Jamaica

Florida
Ponce de Leon 1513
Pineda 1519

GULF OF MEXICO

Cordoba 1517
Cozumel I.
Catoche
Cortes 1519
Grijalva 1518
L. Mayapan
L. Chichen Itza
Yucatan
Gulf of Campeche
L. Palenque
Laguna de Terminos
Rio Grijalva
Cortes 1524-25
Alvarado 1524
Quezaltenango 1524
Guatemala
L. Copan
Taysal
Honduras
G. of Honduras
Puerto de Caballos
Trujillo 1525

Evangelista (I. de Pinos)
Columbus 4th voyage

Pinzon and Solis 1508

C a s t i l l a   d e l   O r o

Leon 1523
Granada 1522
L. Nicaragua
Nicaragua
Veragua
Carabaro

Nombre de Dios
Panama 1519
G. of Darien
San Sebastian 1510
Santa Maria la Antigua 1510
Darien
Ojeda 1509
Balboa
Espinosa 1517

P A C I F I C   O C E A N

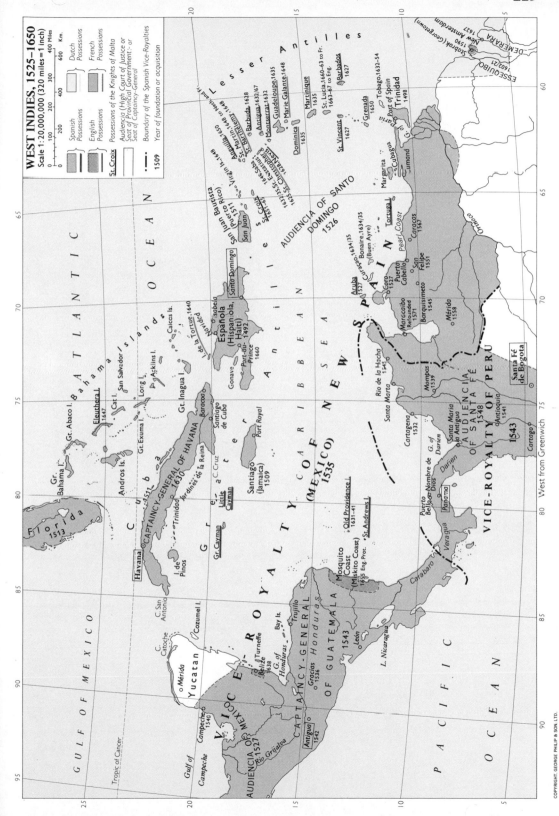

WEST INDIES, 1525–1650

Scale 1:20,000,000 (320 miles=1 inch)

0	200	300	400	600 Miles
0	200	400	600	Km.

Spanish Possessions

Dutch Possessions

English Possessions

French Possessions

St. Croix — Possessions of the Knights of Malta

Audiencia (High Court of Justice or Seat of Provincial Government)- or Seat of Captaincy-General

Boundary of the Spanish Vice-Royalties

1509 — Year of foundation or acquisition

COPYRIGHT GEORGE PHILIP & SON, LTD.

West from Greenwich

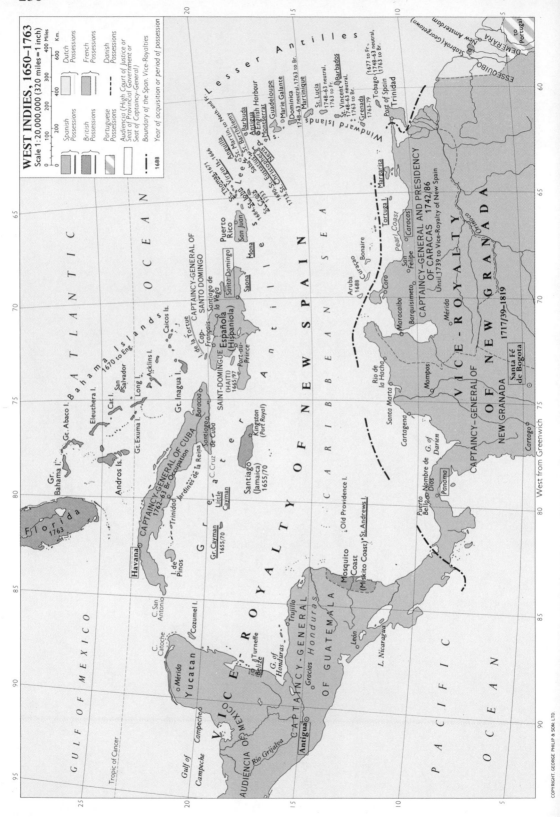

WEST INDIES, 1650–1763

Scale 1:20,000,000 (320 miles=1 inch)

0	100	200	300	400 Miles
0	200	400	600	Km.

Spanish Possessions

British Possessions

Portuguese Possessions

Dutch Possessions

French Possessions

Danish Possessions

Audiencia (High Court of Justice or Seat of Provincial Government or Seat of Captaincy-General)

Boundary of the Span. Vice-Royalties

1688   Year of acquisition or period of possession

Lesser Antilles

Windward Islands

Marie Galante

Dominica 1748–63 neutral, 1763 to Br.

Guadeloupe

Martinique

St. Lucia 1748–63 neutral, 1763 to Fr.

Barbuda

English Harbour

Antigua

Montserrat

Barbados

St. Vincent 1748–63 neutral, 1763 to Br.

Grenada 1763–79

Tobago (1677 to Fr. 1748–63 neutral, 1763 to Br.)

Trinidad

Port of Spain

St. Kitts

Nevis

St. Christopher

St. Eustatius

Saba

St. Martin 1648 Du. and Fr.

St. Barthelemy

St. Thomas 1671 St. John 1717 St. Croix 1733–4

Anguilla

Leeward Islands

Puerto Rico

San Juan 1898

Mona

Saona

Margarita

Tortuga I.

Pearl Coast

San Felipe

Curaçao

Bonaire

Aruba 1688

Coro

Caracas

CAPTAINCY-GENERAL AND PRESIDENCY OF CARACAS 1742/86

Until 1739 to Vice-Royalty of New Spain

CAPTAINCY-GENERAL OF SANTO DOMINGO

Santo Domingo

Santiago de la Vega

Española (Hispaniola)

Port-au-Prince

Cap-Français

de la Tortue

SAINT-DOMINGUE (HAITI) 1665/97

Maracaibo

Barquisimeto

Mérida

Santa Marta

Rio de la Hacha

Mompos

VICE-ROYALTY OF NEW GRANADA 1717/39–1819

Santa Fé de Bogotá

CAPTAINCY-GENERAL OF NEW GRANADA

NEW GRANADA

Cartagena

Cartago

ESSEQUIBO

DEMERARA

Stabrok (Georgetown)

New Amsterdam

to PORTUGAL

ATLANTIC OCEAN

Gr. Bahama I.

Gr. Abaco I.

Bahama Islands

Eleuthera I.

Cat I.

San Salvador

Long I.

Acklins I.

Gt. Exuma I.

Gt. Inagua I.

Caicos Is.

Andros Is.

CAPTAINCY-GENERAL OF CUBA 1762–63 Br. Occupation

Jardines de la Reina

Santiago de Cuba

Baracoa

Trinidad

Havana

I. de Pinos

C. San Antonio

C. Catoche

Cozumel I.

Mérida

Campeche

Yucatan

AUDIENCIA OF MEXICO

VICE-ROYALTY OF NEW SPAIN

Gulf of Campeche

GULF OF MEXICO

Tropic of Cancer

Florida 1763

CARIBBEAN SEA

Gr. Cayman 1655/70

Little Cayman

Kingston (Port Royal)

Santiago (Jamaica) 1655/70

Greater Antilles

Old Providence I.

St. Andrews I.

Mosquito Coast (Miskito Coast)

Puerto Bello

Nombre de Dios

G. of Darien

Panama

Río Grijalva

Belize

Turneffe

G. of Honduras

Gulf of Honduras

Trujillo

Gracias Honduras

León

L. Nicaragua

CAPTAINCY-GENERAL OF GUATEMALA

Antigua

PACIFIC OCEAN

West from Greenwich

COPYRIGHT. GEORGE PHILIP & SON, LTD.

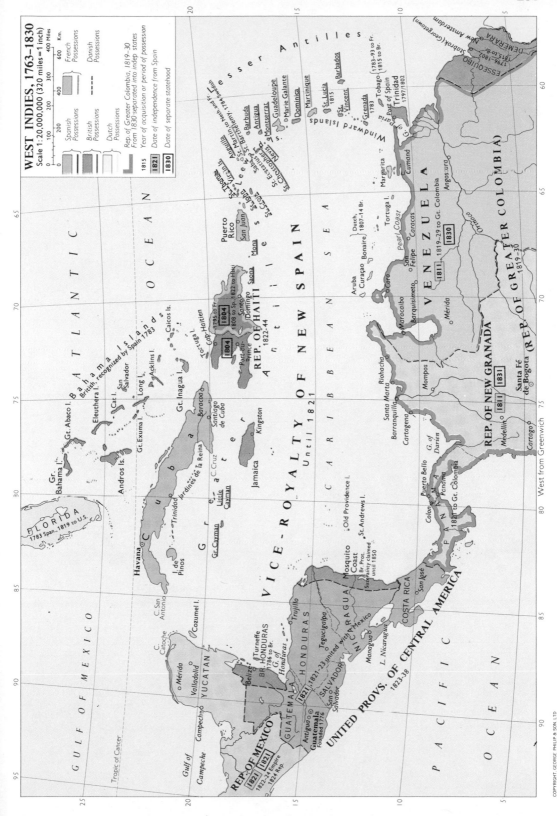

WEST INDIES, 1763–1830

Scale 1:20,000,000 (320 miles=1 inch)

0 | 200 | 400 | 600 Km.

0 | 200 | 300 | 400 Miles

Spanish Possessions
French Possessions
British Possessions
Danish Possessions
Dutch Possessions

Rep. of Greater Colombia, 1819–30
From 1830 separated into indep states

1815 — Year of acquisition or period of possession
1821 — Date of independence from Spain
1830 — Date of separate statehood

ATLANTIC OCEAN

GULF OF MEXICO

FLORIDA
1783 Span.–1819 to U.S.

Tropic of Cancer

Gr. Bahama I.
Gt. Abaco I.
B a h a m a I s l a n d s
British, recognized by Spain 1783
Eleuthera I.
Andros Is.
Cat I.
San Salvador
Long I.
Gt. Exuma I.
Acklins I.
Gt. Inagua I.
Caicos Is.
Tortuga I.

C u b a
Havana
I. de Pinos
Gr. Cayman
Little Cayman
Trinidad
Jardines de la Reina
C. Cruz
Santiago de Cuba
Baracoa
Jamaica
Kingston
G r e a t e r
C. San Antonio

1795 to Fr.
Cap-Haitien
1808 to Sp.–1822 to Haiti
REP. OF HAITI
1822–44
Port-au-Prince
1804
1804
Santo Domingo
Saona
A n t i l l e s

Puerto Rico
San Juan
Mona I.
Mona Passage

V I C E - R O Y A L T Y   O F   N E W   S P A I N
Until 1821

C A R I B B E A N   S E A

Old Providence I.
St. Andrews I.

Mosquito Coast
Br. Prot.
Sovereignty claimed until 1850

C. Catoche
Cozumel I.
C. Merida
Valladolid
Campeche
Y U C A T A N
Gulf of Campeche

REP. OF MEXICO
1821 1821
1822–24 Empire
1824 Resp.

Antigua
Guatemala
Founded 1776
U N I T E D   P R O V S .   O F   C E N T R A L   A M E R I C A
1823–38

G U A T E M A L A
1821/1821–23 united with Mexico

Turneffe
BR. HONDURAS
1786 to Br.
Belize
G. of Honduras
H O N D U R A S
Trujillo
Tegucigalpa
N I C A R A G U A
Managua
L. Nicaragua
San Salvador
SALVADOR
San José
COSTA RICA

Colon
Puerto Bello
G. of Darién
P A N A M A
1821 to Gt. Colombia

L e s s e r   A n t i l l e s

St. Martin, to Fr. 1648/Neth. 1648
St. Barthélemy, 1784 to Fr.
Anguilla
Barbuda
St. Martin
St. Bartholomew
Saba
St. Eustatius
St. Christopher
Nevis
L e e w a r d   I s.
Antigua
Montserrat
Guadeloupe
Marie Galante
Dominica
Martinique
St. Lucia 1815
St. Vincent
Barbados
Grenada 1783
Tobago (1783–93 to Fr.)
1815 to Br.
Trinidad
1797/1802
Port of Spain
W i n d w a r d   I s l a n d s

St. Thomas
St. John
St. Croix

Margarita
Cumaná
Caracas
Barcelona
Pearl Coast
Tortuga I.
Curaçao Bonaire, 1807–14 Br.
Aruba
Dutch, 1807–14 Br.

V E N E Z U E L A
1811
1819–29 to Gt. Colombia
1830

Coro
S. Felipe
Barquisimeto
Angostura

STABROEK (Georgetown)
New Amsterdam
DEMERARA
1796–1802
1815 to Br.
ESSEQUIBO
1781–1803
1815 to Br.

Maracaibo
Mérida
Riohacha
Santa Marta
Barranquilla
Cartagena
Mompos

REP. OF NEW GRANADA
1811 1831

Medellín
Cartago
Santa Fé de Bogotá
(REP. OF GREATER COLOMBIA)
1819–30

A T L A N T I C   O C E A N

P A C I F I C   O C E A N

West from Greenwich

232

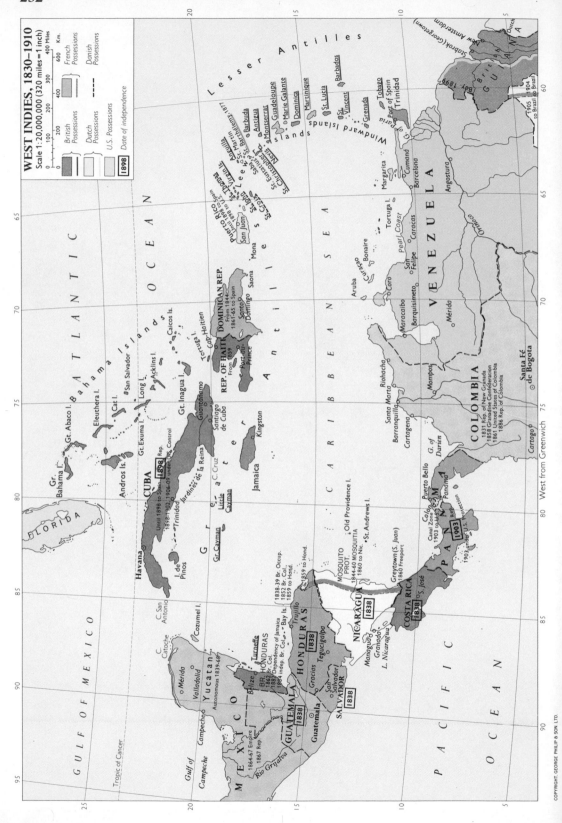

WEST INDIES, 1830–1910
Scale 1:20,000,000 (320 miles=1 inch)

British Possessions
Dutch Possessions
U.S. Possessions
French Possessions
Danish Possessions
1898 Date of independence

COPYRIGHT. GEORGE PHILIP & SON LTD.

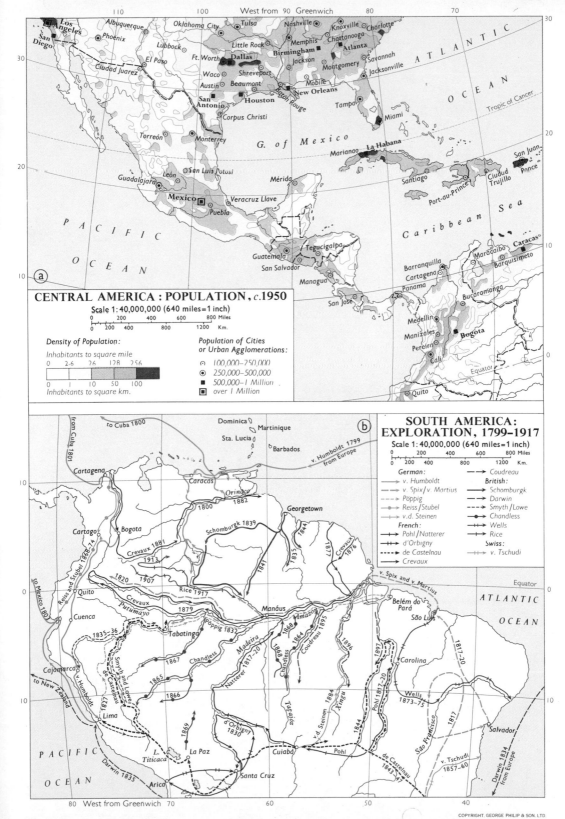

(a) CENTRAL AMERICA : POPULATION, c.1950

Scale 1:40,000,000 (640 miles=1 inch)

0   200   400   600   800 Miles
0 200 400   800   1200 Km.

Density of Population:

Inhabitants to square mile
0 2·6   26   128   256
0   1   10   50   100
Inhabitants to square km.

Population of Cities
or Urban Agglomerations:
⊙ 100,000–250,000
⊙ 250,000–500,000
■ 500,000–1 Million
▣ over 1 Million

(b) SOUTH AMERICA: EXPLORATION, 1799–1917

Scale 1:40,000,000 (640 miles=1 inch)

0   200   400   600   800 Miles
0 200 400   800   1200 Km.

German:
→ v. Humboldt
→ v. Spix/v. Martius
→ Pöppig
→ Reiss/Stubel
→ v.d. Steinen

French:
→ Pohl/Natterer
→ d'Orbigny
→ de Castelnau
→ Crevaux

→ Coudreau

British:
→ Schomburgk
→ Darwin
→ Smyth/Lowe
→ Chandless
→ Wells
→ Rice

Swiss:
→ v. Tschudi

COPYRIGHT. GEORGE PHILIP & SON. LTD.

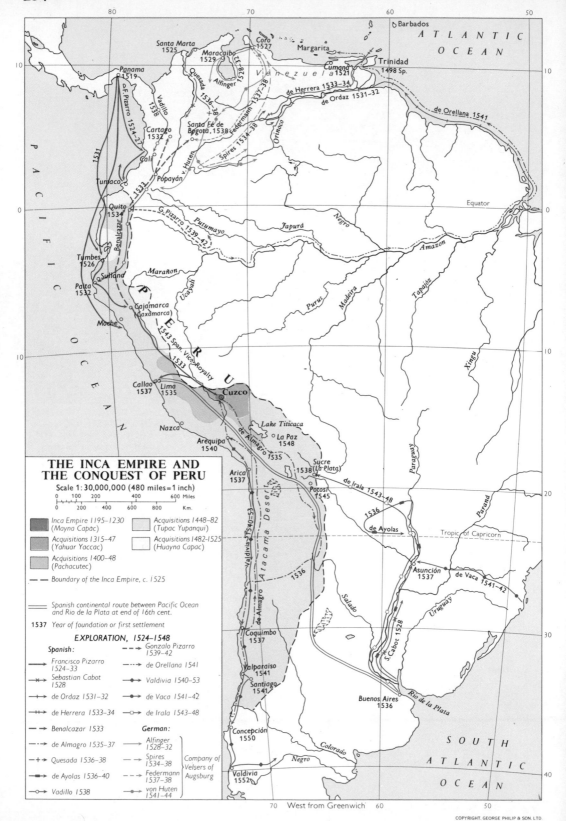

THE INCA EMPIRE AND
THE CONQUEST OF PERU

Scale 1:30,000,000 (480 miles=1 inch)

0   100   200   300   400   500   600 Miles
0   200   400   600   800 Km.

Inca Empire 1195–1230
(Mayna Capac)

Acquisitions 1315–47
(Yahuar Yaccac)

Acquisitions 1400–48
(Pachacutec)

Acquisitions 1448–82
(Tupac Yupanqui)

Acquisitions 1482–1525
(Huayna Capac)

— — — Boundary of the Inca Empire, c. 1525

══════ Spanish continental route between Pacific Ocean
and Rio de la Plata at end of 16th cent.

1537   Year of foundation or first settlement

EXPLORATION, 1524–1548

Spanish:

Francisco Pizarro
1524–33

Sebastian Cabot
1528

de Ordaz 1531–32

de Herrera 1533–34

Benalcazar 1533

de Almagro 1535–37

Quesada 1536–38

de Ayolas 1536–40

Vadillo 1538

Gonzalo Pizarro
1539–42

de Orellana 1541

Valdivia 1540–53

de Vaca 1541–42

de Irala 1543–48

German:

Alfinger
1528–32

Spires
1534–38

Federmann
1537–38

von Huten
1541–44

Company of
Velsers of
Augsburg

COPYRIGHT. GEORGE PHILIP & SON. LTD.

VICE-ROYALTY OF NEW SPAIN
1535

Dominica 1635 Fr.
Martinique, 1635 Fr.
St. Lucia, 1627–60 Eng.
St. Vincent 1627 Eng.
Barbados, 1627 Eng.

Rio de la Hacha
Santa Marta
Cartagena 1532
Panama 1538
1519
Mómpos
Maracaibo
Coro
Puerto Cabello
Barquisimeto
Mérida
Caracas 1567
Cumaná
Trinidad 1498 Span.
Tobago, 1632–54 Dutch

AUDIENCIA
Antioquia
Cartago
OF
SANTA FÉ
1548
Santa Fé de Bogota
1538
Cali
Neiva
Pasto
Popayán
Ibarra
PRESIDENCIA
1638
1534
OF QUITO
1563
Quito
Portoviejo
Guayaquil
Túmbes 1526
Cuenca
Piura
AUDIENCIA
Cajamarca
OF LIMA
1543
Trujillo
Huánuco
Lima 1535
Huancavelica
Callao
Cuzco
L. Titicaca
Arequipa
La Paz
Arica
PRESIDENCIA OF LA PLATA
Santa Cruz
1538
Potosí 1545
CHARCAS 1559

ESSEQUIBO 1602/21 Dutch
DEMERARA, 1590 Dutch (Stabroek (Georgetown) Eng.)
New Amsterdam, 1627 Dutch
SURINAM, 1650 Eng.
Paramaribo 1613 Dutch
GUIANA 1596 Span.
Cayenne 1635

1494
Spanish
Portuguese

ATLANTIC
Equator

Belém do Pará 1616
Gurupá 1624
C. OF PARÁ 1616
C. OF MARANHÃO 1615
Maranhão (São Luis) Port.
DUTCH BRAZIL 1630–1654
C. OF CEARÁ 1613 Port.
Ceará Port.
Natal 1597
C. OF PARAIBA 1532
Paraiba Port.
Olinda Port.
C. OF PERNAMBUCO 1532
Recife Port.
1637
Ft. Maurits
C. OF SERGIPE 1532
Sergipe del Rey
C. OF BAHIA 1532
Bahia Capital 1549–1763
Ilhéus 1534
C. OF PORTO SEGURO 1532
Santa Cruz
Porto Seguro
C. OF ESPIRITO SANTO 1532
C. OF RIO DE JANEIRO 1532
Rio de Janeiro 1565

PRESIDENCIA OF CHARCAS 1559
Fort Olimpo
1609–31
1630–31
Ciudad Real
Asunción 1537
São Paulo 1532
São Vicente
Santos 1545
C. OF SANTA CATARINA 1532
Santa Catarina I.
Destêrro 1640

Jujuy
Salta
Tucumán
Catamarca
La Rioja
Santiago del Estero
Córdoba 1573
Santa Fé

CAPTAINCY-GENERAL AND PRESIDENCIA OF CHILE 1606
La Serena
San Juan
Mendoza
San Luis
Valparaiso 1536
Santiago 1541
Juan Fernandez Is. 1563
Chillán
Concepción
Ft. Arauco
Valdivia 1552
Osorno
Chiloé I.

Buenos Aires 1536

PACIFIC OCEAN

Tropic of Capricorn

OCEAN

Magellan's Str.

West from Greenwich

SOUTH AMERICA, c.1650
Scale 1: 40,000,000 (640 miles=1 inch)

0   200   400   600   800 Miles
0   200 400   600   800 1000 1200 Km.

Spanish Lands   Dutch Lands
Portuguese Lands   French Lands
English Lands
Jesuit mission states with dates
Demarcation line according to the Treaty of Tordesillas, 1494
Division between Spanish and Portuguese influence at the end of the 16th cent.
Audiencia (High Court of Justice or Seat of Provincial Government or Seat of Captaincy-General)
1511 Year of foundation of an Audiencia, a Captaincy-General, or a Captaincy
1535 Year of foundation or first settlement
C.   Captaincy

COPYRIGHT, GEORGE PHILIP & SON, LTD.

80   70   60   50   40

Dominica
1763 Br.
Martinique
St. Lucia, disputed from 1763
St. Vincent
1763 Br.
Barbados

Rio de la Hacha
Santa Marta
Cartagena
Coro
Puerto
Cabello
La Guaira
Tobago, 1783–93 Fr.
Trinidad
1797/1802 Br.

Panama
Barquisimeto
Mompos
Mérida
CAPTAINCY-GENERAL AND
PRESIDENCIA OF CARACAS
CAPTAINCY-GENERAL
Caracas
Cumaná
Stabrok
(Georgetown)
New Amsterdam
SURINAM, 1667 Dutch

A T L A N T I C

Antioquia
Cúcuta
1742/86
Until 1739 to New Spain
Paramaribo
OF
CAPTAINCY-GENERAL
Santa Fé de
Bogota
Cartago
NEW GRANADA
VICE-ROYALTY
OF NEW-GRANADA
1717/39 - 1819
Cayenne, 1674 to Fr. Crown
Cali
Neiva
GUIANA
Pasto
Popayán
Ibarra
Quito
Equator

Portoviejo
Guayaquil
PRESIDENCIA
OF QUITO
Putumayo
Japurá
Negro
Belém do Pará
Amazon
Gurupá
C. OF
PARÁ
Maranhão
(São Luis)
C. OF
MARANHÃO
C. OF
Ceará
CEARÁ

Túmbes
Cuenca
1638
Tabatinga
Manáus
1674
Amazon
Natal

Piura
Marañon
Purus
Madeira
Tapajóz
Xingu
C. OF
PIAUÍ
C. OF PARAIBA
Olinda
Panaiba
C. OF PERNAMBUCO
Recife

AUDIENCIA
Cajamarca
Ucayali
VICE-ROYALTY OF
BRAZIL
1760
C. OF SERGIPE
Ft. Maurits
Sergipe
del Rey

Trujillo
Huánuco
Ft. da Beira
1760
C. OF MATO GROSSO
1748
São Francisco
C. OF
GOIAZ
1746
C. OF
BAHIA
Bahia
(Salvador)
Capital until 1763

OF LIMA
Lima
Huancavelica
Cuzco
1684
Mato Grosso
(Vila Bela)
1752
Cuiabá
C. OF
PORTO
SEGURO
Ilhéus
Santa Cruz
Porto Seguro

Callao
AUDIENCIA
VICE-
Titicaca
OF
Santa Cruz
Arequipa
La Paz
PRESIDENCIA
OF
1691
Santa Anna
(Goiaz)
Paracatu
1730
Diamantina
Minas Novas
1727
C. OF
ESPIRITO
SANTO

Arica
1543
ROYALTY
CUZCO
1787
La Plata
Potosí
CHARCAS
Corumbá
1788
Nueva Coimbra
1775
Paraná
C. OF MINAS GERAIS
1720
Sabará
Vila Rica
C. OF
SÃO PAOLO
1709
C. OF
RIO DE JANEIRO

OF PERU
VICE-ROYALTY
OF
Jujuy
Salta
1630
Asunción
Ciudad Real
São Paulo
Santos
São
Vicente
Rio de Janeiro
Capital since 1763

CAPTAINCY-
GENERAL
Tucumán
Copiapó
AND
La Serena
RIO DE LA PLATA
1776
Santiago
del Estero
Catamarca
La Rioja
AUDIENCIA
Córdoba
OF
Uruguay
C. OF
RIO GRANDE
DO SUL
1777
Santa Catarina
Santa Catarina I.
Laguna 1654

PRESIDENCIA
OF CHILE
Valparaíso
San Juan
Mendoza
Santa Fé
BUENOS AIRES
1776
Paraná
Banda
Oriental
Porto Alegre
Rio Grande
1737

Santiago
Rancagua
San Luis
Buenos Aires
Colonia
do Sacramento
1680-1705
1715-1750
1762-1777 Port.
Montevideo
1726
Rio de la Plata
Direct traffic with Spain since 1778

Chillán
Concepción
Ft. Arauco
Negro
O C E A N

Valdivia
Carmen de Patagones
1779 Span.

Osorno
1763 San Carlos
de Ancud
Chiloé I.

Juan Fernandez Is.
P A C I F I C
O C E A N

Islas Malvinas
(Falkland Is.)
1763 Fr.
1765 Br.
1770 Span.

Magellan's Str.

C. Horn

SOUTH AMERICA
IN THE 18TH CENTURY
Scale 1: 40,000,000 (640 miles=1 inch)

0   200   400   600   800 Miles
0   200   400   800   1200 Km.

Possessions up to 1650
and later acquisitions:
       British Lands
   Spanish Lands   Dutch Lands
   Portuguese Lands   French Lands
   Jesuit mission states (until 1767)
– · – · – Boundary of the Spanish Vice-
      Royalties 1777
      Audiencia (High Court of Justice or
      Seat of Provincial Government or
      Seat of Captaincy - General)
1709   Year of foundation of an Audiencia,
      a Captaincy–General, or a Captaincy
1726   Year of foundation or first settlement
C.   Captaincy

90   West from 80 Greenwich   70   60   50

Tropic of Capricorn

**SOUTH AMERICA
1800–30**

Scale 1:40,000,000 (640 miles=1 inch)

| 0 | | 200 | 400 | 600 | 800 Miles |

| 0 | 200 | 400 | | 800 | 1200 Km. |

Rep. of Greater Colombia, 1819–30, from 1830 separated into indep. states

1811 Date of independence from Spain

1811 Date of separate statehood

☆ Last Spanish fortresses 1826

✗ Battle in the wars of independence 1810–27

COPYRIGHT. GEORGE PHILIP & SON. LTD.

Caribbean Sea

Dominica to Br.
Martinique, to Fr.
Aruba to Neth.
Curaçao to Neth.
Bonaire
Sta. Lucia, to Br.
St. Vincent to Br.
Barbados, to Br.
Grenada to Br.
Tobago, to Br.
Trinidad, to Br.

Caracas 1954

Maracaibo

ATLANTIC

Canal Zone 1903 to U.S.
Cartagena 1939, 1956
Panama
PANAMA **1903** Rep.
1903–39 under U.S. Prot.

VENEZUELA

Ciudad Bolivar (Angostura)
Orinoco

Georgetown
New Amsterdam
Paramaribo
British GUIANA
Dutch GUIANA SURINAM
French GUIANA
Cayenne

Medellin
Cartago
Bogotá 1948
Cali

COLOMBIA
1858 Granadine Confederation
1861 United States of Colombia
1886 Rep. of Colombia

1905 to Brazil
1905/29
1929

RIO BRANCO

AMAPÁ
Macapá

Equator

Quito
ECUADOR
Guayaquil
1942

1880
1880–1922 to Ecuador

1907
1905/29

1905 to Brazil
1904 to Brazil

Amazon

Negro

Belém do Pará
São Luis
Fortaleza (Ceará)

Tumbes
1880 to Ecuador
1942 to Peru
1880
Leticia
1909

Amazon
Manáus

Gurupá

PARÁ
MARANHÃO
CEARÁ

Piura

AMAZONAS

Purus

Tapajóz

Xingu

RIO GRANDE DO NORTE
PARAÍBA
Pernámbuco
PERNAMBUCO
ALAGÔAS

Trujillo
Huánuco
1857
1903
1909 to Peru 1867 to Brazil

Ucayali
Acre

UNITED   STATES
OF   BRAZIL
Until 1889 Empire of Brazil

Tocantins

SERGIPE
Sergipe del Rey

PERU

1902 to Peru

GUAPORÉ Formed 1943
Guaporé

MATO GROSSO
GOIÁS
BAHIA
Salvador (Bahia)

Callao
Lima 1938
Chincha Is.
1864–66 Span. Occup.

Cuzco
Arequipa

L. Titicaca
La Paz
BOLIVIA

1927 to Brazil

Brasília Founded 1960 New Capital

Santa Cruz
Minas Novas
Diamantina

1880

1929 to Peru, Tacna
1929 to Chile, Arica
1879, Pisagua
1883 to Chile
Tarapacá
Iquique
Calama
Atacama Desert

Paraguay
La Plata 1938
Potosí
1879
1925

Chaco 1932/35 to Par.
1879
1880 to Bol.
1870 to Brazil

MINAS GERAIS
ESPÍRITO SANTO

San Francisco

Paraná

SÃO PAULO
Sao Paulo
1870
Santos

RIO DE JANEIRO
Rio de Janeiro
1906, 1942, 1947

Antofagasta
1884 to Chile

Jujuy
Salta
1874 to Arg.
Concepción
PARAGUAY
Asunción

PARANÁ Formed 1853
São Vicente
1892 to Brazil
SANTA CATARINA
Florianópolis (Destêrro)

S. Felix
S. Ambrosio to Chile
Caldera
Copiapó

Catamarca
Santiago del Estero

Paraná
Uruguay
1874 to Arg.

RIO GRANDE DO SUL
Porto Alegre

OCEAN

La Serena

CHILE

Cordoba
Santa Fé
1861, Pavon
1859, Cepeda
Rosario

Caseros
1852
Rio Grande

Juan Fernandez Is. to Chile
Valparaiso
Santiago 1923

San Luis
Buenos Aires 1910, 1936
URUGUAY
Fray Bentos
1909
Montevideo 1933
Dec. 13, 1939

Nov. 1, 1914
Concepción
Chillan

ARGENTINA
From 1853 Rep.

Salado
Bahia Blanca Founded 1863
Rio de la Plata

Valdivia
Osorno
Puerto Montt Founded 1853
Chiloé I.

Negro

Carmen de Patagones

PACIFIC

Rawson (Chubut) Founded 1865

Tropic of Capricorn

1861 to Arg.

Disputed between Chile and Arg. 1899–1902

Santa Cruz

Falkland Is. 1833 to Br. Disputed between Britain/Arg.
Dec. 8, 1914

Punta Arenas Founded 1847
Magellan's Str.
Tierra del Fuego

C. Horn

OCEAN

SOUTH AMERICA 1830–1956

Scale 1:40,000,000 (640 miles=1 inch)

0   200   400   800   1200 Miles
0 200 400   800   Km.

Confederation of Peru and Bolivia 1836–39
Battle of the War of the Pacific 1879–84
Sea battle of World War I or II with date
1903 Date of independence
1907 Boundary with date of final agreement
Lima 1938 Seat of Pan-American Congress with date

Essequibo, Demerara and Berbice were united to form British Guiana from 1831

SOUTH AMERICA : POPULATION, *c.*1950

Scale 1:40,000,000 (640 miles=1 inch)

0   200   400   600   800 Miles

0   200   400   600   800   1200 Km.

Density of Population:

Inhabitants to square mile

| | 0 | 2·6 | 26 | 128 | 256 |

Unpopulated

0   1   10   50   100

Inhabitants to square km.

Population of Cities
or Urban Agglomerations:

⊙ 100,000 – 250,000

◉ 250,000 – 500,000

■ 500,000 – 1 Million

▣ over 1 Million

COPYRIGHT. GEORGE PHILIP & SON, LTD.

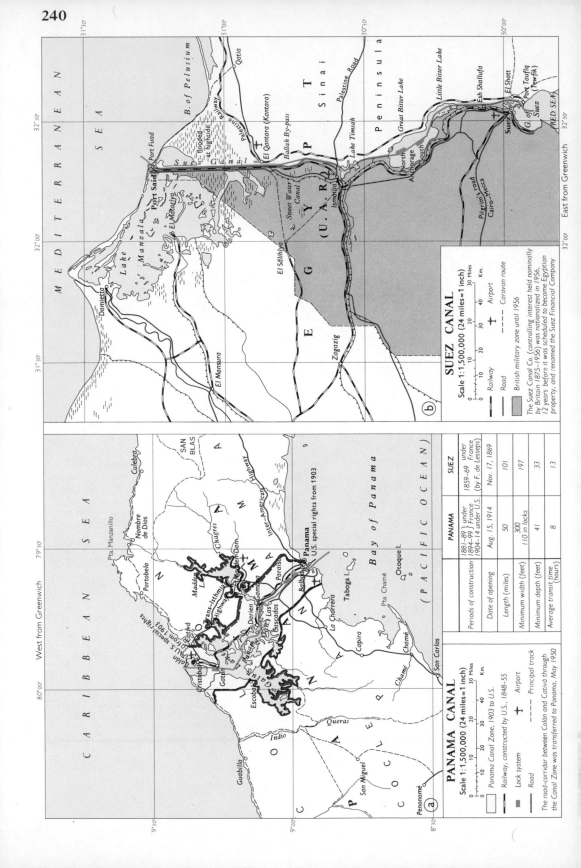

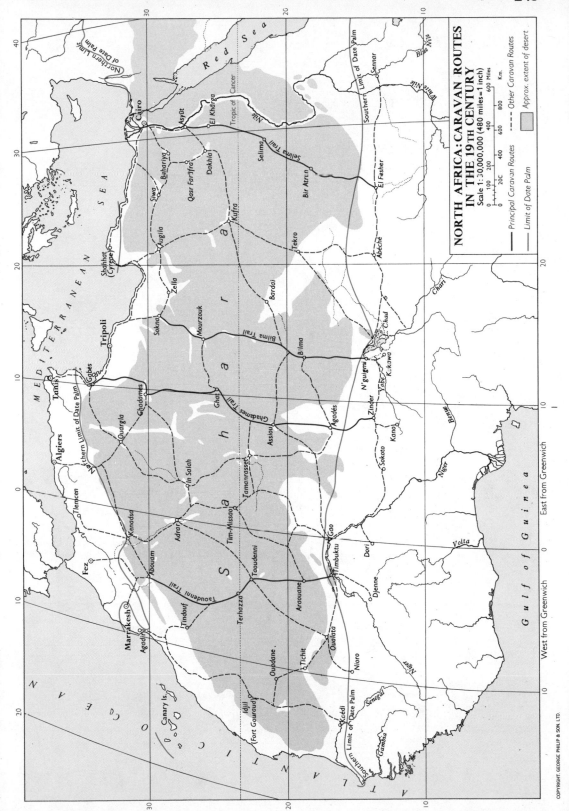

NORTH AFRICA: CARAVAN ROUTES
IN THE 19TH CENTURY
Scale 1:30,000,000 (480 miles=1 inch)

Principal Caravan Routes
Other Caravan Routes
Limit of Date Palm
Approx. extent of desert

COPYRIGHT. GEORGE PHILIP & SON, LTD.

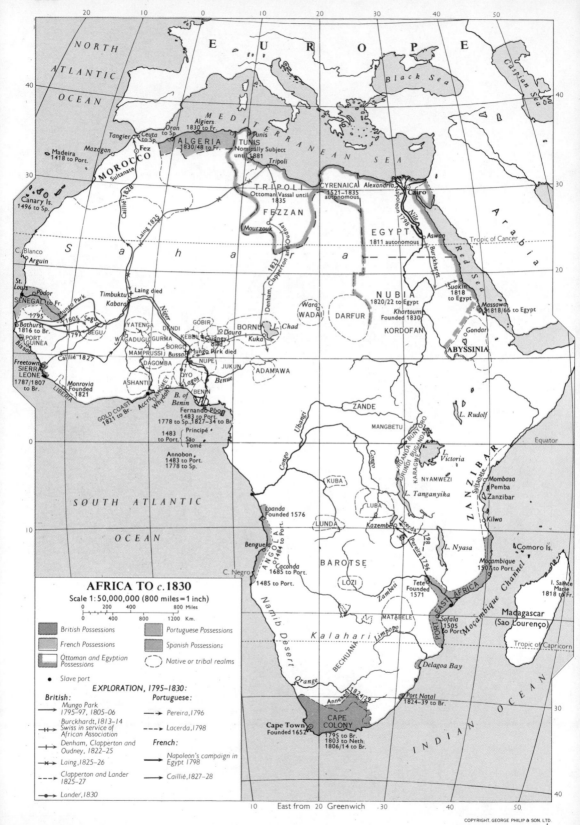

AFRICA TO c.1830

Scale 1:50,000,000 (800 miles = 1 inch)

| 0 | 200 | 400 | | 800 Miles |
| 0 | 400 | 800 | 1200 Km. |

British Possessions

Portuguese Possessions

French Possessions

Spanish Possessions

Ottoman and Egyptian Possessions

Native or tribal realms

• Slave port

EXPLORATION, 1795–1830:

British:
Mungo Park 1795–97, 1805–06
Burckhardt, 1813–14 Swiss in service of African Association
Denham, Clapperton and Oudney, 1822–25
Laing, 1825–26
Clapperton and Lander 1825–27
Lander, 1830

Portuguese:
Pereira, 1796
Lacerda, 1798

French:
Napoleon's campaign in Egypt 1798
Caillié, 1827–28

COPYRIGHT. GEORGE PHILIP & SON. LTD.

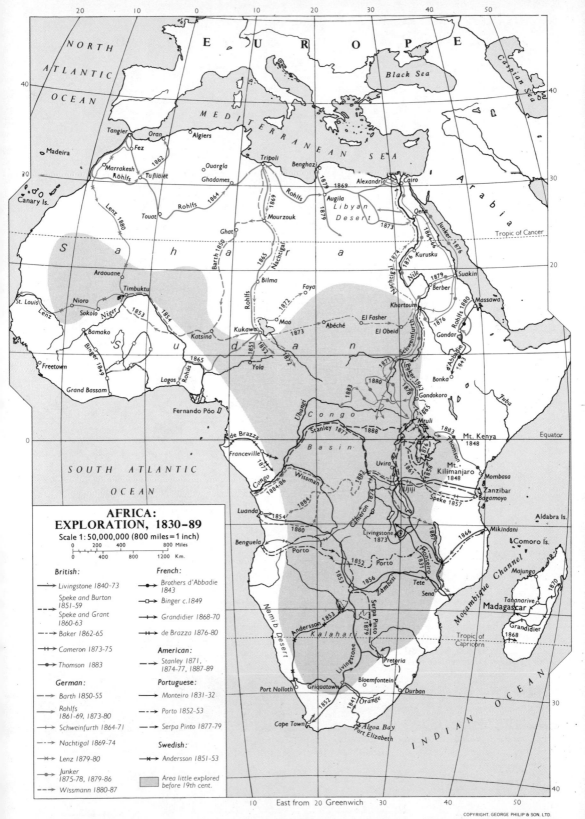

**AFRICA:
EXPLORATION, 1830–89**

Scale 1:50,000,000 (800 miles = 1 inch)

0   200   400   800 Miles
0   400   800   1200 Km.

British:

→ Livingstone 1840–73

Speke and Burton
1851–59

Speke and Grant
1860–63

-·-·- Baker 1862–65

⊢+++ Cameron 1873–75

•——• Thomson 1883

German:

→ Barth 1850–55

Rohlfs
1861–69, 1873–80

⊢+⊢+ Schweinfurth 1864–71

-·-·- Nachtigal 1869–74

×—×—× Lenz 1879–80

•——• Junker
1875–78, 1879–86

-·-·- Wissmann 1880–87

French:

●——● Brothers d'Abbadie
1843

□——□ Binger c.1849

+——+ Grandidier 1868–70

⊢+—+⊣ de Brazza 1876–80

American:

→ Stanley 1871,
1874–77, 1887–89

Portuguese:

→ Monteiro 1831–32

-·-·- Porto 1852–53

→ Serpa Pinto 1877–79

Swedish:

×—×—× Andersson 1851–53

▓ Area little explored
before 19th cent.

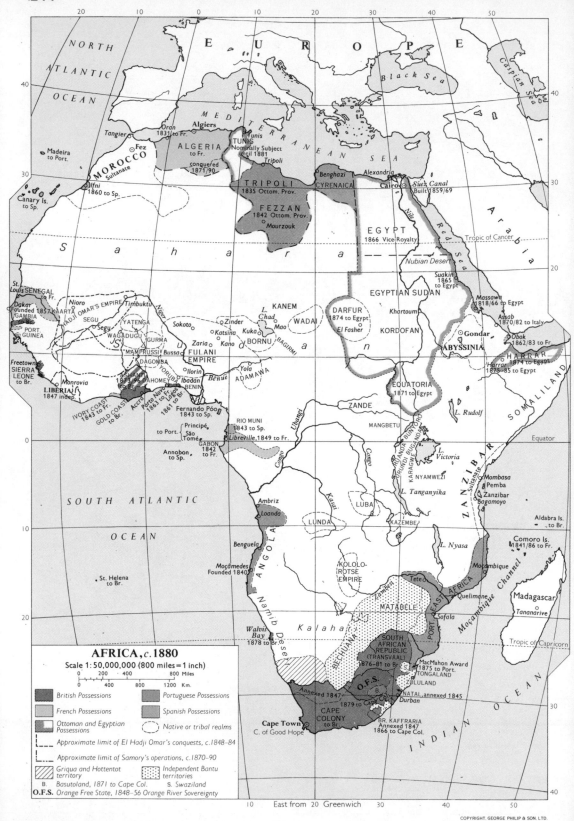

NORTH
ATLANTIC
OCEAN

E U R O P E

Black Sea

Caspian Sea

M E D I T E R R A N E A N   S E A

Tangier
Oran
1831 to Fr.
Algiers
Tunis
Nominally Subject
until 1881
Tripoli
Benghazi
Alexandria
Cairo
Suez Canal
Built 1859/69

○ Madeira
to Port.

○ Fez
MOROCCO
Sultanate
Ifni
1860 to Sp.

ALGERIA
to Fr.
conquered
1871/90

TRIPOLI
1835 Ottom. Prov.
CYRENAICA

Canary Is.
to Sp.

FEZZAN
1842 Ottom. Prov.
● Mourzouk

S   a   h   a   r   a

EGYPT
1866 Vice-Royalty

Red Sea

A r a b i a

Tropic of Cancer

Nubian Desert

Suakin
1865
to Egypt

St. Louis
SENEGAL
to Fr.
Dakar
Founded 1857
GAMBIA
PORT.
GUINEA

Nioro
HADJ OMAR'S EMPIRE
SEGU
SEGU
Timbuktu

L. KANEM
Chad
Mao

WADAI

DARFUR
1874 to Egypt
El Fasher

EGYPTIAN SUDAN

Khartoum

Massowa
1818/66 to Egypt
Assab
1870/82 to Italy
Obok
1862/83 to Egypt

KAARTA
YATENGA
WAGADUGU
GURMA
MAMPRUSSI
DAGOMBA

Zinder
Sokoto

Katsina
Zaria
Kano

Kuka
BORNU
BAGIRMI

KORDOFAN

Gondar
ABYSSINIA

HARRAR
Harrar
1874 to Egypt
1875–85 to Egypt

Freetown
SIERRA
LEONE
to Br.
Monrovia
LIBERIA
1847 indep.

ASHANTI
1896 to Br.
DAHOMEY
IVORY COAST
1843 to Fr.
GOLD COAST
to Br.

FULANI
EMPIRE
Bussa
Ilorin
YORUBA
Ibadan
BENIN
Accra
Porto Novo
1863 to Fr.
Lagos
1861 to Br.
Fernando Póo
1843 to Sp.

Benue
ADAMAWA
Yola

EQUATORIA
1871 to Egypt

L. Rudolf

SOMALILAND

ZANDE

MANGBETU

RIO MUNI
1843 to Sp.
Libreville, 1849 to Fr.

Principé
to Port.
São
Tomé
Annobon
to Sp.
GABON
1842
to Fr.

Ubangi

RUANDA
BURUNDI
KARAGWE
BUGANDA
BUNYORO

L.
Victoria

NYAMWEZI

Equator

ZANZIBAR Sultanate

Mombasa
Pemba
Zanzibar
Bagamoyo

SOUTH ATLANTIC

OCEAN

Congo

Kasai

LUBA
KAZEMBE

LUNDA

L. Tanganyika

Aldabra Is.
to Br.

Ambriz
Loanda

Benguela

ANGOLA

Moçâmedes
Founded 1840

KOLOLO-
ROTSE
EMPIRE

L. Nyasa

Comoro Is.
1841/86 to Fr.

St. Helena
to Br.

Zambezi
Tete
PORT. EAST AFRICA
Quelimane

Moçambique

Mozambique Channel

Madagascar
Tananarive

Namib Desert

Kalahari

Walvis
Bay
1878 to Br.

BECHUANA

MATABELE

SOUTH
AFRICAN
REPUBLIC
(TRANSVAAL)
1876–81 to Br.

Sofala

Tropic of Capricorn

MacMahon Award
1875 to Port.
TONGALAND

O.F.S.

ZULULAND

Annexed 1847
1879 to

NATAL, annexed 1845
Durban

Cape Town
C. of Good Hope

CAPE
COLONY
to Br.

BR. KAFFRARIA
Annexed 1847
1866 to Cape Col.

INDIAN   OCEAN

AFRICA, *c.1880*
Scale 1 : 50,000,000 (800 miles = 1 inch)

0   200   400   800 Miles
0   400   800   1200 Km.

British Possessions
French Possessions
Ottoman and Egyptian
Possessions
Portuguese Possessions
Spanish Possessions
Native or tribal realms

Approximate limit of El Hadji Omar's conquests, c.1848–84
Approximate limit of Samory's operations, c.1870–90
Griqua and Hottentot
territory
Independent Bantu
territories
B. Basutoland, 1871 to Cape Col.   **S.** Swaziland
O.F.S. Orange Free State, 1848–56 Orange River Sovereignty

10   East from 20 Greenwich   30   40   50

COPYRIGHT, GEORGE PHILIP & SON, LTD.

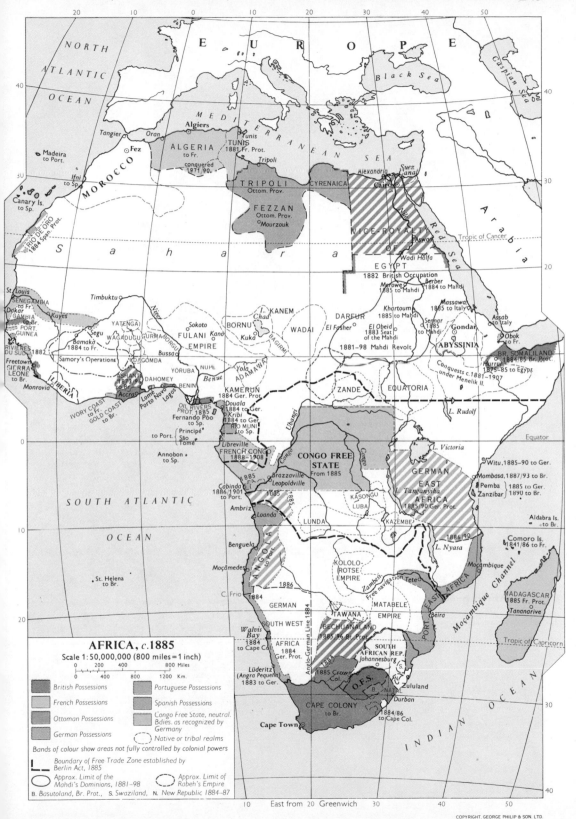

AFRICA, c.1885

Scale 1:50,000,000 (800 miles = 1 inch)

0   200   400   800 Miles

0   400   800   1200 Km.

British Possessions

French Possessions

Ottoman Possessions

German Possessions

Portuguese Possessions

Spanish Possessions

Congo Free State, neutral. Bdies. as recognized by Germany

Native or tribal realms

Bands of colour show areas not fully controlled by colonial powers

Boundary of Free Trade Zone established by Berlin Act, 1885

Approx. Limit of the Mahdi's Dominions, 1881–98

Approx. Limit of Rabeh's Empire

B. Basutoland, Br. Prot., S. Swaziland, N. New Republic 1884–87

East from 20 Greenwich

COPYRIGHT. GEORGE PHILIP & SON. LTD.

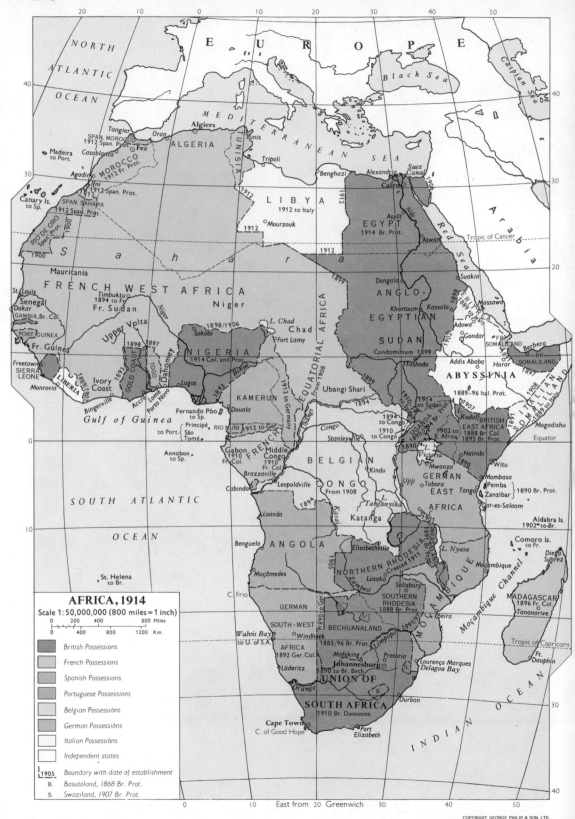

AFRICA, 1914

Scale 1:50,000,000 (800 miles=1 inch)

0 200 400 800 Miles
0 400 800 1200 Km.

British Possessions
French Possessions
Spanish Possessions
Portuguese Possessions
Belgian Possessions
German Possessions
Italian Possessions
Independent states

1905 Boundary with date of establishment
B. Basutoland, 1868 Br. Prot.
S. Swaziland, 1907 Br. Prot.

COPYRIGHT. GEORGE PHILIP & SON. LTD.

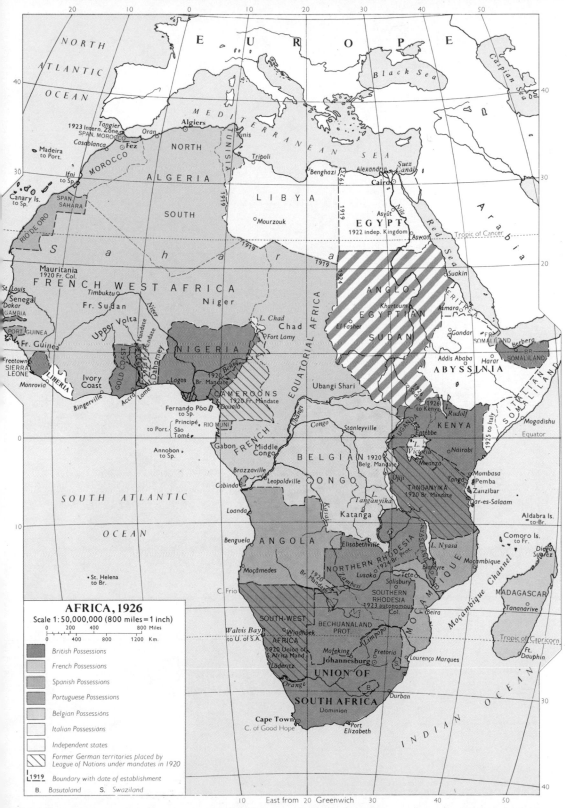

AFRICA, 1926
Scale 1:50,000,000 (800 miles = 1 inch)

| | 200 | 400 | 800 Miles |
| 0 | 400 | 800 | 1200 Km. |

British Possessions
French Possessions
Spanish Possessions
Portuguese Possessions
Belgian Possessions
Italian Possessions
Independent states
Former German territories placed by League of Nations under mandates in 1920
1919 Boundary with date of establishment
B. Basutoland   S. Swaziland

EUROPE

NORTH ATLANTIC OCEAN

MEDITERRANEAN SEA

Black Sea

Caspian Sea

Arabia

Tangier
1923 Intern. Zone
SPAN. MOROCCO
Casablanca
Fez
Algiers
Tunis
Tripoli
Benghazi
Alexandria
Suez Canal
Cairo

Oran
TUNISIA

Ifni
to Sp.
MOROCCO

Madeira
to Port.

Canary Is.
to Sp.
SPAN.
SAHARA

RIO DE ORO

NORTH
ALGERIA
SOUTH

LIBYA

Mourzouk

EGYPT
1922 indep. Kingdom

Asyût

Aswân

Tropic of Cancer

Red Sea

Suakin

ERITREA

Sahara

Mauritania
1920 Fr. Col.

St. Louis
Senegal
Dakar
GAMBIA

PORT. GUINEA

Fr. Guinea

Freetown
SIERRA LEONE

Monrovia
LIBERIA

Bingerville

FRENCH WEST AFRICA

Timbuktu

Fr. Sudan

Upper Volta

Niger

L. Chad
Fort Lamy

Chad

NIGERIA

Ivory
Coast

GOLD COAST
Dahomey
Lomé
Accra

Lagos
Br. Mandate
1920

CAMEROONS
1920 Fr. Mandate

Fernando Póo
to Sp.
Douala

Principé
to Port. São
Tomé

RIO MUNI

Annobon
to Sp.

Gabon

FRENCH
Middle
Congo

Brazzaville

Cabinda

Loanda

Benguela

Moçâmedes

ANGOLA

C. Frio

Walvis Bay
to U. of S.A.

Windhoek

SOUTH-WEST
AFRICA
1920 Union of
S. Africa Mand.

Lüderitz

EQUATORIAL AFRICA

Ubangi Shari

Congo
Stanleyville

BELGIAN
CONGO
1920
Belg. Mandate

Leopoldville

Katanga

Elisabethville

Kasai

L.
Tanganyika

Ujiji

UGANDA

Entebbe
L.
Victoria

Mwanza

TANGANYIKA
1920 Br. Mandate

Rudolf

KENYA
1926
to Kenya

Nairobi

Mombasa
Pemba
Zanzibar
Dar-es-Salaam

1925 to Italy

1926
to Kenya

SOMALILAND

Addis Ababa
Harar

ABYSSINIA

FR.
SOMALILAND
Berbera
BR.
SOMALILAND

Asmara
Gondar

El Fasher

Khartoum

ANGLO-
EGYPTIAN
SUDAN

Mogadishu

Equator

Tanga

Comoro Is.
to Fr.

Aldabra Is.
to Br.

Diego
Suárez

NORTHERN RHODESIA
1924 Br. Prot.

Lusaka

Zambesi

L. Nyasa

Tete

Blantyre

Salisbury

SOUTHERN
RHODESIA
1923 autonomous
Col.

Beira

MOZAMBIQUE

Moçambique

Lourenço Marques

Moçambique Channel

MADAGASCAR

Tananarive

Tropic of Capricorn

Ft.
Dauphin

BECHUANALAND
PROT.

Mafeking
1920 Union of
S. Africa

Johannesburg
Pretoria

Limpopo

Durban

UNION OF
SOUTH AFRICA
Dominion

Orange

Cape Town
C. of Good Hope

Port
Elizabeth

INDIAN OCEAN

St. Helena
to Br.

SOUTH ATLANTIC OCEAN

East from Greenwich

COPYRIGHT. GEORGE PHILIP & SON. LTD.

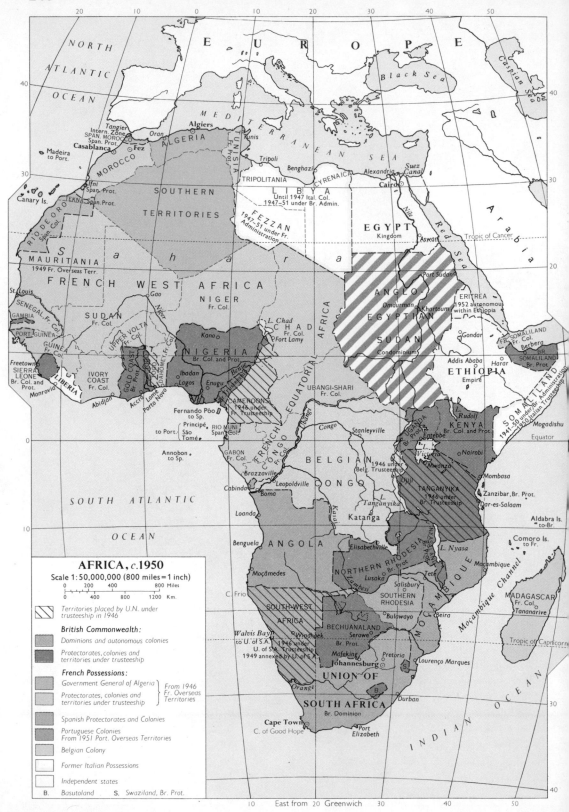

AFRICA, c.1950

Scale 1:50,000,000 (800 miles=1 inch)

Territories placed by U.N. under trusteeship in 1946

British Commonwealth:
Dominions and autonomous colonies
Protectorates, colonies and territories under trusteeship

French Possessions:
Government General of Algeria ⎱ From 1946
Protectorates, colonies and ⎰ Fr. Overseas
territories under trusteeship   Territories

Spanish Protectorates and Colonies
Portuguese Colonies
From 1951 Port. Overseas Territories
Belgian Colony
Former Italian Possessions
Independent states

B. Basutoland   S. Swaziland, Br. Prot.

COPYRIGHT. GEORGE PHILIP & SON. LTD.

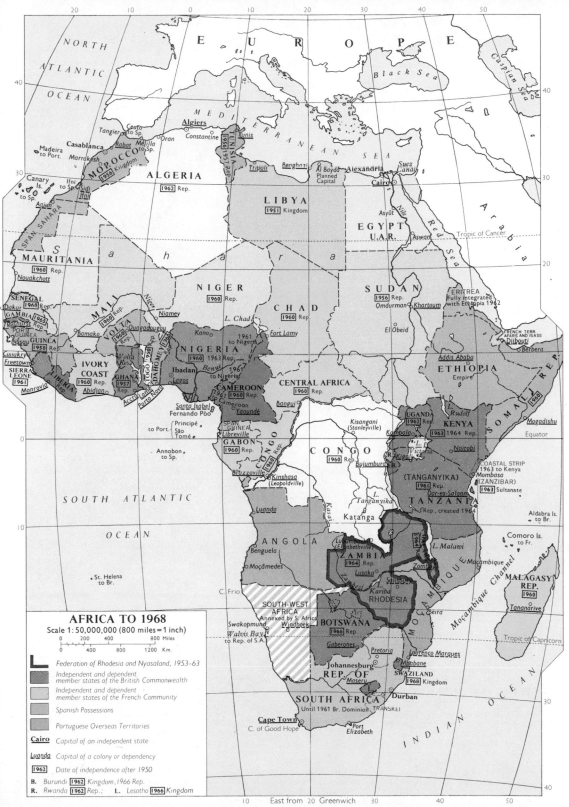

AFRICA TO 1968

Scale 1:50,000,000 (800 miles=1 inch)

| 0 | 200 | 400 | | 800 Miles |

| 0 | 400 | 800 | 1200 Km. |

Federation of Rhodesia and Nyasaland, 1953–63

Independent and dependent
member states of the British Commonwealth

Independent and dependent
member states of the French Community

Spanish Possessions

Portuguese Overseas Territories

Cairo — Capital of an independent state

Luanda — Capital of a colony or dependency

1962 — Date of independence after 1950

B. — Burundi 1962 Kingdom, 1966 Rep.

R. — Rwanda 1962 Rep.;   L. — Lesotho 1966 Kingdom

East from 20 Greenwich

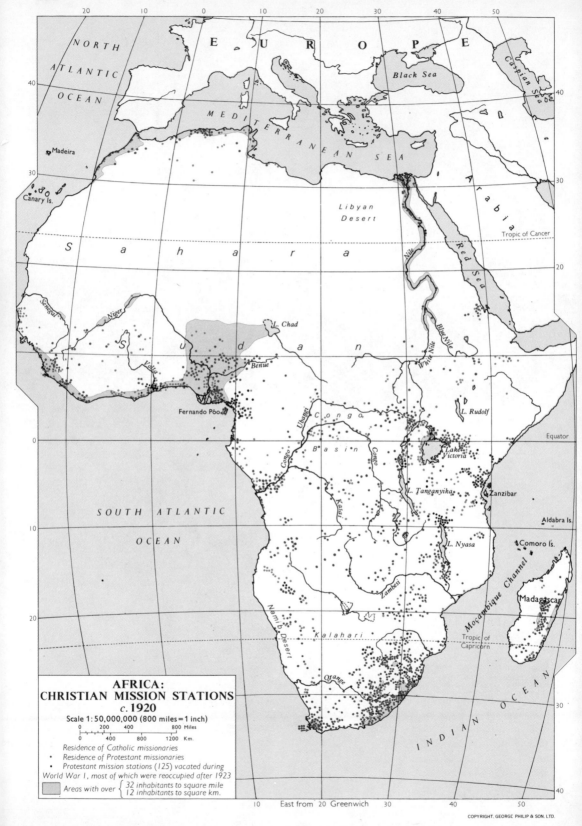

AFRICA:
CHRISTIAN MISSION STATIONS
c. 1920

Scale 1:50,000,000 (800 miles = 1 inch)

0   200   400   800 Miles
0   400   800   1200 Km.

Residence of Catholic missionaries
• *Residence of Protestant missionaries*
• *Protestant mission stations (125) vacated during*
World War 1, most of which were reoccupied after 1923

Areas with over { 32 inhabitants to square mile
                  12 inhabitants to square km.

COPYRIGHT. GEORGE PHILIP & SON. LTD.

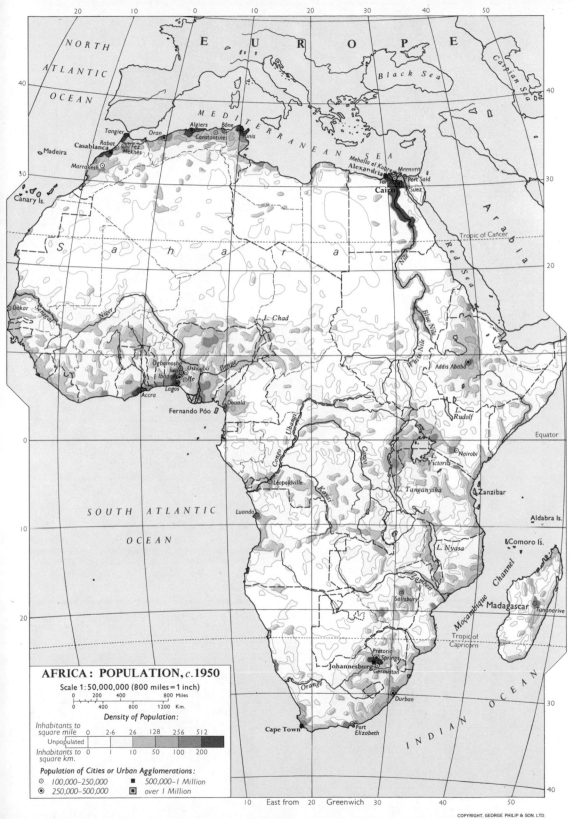

AFRICA : POPULATION, *c.*1950

Scale 1:50,000,000 (800 miles = 1 inch)

Density of Population:

Inhabitants to square mile   0   2·6   26   128   256   512

Unpopulated

Inhabitants to square km.   0   1   10   50   100   200

Population of Cities or Urban Agglomerations:

⊙ 100,000–250,000   ■ 500,000–1 Million
◉ 250,000–500,000   ▣ over 1 Million

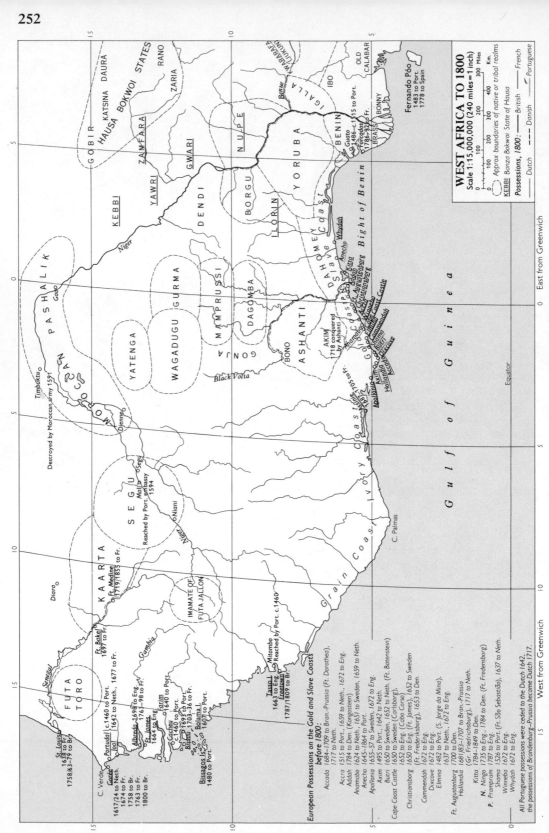

KEBBI Bonza Bokwoi State of Hausa

WEST AFRICA TO 1800

Scale 1:15,000,000 (240 miles = 1 inch)

0 100 200 300 400 Miles
0 100 200 300 400 500 Km.

Approx boundaries of native or tribal realms

Possessions, 1800:

— British — French
— Dutch --- Danish — Portuguese

HAUSA STATES
GOBIR DAURA KATSINA BOKWOI RANO ZAMFARA ZARIA GWIARI NUPE YAWRI KEBBI DENDI BORGU LORIN YORUBA BENIN IGALLA IBO OLD CALABAR KWARAFA (JUKON)

Fernando Póo
1483 to Port.
1778 to Spain

BONNY BRASS
Benue
Guato
c 1486–c1515 to Port.
Forcados 1786–92 to Fr.

Bight of Benin

DAHOMEY
Slave Coast
Whydah Anecho Kitta
Porto Novo

ASHANTI
AKIM 1718 conquered by Ashanti
Gold Coast
BONO

Ivory Coast

Grain Coast

Gulf of Guinea

KAARTA
SEGU
Reached by Port. embassy 1594
Niani
Segu Kongostem

PASHALIK
Timbúktu
Gao
Djenné
Destroyed by Moroccan army 1591
Niger

YATENGA WAGADUGU GURMA MAMPRUSSI GONJA DAGOMBA
Black Volta

FUTA TORO
Diara
IMAMATE OF FUTA JALLON

Senegal
Gambia
Niger
Bafing

C. Palmas

Tasso I. Mitombo
1663 to Eng. Reached by Port. c.1460
Freetown
1787/1809 to Br.

European Possessions on the Gold and Slave Coasts before 1800:

Accada 1684–1709 to Bran.-Prussia (Ft. Dorothea), 1717 to Neth.
Accra 1515 to Port., 1659 to Neth., 1672 to Eng.
Addah 1784 to Den. (Kongosten)
Anamabo 1624 to Neth., 1651 to Sweden, 1659 to Neth.
Anecho 1645–1864 to Port.
Apollonia 1655–57 to Sweden, 1672 to Eng.
Axim 495 to Port., 1642 to Neth.
Butri 1650 to Sweden, 1652 to Neth. (Ft. Batenstein)
Cape Coast Castle 1650 to Sweden (Carlsborg), 1652 to Eng. (Ft. James), 1652 to Sweden
Christiansborg 1650 to Eng. (Ft. Frederiksborg), 1653 to Den.
Commendah 1672 to Eng.
Dixcove 1672 to Eng.
Elmina 482 to Port. (S. Jorge da Mina), 1637 to Neth., 1672 to Eng.

Ft. Augustenborg 1700 to Den.
Hollandia 1681/83–1707 to Bran.-Prussia (Gr. Friedrichsburg), 1717 to Neth.
Kitta 1784 to Eng., 1849 to Den.
N. Ningo 1735 to Eng. 1784 to Den. (Ft. Fredensborg)
P. Prompram 1787 to Eng.
Shama 526 to Port. (Ft. Sáo Sebastião), 1637 to Neth.
Winnebo 1672 to Eng.
Whydah 1672 to Eng.

All Portuguese possessions were ceded to the Dutch 1642, the possessions of Brandenburg-Prussia became Dutch 1717.

St. Louis 1638 to Fr.
1758/63–79 to Br.
C. Verde, Gorée 1617/24 to Port.
Portudal c.1460 to Port.
1674 to Fr.
1758 to Fr.
1763 to Fr.
1800 to Br.
1652 to Neth., 1677 to Fr.
Ft. Bakel 1697 to Fr.
Ft. Medine 1719/1855 to Fr.
Albreda 1698 to Eng., 1659 to Fr.
Ft. James 1664 to Eng.
Cacheu c.1460 to Port.
Geba 1640 to Port.
Bissao 1693 to Port., 1703–36 to Fr.
Bolama I. 1607 to Port.
Bissagos Is. 1480 to Port.

West from Greenwich

East from Greenwich

Equator

COPYRIGHT. GEORGE PHILIP & SON. LTD.

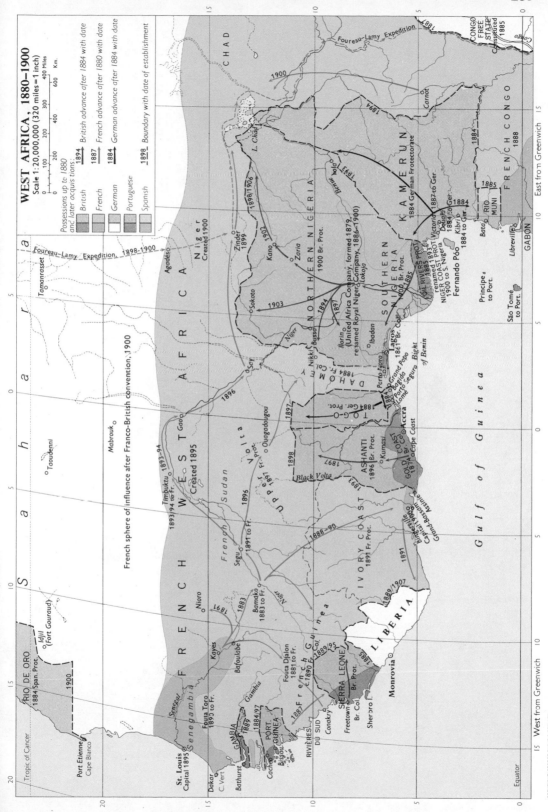

WEST AFRICA, 1880–1900
Scale 1:20,000,000 (320 miles=1 inch)

British advance after 1884 with date	1894
French advance after 1880 with date	1887
German advance after 1884 with date	1884
Boundary with date of establishment	1898

Possessions up to 1880
and later acquisitions

British French German Portuguese Spanish

S a h a r a

French sphere of influence after Franco-British convention, 1900

Foureau–Lamy Expedition, 1898–1900

Tamanrasset

Mabrouk

Taoudenni

Agadès

Zinder 1899

Niger Created 1900

Sokoto

1903

Timbuktu 1893–94

Created 1895

French Sudan

Ségu 1891 to Fr.

Nioro

Bamako 1883 to Fr.

Kayes

1883

Bafoulabé

Fouta Toro 1891 to Fr.

Senegal

Senegambia

St. Louis Capital 1895

Dakar C. Vert

Bathurst

GAMBIA 1884/97

PORT. GUINEA

Cacheu Bissau

Fouta Djalon 1881 to Fr.

Conakry

RIVIÈRES DU SUD

French Guinea c.1890 Fr. Col. 1889/95

SIERRA LEONE Freetown Br. Col. Br. Prot.

Sherbro

LIBERIA

Monrovia

1895

1889/1907

1891

IVORY COAST 1891 Fr. Prot.

Bingerville Capital 1900 Grand-Bassam 1842 to Fr. Assinie 1842 to Fr.

1888–90

1892

Upper Volta Created 1895

Ouagadougou

Black Volta

Gao

Sey

1896

1897

1897

DAHOMEY 1884 Fr. Col.

Nikki Bussa

Ouidah Grand Popo Porto Novo Porto Seguro Lomé Bight of Benin

TOGO 1884 Ger. Prot.

Accra

GOLD COAST Br. Col. 1871 Cape Coast

ASHANTI 1896 Br. Prot.

Kumasi 1896

1897

1898

Florin 1897

Ibadan

Lagos 1861 Br. Col.

SOUTHERN NIGERIA 1900 Br. Prot.

OIL RIVERS PROT. 1885 renamed 1893 NIGER COAST PROT. 1900 to S. Nigeria

NORTHERN NIGERIA 1900 Br. Prot.

Lokoja

United Africa Company, formed 1879, renamed Royal Niger Company, 1886–1900

1894

Kano 1903

Zaria

Benue

1893

CHAD

L. Chad

1900

Foureau-Lamy Expedition

1887

KAMERUN 1884 German Protectorate

1884 to Ger. 1887 to Ger. Victoria Douala Kribi 1884 to Ger.

RIO MUNI 1885

Bata

Fernando Póo 1884 to Sp.

Principe to Port.

São Tomé to Port.

Librerville

GABON

FRENCH CONGO 1888

1884

Carnot 1894

CONGO FREE STATE 1885 Constituted

Congo

1898/1906

F R E N C H   W E S T   A F R I C A

Gulf of Guinea

Equator

Tropic of Cancer

RIO DE ORO 1884 Span. Prot.

1900

Port Etienne Cape Blanco

Djil (Fort Gouraud)

West from Greenwich

East from Greenwich

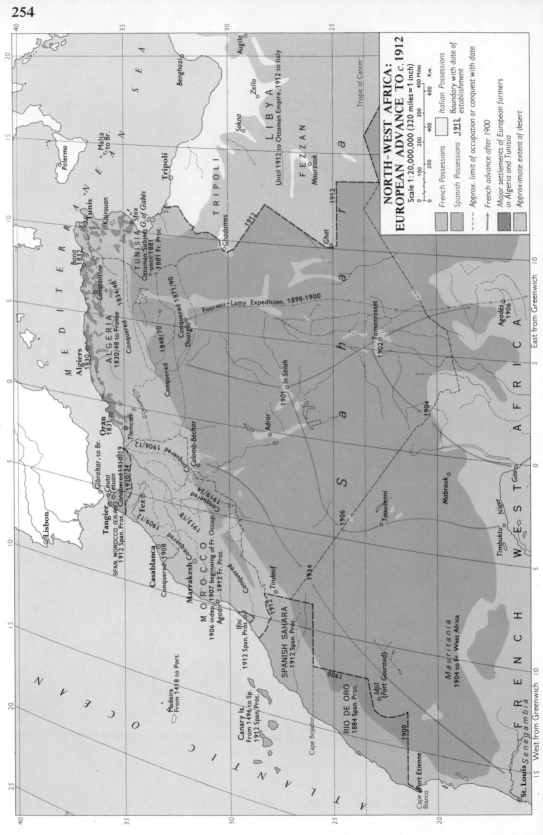

NORTH-WEST AFRICA:
EUROPEAN ADVANCE TO c.1912
Scale 1:20,000,000 (320 miles =1 inch)

French Possessions
Spanish Possessions
Italian Possessions
1912 Boundary with date of establishment
Approx. limit of occupation or conquest with date
French advance after 1900
Major settlements of European farmers in Algeria and Tunisia
Approximate extent of desert

0   100 200 300 400 Miles
0 200 400 600 Km.

Tropic of Cancer

East from Greenwich

MEDITERRANEAN SEA

Palermo
Malta to Br.
Tunis
Kairouan
Tripoli
Benghazi
Augila
Zella
Sokna
LIBYA
Until 1912 to Ottoman Empire,1912 to Italy
FEZZAN
Maurzouk
TRIPOLI
Ghadames
1912
1912
Ghat

TUNISIA
Sfax
G. of Gabes
Ottoman. Subject 1881
1881 Fr. Prot.

Constantine
1834/48
ALGERIA
1830/48 to France
Conquered 1871/90
Conquered 1848/70
Ouargla
Foureau–Lamy Expedition, 1898-1900
Tamanrasset
1902
Agadès
1906

Algiers
1830
Conquered

Oran
1831
Tlemcen
Conquered 1910/19
Conquered 1906/12
Colomb-Béchar
Adrar
1901
In Salah
1904

Gibraltar. to Br.
Ceuta
Tetuan
Conquered 1920/34
Tangier
SPAN.MOROCCO (ER-RIF)
1912 Span.Prot.
Fez
1909/12
1913/18
Conquered 1919/34

Casablanca
Conquered 1908
Marrakesh
MOROCCO
1906 indep./1907 beginning of Fr. Occup./1912 Fr. Prot.
Agadir

Ifni
1912 Span.Prot.
Tindouf
1912
1934

SPANISH SAHARA
1912 Span. Prot.

Idjil
(Fort Gouraud)
1900

Taoudenni
Mabrouk

Mauritania
1904 to Fr. West Africa

Timbuktu
Gao
Niger
WEST AFRICA

Lisbon

Madeira
From 1418 to Port.

Canary Is.
From 1496/to Sp.
1912 Span/Prot.

Cape Bojador

RIO DE ORO
1884 Span. Prot.
1900

Cape Blanco
Port Etienne
St.Louis
Senegambia
FRENCH

ATLANTIC OCEAN

S   a   h   a   r   a

West from Greenwich

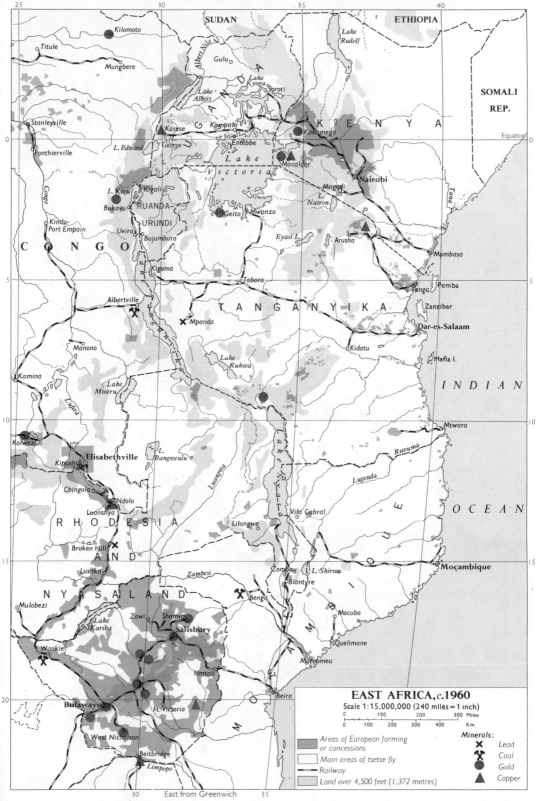

EAST AFRICA, c.1960

Scale 1:15,000,000 (240 miles = 1 inch)

0   100   200   300   Miles
0   100   200   300   400   Km.

Areas of European farming
or concessions

Main areas of tsetse fly

Railway

Land over 4,500 feet (1,372 metres)

Minerals:
X   Lead
     Coal
●   Gold
▲   Copper

East from Greenwich

COPYRIGHT. GEORGE PHILIP & SON. LTD.

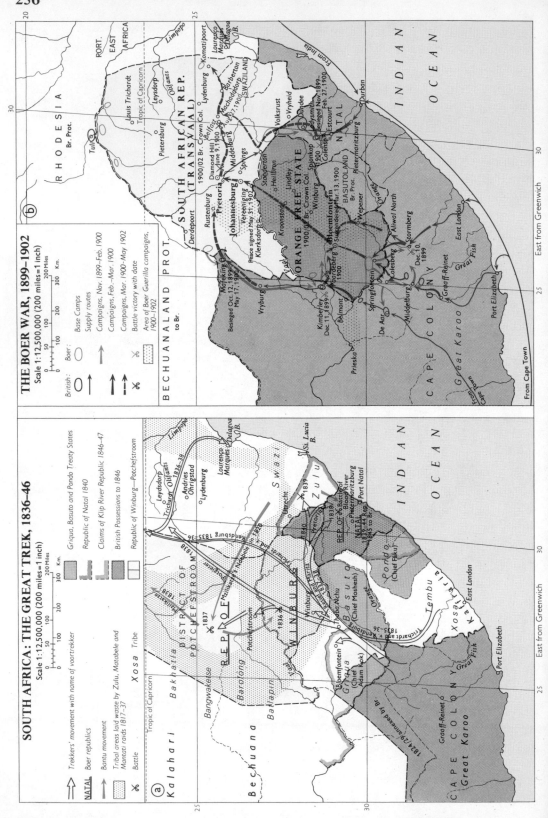

SOUTH AFRICA: THE GREAT TREK, 1836–46

(a)

Scale 1:12,500,000 (200 miles=1 inch)

0 50 100 200 300 Miles

0 100 200 300 Km.

Trekkers' movement with name of voortrekker

NATAL Boer republics

Bantu movement

Tribal areas laid waste by Zulu, Matabele and
Mantati raids 1817–37

Battle

Griqua, Basuto and Pondo Treaty States

Republic of Natal 1840

Claims of Klip River Republic 1846–47

British Possessions to 1846

Republic of Winburg—Potche[f]stroom

THE BOER WAR, 1899–1902

(b)

Scale 1:12,500,000 (200 miles=1 inch)

0 50 100 200 300 Miles

0 100 200 300 Km.

British: Boer:

Base Camps

Supply routes

Campaigns, Nov. 1899–Feb. 1900

Campaigns, Feb.–Mar. 1900

Campaigns, Mar. 1900–May 1902

Battle/Boer victory with date

Area of Boer Guerilla campaigns,
1900–1902

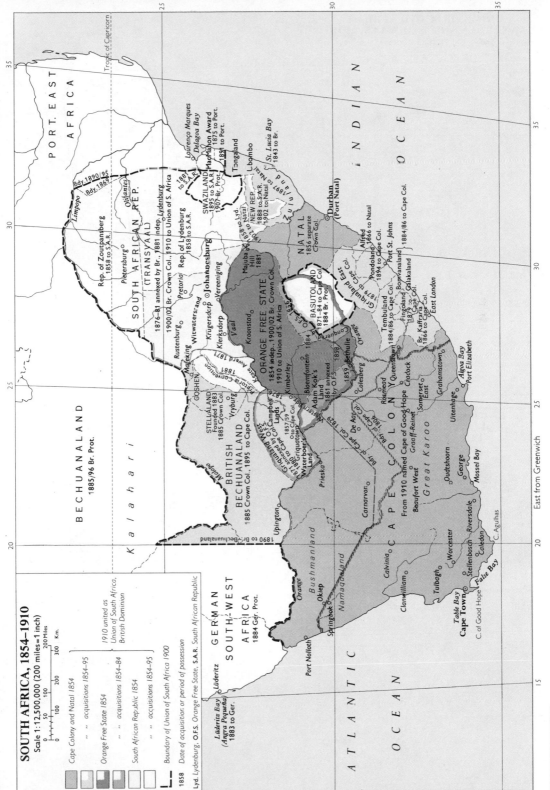

SOUTH AFRICA, 1854–1910

Scale 1:12,500,000 (200 miles=1 inch)

0 50 100 150 200 Miles

0 50 100 150 200 300 Km.

Cape Colony and Natal 1854

   ,,   ,,   acquisitions 1854–95

Orange Free State 1854

   ,,   ,,   acquisitions 1854–84

South African Republic 1854

   ,,   ,,   acquisitions 1854–95

Boundary of Union of South Africa 1900

1858 Date of acquisition or period of possession

Lyd. Lydenburg, O.F.S. Orange Free State, S.A.R. South African Republic

1910 united as
Union of South Africa,
British Dominion

COPYRIGHT. GEORGE PHILIP & SON, LTD.

258

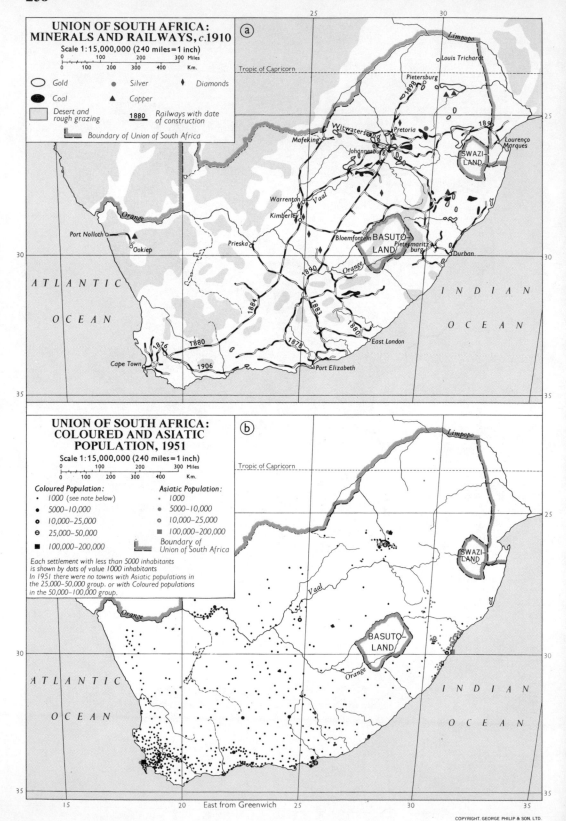

UNION OF SOUTH AFRICA:
MINERALS AND RAILWAYS, c.1910

UNION OF SOUTH AFRICA:
COLOURED AND ASIATIC
POPULATION, 1951

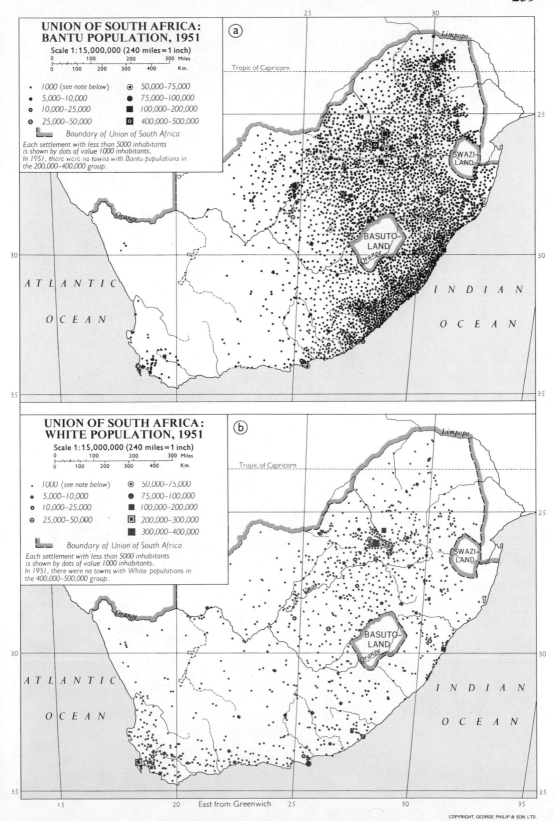

UNION OF SOUTH AFRICA: BANTU POPULATION, 1951

Scale 1:15,000,000 (240 miles = 1 inch)

| 0 | 100 | 200 | 300 Miles |

| 0 | 100 | 200 | 300 | 400 Km. |

- 1000 (see note below)
- 5,000–10,000
- 10,000–25,000
- 25,000–50,000
- 50,000–75,000
- 75,000–100,000
- 100,000–200,000
- 400,000–500,000

Boundary of Union of South Africa

Each settlement with less than 5000 inhabitants is shown by dots of value 1000 inhabitants.
In 1951, there were no towns with Bantu populations in the 200,000–400,000 group.

UNION OF SOUTH AFRICA: WHITE POPULATION, 1951

Scale 1:15,000,000 (240 miles = 1 inch)

| 0 | 100 | 200 | 300 Miles |

| 0 | 100 | 200 | 300 | 400 Km. |

- 1000 (see note below)
- 5,000–10,000
- 10,000–25,000
- 25,000–50,000
- 50,000–75,000
- 75,000–100,000
- 100,000–200,000
- 200,000–300,000
- 300,000–400,000

Boundary of Union of South Africa

Each settlement with less than 5000 inhabitants is shown by dots of value 1000 inhabitants.
In 1951, there were no towns with White populations in the 400,000–500,000 group.

East from Greenwich

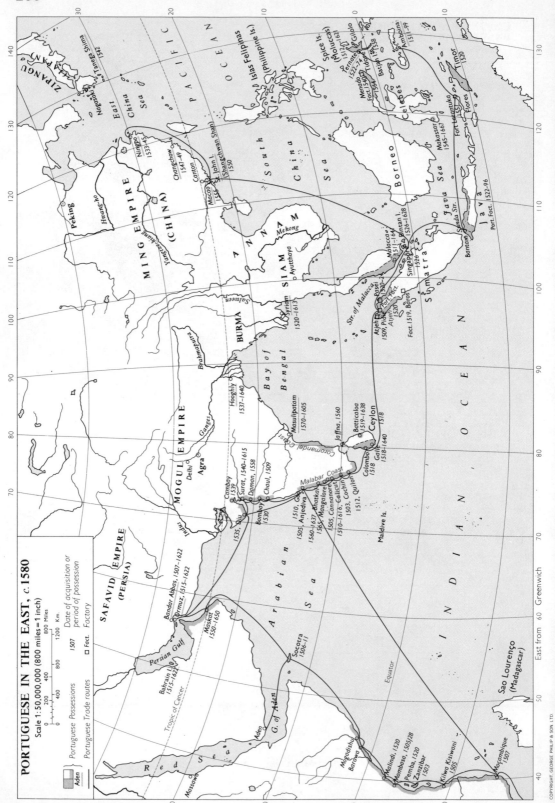

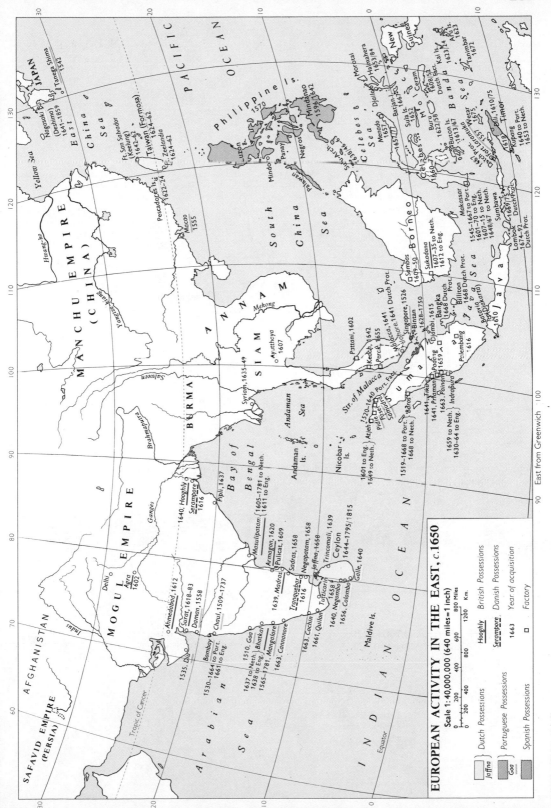

EUROPEAN ACTIVITY IN THE EAST, c.1650

Scale 1:40,000,000 (640 miles=1 inch)

Dutch Possessions

Portuguese Possessions

Spanish Possessions

British Possessions — *Hooghly*

Danish Possessions — *Serampore*

Jaffna / *Goa*

1663 — Year of acquisition

☐ Factory

Scale 0 200 400 600 800 Miles
0 400 800 1200 Km.

EAST INDIES, 1700–1820

Scale 1 : 22,500,000 (360 miles = 1 inch)

| 0 | 100 | 200 | 300 | 400 | 500 Miles |

| 0 | 200 | 400 | 600 | 800 Km. |

Native states or unsettled areas

Dutch Possessions in 17th cent.

Dutch acquisitions to 1820

Spanish Possessions

Portuguese Possessions

Acquisitions of Dutch
East India Company,
from 1795
Dutch East Indies

British Possessions

Danish Possessions

1797 Date of acquisition or period of possession

□ Dutch factory

■ English factory

The colours also include protectorates and areas of privileged factories

East from Greenwich

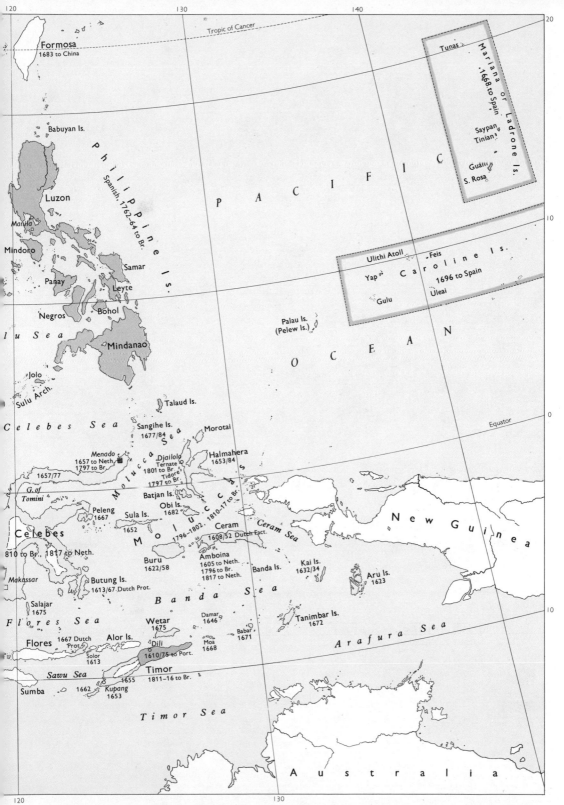

Tropic of Cancer

120   130   140

20

Formosa
1683 to China

Tunas

Mariana or Ladrone Is.
1668 to Spain

P   A   C   I   F   I   C

Babuyan Is.

Saypan
Tinian

Luzon

Guam
S. Rosa

Manila

10

Mindoro

Ulithi Atoll   Feis

Panay   Samar

Yap   C a r o l i n e I s.
1696 to Spain

Negros   Leyte

Gulu   Uleai

Bohol

lu Sea

Mindanao

Jolo

Palau Is.
(Pelew Is.)

O   C   E   A   N

Sulu Arch.

Talaud Is.

Equator   0

Celebes Sea

Sangihe Is.
1677/84

Morotai

Menado
1657 to Neth.
1797 to Br.

Djailolo
Ternate
1801 to Br.
Tidore
1797 to Br.

Halmahera
1653/84

1657/77

G. of
Tomini

Batjan Is.

Peleng
1667

Obi Is.
1682

N e w   G u i n e a

Sula Is.
1652

1796–1802. 1810–17 to Br.

Celebes

Ceram
1608/52 Dutch Fact.

Ceram Sea

810 to Br., 1817 to Neth.

Buru
1622/58

Amboina
1605 to Neth.
1796 to Br.
1817 to Neth.

Banda Is.

Kai Is.
1632/34

Aru Is.
1623

Makassar

Butung Is.
1613/67 Dutch Prot.

B a n d a   S e a

Salajar
1675

Damar
1646

F l o r e s   S e a

Wetar
1675

Babar
1671

Tanimbar Is.
1672

A r a f u r a   S e a

Flores
1667 Dutch
Prot.

Alor Is.

Dili
1610/75 to Port.

Moa
1668

Solor
1613

Timor

Sawu Sea
1655

1811–16 to Br.

Sumba   1662   Kupang
1653

T i m o r   S e a

A u s t r a l i a

120   130

EAST INDIES, 1820–1914
Scale 1 : 22,500,000 (360 miles = 1 inch)

0   100   200   300   400   500 Miles

0   200   400   600   800 Km.

British Possessions

British sphere of influence 1896

Straits Settlements, established
1826 by Br. East India Co.,
1867 Br. Crown Col.

Malay States under Br. Prot.:

Federated from 1895

Unfederated

Malay Provinces:
J. Johore, K. Kedah, KE. Kelantan,
N.S. Negri Sembilan, PA. Pahang, PE. Perak, P. Perlis, S. Selangor, T. Trengganu

Dutch Possessions

French Possessions

French sphere of influence 1898

Portuguese Possessions

German Possessions

United States Possessions

1824   Year of acquisition or
period of possession

East from Greenwich

120 130 140

Tropic of Cancer

20

Taiwan
(Formosa)
Chinese,
1895 to Jap.

s.

Mariana or Ladrone Is.
Spanish, 1899 to Germany

Babuyan Is.

P A C I F I C

Guam
1898 to U.S.

10

Luzon

Manila

Spanish, 1898 to U.S.

Mindoro

Samar

Caroline Is.
Spanish, 1899 to Germany

Calamian
Group Panay

Leyte

O C E A N

Negros Bohol

Palau Is.
1899 to Germany

lu Sea

Mindanao

Jolo Zamboanga Davao

Sulu Arch.
1876–99 to Spain
1899–1910 to Sultanate

Talaud Is.

Equator 0

Celebes Sea

Sangihe Is.

Morotai

Menado
1824

Djailolo

Halmahera

1884/99
to Germany

Tontoli

1824

Ternate,
Tidore

KAISER
WILHELM
LAND

Gorontalo

G. of
Tomini

Batjan Is.

Peleng

Obi Is.

D   I   E   S

New Guinea

S T

Sula Is.

1828

Celebes

Ceram

Ceram Sea

1886 Br.Crown Col.

M o l u c c a s

Buru

Amboina

TERR.
OF
PAPUA

Makassar

Butung Is.

Kai Is.

Aru Is.

Fredrik
Hendrik I.

Salajar

B a n d a   S e a

1884 Br. Prot.
1886 Br.Crown Col.
1906 to Australia

10

Flores Sea

Wetar

Tanimbar Is.

Alor Is.

A r a f u r a   S e a

Flores

Dili

1859

Ambeno
1859/1904

Timor

Melville I.
1824

Sawu Sea

Sumba

Kupang

Darwin

Gulf of

Timor   Sea

Carpentaria

COMMONWEALTH OF AUSTRALIA
Proclaimed 1901

120 130

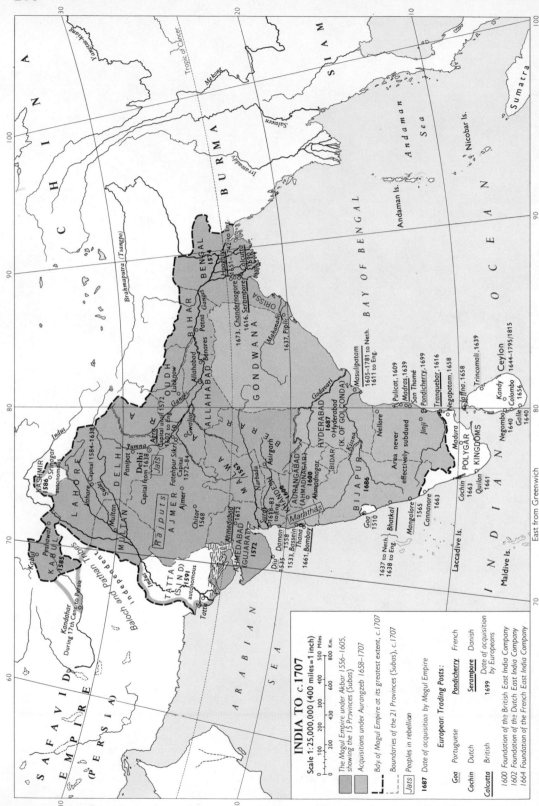

INDIA TO c.1707

Scale 1:25,000,000 (400 miles=1 inch)

```
0   100  200  300  400  500 Miles
0  200  400   600   800 Km.
```

The Mogul Empire under Akbar 1556–1605,
showing the 15 Provinces (Subas)

Acquisitions under Aurangzeb 1658–1707

Bdy. of Mogul Empire at its greatest extent, c.1707

Boundaries of the 21 Provinces (Subas), c.1707

Jats   Peoples in rebellion

1687   Date of acquisition by Mogul Empire

European Trading Posts:

Goa	*Portuguese*	**Pondicherry** *French*
Cochin	Dutch	**Serampore** *Danish*
<u>Calcutta</u>	British	1699 Date of acquisition by Europeans

1600 Foundation of the British East India Company
1602 Foundation of the Dutch East India Company
1664 Foundation of the French East India Company

COPYRIGHT. GEORGE PHILIP & SON, LTD.

East from Greenwich

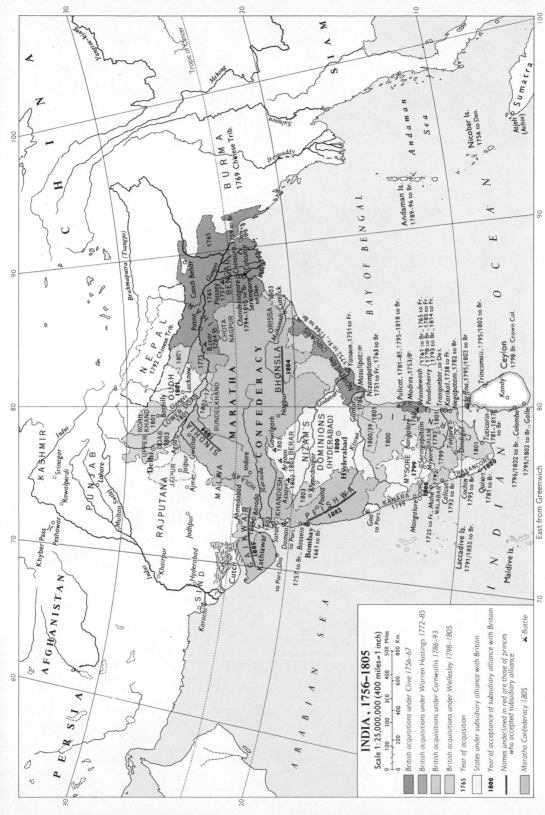

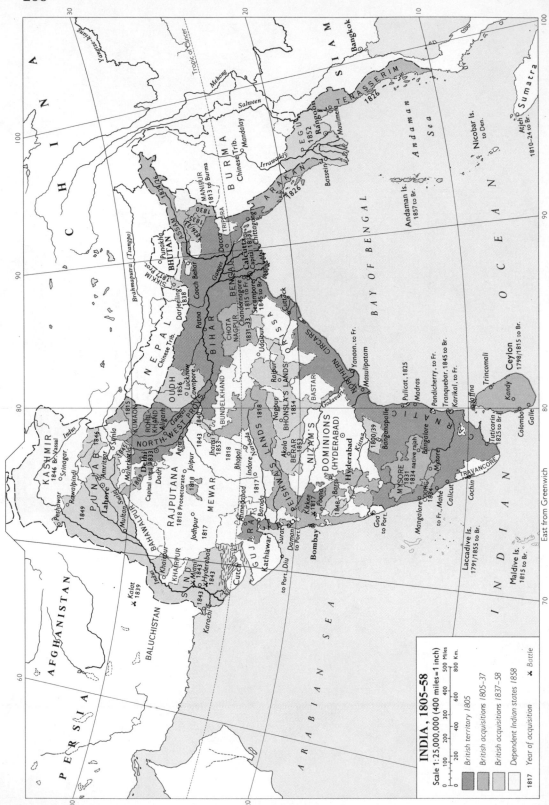

INDIA, 1805-58

Scale 1:25,000,000 (400 miles=1 inch)

British territory 1805
British acquisitions 1805-37
British acquisitions 1837-58
Dependent Indian states 1858
1817 Year of acquisition
✕ Battle

East from Greenwich

COPYRIGHT. GEORGE PHILIP & SON, LTD.

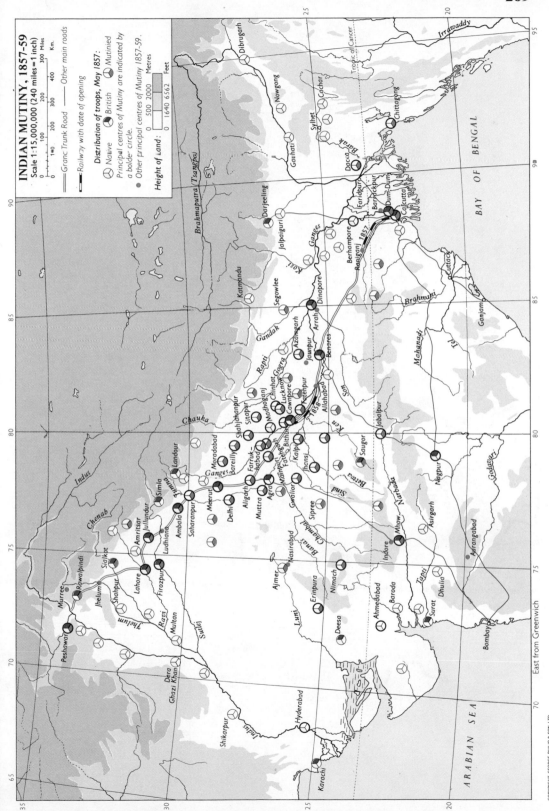

INDIAN MUTINY, 1857-59
Scale 1:15,000,000 (240 miles=1 inch)

═══ Grand Trunk Road ─── Other main roads

▭ Railway with date of opening

Distribution of troops, May 1857:
◔ Native ◑ British ◕ Mutinied
● Principal centres of Mutiny are indicated by
   a bolder circle.
• Other principal centres of Mutiny 1857-59.

Height of land:

| Metres | 0 | 500 | 2000 |
| Feet | 0 | 1640 | 6562 |

East from Greenwich

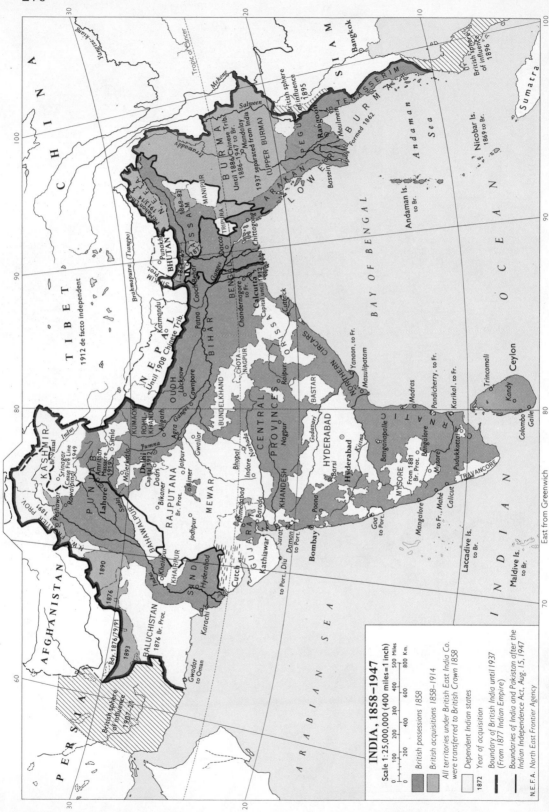

INDIA, 1858–1947
Scale 1:25,000,000 (400 miles=1 inch)

British possessions 1858

British acquisitions 1858–1914

All territories under British East India Co.
were transferred to British Crown 1858

Dependent Indian states

1872 Year of acquisition

Boundary of British India until 1937
(From 1877 Indian Empire)

Boundaries of India and Pakistan after the
Indian Independence Act, Aug. 15, 1947

N.E.F.A. = North East Frontier Agency

0 100 200 300 400 500 Miles
0 200 400 600 800 Km.

COPYRIGHT GEORGE PHILIP & SON LTD.

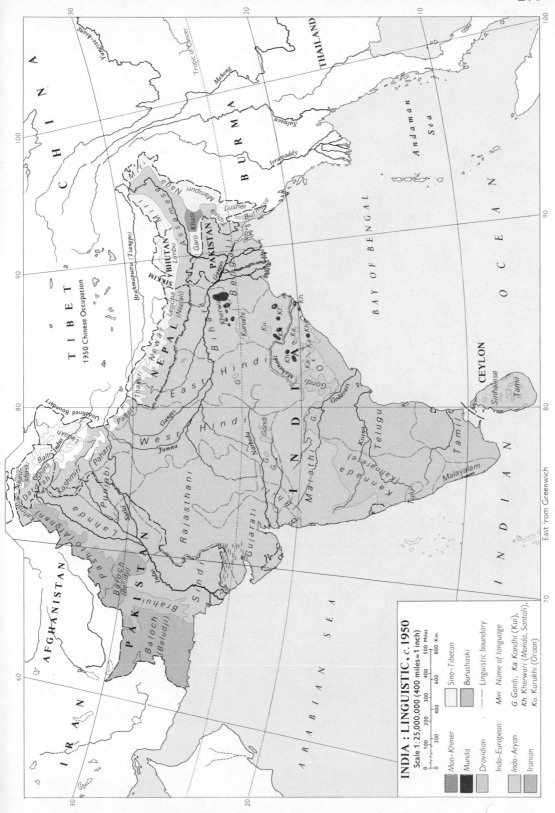

INDIA : LINGUISTIC, c.1950

Scale 1:25,000,000 (400 miles=1 inch)

0 100 200 300 400 500 Miles
0 200 400 600 800 Km.

Sino–Tibetan

Burushaski

— — — Linguistic boundary

Miri Name of language

G. Gondi, Ka Kandhi (Kui),
Kh. Kherwari (Monda, Santali),
Ku. Kurukhi (Oraon)

Mon–Khmer

Munda

Dravidian

Indo-European:

Indo-Aryan

Iranian

COPYRIGHT GEORGE PHILIP & SON, LTD.

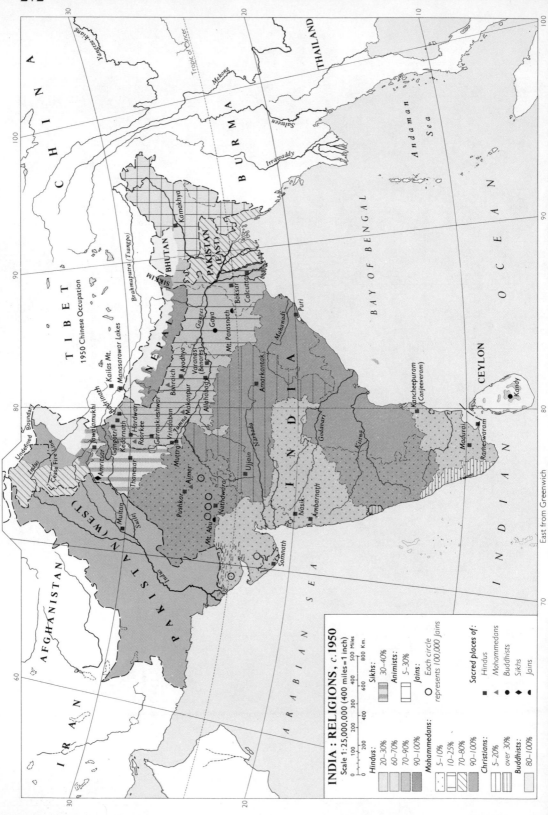

INDIA : RELIGIONS, c. 1950

Scale 1:25,000,000 (400 miles=1 inch)

0 100 200 300 400 500 Miles
0 200 400 600 800 Km.

Hindus:
20–30%
60–70%
70–90%
90–100%

Mohammedans:
5–10%
10–25%
70–80%
90–100%

Christians:
5–20%
over 30%

Buddhists:
80–100%

Sikhs:
30–40%

Animists:
5–30%

Jains:
○ Each circle represents 100,000 Jains

Sacred places of:
Hindus ■
Mohammedans ▲
Buddhists ●
Sikhs ◆
Jains

East from Greenwich

COPYRIGHT GEORGE PHILIP & SON, LTD.

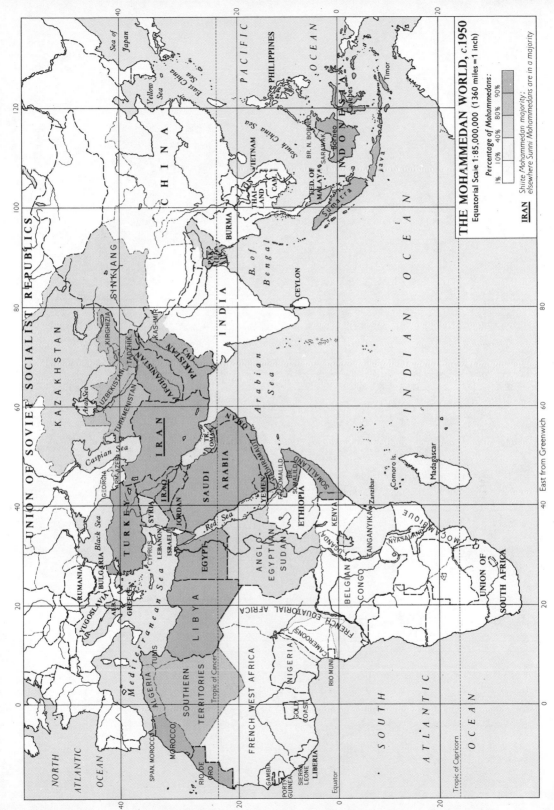

THE MOHAMMEDAN WORLD, c.1950
Equatorial Scale 1:85,000,000 (1360 miles = 1 inch)

Percentage of Mohammedans:
1%   10%   40%   80%   90%

*Shiite Mohammedan majority;
elsewhere Sunni Mohammedans are in a majority*

IRAN

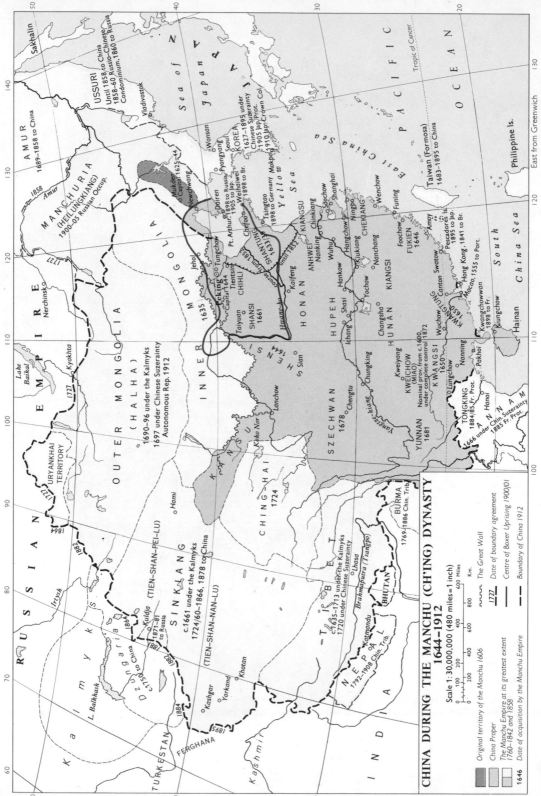

CHINA DURING THE MANCHU (CH'ING) DYNASTY 1644-1912

Scale 1:30,000,000 (480 miles=1 inch)

0 100 200 300 400 500 600 Km.
0 100 200 300 400 500 600 Miles

1727	Date of boundary agreement
⸺⸺⸺	The Great Wall
○	Centre of Boxer Uprising 1900/01
▬ ▬ ▬	Boundary of China 1912

Original territory of the Manchu 1606

China Proper

The Manchu Empire at its greatest extent 1760-1842 and 1858

1646 Date of acquisition by the Manchu Empire

COPYRIGHT GEORGE PHILIP & SON LTD.

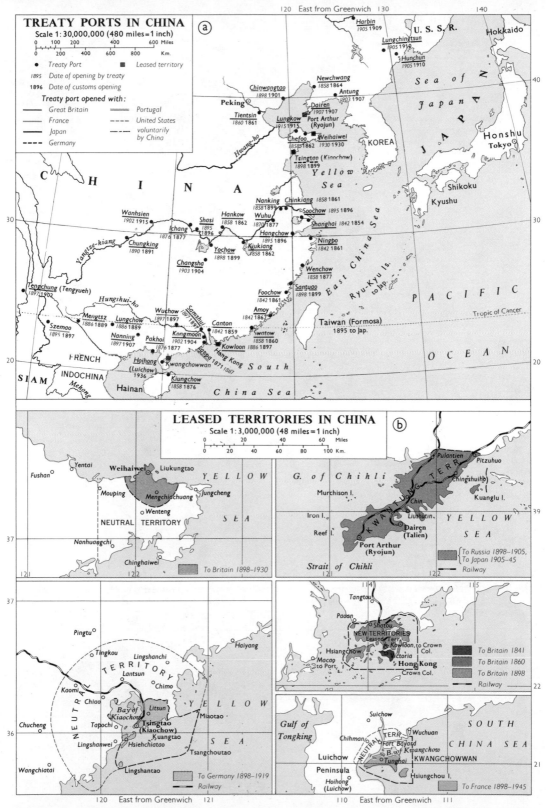

TREATY PORTS IN CHINA
Scale 1:30,000,000 (480 miles=1 inch)

0 100 200 400 600 Miles

0 200 400 600 800 Km.

- Treaty Port ■ Leased territory

1895 Date of opening by treaty

1896 Date of customs opening

Treaty port opened with:

Great Britain ――― Portugal

France ――― United States

Japan ――― voluntarily by China

Germany ---

(a)

120 East from Greenwich 130 140

Harbin *1905 1909*

U.S.S.R.

Hokkaido

Lungchingtsun *1905 1919*

Hunchun *1905 1910*

Sea of Japan

Newchwang *1858 1864*

Antung *1903 1907*

Chinwangtao *1898 1901*

Peking

Tientsin *1860 1861*

Dairen *1907 1907*

Port Arthur (Ryojun)

Lungkow *1915 1915*

Hwang-ho

Chefoo *1858 1862*

Weihaiwei *1930 1930*

KOREA

JAPAN

Honshu

Tokyo

Tsingtao (Kiaochow) *1898 1899*

Yellow Sea

Shikoku

Kyushu

Nanking *1858 1899*

Chinkiang *1858 1861*

Soochow *1895 1896*

Wanhsien *1902 1915*

Hankow *1858 1862*

Wuhu *1870 1877*

Shasi *1895 1896*

Hangchow *1895 1896*

Shanghai *1842 1854*

Ichang *1876 1877*

East China Sea

Chungking *1890 1891*

Yangtze-kiang

Yochow *1898 1899*

Kiukiang *1858 1862*

Ningpo *1842 1861*

Changsha *1903 1904*

Wenchow *1858 1877*

Ryu-Kyu Is. to Jap.

PACIFIC

Tengchung (Tengyueh) *1897 1902*

Hungshui-ho

Foochow *1842 1861*

Santuao *1898 1899*

Tropic of Cancer

Mengtsz *1886 1889*

Lungchow *1886 1889*

Wuchow *1897 1897*

Samshui *1897 1897*

Canton *1842 1859*

Amoy *1842 1862*

Taiwan (Formosa) *1895 to Jap.*

Szemao *1895 1897*

Nanning *1897 1907*

Pakhoi *1876 1877*

Kongmoon *1902 1904*

Swatow *1858 1860*

OCEAN

Kowloon *1886 1897*

Macao *1871 1887*

Hoihong (Luichow) *1936*

Kwangchowwan

Hong Kong

South China Sea

SIAM

FRENCH INDOCHINA

Mekong

Kiungchow *1858 1876*

Hainan

CHINA

LEASED TERRITORIES IN CHINA
Scale 1:3,000,000 (48 miles=1 inch)

0 20 40 60 Miles

0 20 40 60 80 100 Km.

(b)

Fushan

Yentai

Weihaiwei

Liukungtao

YELLOW SEA

Mouping

Mengchiachuang

Jungcheng

Wenteng

NEUTRAL TERRITORY

Nanhuangchi

Chinghaiwei

To Britain 1898-1930

121 122

G. of Chihli

Pulantien

Pitzuhuo

KWANTUNG TERR.

Chingshuiho

Murchison I.

Chin

Kuanglu I.

Iron I.

Liushutin

Reef I.

Dairen (Talien)

YELLOW SEA

Port Arthur (Ryojun)

Strait of Chihli

To Russia 1898-1905, To Japan 1905-45

Railway

121 122

39

37

Pingtu

Tangtou

Tingkou

Lingshanchi

NEUTRAL TERRITORY

Lantsun

Padou

Shatou

NEW TERRITORIES Leased Terr.

Haiyang

Kowloon, to Crown Col.

Chimo

Hsiangchow

Victoria

Hong Kong

Kaomi

Chiao

Bay of Kiaochow

Litsun

Macao to Port.

Crown Col.

Chucheng

Tapochi

Tsingtao (Kiaochow)

Miaotao

To Britain 1841

To Britain 1860

To Britain 1898

Railway

Lingshanwei

Hsiehchiatao

Kuangtao

YELLOW SEA

Gulf of Tongking

Suichow

Wuchuan

SOUTH CHINA SEA

Wangchiatai

Tsangchoutao

Chihman

NEUTRAL TERR.

Fort Bayard

B. of Kwangchow

Tunghai

KWANGCHOWWAN

Lingshantao

To Germany 1898-1919

Railway

Luichow Peninsula

Hoihong (Luichow)

Hsiungchou I.

To France 1898-1945

36

120 East from Greenwich 121

110 East from Greenwich 111

21

22

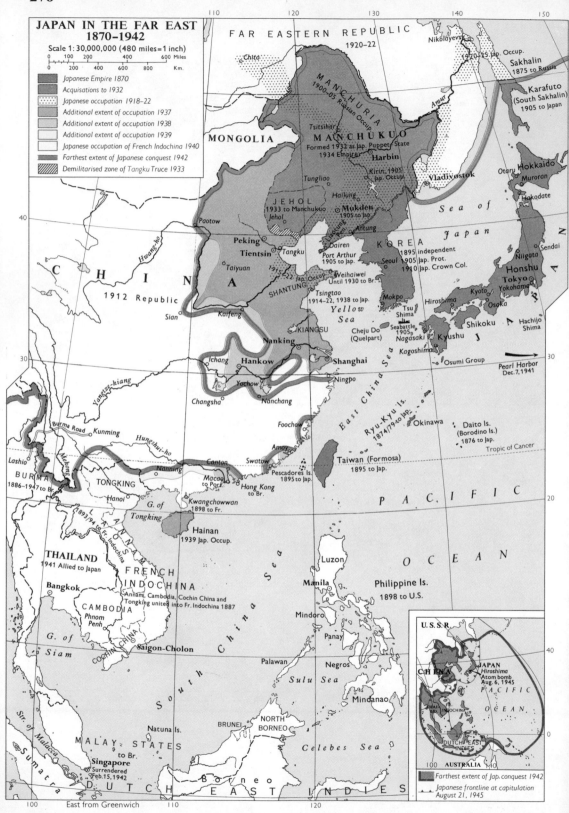

JAPAN IN THE FAR EAST 1870–1942

Scale 1:30,000,000 (480 miles = 1 inch)

0 100 200 400 600 Miles

0 200 400 800 Km.

- Japanese Empire 1870
- Acquisitions to 1932
- Japanese occupation 1918–22
- Additional extent of occupation 1937
- Additional extent of occupation 1938
- Additional extent of occupation 1939
- Japanese occupation of French Indochina 1940
- Farthest extent of Japanese conquest 1942
- Demilitarised zone of Tangku Truce 1933

FAR EASTERN REPUBLIC 1920–22

Nikolayevsk

1920–25 Jap. Occup.

Sakhalin 1875 to Russia

Karafuto (South Sakhalin) 1905 to Jap.

Chita

MANCHURIA 1900–05 Russian Occup.

Amur

MONGOLIA

MANCHUKUO Formed 1932 as Jap. Puppet State 1934 Empire

Tsitsihar

Harbin

Kirin. 1905 Jap. Occup.

Tungliao

Hailung

Otaru Hokkaido Muroran

Hakodate

Vladivostok

Sea of Japan

JEHOL 1933 to Manchukuo

Jehol

Mukden 1905 to Jap.

Antung

Liaoyang

Sendai

CHINA

Paotow

40

Peking

Tientsin Tangku

Taiyuan

1913–22 Jap. Occup.

SHANTUNG

Port Arthur 1905 to Jap.

Dairen

Weihaiwei Until 1930 to Br.

Tsingtao 1914–22, 1938 to Jap.

KOREA

Seoul

1895 independent 1905 Jap. Prot. 1910 Jap. Crown Col.

Niigata

Honshu

Tokyo Yokohama

Kyoto

Osaka

1912 Republic

Sian

Kaifeng

Yellow Sea

Cheju Do (Quelpart)

Sea battle 1905

Mokpo

Tsu Shima

Hiroshima

Nagasaki

Kyushu

Shikoku

Hachijo Shima

Nanking

KIANGSU

Kagoshima

Osumi Group

Pearl Harbor Dec. 7, 1941

30

Ichang Hankow

Yochow

Changsha Nanchang

Shanghai

Ningpo

East China Sea

Ryu-Kyu Is. 1874/79 to Jap.

Okinawa

Daito Is. (Borodino Is.) 1876 to Jap.

Tropic of Cancer

Yangtze-kiang

Hung-shui-ho

Burma Road Kunming

Lashio

BURMA 1886–1947 to Br.

TONGKING

Nanning

Hanoi

G. of Tongking

Foochow

Amoy

Swatow

Canton

Macao to Port.

Pescadores Is. 1895 to Jap.

Hong Kong to Br.

Taiwan (Formosa) 1895 to Jap.

PACIFIC OCEAN

Kwangchowwan 1898 to Fr.

Hainan 1939 Jap. Occup.

Luzon

20

THAILAND 1941 Allied to Japan

Bangkok

CAMBODIA

Phnom Penh

FRENCH INDOCHINA

Annam, Cambodia, Cochin China and Tongking united into Fr. Indochina 1887

COCHIN CHINA

Saigon-Cholon

G. of Siam

Str. of Malacca

MALAY STATES to Br.

Singapore Surrendered Feb. 15, 1942

Sumatra

DUTCH

Natuna Is.

BRUNEI

NORTH BORNEO

Borneo

Manila

Mindoro

Panay

Palawan

Negros

Sulu Sea

Mindanao

Celebes Sea

EAST

Philippine Is. 1898 to U.S.

INDIES

U.S.S.R.

CHINA

JAPAN Hiroshima Atom bomb Aug. 6, 1945

PACIFIC OCEAN

INDOCHINA

DUTCH EAST INDIES

AUSTRALIA

- Farthest extent of Jap. conquest 1942
- Japanese frontline at capitulation August 21, 1945

100 East from Greenwich 110 120

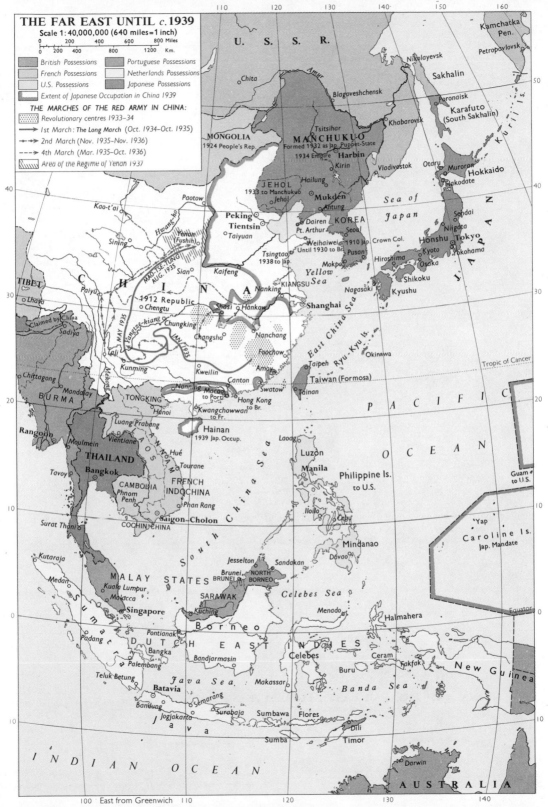

THE FAR EAST UNTIL c.1939

Scale 1:40,000,000 (640 miles=1 inch)

0 200 400 600 800 Miles
0 200 400 800 1200 Km.

British Possessions
French Possessions
U.S. Possessions
Portuguese Possessions
Netherlands Possessions
Japanese Possessions

Extent of Japanese Occupation in China 1939

THE MARCHES OF THE RED ARMY IN CHINA:

Revolutionary centres 1933–34
1st March: The Long March (Oct. 1934–Oct. 1935)
2nd March (Nov. 1935–Nov. 1936)
4th March (Mar. 1935–Oct. 1936)
Area of the Regime of Yenan 1937

U. S. S. R.

Kamchatka Pen.

Petropavlovsk

Chita

Blagoveshchensk

Nikolayevsk

Sakhalin

Paronaisk

Karafuto (South Sakhalin)

Amur

MONGOLIA
1924 People's Rep.

Tsitsihar

MANCHUKUO
Formed 1932 as Jap. Puppet-State
1934 Empire Harbin

Khabarovsk

Kuril Is.

Kao-t'ai

Paotow

Hailung

Kirin

Vladivostok

Otaru
Muroran

Hokkaido

JEHOL
1933 to Manchukuo
Jehol

Mukden

Hakodate

Sining

Yenan
(Fushih)

Peking
Tientsin

Taiyuan

Antung

KOREA

Dairen
Pt. Arthur

Weihaiwei
Until 1930 to Br.

Seoul

1910 Jap. Crown Col.

Pusan

Sea of
Japan

Sendai

Niigata

Honshu

Tokyo
Yokohama

TIBET

Lhasa

CHINA

MAO-TSE-TUNG
AUG. 1935

Sian

Kaifeng

KIANGSU

Nanking

Tsingtao
1938 to Jap.

Hiroshima
Osaka

Kyoto

Yellow
Sea

Nagasaki

Mokpo

Kyushu

Shikoku

East China Sea

Paiyu

1912 Republic

Chengtu

MAY 1935

Yangtze-kiang

Chungking

Shasi

Hankow

Shanghai

Claimed by China

Sadiya

Tali

JAN. 1935

Changsha

Nanchang

Foochow

Taipeh

Ryu-kyu Is.

Okinawa

Tropic of Cancer

Chittagong

Mandalay

BURMA

TONGKING

Kunming

Kweilin

Canton

Amoy

Swatow

Taiwan (Formosa)

Tainan

PACIFIC

Rangoon

Moulmein

Luang Prabang

Vientiane

LAOS

Hanoi

Nanning

Kwangchowan
to Fr.

Macao
to Port.

Hong Kong
to Br.

Hainan
1939 Jap. Occup.

Laoag

OCEAN

Guam
to U.S.

Tavoy

THAILAND

Bangkok

Hué

Tourane

ANNAM

Phan Rang

Luzon

Manila

Philippine Is.
to U.S.

Yap

Caroline Is.
Jap. Mandate

Surat Thani

CAMBODIA
Phnom
Penh

FRENCH
INDOCHINA

Saigon–Cholon

COCHIN CHINA

Iloilo

Cebu

Mindanao

Davao

Kutaraja

Medan

MALAY STATES

Kuala Lumpur

Malacca

Jesselton

Brunei
BRUNEI

Sandakan

NORTH
BORNEO

Singapore

SARAWAK

Kuching

Celebes Sea

Menado

Halmahera

Equator

Padang

Pontianak

Borneo

Bangka

DUTCH EAST INDIES

Celebes

Ceram

Fakfak

New Guinea

Palembang

Bandjarmasin

Makassar

Buru

Banda Sea

Teluk Betung

Batavia

Java Sea

Bandung

Semarang

Surabaja

Sumbawa

Flores

Bali

Dili

Jogjakarta

Java

Sumba

Timor

Darwin

INDIAN OCEAN

AUSTRALIA

Hwang-ho

South China Sea

East from Greenwich

COPYRIGHT, GEORGE PHILIP & SON, LTD.

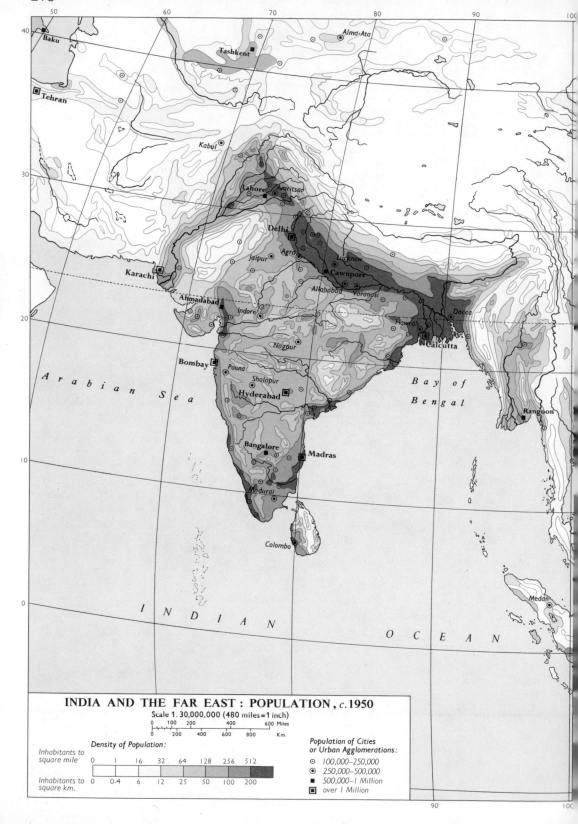

INDIA AND THE FAR EAST : POPULATION, *c.*1950

Scale 1:30,000,000 (480 miles=1 inch)

0   100   200   400   600 Miles
0   200   400   600   800   Km.

Density of Population:

Inhabitants to
square mile

0   1   16   32   64   128   256   512

Inhabitants to
square km.

0   0.4   6   12   25   50   100   200

Population of Cities
or Urban Agglomerations:

⊙ 100,000–250,000
◉ 250,000–500,000
■ 500,000–1 Million
▣ over 1 Million

East from Greenwich

COPYRIGHT. GEORGE PHILIP & SON. LTD.

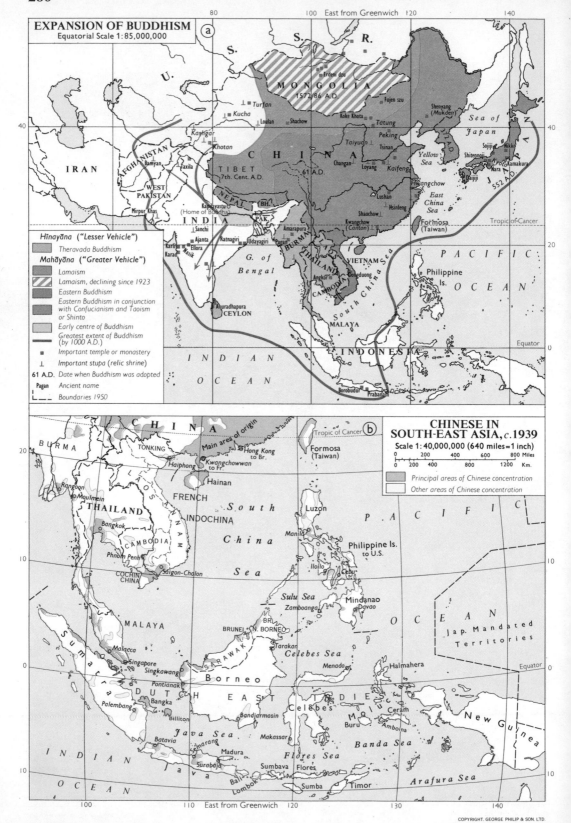

EXPANSION OF BUDDHISM
Equatorial Scale 1:85,000,000 (a)

Hīnayāna ("Lesser Vehicle")
- Theravada Buddhism

Mahāyāna ("Greater Vehicle")
- Lamaism
- Lamaism, declining since 1923
- Eastern Buddhism
- Eastern Buddhism in conjunction with Confucianism and Taoism or Shinto
- Early centre of Buddhism
- Greatest extent of Buddhism (by 1000 A.D.)
- ■ Important temple or monastery
- ⊥ Important stupa (relic shrine)
- 61 A.D. Date when Buddhism was adopted
- Pagan Ancient name
- Boundaries 1950

CHINESE IN SOUTH-EAST ASIA, c.1939 (b)
Scale 1:40,000,000 (640 miles=1 inch)

- Principal areas of Chinese concentration
- Other areas of Chinese concentration

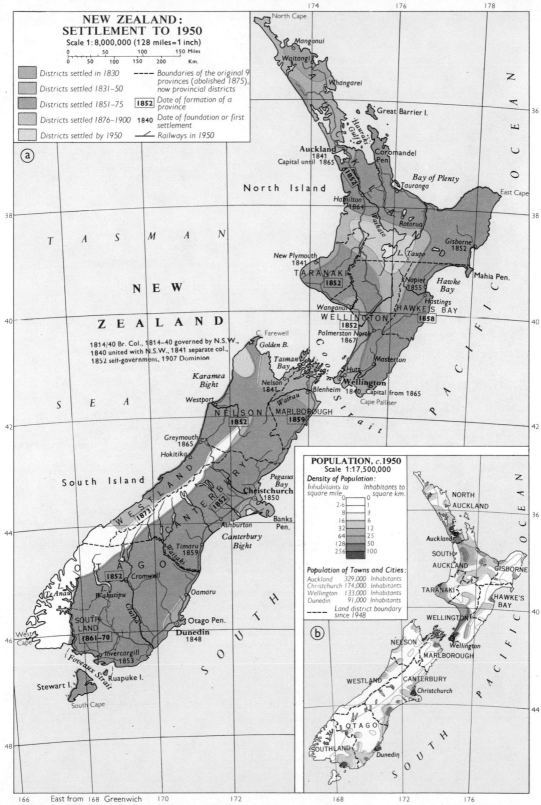

NEW ZEALAND: SETTLEMENT TO 1950

Scale 1:8,000,000 (128 miles=1 inch)

- Districts settled in 1830
- Districts settled 1831–50
- Districts settled 1851–75
- Districts settled 1876–1900
- Districts settled by 1950

- Boundaries of the original 9 provinces (abolished 1875), now provincial districts
- 1852 Date of formation of a province
- 1840 Date of foundation or first settlement
- Railways in 1950

POPULATION, c.1950
Scale 1:17,500,000

Density of Population:

Inhabitants to square mile	Inhabitants to square km.
0	0
2–6	1
8	3
16	6
32	12
64	25
128	50
256	100

Population of Towns and Cities:

Auckland 329,000 Inhabitants
Christchurch 174,000 Inhabitants
Wellington 133,000 Inhabitants
Dunedin 91,000 Inhabitants

Land district boundary since 1948

MOLLWEIDE'S EQUAL AREA PROJECTION

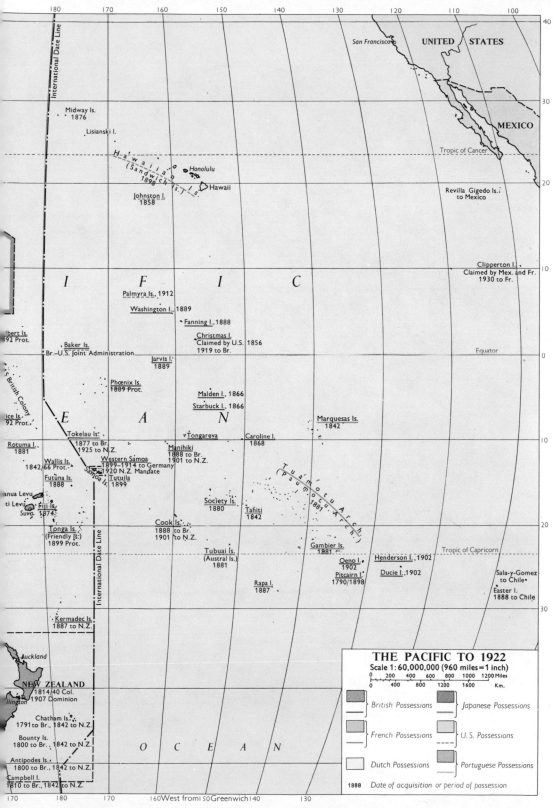

THE PACIFIC TO 1922
Scale 1 : 60,000,000 (960 miles = 1 inch)

British Possessions	Japanese Possessions
French Possessions	U.S. Possessions
Dutch Possessions	Portuguese Possessions

1888 Date of acquisition or period of possession

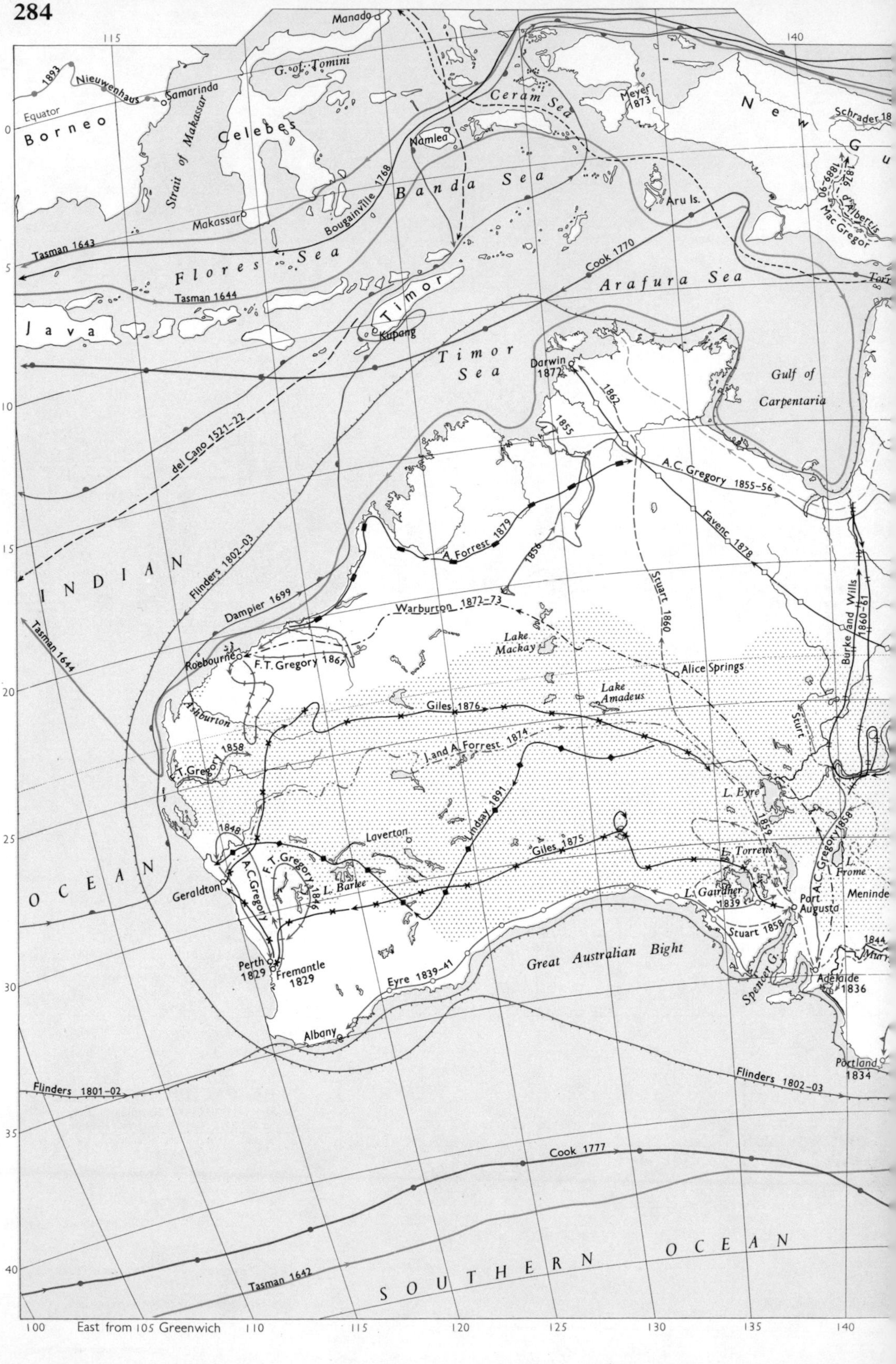

Equator

1893

Nieuwenhaus

Samarinda

Strait of Makassar

Borneo

Celebes

G. of Tomini

Manado

Ceram Sea

Meyer 1873

New Gu

Schrader 18

Banda Sea

Namlea

Bougainville 1768

Makassar

Aru Is.

Alberti 1896 — MacGregor

Tasman 1643

Flores Sea

Cook 1770

Arafura Sea

Torr

Tasman 1644

del Cano 1521–22

Java

Kupang

Timor

Timor Sea

Darwin 1872

1863

1855

Gulf of Carpentaria

INDIAN

A. C. Gregory 1855–56

Favenc 1878

A. Forrest 1879

1856

Stuart 1860

Burke and Wills 1860–61

Flinders 1802–03

Dampier 1699

Warburton 1872–73

Lake Mackay

Roebourne

F. T. Gregory 1861

Alice Springs

Tasman 1644

Giles 1876

Lake Amadeus

Ashburton

Stuart

J. and A. Forrest 1874

L. Eyre

F. Gregory 1858

T. Gregory

Lindsay 1891

1858

L. Eyre 1858

OCEAN

1848

A. C. Gregory

F. T. Gregory 1846

Laverton

Giles 1875

E. Torrens

A. C. Gregory 1858

L. Frome

Geraldton

L. Barlee

L. Gardner 1839

Port Augusta

Meninde

Perth 1829

Fremantle 1829

Eyre 1839–41

Great Australian Bight

Stuart 1858

Spencer G.

1844 Murr.

Adelaide 1836

Albany

Portland 1834

Flinders 1801–02

Flinders 1802–03

Cook 1777

SOUTHERN OCEAN

Tasman 1642

East from 105 Greenwich

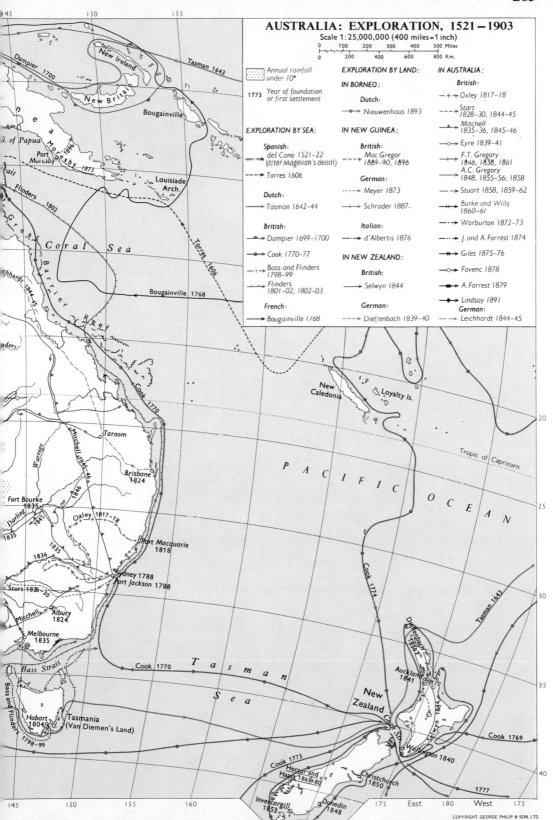

AUSTRALIA: EXPLORATION, 1521–1903
Scale 1:25,000,000 (400 miles=1 inch)

0 100 200 300 400 500 Miles
0 200 400 600 800 Km.

Annual rainfall under 10"

1773 Year of foundation or first settlement

EXPLORATION BY SEA:

Spanish:
— del Cano 1521–22 (after Magellan's death)
---→ Torres 1606

Dutch:
→ Tasman 1642–44

British:
→ Dampier 1699–1700
→ Cook 1770–77
—ı→ Bass and Flinders 1798–99
→ Flinders 1801–02, 1802–03

French:
→ Bougainville 1768

EXPLORATION BY LAND:

IN BORNEO:

Dutch:
→ Nieuwenhaus 1893

IN NEW GUINEA:

British:
---→ Mac Gregor 1889–90, 1898

German:
---→ Meyer 1873
→ Schrader 1887

Italian:
---→ d'Albertis 1876

IN NEW ZEALAND:

British:
→ Selwyn 1844

German:
---→ Dieffenbach 1839–40

IN AUSTRALIA:

British:
—+→ Oxley 1817–18
-----→ Sturt 1828–30, 1844–45
→ Mitchell 1835–36, 1845–46
—o→ Eyre 1839–41
→ F.T. Gregory 1846, 1858, 1861
A.C. Gregory 1848, 1855–56, 1858
—→ Stuart 1858, 1859–62
→→ Burke and Wills 1860–61
—•— Warburton 1872–73
—••→ J. and A. Forrest 1874
—×—× Giles 1875–76
—◇—◇ Favenc 1878
—■—■ A. Forrest 1879
—♦—♦ Lindsay 1891

German:
—•—• Leichhardt 1844–45

COPYRIGHT. GEORGE PHILIP & SON. LTD.

AUSTRALIA : SETTLEMENT TO 1950

Scale 1:25,000,000 (400 miles=1 inch)

```
0    100   200   300   400   500 Miles
0      200      400      600      800 Km.
```

Districts settled 1830

Districts settled 1831–50

Districts settled 1851–75

Districts settled 1876–1900

Districts settled up to 1950

1852 *Date when self-government was granted*

— *Railways 1950*

⊕ *Principal goldfields c.1910*

● *Principal goldfields 1950*

Annual rainfall under 10"

Northern Territory, subdivided 1926 into North Australia and Central Australia, reunited 1931

Penal Colonies 1788–c.1850:

■ *Penal cols. for all grades of convict*

▲ *Penal colonies of serious criminals and recidivists*

⬥ *Penal ship colony*

□ *Areas of settlement for reprieved convicts (Pentonvillains)*

East from 130 Greenwich 135   140

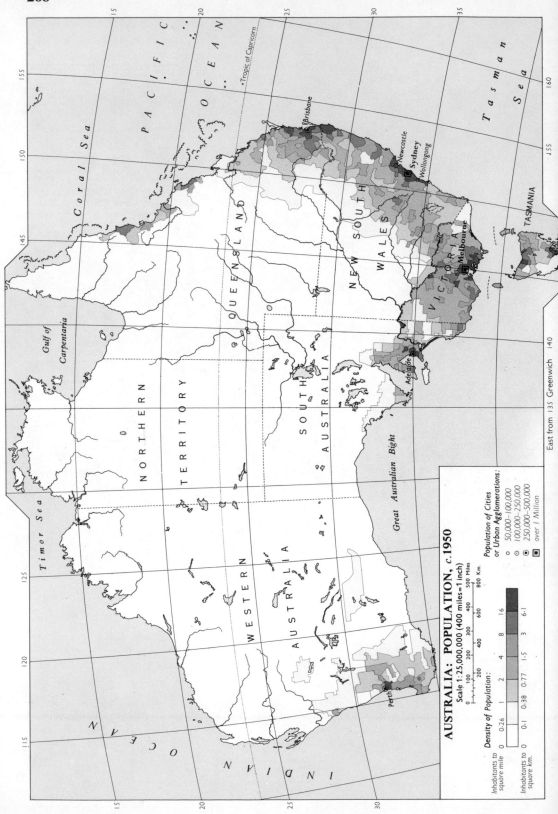

AUSTRALIA: POPULATION, c.1950

Scale 1:25,000,000 (400 miles=1 inch)

0 100 200 300 400 500 Miles

0 200 400 600 800 Km.

Density of Population:

Inhabitants to square mile:
0   0·26   1   2   4   8   16

Inhabitants to square km.:
0   0·1   0·38   0·77   1·5   3   6·1

Population of Cities or Urban Agglomerations:

○ 50,000–100,000
◦ 100,000–250,000
◉ 250,000–500,000
▣ over 1 Million

East from 135 Greenwich

SUBJECT INDEX

For abbreviations, see pages xxiii–xxiv

Abyssinia, *see* Ethiopia
Acadia
  17–18C.: 196
Acarnania
  19C.: 168, 169b
Adam Kok's Land
  19C.: 257
Adams–Onis Treaty or Spanish Treaty
  (1819), 202
Aden Prot.
  16C.: 2, 5, 260
  19–20C.: 15–21, 62, 174, 175
Adrianople (1829), T. of, 166–7
Adwalton Moor (1643), B. of, 96a
Affane (1565), B. of, 94a
Afghanistan
  20C.: 273, 280
Africa
  16C.: 2, 4–6a
  17C.: 6b
  18C.: 7a, 8–11, 41b, 43b, 252
  19C.: 7b, 12–15, 47b, 241–5
  20C.: 16–23, 55a, 62, 246–51
Agnadello (1509), B. of, 159
Agriculture, *see* Economy
Ahmadnagar
  15–16C.: 3, 266
Aix-la-Chapelle (1668), T. of, 33b, 108–9
Aix-la-Chapelle (1748), T. of, 39, 42
Akhaltsikhe (1853), B. of, 51a
Åland Is.
  20C.: 56, 83, 191
Alaska
  18C.: 10, 220
  19C.: 12, 14, 219a, 220, 222, 223a
  20C.: 16–20, 26, 223b, c
Alawites, Terr. of
  20C.: 174
Albania
  15C.: 164
  16–18C.: 71–5
  19C.: 77–9, 168, 170a
  20C.: 53, 57–61, 81, 83, 85, 166, 169,
    170a, 171, 273
Alberta
  19C.: 222c, 223a
  20C.: 223b, c, 224a, b
  See Canada
Alcantara (1706), B. of, 34
Alessandria (1745), B. of, 159
Alexandretta, Sanjak of
  20C.: 174
Alexandria (1798), B. of, 45b

Algeria, Algiers
  16C.: 70, 164
  17C.: 72
  18C.: 74, 166
  19C.: 76–9, 241–5
  20C.: 22–3, 58, 80, 82, 84, 246–51, 254,
    273
Allerheim (1645), B. of, 31b
Almansa (1707), B. of, 34
Almenara (1710), B. of, 34
Alsace
  15C.: 106
  17C.: 108–9, 111
  18C.: 113a, 115a, 132
  19C.: 117, 141a, b
  20C.: 57, 58, 80, 82
Amboina (E. Indies)
  16C.: 260
  17C.: 263
  18C.: 263
  19C.: 265
  20C.: 265, 279, 280
Amiens (1870), B. of, 117
Amiens (1802), T. of, 48, 50b
Amritsar (1809), T. of, 50b
Amur
  17–19C.: 184, 274
Anatolia
  15C.: 164–5
  16C.: 71
  17C.: 73
  18C.: 75
  20C.: 166–7
  See Ottoman Empire, Turkey
Ancona (1798), B. of, 44
Andaman Is.
  18–19C.: 262, 267
  19–20 C.: 264, 268, 270
Andorra
  16C.: 70
  17C.: 72
  18C.: 74
  19C.: 76–9
  20C.: 52, 58, 80, 82, 84, 90, 91
Anglo-Egyptian Sudan, *see* Sudan
Anguilla (W. Indies)
  17–20C.: 22, 229–32
Annam, *see* Indochina
Ansbach
  15C.: 122–3, 138a
  16C.: 124–5
  17C.: 129a, 130–1
  18C.: 134, 139a

289

Ansbach (*cont.*)
  19C.: 135, 139b
Antarctic
  18–20C.: 16–23, 27
Antietam (1862), B. of, 207
Antigua
  16C.: 228
  17C.: 229
  18C.: 230
  19C.: 47b, 231
  20C.: 62, 232
Arab League (1945), 175
Aragon
  15C.: 163a
  16C.: 70, 144
  17C.: 72
  See Spain
Arakan
  19–20C.: 268, 270
Arcole (1796), B. of, 44
Arctic 24–5, 26, 149, 180–5, 188–91, 220,
  222–3
Argaon (1803), B. of, 50a, 267
Argentina
  19C.: 237
  20C.: 238, 239
  See South America
Armenia
  16–17C.: 165
  20C.: 167, 174, 273
  See Turkey
Arras (1579), League of, 150b
Artenay (1870) B. of, 117
Artois
  16C.: 122, 124
  17C.: 32b
  18C.: 113a, 115a
Aruba (W. Indies)
  17–20C.: 229–233a
Ashanti
  19C.: 242, 244, 245, 252, 253
  See Gold Coast
Asia
  16C.: 2–3, 5, 6a
  17C.: 6b
  18C.: 7a, 9, 11
  19C.: 7b, 13, 15
  20C.: 17, 19, 21, 23, 62–3, 273
Ashkiga (1336–1573), Shogunate of, 3
Asir (in Arabia)
  20C.: 174
Aspern (1809), B. of, 45
Aspromonte (1862), B. of, 161
Assam
  19C.: 268, 270
Assaye (1803), B. of, 50a, 267

Assiniboia, District of
  19C.: 222c, 223a
Asti (1746), B. of, 159
Asti, Pr. of
  16C.: 156, 157
Astrakhan
  16C.: 2, 181
  17C.: 182
  18C.: 183
  19C.: 187–190
Athabaska, District of
  19C.: 222c, 223a
Athlone (1691), B. of, 94a
Atlanta (1864), B. of, 207
Atlantic Ocean
  16C.: 4–5, 6a
  17C.: 6b
  18C.: 7a, 8–11
  19C.: 7b, 12–15, 47b
  20C.: 16–23, 62
Auerstedt (1806), B. of, 44
Aughrim (1691), B. of, 33a, 94a
Augsburg
  16C.: 122–6
  17C.: 127, 130
  18C.: 132, 134
Augsburg (1689), League of, 33a
Augusta (1779), B. of, 199
Austerlitz (1805), B. of, 45
Australia
  16C.: 5, 6, 284–5
  17C.: 7, 284–5
  18C.: 8, 9, 11, 284–5
  19C.: 13, 15, 284–7
  20C.: 17–23, 55b, 63, 282–8
Austria
  16C.: 66–7, 123–6, 128, 144
  17C.: 33a, 38a, b, 72–3, 127, 131, 145
  18C.: 39, 42, 48, 74–5, 132–4
  19C.: 49, 68–9, 76–9, 86–9, 93, 135–7
    142, 168
  20C.: 52–3, 57–61, 80–5, 90–3, 146–8
Ava
  16C.: 3
Avignon, *see* Venaissin
Ayacucho (1824), B. of, 237
Azerbaijan
  17C.: 165
  18C.: 167
  20C.: 273
Aztec Empire, 225a

Baden
  16C.: 122–6
  17C.: 127, 130
  18C.: 131, 134

Baden (*cont.*)
  19C.: 49, 78, 135–7, 140–1
Baden (1714), T. of, 35
Bahama Is.
  16C.: 4, 228
  17C.: 229
  18C.: 8, 10, 41a, 43a, 230
  19C.: 12, 14, 198b, 231
  20C.: 16–22, 62, 232, 233a
Bahmani
  16C.: 3
Bahrain
  16C.: 260
  20C.: 174, 175
Bailen (1808), B. of, 44, 46c
Balaklava (1854), B. of, 51b
Balearic Is.
  15C.: 68, 162, 163a
  16C.: 66, 70, 144
  17C.: 72
  18C.: 42, 44, 74
  19C.: 49, 76–9, 86
  20C.: 52, 58–61, 80, 82, 84, 163b
Balkans, The
  16C.: 67, 71
  17C.: 38a, 73, 164
  18C.: 38b, 48, 75, 87
  19C.: 49, 77–81, 168
  20C.: 53, 57–61, 83, 85, 166, 169–72
Ballinamuck (1798), B. of, 94a
Baltic Orders, The, 2, 71, 120, 123, 176a
Banat of Temesvar
  18C.: 38b, 146, 166
  19C.: 168
Bar, D. of
  15C.: 106
  16C.: 122, 124
  17C.: 32b, 108–9, 111, 130
  18C.: 42
Barbados
  17C.: 229, 235
  18C.: 8, 10, 230, 236
  19C.: 12, 14, 47b, 231, 237
  20C.: 16–22, 232, 238, 239
Barbuda (W. Indies)
  17–20C.: 229–32
Barcelonnette
  18C.: 35, 111, 157
Barrois mouvant
  16C.: 122, 124
  17C.: 111, 130
  18C.: 108–9
Bashkirs, Risings of
  17C.: 180–1
  18C.: 182
  19C.: 183

Basing House (1645), B. of, 96b
Basle, Bp. of, Canton of
  16C.: 122, 124, 154
  19C.: 155
Basle (1795), T. of, 48
Bassano (1796), B. of, 44
Bassein (1802), T. of, 50b
Bassignano (1745), B. of, 39, 159
Basutoland
  19C.: 244–5, 256a, 257
  20C.: 246–51, 256b, 273
Batavian Rep.
  18–19C.: 134, 135
  See Netherlands
Bautzen (1813), B. of, 44
Bavaria
  16C.: 70, 121–6, 128
  17C.: 32a, 33a, 72, 127, 131
  18C.: 35, 74, 132, 134
  19C.: 49, 78, 135–7, 140, 141
Bayonne (1808), B. of, 44
Bayreuth
  15C.: 138a
  16C.: 123, 125
  17C.: 129a, 131
  18C.: 134, 139
  19C.: 135–7
Beachy Head (1690), B. of, 33a
Beaugency (1870), B. of, 117
Bechuanaland
  19C.: 242, 244, 245, 257
  20C.: 246–51
Behaim (1492), Martin, Globe of, 1
Belfast, in South Africa (1900), B. of, 256b
Belgian Congo
  20C.: 246–51, 255, 273
Belgium
  16–17C.: *See* Netherlands, Spanish
  18C.: *See* Netherlands, Austrian
  19C.: 68, 80, 88, 89, 93, 117, 140b–142, 152
  20C.: 52, 54, 57–61, 80–93, 147, 148
Belgium Overseas
  20C.: 16–19, 55a, 246–8
Belgrade (1739), T. of, 38b, 42
Belize
  17C.: 229, 230
  18C.: 8, 10, 42a, 230
Bemis Heights (1777), B. of, 199
Benburb (1646), B. of, 94a
Bengal
  16C.: 3
  17C.: 266
  18C.: 41c, 266, 267
  19C.: 50b, 268, 270
  20C.: 270

Bennington (1777), B. of, 199
Berar
  16C.: 3, 266
  18C.: 267
  19C.: 268
Berg
  16C.: 122–6
  17C.: 127, 130
  18C.: 132, 134
  19C.: 76, 78, 135–7, 139b
Berkersdorf (1761), B. of, 40
Berlin (1878), T. of, 166–7
Bermuda Is.
  18–20C.: 8–20
Bessarabia
  16C.: 71, 165, 181
  17C.: 73, 181
  18C.: 75, 133, 182
  19C.: 48, 51, 77, 167, 168, 183
  20C.: 57, 59, 170a, b, 171a, b, 191
Bharatpur (1805), B. of, 50a
Bhonsla
  19C.: 50b, 267, 268
Bhutan
  19C.: 268
  20C.: 270–2
Bidar
  16C.: 3
  17C.: 266
Bideford (1643), B. of, 96a
Bihar
  16C.: 3
  17C.: 266
  18C.: 267
  19C.: 268
  20C.: 270
Bijapur
  16C.: 3
  17C.: 266
Bismarck Arch.
  20C.: 16–23, 55b, 282–3
Blackstock (1780), B. of, 199
Blekinge
  17C.: 36b, 149
Blenheim (1704), B. of, 34
Böblingen (1525), B. of, 28
Bohemia
  15C.: 120
  16C.: 70–1, 121, 123, 125, 126, 144
  17C.: 72–3, 127, 131, 145
  18C.: 39, 40, 74–5, 132–3, 134
  19C.: 76–9, 135–7, 142, 146
  20C.: 58–9, 80, 148, 187
Bohuslän
  17C.: 36b, 149

Bolivia
  19C.: 237, 238
  20C.: 238, 239
  See South America
Bologna (1551), B. of, 159
Bonaire (W. Indies)
  17C.: 229–233a
Borisov (1812), B. of, 45, 46b
Borneo
  16C.: 5, 260
  17C.: 261
  18C.: 9, 11, 262
  19C.: 13, 15, 262, 264
  20C.: 17–23, 63, 264, 273, 277–280, 282
Borodino (1812), B. of, 45, 46a
Bosnia
  16C.: 71, 164
  17C.: 73
  18C.: 38b, 75, 133, 134
  19C.: 77–9, 135–7, 146, 166, 168, 170a
  20C.: 81, 169a, 170b, 171a, b, 172a
Botswana
  20C.: 23, 249
  See Bechuanaland
Bouillon
  15C.: 106
  17–19C.: 108, 111
Boxer Uprising (1900–1), 274
Boyaca (1819), B. of, 237
Boyne (1690), B. of the, 33a
Brabant
  15C.: 106
  16C.: 70, 108, 122, 124, 150a
  17C.: 151b
  19C.: 152
Bradock Down (1643), B. of, 96a
Brandenburg, see Prussia
Brandywine (1777), B. of, 199
Brazil
  17C.: 235
  18C.: 236
  19C.: 237, 238
  20C.: 238, 239
  See South America
Breisgau
  15C.: 106
  16C.: 122, 124, 128, 145
  17C.: 130, 146,
  19C.: 135
Breitenfeld (1631), B. of, 31a
Breitenfeld (1642), B. of, 31b
Bremen, Abp. of
  16C.: 122, 124, 126
  17C.: 32a, 36b, 127, 129a, 130, 149
  18C.: 37b
Brescia (1512), B. of, 159

Breslau (1742), T. of, 42
Briar Creek (1779), B. of, 199
Brihuega (1710), B. of, 34
British Columbia
  19C.: 219a, 222, 223a
  20C.: 223b, c, 224
  See Canada
British Commonwealth
  20C.: 20–1, 248, 249
  See Great Britain Overseas
British East Africa
  20C.: 246
British Guiana
  17C.: 235
  18C.: 236
  19C.: 47b, 232, 233b, 237, 238
  20C.: 23, 239
British Honduras
  18C.: 231
  19C.: 232
  20C.: 233
  See Belize
British North Borneo, *see* Borneo
British Somaliland, *see* Somaliland
Brunei, *see* Borneo
Brunswick–Lüneberg
  16C.: 122, 124, 126, 128
  17C.: 32a, 127, 130
Bucharest (1812), T. of, 48
Bucharest (1913), T. of, 166–7
Buddhists, 272, 280a
Buena Vista (1847), B. of, 227
Bukhara, Khanate of
  19–20C.: 186b
Bulgaria
  16C.: 71
  17C.: 73, 165–6
  18C.: 75, 133
  19C.: 51, 77, 79, 93, 166–7, 168, 169b,
    170a, 187
  20C.: 53, 57, 59–61, 81, 83, 85, 92, 93,
    169a, 170b, 171a, b, 172a, 273
Bundelkhand
  16C.: 3
  19C.: 268, 270
Bunker Hill (1775), B. of, 199
Burgundy, C. of
  15C.: 106
  16C.: 70, 121–6, 128, 144
  17C.: 32b, 33a, b, 72, 109, 111, 127,
    130, 145
  18C.: 74, 115a
Burgundy, D. of
  15C.: 106
  16C.: 107

Burma
  16C.: 260
  17C.: 261
  18C.: 262, 267
  19C.: 264, 268, 270
  20C.: 23, 270, 273, 276–80, 282
Burma Road, 276
Burundi
  20C.: 23, 239
  See Ruanda-Urundi
Busacco (1810), B. of, 44, 46c
Buxar (1764), B. of, 267

Calama (1879), B. of, 238
Calcinato (1706), B. of, 159
California
  19C.: 201a, 202, 203, 206, 227
  See United States
Calmar (1397–1523), Union of, 70–1
Cambodia
  20C.: 23, 264, 273, 276–80
  See Indochina
Cambrai (1677), B. of, 33a
Cambrai (1917), B. of, 54
Cambrai, Bp. of, C. of
  15C.: 106
  16C.: 108, 110, 122, 124, 150a, b
  17C.: 151b
Cameroons
  20C.: 22, 55, 247–51, 273
  See Kamerun
Camisards (1702–5), Revolt of, 34
Camperdown (1673), B. of, 29
Camperdown (1797), B. of, 44
Campo Formio (1797), T. of, 48
Campo Santo (1743), B. of, 39
Canada
  18C.: 41a, 43a, 198–200, 220, 221a
  19C.: 26, 219a, b, 200a, 220–2, 223a
  20C.: 26, 220, 223b, c, 224 a, b
  See North America
Canary Is.
  19C.: 47b, 242, 244, 245
  20C.: 246–250, 254
Cannstadt (1796), B. of, 44
Cape Colony
  19C.: 50c, 242, 244, 245, 256a, 257
  20C.: 256b
Cape Finesterre (1805), B. of, 47b
Carabobo (1821), B. of, 237
Carelia
  17C.: 36b, 149, 180, 182
  18C.: 37a, b
Carinthia
  16C.: 70, 123, 125, 126, 128

Carinthia (*cont.*)
  17C.: 72, 127, 131, 145
  18C.: 74, 132–3, 134
  19C.: 76–7, 135–7, 142, 146
Carlowitz (1699), T. of, 38b, 166–7
Carniola
  16C.: 70, 123, 125, 126, 128
  17C.: 72, 127, 131, 145
  18C.: 74, 132–3, 134
  19C.: 135, 136, 142, 146
Caroline Is.
  16C.: 5
  18C.: 9, 11, 263
  19C.: 13, 15, 265
  20C.: 17–23, 55b, 63, 277, 282
Carpatho-Ukraine
  20C.: 148a, b
Carpi (1701), B. of, 34, 159
Casale (1681), B. of, 159
Caseros (1852), B. of, 238
Cassano (1705), B. of, 34, 159
Cassel (1675), B. of, 33a
Cassel (1758), B. of, 40
Castiglione (1796), B. of, 44
Castile
  15C.: 163a
  16C.: 70, 144
  17C.: 72
  See Spain
Catalonia
  15C.: 163a
  17C.: 32b
  18C.: 34, 74
  19C.: 76
  See Spain
Cayman Is.
  16–20C.: 228–32
Celebes
  16C.: 260
  17C.: 261
  18C.: 9, 11, 262–3
  19C.: 13, 15, 262–5
  20C.: 17–23, 63, 264–5, 273, 279–80,
    282
Cempoala (1520), B. of, 225b
Central Africa, Rep. of
  20C.: 23, 249
  See French Equatorial Africa
Central America (1823–38), United Provs.
  of, 231
Central Europe
  16C.: 66–7, 120–6, 128, 138a
  17C.: 127, 129–31, 138b, 145
  18C.: 34, 35, 39, 40, 132-4, 139a, b
  19C.: 48, 49, 68–9, 89, 135–7, 140–2

  20C.: 56–7, 146–8
  See Europe
Cepeda (1859), B. of, 238
Ceram (E. Indies)
  17C.: 261, 263
  18C.: 9, 11, 263
  19C.: 265
  20C.: 265, 277, 279, 280, 282
Cerdagne
  15–16C.: 107, 163
  17C.: 32b
Ceresole (1544), B. of, 159
Cerigo (Kythira)
  16C.: 71, 158a
  17C.: 73, 164
  18C.: 48, 75
  19C.: 77, 79, 81, 168, 170a
  20C.: 83, 85, 169b, 170b, 171
Ceuta
  16C.: 70
  17C.: 72
  18C.: 74
  19C.: 76, 78, 80, 242
  20C.: 84, 249
Ceylon
  16C.: 260
  17C.: 261
  18C.: 50a, b, 266, 267
  19C.: 268, 270
  20C.: 271–3, 278, 280a
Chacabuco (1817), B. of, 237
Chad
  20C.: 22, 246–51, 253
Chalgrove (1643), B. of, 96a
Chancellorsville (1863), B. of, 207
Charolais
  15C.: 106
  16C.: 70, 107
  17C.: 32b, 33b, 109, 111
Chashniki (1812), B. of, 45, 46b
Chatham Is.
  19C.: 12, 14
  20C.: 17–21, 283
Château-Thierry (1918), B. of, 54
Chattanooga (1863), B. of, 207
Chemnitz (1639), B. of, 31b
Chenla Khmer
  16C.: 3
Chiari (1701), B. of, 159
Chickamauga (1863), B. of, 207
Chile
  17C.: 235
  18C.: 236
  19C.: 237, 238
  20C.: 238, 239
  See South America

China
  16C.: 3
  17C.: 261, 274
  18C.: 274
  19C.: 274, 275
  20C.: 273, 275–80, 282
Chios
  16C.: 71, 164
  17C.: 38, 158, 166
  19C.: 168, 170a
  20C.: 169b, 170b, 171a, b, 172
Chorgum (1854), B. of, 51b
Chotusitz (1742), B. of, 39
Christmas I.
  20C.: 283
Circassians
  16C.: 71
  17C.: 73, 165, 181
  18C.: 75, 183
  19C.: 79, 81, 183, 186a
  20C.: 81, 167
Cisalpine Rep. (1797–1802), 134
Ciudad Rodrigo (1706), B. of, 34
Clonmel (1650), B. of, 94a
Coal industry
  East Africa: 225
  England: 92, 93, 97, 102b, 103b
  Europe: 92, 93
  Poland: 92, 93, 179b
  Russia in Asia: 192, 193
  Russia in Europe: 92, 93, 188, 189
  Scotland: 92, 93, 102b, 103b
  South Africa: 258
  United States: 213
  Wales: 92, 93, 102b, 103b
Cochin China
  See Indochina
Colenso (1900), B. of, 256b
Colmar (1675), B. of, 33a
Cologne, Abp. of
  16C.: 122, 124
  17C.: 130
  18C.: 132
Colombia
  18C.: 231
  19C.: 232, 237, 238
  20C.: 233a, 238, 239
  See South America
Concentration Camps (1939–45), 60, 179b
Confederation of the Rhine (1806), 48, 76,
  136, 137
Congo, formerly Belgian Congo
  20C.: 23, 246–51, 255, 273
Congo, formerly French Congo
  20C.: 23, 246–51

Congo Free State
  19C.: 245
Connecticut
  17C.: 194, 196
  18C.: 197, 198a, b, 200a, b
  19C.: 202, 205, 206
  See United States
Cook Is.
  20C.: 16–20, 283
Copenhagen (1801, 1807), B. of, 44
Copenhagen (1660), T. of, 36b
Corfu
  16C.: 67, 168
  17C.: 168
  18C.: 38b, 158, 168
  19C.: 48, 49, 169b, 170a
  20C.: 170b, 171b.
Corsica
  16C.: 66, 70, 126, 156
  17C.: 72, 112a, 127
  18C.: 44, 74, 112b, 113a, b, 114a, 115a,
    132, 160, 161
  19C.: 76, 78, 86, 114b, 115b
  20C.: 52, 58, 80, 82, 84, 90, 91
Cossacks
  16C.: 71
  17C.: 73, 177a, 181
  18C.: 75, 177b, 182, 183
  19C.: 183
Costa Rica
  18–19C.: 231
  19–20C.: 232, 233a
Coulmiers (1870), B. of, 117
Courland
  16C.: 71, 176a
  17C.: 73, 177a
  18C.: 37a, 75, 177b, 183
  19C.: 187
Cowpens (1781), B. of, 199
Cremona (1526), B. of, 159
Crete
  16C.: 71
  17C.: 73, 158a, 164
  18C.: 75, 158a, 166
  19C.: 77–9, 166, 168, 170a
  20C.: 53, 59, 81, 83, 85, 169b, 170b,
    171a, b
Crimea
  16C.: 2, 71
  17C.: 73, 165, 181
  18C.: 75, 167, 183, 186a
  19C.: 51, 187, 188
  20C.: 189–91
Crim Tartars
  16C.: 71
  17C.: 73, 165, 181

Croatia
  16C.: 71, 164
  17C.: 73, 165
  18C.: 75, 132–4
  19C.: 135–6
  20C.: 58–9, 169
Cropredy Bridge (1644), B. of, 96b
Crown Point (1758), B. of, 41a
Cuba
  16C.: 4, 228
  17C.: 229, 230
  18C.: 8, 10, 41a, 43a, 230, 231
  19C.: 12, 14, 231, 232
  20C.: 16–20, 232, 233a
Culloden (1746), B. of, 95b
Curaçao (W. Indies)
  17–20C.: 16–20, 229–233a
Curzon Line (1919), 179a, 191
Cyprus
  16C.: 71, 158a
  17C.: 73, 165
  18C.: 75
  19C.: 77–9, 167
  20C.: 23, 53, 59, 81–5, 174, 175
Cyrenaica
  16–18C.: 164
  19C.: 166, 242–5
  20C.: 248
Czechoslovakia
  20C.: 57–61, 82–5, 90–3, 147, 148b,
    178b, 179a, b
  See Bohemia, Moravia, Slovakia

Daghestan
  17C.: 165
  18C.: 167
  19C.: 186a
  20C.: 187
Dahomey
  19C.: 244, 245, 252, 253
  20C.: 246–51
Dalmatia
  16C.: 67, 121, 126, 156, 164
  17C.: 38a, 127, 158a, 166
  18C.: 38b, 133, 134, 142, 160, 166
  19C.: 79, 135, 136, 146, 168
  20C.: 81, 169a
Danzig
  16–17C.: 176
  18C.: 48, 133, 176
  19C.: 49, 77, 137, 139
  20C.: 56, 179a
Darfur
  19C.: 2, 42, 244, 245
Dartmouth (1643), B. of, 96a

Delaware
  17C.: 194, 196
  18C.: 197, 198, 200
  19C.: 202, 206, 207
  See United States
Delhi, Prov. of, Sultanate of
  16C.: 3
  18C.: 266
Demerara, See British Guiana
Denain (1712), B. of, 34
Denmark
  16C.: 2, 66–7, 70, 126, 128, 149
  17C.: 36a, b, 72, 127, 149
  18C.: 37a, b, 132, 134
  19C.: 49, 68–9, 76–9, 86–8, 93, 135–7,
    143a
  20C.: 52, 56–61, 80–4, 90–3, 143b
Denmark Overseas
  17C.: 261
  18C.: 8–11, 230, 266
  19C.: 12–15, 231, 262–3
  20C.: 16–21, 232
Deogaon (1803), T. of, 50b
Désirade (W. Indies)
  18C.: 43a
Dessau (1626), B. of, 30b
Dettingen (1743), B. of, 39
Diamond Hill (1900), B. of, 256b
Dig (1804), B. of, 50a
Dobruja
  16–18C.: 71–5, 165
  19C.: 77–9, 167, 170a
  20C.: 81, 170b, 171a, b
Dodecanese
  19C.: 168, 170a
  20C.: 166, 169b, 170b, 171a, b, 172
Dominica I.
  16C.: 228
  17C.: 229
  18C.: 41a, 43a, 230
  19C.: 231
  20C.: 22, 232
Dominican Rep.
  19C.: 14, 232
  20C.: 16–20, 232, 233a
Domnitz (1635), B. of, 31b
Donauwörth (1632), B. of, 31a
Donauwörth (1809), B. of, 44
Downs (1652), B. of, 29
Dresden (1745), T. of, 42
Dreux (1870), B. of, 117
Drissa (1812), B. of, 45, 46a
Drogheda (1649), B. of, 94a
Dublin (1649), B. of, 94a
Duchovshchina (1812), B. of, 46b
Dunamünde (1701), B. of, 37a

Dungeness (1652), B. of, 29
Dusseldorf (1758), B. of, 40
Dutch Guiana
  17C.: 235
  18C.: 236
  19C.: 237, 238
  20C.: 239

East Indies
  16C.: 5, 260
  17C.: 261
  18C.: 9, 11, 262–3
  19C.: 13, 15, 262–5
  20C.: 17–23, 62–3, 265–5, 273, 277–280,
    282–3
Ecclesiastical Divisions
  Europe: 16C.: 66–7
  France: 18–19C.: 114
Economy
  California: 201a
  East Africa: 255
  East India: 261–3
  England: 97, 102, 103
  Europe: 92, 93, 118–9
  Iberian Pen.: 162a
  Middle East: 175
  North America: 201b
  Poland: 179b
  Russia in Asia: 192, 193
  Russia in Europe: 182, 188, 189
  Scandinavia: 149
  Scotland: 97, 102, 103
  South Africa: 258a
  United States: 208–13
  Wales: 97, 102, 103
Ecuador
  19C.: 237, 238
  20C.: 238, 239
  See South America
Edge Hill (1642), B. of, 96a
Egypt
  16–17C.: 164–5
  18–19C.: 45b, 166–7
  19C.: 242–5
  20C.: 53, 173–5, 240b, 246–51, 273
Eire
  20C.: 94b
  See Ireland
El Faiyum (1798), B. of, 45b
El Gîzah (1798), B. of, 45b
Ellice Is.
  20C.: 17–21, 283
England
  16C.: 2, 24–5, 66, 70, 118
  17C.: 24–5, 29, 33a, 72, 96a, b
  18C.: 34, 35, 41b, 74, 97

  19C.: 24–5, 47b, 49, 68, 76–9, 86, 88,
    98–102
  20C.: 52, 58, 61, 80, 82, 84, 90–3,
    103, 104
Enniskillen (1689), B. of, 94a
Enzheim (1674), B. of, 33a
Equatoria
  19C.: 244, 245
Erfurt (1808), B. of, 44
Eritrea
  20C.: 174, 175, 246–51
Ermes (1560), B. of, 176a
Ermland
  15–16C.: 123, 125, 126, 176a
  17C.: 127, 131
  18C.: 133, 139a, 177b
Española (Hispaniola, Haiti)
  16C.: 4, 228
  17C.: 229
  18C.: 8, 10, 43a, 230
Espinasa (1808), B. of, 46c
Essequibo, See British Guiana
Esslingen (1809), B. of, 45
Estonia
  16C.: 71, 119, 149, 176a
  17C.: 36b, 73
  18C.: 37a, b, 74, 182, 183
  20C.: 56, 81, 83, 85, 178b, 187, 191
Ethiopia (Abyssinia)
  16C.: 2
  19C.: 242–5
  20C.: 246–51, 273
Etruria, K. of
  19C.: 135, 136
Euboea
  19C.: 166, 168, 169b
  20C.: 170–2
  See Negroponte
Eupatoria (1855), B. of, 51b
Europe
  16C.: 2–6a, 66–7, 70–1
  17C.: 6b, 72–3
  18C.: 7a, 8–11, 34, 35, 42, 44, 74–5
  19C.: 7b, 12–15, 48, 49, 68–9, 76–9,
    86–7, 93, 216
  20C.: 16–25, 52–3, 56–63, 80–5, 90–3
  Physical: 64–5
Eutaw Springs (1781), B. of, 199
Exploration
  Africa: 242, 243
  Antarctic: 27
  Arctic: 24–6
  Australia: 284–5
  Canada: 24, 196, 220
  Mexico: 225a, 226
  New Zealand: 284–5

Exploration (*cont.*)
  North America: 24, 196, 203, 220, 225a, 226
  Russia in Asia: 184
  South America: 233b, 234
  United States: 196, 203, 226
  West Indies: 228
  World: 4–7
Eylau (1807), B. of, 45
Falkirk (1746), B. of, 95b
Falkland Is.
  18C.: 10, 236
  19C.: 12, 14, 237, 238
  20C.: 16–22
Farruckhabad (1804), B. of, 50a
Fehrbellion (1675), B. of, 33a
Fernando Póo
  18C.: 252
  19C.: 242–5, 253
  20C.: 246–51
Fezzan
  19C.: 166, 242, 244, 245
  20C.: 248, 254
Fiji Is.
  20C.: 17–21, 63, 283
Finland
  16C.: 71, 119
  17C.: 36b, 73, 149
  18C.: 37a, b, 75
  19C.: 48, 49, 77, 79, 183, 188
  20C.: 53, 56, 59, 61, 62, 81, 83, 85, 191
Flanders
  16C.: 70, 106, 122, 124, 150a
  17C.: 108, 111, 151b
  18C.: 113a, 115a
  19C.: 152
  20C.: 54
Fleurus (1622), B. of, 30a
Fleurus (1690), B. of, 33a
Fleurus (1794), B. of, 44
Florence, Rep. of
  16C.: 70, 126, 127, 156a, b
  See Tuscany
Florida
  16C.: 228, 229
  17C.: 196, 229
  18C.: 43a, 196, 198a, b, 200a, 230, 231
  19C.: 202, 206, 207, 231
  20C.: 232, 233a
  See United States
Fontenoy (1749), B. of, 39
Formosa: *see* Taiwan
Fort Duquesne (1755), B. of, 41a
Fort Jackson (1862), B. of, 207
Fort Monroe (1862), B. of, 207
Fort Morgan (1864), B. of, 207

Fort Ontario (1756), B. of, 41a
Fra Mauro (1459), Globe of, 1
France
  15C.: 106
  16C.: 66, 70, 107–10, 118, 121, 144
  17C.: 32a, b, 33a, b, 72, 108–9, 111, 112a
  18C.: 34, 35, 39, 42, 74, 108–9, 112b–114a, 115a
  19C.: 44, 47b, 48, 68, 76–9, 86, 88, 89, 93, 114b, 115b, 117
  20C.: 52, 54, 57–61, 80, 82, 84, 90–3
France Overseas
  17C.: 229, 235
  18C.: 8–11, 43, 196–8, 221a, 230, 236, 266
  19C.: 12–15, 50b, 80, 166–7, 231, 237, 242–5, 252, 253, 275
  20C.: 16–21, 55a, 58, 82–5, 174, 232, 238, 246–9, 254, 264–5, 275, 277, 282–3
Franche Comté, *See* Burgundy, C. of
Frankenhausen (1525), B. of, 28
Franklin, District of
  19C.: 223a
  20C.: 223b, c
Fraustadt (1706), B. of, 37a
Fredericksburg (1862), B. of, 207
Fredrikshamn (1809), T. of, 48
Freemans Farm (1777), B. of, 199
Freiberg (1762), B. of, 40
Freiburg (1525), B. of, 28
Freiburg (1644), B. of, 31b
French Congo
  19C.: 245, 253
  20C.: 246–51
French Equatorial Africa
  20C.: 246–8, 273
French Guiana
  17C.: 235
  18C.: 236
  19C.: 47b, 237, 238
French Guinea
  19C.: 253
  20C.: 246–8
French Sudan
  19C.: 253
  20C.: 246–8
French West Africa
  19C.: 253
  20C.: 246–8, 254, 273
Friedland (1807), B. of, 45
Friesland (in Holland)
  16C.: 122, 124, 150a
  17C.: 151b
  19C.: 152
Friesland, East
  16C.: 122, 124

Friesland, East (*cont.*)
  17C.: 130
  18C.: 42, 139a
Fulani Empire
  19C.: 244, 245
Fulda (1525), B. of, 28

Gabbard (1653), B. of, 29
Gabon
  19C.: 253
  20C.: 22–3, 246–9
Gadebusch (1712), B. of, 37a
Gadsen Purchase (1853), 202, 227
Gaeta (1806), B. of, 44
Gaikwar
  19C.: 50b, 267
  See Gujarat
Galapagos Is.
  16C.: 4
  18C.: 8, 10
  19C.: 12, 14
  20C.: 16–22
Galicia and Lodomeria, K. of
  18C.: 133, 177b
  19C.: 48, 77, 142, 146, 178a
  20C.: 179a
Gambia
  19C.: 244, 245, 253
  20C.: 22, 246–9, 273
Gawilgarh (1803), B. of, 50a, 267
Gelderland
  15C.: 106
  16C.: 122, 124, 150a
  17C.: 151b
  19C.: 152
Genoa (1538, 1548), B. of, 159
Genoa, Rep. of
  16C.: 70, 156
  17C.: 72
  18C.: 74, 132, 160
Georgia (in Russia)
  16C.: 165
  18C.: 167
  19C.: 183, 186a
  20C.: 273
Georgia (in U.S.A.)
  18C.: 196, 198a, b, 200
  19C.: 202, 206, 207
  See United States
German Confederation (1815–66), 49,
    78–79, 139b–42, 152
German East Africa
  19C.: 245
  20C.: 55a, 246

German South-West Africa
  19C.: 245
  20C.: 55a, 246
Germantown (1777), B. of, 199
Germany
  19C.: 68–9, 86–9, 93, 140–2
  20C.: 52–61, 80–5, 90–3, 147, 148a, b,
    178b, 187
  See Central Europe, Europe
Germany Overseas
  19C.: 221a, 245, 253, 275
  20C.: 16–17, 55, 246, 264–5, 275
Gerona (1694), B. of, 33a
Gerona (1809), B. of, 44
Gettysburg (1863), B. of, 207
Ghana
  20C.: 22, 249
  See Gold Coast
Gilbert Is.
  20C.: 17–21, 283
Gmunden (1626), B. of, 30b
Goa
  16C.: 260
  17C.: 261
  18C.: 266, 267
  19C.: 268
  20C.: 270–2, 278
Golconda
  16C.: 3
  17C.: 266
Goldberg (1635), B. of, 31b
Gold Coast
  19C.: 47b, 242, 244, 245, 252, 253
  20C.: 246–51, 273
Golden Horde, 71, 180–1
Gold mining
  Australia: 286–7
  California: 201a
  East Africa: 255
  Russia in Asia: 192, 193
  Russia in Europe: 188, 189
  Scandinavia: 149
  South Africa: 258a
  United States: 209b
Golymin (1806), B. of, 45
Gondwana
  16C.: 3
  17C.: 266
Granada, *see* Spain
Grandson (1476), B. of, 106
Great Britain, *see* England, Ireland,
    Scotland, Wales
Great Britain Overseas
  17C.: 74, 194–5, 229, 235, 261
  18C.: 8–11, 43, 196–8, 200a, 221a, 230,
    236, 266, 267

Great Britain Overseas (*cont.*)
19C.: 12–15, 48–50, 76–80 166–8, 231, 237, 242–5, 252, 253, 262–3, 267, 268, 275
20C.: 16–21, 55, 82–5, 174, 232, 238, 240, 246–9, 257, 264–5, 270, 275, 277, 282–3
Great Kabardia
18–19C.: 77, 79, 183, 186a
Great Trek (1836–46), 256a
Greece
16C.: 71, 164
17C.: 73
18C.: 38a, b, 75, 158a
19C.: 77–81, 166–170a
20C.: 53, 57–61, 81–5, 170b–172a, 273
Greek Orthodox
16C.: 66–7, 126
17C.: 127
Greenland
16–20C.: 24–6, 220, 222, 223
Grenada (W. Indies)
17C.: 229
18C.: 41a, 43a, 230
19C.: 231
20C.: 22, 232
Groningen (1672), B. of, 33a
Gross Jägersdorf (1757), B. of, 40
Grünberg (1761), B. of, 40
Guadalupe Hidalgo (1848), T. of, 227
Guadeloupe
16C.: 228
17C.: 229
18C.: 8, 10, 41a, 43a, 230
19C.: 12, 14, 231
20C.: 16, 18, 20, 22
Guam
19C.: 265
20C.: 282
Guastalla (1734), B. of, 159
Guatemala
16C.: 228, 229
17C.: 230
18C.: 231
19–20C.: 232, 233a
Guiana, *see* British, Dutch and French Guiana
Guilford (1781), B. of, 199
Guinea
20C.: 22, 249
See French Guinea
Gujarat
16C.: 3
17C.: 266
19C.: 267, 268
20C.: 270

Guyana
20C.: 22, 239
See British Guiana

Habsburg possessions
16C.: 70–1, 122–5, 144
17C.: 72–3, 130–1, 145
18C.: 74–5, 132–4, 160
19C.: 135
20C.: 146
See Austria
Hadhramaut
16C.: 2
19–20C.: 174, 273
Hainan
19C.: 274
20C.: 276, 277, 279, 280
Hainaut
15C.: 106
16C.: 70, 122, 124, 150a
17C.: 151b
18C.: 115a
19C.: 152
Haiti
19C.: 12, 14, 231
20C.: 16–21, 232, 233a
See Española
Halberstadt, Bp. of
16C.: 122–5
17C.: 32a
Halland
17C.: 36b, 149
Halle (1806), B. of, 44
Halmahera
17C.: 261, 263
18C.: 9, 11, 263
19C.: 13, 15, 265
20C.: 17–23, 265, 277, 279, 280, 282
Hanover, El. of; K. of
18C.: 37b, 40, 74, 132, 134
19C.: 49, 78, 135–7, 139b, 140–2
Hanseatic League
14–15C.: 118–9
Hastenbeck (1757), B. of, 40
Hateg (1690), B. of, 38a
Hausa states
18C.: 252
Havana, Captaincy General of, 229
Hawaiian Is.
19–20C.: 12–22, 63, 283
Hejaz
16–20C.: 165, 167, 174
Heligoland
16C.: 122, 124
17C.: 130
18C.: 74, 132

Heligoland (*cont*.)
  19C.: 48, 49, 76–9, 136, 137
  20C.: 52, 80
Heligoland (1914), B. of, 52
Helsinborg (1710), B. of, 37a
Helvetia, Helvetic Rep., *see* Switzerland
Herbsthausen (1645), B. of, 31b
Héricourt (1474), B. of, 106
Herzegovina
  16C.: 71
  17C.: 73, 165
  18C.: 75, 133
  19C.: 77–9, 146, 168, 170a
  20C.: 81, 170b, 171a, b
Hesse, Hesse-Cassel, Hesse-Darmstadt
  16C.: 122–6, 128
  17C.: 32, 127, 129, 130
  18C.: 132, 134
  19C.: 49, 135–7, 140–2
Hindenburg Line (Siegfriedstellung), (1917),
  54
Hiroshima (1945), 63
Hispanola, *see* Española
Hobkirk's Hill (1781), B. of, 199
Hochkirch (1758), B. of, 40
Höchst (1622), B. of, 30a
Hohenfriedberg (1745), B. of, 39
Hohenlinden (1800), B. of, 44
Hohenzollern possessions
  16C.: 122–5
  17C.: 130–1
  18C.: 132–3
  See Prussia
Hollabrunn (1805), B. of, 45
Holland, *see* Netherlands
Holowczyn (1708), B. of, 37a
Holstein
  16C.: 70, 122–6
  17C.: 127, 130, 132
  18C.: 134
  19C.: 135, 140–143a
  20C.: 80, 143b
Holy Roman Empire
  16C.: 2, 70–1, 121–6, 128, 145
  17C.: 30–3, 36a, b, 72–3, 127, 129–31,
    145
  18C.: 34, 35, 37, 39, 42, 44–5, 74–5,
    132–4, 146
  19C.: 135
Honduras
  16C.: 228
  17C.: 229
  18C.: 230
  19C.: 231, 232
  20C.: 232, 233a

Hong Kong
  19C.: 274, 275b
  20C.: 276, 277, 279, 280b, 282
Hubertusburg (1763), T. of, 42
Huguenots
  16C.: 110
Hull (1643), B. of, 96a
Hungary
  16C.: 2, 67, 71, 121, 125, 126, 144, 164
  17C.: 33a, 38, 73, 127, 131, 145, 146, 166
  18C.: 35, 42, 75, 133, 134
  19C.: 49, 69, 77–9, 86–9, 135–7, 142, 168
  20C.: 53, 57–61, 81, 83, 85, 90–3, 147,
    148, 178, 187
Hyderabad
  17C.: 266
  18C.: 267
  19C.: 50b, 268
  20C.: 270
Hyderabad, in Sind (1843), B. of, 268

Iberian Peninsula
  15C.: 162a, b, 163a
  16C.: 66, 70, 144
  17C.: 72
  18C.: 34, 35, 42, 44, 74
  19C.: 46c, 47b, 76–80, 86
  20C.: 52, 58, 69, 82, 84, 163b
Iceland
  16–20C.: 2, 23, 25, 26, 64
Ifni
  19C.: 244, 245
  20C.: 246–51, 254
Illyrian Provinces
  19C.: 48, 76–8, 137
Inca Empire (1195–1525), 234
India
  16C.: 2–5, 260
  17C.: 261, 266
  18C.: 9, 11, 41c, 43b, 50a, b, 266, 267
  19C.: 13, 15, 50b, 268–70
  20C.: 17–23, 62, 270–3, 278, 280a
Indian Ocean
  16C.: 4–5, 260
  17C.: 6b, 261
  18C.: 7a, 9, 11
  19C.: 7b, 13, 15
  20C.: 15–23, 62–3
Indochina
  16C.: 3, 260
  17C.: 261
  18C.: 262
  19C.: 264
  20C.: 273, 276–80, 282

Indonesia
  20C.: 23, 273, 280
  See East Indies
Industry, *see* Economy
Ingria
  16C.: 149
  17C.: 36b, 180
  18C.: 37a, b, 182
Inkerman (1854), B. of, 55b
Innsbruck (1809), B. of, 44
Ionian Is.
  16C.: 71
  17C.: 73
  18C.: 75, 166
  19C.: 48, 77–81, 166, 168, 169b, 170a
  20C.: 53, 59, 83, 85, 170b, 171
Iran
  16C.: 260
  19C.: 270
  20C.: 174, 175, 184, 186b, 273
Iraq
  16–20C.: 165, 167, 174, 175, 273
Ireland
  16C.: 2, 66, 70, 94a
  17C.: 33a, 72, 94a
  18C.: 41b, 74, 94a
  19C.: 68, 76–9, 86, 88, 98–101
  20C.: 22–3, 52, 58, 80–4, 90–3, 94b, 104
Iron industry
  England: 92, 93, 102b, 103b
  Europe: 92, 93
  North America: 201b
  Poland: 92, 93, 179b
  Russia in Asia: 192, 193
  Russia in Europe: 92, 93, 182, 188, 189
  Scandinavia: 92, 93, 149
  Scotland: 92, 93, 102b, 103b
  United States: 212, 213
  Wales: 92, 93, 102b, 103b
Iroquois
  17C.: 194–5
Islam, *see* Mohammedans
Israel
  20C.: 167, 173, 175, 273
Isola della Scala (1512), B. of, 159
Italy
  16C.: 66–7, 70–1, 144, 156
  17C.: 72–3
  18C.: 35, 42, 48, 74–5, 132, 134, 158–60
  19C.: 49, 68–9, 76–9, 86, 88, 93, 135–7, 161
  20C.: 52, 57–61, 80–5, 92, 93, 147, 161
Italy Overseas
  20C.: 16–19, 174, 246–8, 254
Ituzaingú (1827), B. of, 237

Ivory Coast
  19C.: 244, 245, 252, 253
  20C.: 22, 246–51

Jamaica
  16C.: 228
  17C.: 229
  18C.: 8, 10, 230
  19C.: 12, 14, 231
  20C.: 16–20, 232, 233a
Jamestown (1781), B. of, 199
Jankau (1645), B. of, 31b
Japan
  16C.: 3
  17C.: 261
  18C.: 9, 11
  19C.: 13, 15
  20C.: 17–21, 63, 276–280a, 282
Java
  16C.: 260
  17C.: 261
  18C.: 9, 11, 262
  19C.: 13, 15, 264
  20C.: 17–23, 63, 264, 273, 277–80
Jedisan
  16C.: 165
  17C.: 181
  18C.: 167, 182
Jena (1806), B. of, 44
Jews
  Europe: 60, 187
  Palestine: 173
Jordan
  20C.: 175, 273
  See Transjordan
Juana, *see* Cuba
Jülich
  16C.: 122, 124, 126
  17C.: 127, 130
  18C.: 132
  19C.: 139b
Jungfernhof (1700), B. of, 37a
Junin (1824), B. of, 237
Jüterbok (1644), B. of, 31b

Kaiser Wilhelm Land
  19–20C.: 265
  See New Guinea
Kalat (1839), B. of, 268
Kalisz (1706), B. of, 37a
Kamchatka Pen.
  17–18C.: 184
  20C.: 185
Kamerun
  19–20C.: 246, 253

Kammin, Bp. of
  16C.: 123, 125
  17C.: 129a, 131, 138b
Karabagh
  17C.: 165
  18C.: 167
  19C.: 186
Karafuto
  20C.: 276, 277
Karaman
  16–17C.: 71, 73, 165
  18C.: 75
Kardis (1661), T. of, 36b
Karelian A.S.S.R.
  20C.: 191
  See Carelia
Kars (1855), B. of, 51a
Kashmir
  16C.: 3, 266
  17C.: 266
  19C.: 268
  20C.: 270, 273, 278
Kath-Hennersdorf (1745), B. of, 39
Kazan, Khanate of, Tatars of
  16C.: 3, 71
  17C.: 180–1
Keewatin, District of
  19C.: 222c, 223a
  20C.: 223b, c
Kempen (1642), B. of, 31b
Kempten (1525), B. of, 28
Kentish Knock (1652), B. of, 29
Kentucky
  18C.: 200
  19C.: 202, 206, 207
  See United States
Kenya
  20C.: 23, 246–51, 255, 273
Kesselsdorf (1745), B. of, 39
Khandesh
  16C.: 3
Khorasan
  16C.: 2
Kiaochow (Tsingtao)
  19–20C.: 275b
Kiel (1814), T. of, 49
Kimberley (1899), B. of, 256b
King's Mtn. (1780), B. of, 199
Kinsale (1601), B. of, 94a
Kirkee (1817), B. of, 268
Kleve
  16C.: 122, 124, 126
  17C.: 127, 130, 138
Klissow (1702), B. of, 37a
Kolberg (1761), B. of, 40
Kolberg Heath (1644), B. of, 31b

Kolin (1757), B. of, 40
Königshofen (1525), B. of, 28
Korbach (1760), B. of, 40
Korea
  16C.: 3
  17–19C.: 274
  20C.: 23, 276–80, 282
Kosovo Polje (1389), B. of, 164
Krakow, Rep. of
  19C.: 49, 79, 142, 146, 178a
Krasnoj (1812), B. of, 45, 46b
Kutchuk–Kainarji (1774), T. of, 166–7
Kuwait
  19C.: 167
  20C.: 174, 175
Kwangchow
  19–20C.: 275b
Kwangtung Terr.
  19–20C.: 275b
Kyritz (1635), B. of, 31b
Kythira, see Cerigo

La Albuera (1809), B. of, 44, 46c
Labrador
  17C.: 24
  18C.: 43a
  19C.: 220
  See Canada
La Coruña (1809), B. of, 44, 46c
Ladrone Is. See Mariana Is.
  16C.: 5
Ladysmith (1899–1900), Siege of, 256b
Lagos, in Portugal (1759), B. of, 41b
La Hogue (1692), B. of, 33a
Landriano (1529), B. of, 159
Landshut (1760), B. of, 40
Langport (1645), B. of, 96b
Languages and Peoples
  Balkans: 60, 61, 171a
  Belgium: 60, 108–9, 113b, 150b, 151a, 152
  Canada: 221, 224a
  Central Europe: 60, 61, 120
  Finland: 149
  France: 108–9, 113b
  Habsburg Empire: 147
  India: 271
  Macedonia: 172b
  Poland: 60, 61, 176b, 178b
  Schleswig-Holstein: 143b
  South-East Asia: 280b
  Switzerland: 109, 113b, 155
Lansdown Hill (1643), B. of, 96a
Laos
  16C.: 3
  19–20C.: 23, 264, 273, 276–80
  See Indochina

Laswari (1803), B. of, 50a
Latvia
    20C.: 56, 81, 83, 85, 178b, 179, 191
Lauenburg
    19C.: 49, 142, 143a
Lauffeldt (1747), B. of, 39
Lausanne (1923), T. of, 166–7, 174
Lebanon
    20C.: 59, 167, 173–5, 273
Le Cateau (1914), B. of, 54
Leipheim (1525), B. of, 28
Leipzig (1813), B. of, 44
Le Mans (1871), B. of, 117
Lemnos
    15–17C.: 158, 164
    19C.: 168, 170a
    20C.: 169b, 170b, 171a, b, 172a
León, see Spain
Lepanto (1571), B. of, 158, 164
Lesbos, see Mitilini
Lesna (1708), B. of, 37a
Lesotho
    20C.: 23, 249
    See Basutoland
Leuthen (1757), B. of, 40
Lexington (1775), B. of, 199
Liberia
    19C.: 242–5, 253
    20C.: 246–51, 273
Libya
    20C.: 23, 53–4, 246–51, 254, 273
    See Fezzan, Tripoli
Lichfield (1643), B. of, 96a
Liechtenstein
    18C.: 132, 134
    19C.: 135–7, 142
    20C.: 58, 80, 82, 84, 148
Liège (1914), B. of, 54
Liège, Bp. of, Prov. of
    15C.: 106
    16C.: 122, 124, 150a
    17C.: 130
    18C.: 132
    19C.: 152
Liegnitz (1760), B. of, 40
Ligurian Rep.
    18C.: 48, 134
    19C.: 135, 136, 161
Limburg, D. of,
    16C.: 150a
    17C.: 151
    19C.: 152
Limerick (1690–91), B. of, 94a
Lithuania
    16C.: 2, 70
    17C.: 73, 177a

18C.: 37a, 75, 177b
20C.: 56, 81, 83, 85, 148, 178b, 179, 191
Livonia
    16C.: 176a
    17C.: 36b, 149, 177a, 180
    18C.: 37a, b, 177b, 182
    19C.: 183
    20C.: 187
Ljachovo (1812), B. of, 46b
Lobositz (1756), B. of, 40
Lodi (1523), B. of, 159
Lodi (1796), B. of, 44
Lodomeria, Galicia and, K. of
    18C.: 133, 177b
    19C.: 142, 146, 178a
    20C.: 179a
Loigny (1870), B. of, 117
Lombardy and Venetia, K. of
    19C.: 49, 78, 142, 146, 161
Lomnitz (1618), B. of, 30a
London
    18C.: 105a
    20C.: 104
London (1913), T. of, 166–7
Londonderry (1689), B. of, 94a
Loos (1917), B. of, 54
Lorraine
    15C.: 106
    16C.: 70, 122–6
    17C.: 32b, 72, 108–9, 111, 127, 130
    18C.: 42, 74, 113a, 115a, 132
    19C.: 117, 141a, b
    20C.: 54, 57, 58, 80, 82
Lostwithiel (1644), B. of, 96b
Louisiana
    17C.: 196
    18C.: 43a, 198
    19C.: 202, 206, 207
    See United States
Lowestoft (1665), B. of, 29
Lublin (1569), Union of, 177a
Lucca
    16C.: 156
    18C.: 48, 132, 134, 160
    19C.: 49, 76, 78, 135–7, 142, 146, 161
Lunéville (1801), T. of, 48
Lusatia
    15C.: 120
    17C.: 32a, 131, 145
Lutter (1626), B. of, 30b
Lutternberg (1762), B. of, 40
Lützen (1632), B. of, 31a
Luxemburg
    15C.: 106
    16C.: 70, 122–6, 128, 144, 150
    17C.: 127, 145, 151

Luxemburg (*cont.*)
  19C.: 49, 78, 117, 140–2, 152
  20C.: 52, 54, 57–61, 80, 82, 84, 147, 148
Luzzara (1702), B. of, 34, 159

Macao
  16C.: 260
  17C.: 261
  18C.: 262
  19C.: 264
  20C.: 276, 277
Macedonia
  19C.: 77, 79, 168, 170a
  20C.: 81, 83, 166, 169b, 170b, 171, 172
Mackenzie, District of
  19C.: 223a
  20C.: 223b, c
Madagascar
  16C.: 5
  18C.: 9, 11
  19C.: 13, 15, 242–5
  20C.: 17–23, 62, 246–51, 273
Madeira
  19C.: 242–5
  20C.: 246–51, 254
Mafeking (1899–1900), Siege of, 256b
Magdeburg, Abp. of
  16C.: 123, 125
  17C.: 32a, 129a, 131, 138b
Maine
  17C.: 194
  18C.: 197
  19C.: 202, 206, 219
  See United States
Mainz, Abp. of
  16C.: 122, 124, 126, 128
  17C.: 127, 130
  18C.: 132, 134
Maipu (1818), B. of, 237
Majorca
  15C.: 162, 163a
  16C.: 66
  19C.: 68
  20C.: 163b
  See Balearic Is.
Malacca
  16C.: 260
  17C.: 261
  18C.: 262
  19C.: 264
Malaga (1704), B. of, 34
Malaga (1809), B. of, 44
Malagasy
  20C.: 23, 249
  See Madagascar

Malawi
  20C.: 23, 249
  See Nyasaland
Malaya
  18–19C.: 262
  19C.: 264
  20C.: 273, 277, 279, 280, 282
Malaysia
  20C.: 23
  See Malaya
Mali
  20C.: 22, 249
  See French Sudan
Maloyaroslavets (1812), B. of, 45, 46b
Malplaquet (1709), B. of, 34
Malta
  16C.: 70, 156
  17C.: 72
  18C.: 48, 49, 74, 160
  19C.: 23, 76, 161
Malvalli (1799), B. of, 50a
Malwa
  16C.: 3, 266
  17C.: 266
Mamelukes (1257–1517), Empire of, 2
Manassas (1862), B. of, 207
Manchu (Ch'ing) Empire (1644–1912), 274
Manchukuo, Manchuria
  20C.: 184, 274, 276, 277
Manitoba
  19C.: 222c, 223a
  20C.: 223b, c, 224a, b
  See Canada
Mantua, Mar. of
  16C.: 156
  18C.: 35, 160
Mantua (1801), B. of, 44
Maratha Confederacy (1805), 50a, 50b, 267
Marciano (1554), B. of, 159
Marengo (1800), B. of, 44
Mariana Is.
  17–18C.: 9, 11, 263
  19C.: 13, 15, 265
  20C.: 17–23, 55b, 63, 282
Marie Galante (W. Indies)
  16C.: 228
  17C.: 229
  18C.: 43a, 230
  19C.: 231
  20C.: 232
Marignano (1515), B. of, 159
Mark, C. of
  16C.: 122, 124, 126
  17C.: 127, 130, 138a
Marquesas Is.
  19C.: 14

Marquesas Is. (*cont.*)
  20C.: 16–20, 283
Marsaglia (1693), B. of, 159
Marshall Is.
  20C.: 17–23, 55b, 282
Mars-la-Tour (1870), B. of, 117
Marston Moor (1644), B. of, 96b
Martinique
  16C.: 228
  17C.: 229, 235
  18C.: 41a, 43a, 230, 236
  19C.: 47b, 231, 237
  20C.: 232, 239
Maryland
  17C.: 195
  18C.: 196–8, 200
  19C.: 202, 206, 207
  See United States
Mason-Dixon Line (1763–7), 206
Massachusetts
  17–18C.: 196–8, 200
  19C.: 202, 206
  See United States
Massachusetts Bay
  17C.: 194, 195b
Mauritania
  20C.: 22, 246–51, 254
Maxen (1759), B. of, 40
Maya Civilization, 225a
Mecklenburg, Mecklenburg-Schwerin
  16C.: 123, 125, 126
  17C.: 32a, 127, 131
  18C.: 40, 132, 134
  19C.: 135–7, 140, 141
Memel Terr.
  20C.: 56, 82, 191
Memmingen (1800), B. of, 44
Memphis (1862), B. of, 207
Mesta Routes in Iberian Peninsula, 162
Metz, Bp of
  16C.: 108–9, 122, 124
  17C.: 32a, 111, 130
  18C.: 115a
Mexico
  16C.: 225
  17C.: 226
  19C.: 227
  20C.: 233a
Mexico City (1847), B. of, 227
Miani (1843), B. of, 268
Milan, D. of
  16C.: 122, 124, 126, 128, 144, 156
  17C.: 127, 130
  18C.: 35, 160
Minden (1759), B. of, 40

Minden, Bp. of
  16C.: 122, 124
  17C.: 32a, 129, 130, 138b
Ming Empire (1368–1644), 3
Minorca
  15C.: 162, 163a
  16C.: 66
  18C.: 34, 35, 41b, 42, 44, 48
  20C.: 163b
  See Balearic Is.
Miquelon
  18C.: 43a, 198b
Mirandola (1710), B. of, 159
Missouri Compromise Line (1820), 206
Mitilini (Lesbos)
  16–17C.: 164
  19C.: 168, 170a
  20C.: 169b, 170b, 171a, b, 172
Moçambique
  20C.: 246–51, 255, 273
  See Portuguese East Africa
Modena
  16C.: 156
  18C.: 132, 160, 161
  19C.: 49, 78, 142, 146
Mogul Empire
  16C.: 260, 261, 266
Mohacs (1526), B. of, 164
Mohammedans, 66–7, 126, 127, 162b
    172b, 272, 273
  See Ottoman Empire
Mohilev (1812), B. of, 45, 46a
Moldavia
  16C.: 2, 71, 164–5
  17C.: 72
  18C.: 48, 75, 133, 183
  19C.: 77, 79, 166–7, 168
  20C.: 81, 83, 85
Mollwitz (1741), B. of, 39
Moluccas
  16C.: 5, 260
  17C.: 261
  18C.: 263
  19C.: 265
  20C.: 279, 280b, 282
Monaco
  16C.: 156
  17C.: 157
  18C.: 160
  19C.: 49, 78, 117, 161
  20C.: 80, 82, 84
Monaco (1507), B. of, 159
Mondovi (1796), B. of, 44
Mongolia
  17C.: 274
  20C.: 184, 277, 280

Monmouth, in United States (1778), B. of, 199
Mons (1691), B. of, 33a
Mons (1914), B. of, 54
Montenegro
  16C.: 71
  17C.: 73, 164
  18C.: 75, 133
  19C.: 77, 79, 166, 168, 170a
  20C.: 53, 57, 59, 81, 169a, 170b, 171, 172a
Montferrat, Mar. of
  16C.: 156
  17–18C.: 157
Montmirail (1814), B. of, 44
Moravia
  15C.: 120
  16C.: 71, 121, 123, 125, 126, 144
  17C.: 73, 127, 131, 145
  18C.: 39, 75, 133, 134
  19C.: 77, 79, 135–7, 142
  20C.: 58–9, 81, 146, 148a
Morea, see Peloponnese
Morhange (1914), B. of, 54
Morocco
  19C.: 242–5
  20C.: 22, 52, 58, 246–51, 254, 273
Moslems, see Mohammedans
Mosquito Coast; Prot. of
  16–17C.: 229
  17–18C.: 230
  19C.: 231, 232
Mt. Tabor (1799), B. of, 45b
Münster (in Germany), Bp. of
  16C.: 122, 124, 126
  17C.: 127, 130
  18C.: 132, 134, 136
Murten (1476), B. of, 106
Murviedro (1811), B. of, 44, 46b
Muscovy, Gr. Pr. of
  16C.: 180
Mysore
  18C.: 50a, b, 267
  19C.: 268
  20C.: 270
  See India

Nagasaki (1945), 63
Namur (1692), B. of, 33a
Namur (1914), B. of, 54
Nancy (1477), B. of, 106
Nantwich (1644), B. of, 96b
Naples (1799), B. of, 44
Naples, K. of
  16C.: 2, 70–1, 126, 144, 156
  17C.: 72–3, 127

18C.: 35, 42, 74–5, 132–3, 134, 160
  19C.: 48, 76–9, 135–7, 161
Naseby (1645), B. of, 96b
Nashville (1864), B. of, 207
Natal
  19C.: 256a, 257
  20C.: 256b
  See South Africa
Nauru I.
  20C.: 55b, 282
Navarre
  15C.: 163a
  16C.: 70, 107
  17C.: 72
Naxos
  16C.: 71, 158a, 164
Neerwinden (1693), B. of, 33a
Negroponte (Euboea)
  17C.: 38a, 164
  18C.: 158
  19C.: 166
Nepal
  16C.: 3
  18C.: 267
  19C.: 50a, 268, 274
  20C.: 23, 270–2, 279, 280a
Nesvizh (1812), B. of, 46a
Netherlands
  16C.: 144, 150, 151a; see Netherlands, Spanish
  17C.: 145, 151b; see United Provinces
  18C.: See Batavian Rep., United Provinces
  19C.: 48, 68, 86, 88, 89, 93, 117, 136, 137, 140b–2, 152, 153; see Netherlands, United
  20C.: 52, 54, 56–61, 80, 82, 84, 90–3, 147, 148
Netherlands, Austrian
  18C.: 35, 132, 146
Netherlands Overseas
  16C.: 229
  17C.: 194–5, 229, 235, 261
  18C.: 8–11, 230, 236, 266
  19C.: 12–15, 231, 237, 262–3
  20C.: 16–21, 232, 238, 264–5, 277, 282–3
Netherlands, Spanish
  16C.: 124–6
  17C.: 29, 32b, 33b, 72, 127, 130
Netherlands, United (1815–30), 49, 78, 140a, 152
Neuchâtel, Canton of, Pr. of,
  18C.: 132, 134, 138b, 139a, 154
  19C.: 48, 135, 136, 139b, 142, 155
Neuss (1474), B. of, 106

Nevers
  15C.: 106
  16C.: 107
Nevis (W. Indies)
  16–20C.: 228–32
New Brunswick
  18C.: 221a
  19C.: 219b, 222, 223a
  20C.: 223b, c, 224
Newburn (1640), B. of, 96a
Newbury (1643), B. of, 96a
Newbury (1644), B. of, 96b
New Caledonia
  16–19C.: 15, 285
  20C.: 17–21, 63, 282
New England
  17–18C.: 196–9
  See United States
Newfoundland
  16C.: 4
  18C.: 43a, 198
  19C.: 222, 223a
  20C.: 223b, c, 224
  See Canada
New France
  17–18C.: 196–198a
New Granada, Vice-Royalty of
  17–18C.: 230, 236
  19C.: 231, 237
New Guinea
  18–20C.: 11–23, 265, 277, 282, 284–5
New Hampshire
  17C.: 194–5
  18C.: 196–7, 200
  19C.: 202, 206
  See United States
New Haven
  17C.: 194
New Hebrides
  20C.: 17–21, 282
New Jersey
  17C.: 196
  18C.: 197, 198
  19C.: 200, 202, 206, 207
  See United States
New Mexico
  19C.: 202, 206, 207
  See United States
New Netherland
  17C.: 194
New Plymouth
  17C.: 194, 195b
New South Wales
  19–20C.: 13, 15, 286–7, 288
New Spain, Vice-Royalty of
  16–17C.: 229

  17–18C.: 230, 235
  18–19C.: 231
New Sweden
  17C.: 194
Newtown Butler (1689), B. of, 33a, 94a
New York State
  17C.: 196
  18C.: 197, 198, 200
  19C.: 202, 206
  See United States
New Zealand
  18C.: 9, 11, 285
  19C.: 13, 15, 281a, 285
  20C.: 17–23, 63, 281b, 282–3
Nicaragua
  16C.: 228
  19–20C.: 231–233a
  See Mosquito Coast
Nice (1538, 1548), B. of, 159
Nicobar Is.
  18C.: 262
  19C.: 264
Nieuport (1653), B. of, 29
Niger
  20C.: 22–3, 246–51, 253
Niger Coast Prot.
  19C.: 253
Nigeria
  20C.: 22, 246–51, 253, 273
Nijmegen (1678–9), T. of, 33b, 108–9
Nile (1798), B. of the, 45b
Nördlingen (1634), B. of, 31a
Norfolk, in United States (1781), B. of, 199
Norfolk I.
  20C.: 17–23, 282
North America
  16C.: 4, 6a, 24
  17C.: 6b, 24, 195, 196, 226
  18C.: 7a, 8, 10, 41a, 43a, 196–9
  19C.: 7b, 12, 14, 24
  20C.: 16–24, 62–3
  See Canada, United States
North Carolina
  17–18C.: 196–8, 200
  19C.: 202, 206, 207
  See United States
Northern Ireland (Ulster)
  20C.: 58, 82, 84, 94b
  See Ireland
Northern Rhodesia
  20C.: 246–51, 255
Northern Territory (in Australia)
  19–20C.: 286–8,
North Foreland (1666), B. of, 29
Northwest Territories
  19C.: 222, 223a

Northwest Territories (*cont.*)
  20C.: 223b, c
  See Canada
Norway
  16C.: 2, 70, 118, 120
  17C.: 36a, b, 72, 149
  18C.: 37a, 74
  19C.: 26, 49, 52, 56, 58, 76, 78, 86, 93
  20C.: 80, 82, 84, 90–3
Novara (1500, 1513), B. of, 159
Nova Scotia
  18C.: 43a, 198
  19C.: 221a, 222, 223a
  20C.: 223b, c, 224
  See Canada
Novgorod
  15–17C.: 180
  18C.: 182, 183
  19C.: 183
  20C.: 187
Novi (1799), B. of, 44
Novipazar, Sanjak of
  19C.: 146, 170a
Nubia
  19C.: 242
Nuremberg (1632), B. of, 31a
Nuremberg (1538), Catholic League of, 128
Nuremberg Globe (c. 1530), 1
Nyasaland
  20C.: 246–51, 255, 273
Nystad (1721), T. of, 37b

Ohio
  18C.: 200
  19C.: 202, 206, 207
  See United States
Oil fields
  Middle East: 175
  Poland: 179b
  Russia in Asia: 192, 193
  Russia in Europe: 188, 189
  United States: 209b
Oil Rivers Prot.
  19C.: 245, 253
Oirat, Khanate of the
  16C.: 3
Oldenburg
  16C.: 122, 124
  17C.: 130
  18C.: 132–4
  19C.: 49, 78, 135, 136, 140, 141
Old Providence I.
  17–20C.: 229–32
Oliva (1660), T. of, 36b
Oman
  20C.: 174, 175, 273

Ontario
  19C.: 222b, c, 223a
  20C.: 223b, c, 224
  See Canada
Orange, Pr. of
  16C.: 107
  18C.: 35, 74, 111
Orange Free State
  19C.: 244, 245
  20C.: 256b, 257
Oregon
  19C.: 202, 206
  See United States
Oregon Treaty (1846), 202
Oriskany (1777), B. of, 199
Orissa
  16C.: 3
  18C.: 266, 267
  19C.: 268
  20C.: 270
Orléans (1870), B. of, 117
Osnabrück, Bp. of
  16C.: 122, 124
  17C.: 32a, 129, 130
Otricoli (1798), B. of, 44
Ottoman Empire
  16C.: 2, 66–7, 71, 164–5
  17C.: 73, 164–5
  18C.: 38, 42, 75, 166–7
  19C.: 77, 79, 86–7, 166–9a
  20C.: 53, 81, 166–7, 169b
Oudenaarde (1708), B. of, 34
Oudh
  18C.: 50b, 266
  19C.: 267, 268
  20C.: 270

Pacific Ocean
  16C.: 4–5
  17C.: 6b
  18C.: 7a, 8–11
  19C.: 7b, 12–15
  20C.: 16–23, 55b, 63, 282–3
Padua (1500, 1509), B. of, 159
Pakistan
  20C.: 23, 270–3, 289
  See India
Palamos (1694), B. of, 33a
Palatinate, Lower
  16C.: 120, 122–6, 128
  17C.: 127, 130
  19C.: 49, 140–1
Palatinate, Upper
  16C.: 123, 125
  17C.: 32a, 131

Palestine
  20C.: 167, 173, 174
Palo Alto (1846), B. of, 227
Pamplona (1813), B. of, 44
Panama
  16–17C.: 229
  17–18C.: 230, 235
  18–19C.: 231, 236, 237
  19–20C.: 232, 233a, 238, 240a
Panama Canal, 240a
Paoli (1777), B. of, 199
Papal States
  16C.: 70, 126, 156
  17C.: 72, 127
  18C.: 74, 132, 134, 160
  19C.: 48, 49, 76, 78, 135–7, 161
Papua
  20C.: 17–21, 265, 282, 286–7
  See New Guinea
Paraguay
  19C.: 237
  20C.: 238, 239
  See South America
Parapacá (1879), B. of, 238
Paris
  18C.: 105b, 116
Paris (1763), T. of, 43, 198
Paris (1814), T. of, 49, 50c, 117, 152
Paris (1815), T. of, 49, 50b, 117, 152
Parkany (1683), B. of, 38a
Parma (1734), B. of, 159
Parma, D. of
  16C.: 126
  17C.: 127
  18C.: 42, 132, 134, 146, 160
  19C.: 48, 49, 135, 136, 142, 161
Passarowitz (1718), T. of, 38b, 166–7
Patagonia
  18C.: 236
  19C.: 237, 238, 239
  See South America
Pavia (1525), B. of, 159
Pavon (1861), B. of, 238
Pegu
  16C.: 3, 260
  17C.: 261
  19C.: 268
  20C.: 270
Peloponnese
  16C.: 71, 164
  17C.: 73
  18C.: 38a, b, 75, 158a
  19C.: 77–9, 166, 168, 169b, 170a
  20C.: 81, 170b, 171, 172a
Pennsylvania
  17C.: 196

  18C.: 197, 198, 200
  19C.: 202, 206, 207
  See United States
Perryville (1862), B. of, 207
Persia, see Iran
Peru
  16C.: 229, 234
  17C.: 235
  18C.: 236
  19C.: 237
  20C.: 238, 239
  See South America
Pfeddersheim (1525), B. of, 28
Philippines
  16C.: 5, 260
  17C.: 261
  18C.: 9, 11, 263
  19C.: 13, 15, 265, 276
  20C.: 17–23, 63, 273, 277–80, 282
Piacenza (1746), B. of, 159
Picardy
  15C.: 106
  16C.: 107
  18C.: 115
Pichincha (1822), B. of, 237
Piedmont
  16C.: 124, 126, 156, 157
  17C.: 127, 130, 157
  18C.: 35, 42, 48, 74, 132, 134, 157, 160
  19C.: 78, 135, 161
Pilgram (1618), B. of, 30a
Pisagua (1879), B. of, 238
Pitcairn I.
  19C.: 12, 14
  20C.: 16–20, 283
Plassey (1757), B. of, 41c, 267
Podolia
  17C.: 38b, 177a, 164–7, 181
  18C.: 177b, 182
  19C.: 183
  20C.: 187
Poland
  15C.: 120
  16C.: 2, 71, 126, 176a, 177a
  17C.: 30b, 32a, 36a, b, 38b, 73, 127, 177a
  18C.: 37a, b, 40, 75, 133, 177b
  19C.: 49, 69, 79, 87, 93, 142, 146, 178a,
        184, 188
  20C.: 56–9, 81, 83, 85, 90–3, 147, 148,
        176b, 178b, 179, 187, 189–91
Poltava (1709), B. of, 37a
Pomerania
  16C.: 70–1, 123, 125, 126, 128
  17C.: 32a, 36b, 127, 131, 138b, 149
  18C.: 37b, 40, 133
  19C.: 78–9, 141b, 142

Poona (1802), B. of, 50a
Population, Density of
    Africa : 250, 251
    Australia : 288
    British Isles : 88, 90, 91, 98, 99, 101, 104
    Canada : 224
    Central America : 233a
    Europe, Central : 88, 90, 91, 129b
    Europe, Eastern : 90, 91, 187, 188, 190
    Europe, Western : 90, 91
    Far East : 278–9
    India : 278
    New Zealand : 281b
    Russia in Asia : 185
    Russia in Europe : 88, 90, 91, 187, 188,
        190
    South Africa : 258b, 259
    South America : 239
    United States : 200b, 205, 206, 214, 217
    West Indies : 233a
Pordenone (1809), B. of, 44
Portugal
    15C. : 162, 163a
    16C. : 2, 66, 70
    17C. : 72
    18C. : 34, 44, 74
    19C. : 46c, 47b, 68, 76–9, 86
    20C. : 52, 58, 80, 82, 84, 163b
Portugal Overseas
    16C. : 70, 260
    17C. : 72, 235, 261
    18C. : 8–11, 230, 236, 266
    19C. : 12–15, 242–5, 253, 262–3, 267, 275a
    20C. : 16–21, 246–8, 264–5, 277, 282–3
Portuguese East Africa
    19C. : 242–5
Portuguese Guinea
    19C. : 242–5
    20C. : 246–51, 253, 273
Pozzuoli (1800), B. of, 44
Prague (1757), B. of, 40
Pressburg (1805), T. of, 48
Preston (1643), B. of, 96a
Prestonpans (1745), B. of, 95b
Prince Edward Is.
    18C. : 221a, 222, 223a
    19C. : 223b, c
    20C. : 224
    See Canada
Princeton (1777), B. of, 199
Protestants
    16C. : 126, 128
    17C. : 127, 129a
    19C. : 155
    20C. : 94b, 250, 272

Prussia
    15C. : 120, 176a
    16C. : 70–1, 119, 123, 125, 126, 138a, 176a
    17C. : 32a, 33a, 36b, 72–3, 127, 131, 138
    18C. : 35, 37b, 40, 42, 74–5, 132–4, 138b,
        139, 177b
    19C. : 48, 49, 76–9, 135–7, 139b–142
    20C. : 81, 83, 136, 137, 148a, 178a
Puerto Rico
    16–17C. : 228, 229
    17–18C. : 230
    18–19C. : 231
    19–20C. : 232, 233a
Pultusk (1703), B. of, 37a
Punitz (1704), B. of, 37a
Punjab
    16C. : 3
    18C. : 50a, 267
    19C. : 268
    20C. : 270
Pyrenees (1659), T. of, 32b, 108–9

Qatar
    20C. : 174, 175
Quebec (1759), B. of, 41a
Quebec, Pr. of
    18C. : 43a, 198b
    19C. : 219, 222b, c, 223a
    20C. : 223b, c, 224
    See Canada
Queensland
    19–20C. : 15, 286–7, 288
Quiberon Bay (1759), B. of, 41b

Ragusa, Rep. of
    16C. : 2, 67, 71, 126, 156, 158, 164
    17C. : 73, 127
    18C. : 38b, 75, 133, 134, 160, 166
    19C. : 48, 135–7
Railways
    Australia (1950) : 286–7
    Canadian Pacific (1885) : 221b, 223a
    East Africa (1960) : 255
    Egypt (1956) : 240b
    Europe (1870) : 86–7, 89
    India (1857–9) : 269
    New Zealand (1950) : 281a
    Panama (1848–55) : 240a
    Schleswig-Holstein (1864) : 143a
    South Africa (c. 1910) : 258a
    United States (c. 1860) : 204a
Rainfall, Annual
    Asia : 2–3
    Australia : 284–5, 286–7
    Europe : 2
    Iberian Peninsula : 162a

Rainfall, Annual (*cont.*)
   North America (South-West): 226
   Russia: 184
   United States: 213
Rajputana
   16C.: 3
   18C.: 267
   19C.: 50b, 268
   20C.: 270
Rakonitz (1620), B. of, 30a
Ramillies (1706), B. of, 34
Rancagua (1814), B. of, 237
Rastatt (1714), T. of, 35
Ravenna (1512), B. of, 159
Ravensberg, C. of
   16C.: 122, 124
   17C.: 130, 138a
Regensburg (1809), B. of, 44
Religions
   Africa: 250
   Central Europe: 110, 126–9
   Europe: 66–7
   France: 110
   India: 272
   Ireland: 94b
   South-East Asia: 280
   Switzerland: 155
   World: 273
   See Greek Orthodox, Protestants,
     Roman Catholics
Resaca de la Palma (1847), B. of, 227
Restitution (1629), Edict of, 129
Rheinfelden (1638), B. of, 31b
Rhode I.
   17C.: 194
   18C.: 196–8, 200
   19C.: 202, 206
   See United States
Rhodes
   16C.: 67, 71, 165
   17C.: 73
   18C.: 75
   19C.: 77–9
   20C.: 59, 81, 83, 85, 167, 174, 175
Rhodesia
   20C.: 249
   See Southern Rhodesia
Rijswick (1697), T. of, 33b, 108–9
Rio de Oro
   19C.: 245, 253
   20C.: 246–51, 254, 273
Rio Muni
   19C.: 244, 245, 253
   20C.: 246–51, 273
Rivoli (1796–7), B. of, 44
Rocroi (1643), B. of, 31b

Roman Catholics
   16C.: 66–7, 126, 128
   17C.: 127, 129a
   19C.: 155
   20C.: 250, 272
Rome (1799), B. of, 44
Roskilde (1658), T. of, 36b
Rossbach (1757), B. of, 40
Roucoux (1746), B. of, 39
Roundway Down (1643), B. of, 96a
Roussillon
   16C.: 70, 107, 163
   17C.: 32b, 72
   18C.: 115
Rowton (1645), B. of, 96b
Ruanda-Urundi
   20C.: 55a, 255
Ruhr Basin
   20C.: 56–7
Rumania
   19C.: 93, 166–7, 170a
   20C.: 53, 57, 59–61, 81, 83, 85, 92, 93,
     147, 148, 170b, 171, 187, 273
   See Moldavia, Transylvania,
     Wallachia
Rumelia
   19C.: 166–7, 170a
Rupert's Land
   17C.: 8, 10, 43a, 196
   18C.: 43a, 196, 198
   19C.: 12, 222a, b
Russia, *see* U.S.S.R.
Ryu-Kyu Is.
   19–20C.: 276, 282
Rwanda
   20C.: 23, 249
   See Ruanda-Urundi

Saalfeld (1806), B. of, 44
Saar
   20C.: 57, 84, 148
Saba (W. Indies)
   17–20C.: 229–32
Safavid Empire (1499–1736), 2
St. Andrews (W. Indies)
   17–20C.: 229–32
St. Barthélmy (W. Indies)
   17–20C.: 229–32
St. Christopher (W. Indies)
   16C.: 228
   17C.: 229
   18C.: 43a, 230
   19C.: 231
   20C.: 232
St. Croix, Sta. Cruz (W. Indies)
   16C.: 228

St. Croix, Sta. Cruz (W. Indies) (*cont.*)
  17C.: 229
  18C.: 10, 230
  19C.: 12, 14, 231
  20C.: 16, 18, 232
St. Eustatius (W. Indies)
  17–20C.: 229–32
St. Lazaro Arch.
  16C.: 5
St. Lucia (W. Indies)
  17C.: 229
  18C.: 41a, 43a, 230
  19C.: 12, 14, 47b, 231
  20C.: 16, 20, 62, 232
St. Martin (W. Indies)
  16–20C.: 228–32
St. Mihiel (1918), B. of, 54
St. Omer (1677), B, of, 33a
St. Pierre
  18C.: 198b
St. Quentin (1871), B. of, 117
St. Quentin (1918), B. of, 54
St. Thomas (W. Indies)
  17C.: 230
  18C.: 8, 10, 231
  19C.: 12, 14, 232
  20C.: 16, 18, 232
St. Vincent, in Portugal (1797), B. of, 44
St. Vincent (W. Indies)
  17C.: 229
  18C.: 41a, 43a, 230
  19C.: 47b, 231
  20C.: 232
Sakhalin
  19C.: 184, 276
  20C.: 185, 277
Salamanca (1706), B. of, 34
Salamanca (1812), B. of, 46c
Salta (1812), B. of, 237
Saluzzo, Mar. of
  16C.: 110, 156, 157
Salvador
  18–19C.: 231
  19–20C.: 232, 233a
Salzburg, Abp. of
  16C.: 123, 125, 126, 128
  17C.: 127, 131, 132, 134
  18C.: 135–7, 142, 146
Samoa, *see* Western Samoa
Samogitia
  16C.: 176a
  17C.: 177a
  18C.: 177b
Samos
  16C.: 165, 166
  19C.: 168, 170a

  20C.: 169b, 170b, 171a, b, 172a
San Marino
  16C.: 70, 156, 158
  17C.: 72
  18C.: 74, 76, 132, 134, 160
  19C.: 49, 78, 135–7, 161
  20C.: 80, 82, 84
San Pascual (1846), B. of, 227
San Stefano (1878), T. of, 170a
Sta. Cruz (W. Indies), *see* St. Croix
Sta. Maura
  16–18C.: 38a, b, 158a
Sante Fé Trail
  19C.: 203
Saragossa (1710), B. of, 34
Saragossa (1808, 1809), B. of, 44, 46c
Saragossa (1529), T. of, 5, 7
Sarandi (1825), B. of, 237
Sarawak, *see* Borneo
Sardinia, K. of
  16C.: 66, 70, 144, 156
  17C.: 72
  18C.: 35, 39, 42, 74, 132, 157, 160
  19C.: 49, 68, 76, 78, 161
  20C.: 80, 82, 84
Saskatchewan
  19C.: 222c, 223a
  20C.: 223b, c, 224
  See Canada
Saudi Arabia
  20C.: 175, 273
Savannah (1778), B. of, 199
Savona (1800), B. of, 44
Savoy
  16C.: 70, 121, 122, 124, 126, 156, 157
  17C.: 33a, b, 72, 127, 130, 157
  18C.: 35, 42, 74, 132, 134, 157, 160
  19C.: 78, 117, 135, 161
Saxony
  16C.: 28, 70, 121–6, 128
  17C.: 32a, 72, 127, 130–1
  18C.: 40, 74, 132, 134
  19C.: 78, 135–7, 140–2
Scandinavia
  16–17C.: 149
  See Denmark, Norway, Sweden
Schladming (1526), B. of, 28
Schleswig
  16C.: 70, 122, 124
  17C.: 130
  18C.: 132
  19C.: 140–143a
  20C.: 56, 80, 143b
Schmalkaldic League (1530–1), 128
Schönbrunn (1809), T. of, 48
Schooneveld Bank (1673), B. of, 29

Schweidnitz (1642), B. of, 31b
Scotland
  16C.: 2, 66, 70, 95a, 118
  17C.: 72, 95a
  18C.: 74, 95b, 97
  19C.: 68, 76, 78, 86, 88, 98–101, 102
  20C.: 52, 58, 80, 82, 84, 90–2, 103, 104
Senegal, Senegambia
  18C.: 43b
  19C.: 242–4, 253
  20C.: 22, 246–51
Sennheim (1638), B. of, 31b
Serbia
  16C.: 71, 164
  17C.: 73
  18C.: 38b, 42, 75, 146
  19C.: 77, 79, 166, 168, 169, 170a
  20C.: 53, 59, 81, 169, 170b, 171, 172
Serrey, C. of
  17–18C.: 75, 133, 138b, 139a
Sevastopol (1855), B. of, 51a, b
Seven Days' Battle (1862), 207
Sèvres (1920), T. of, 166–7, 174
Sheriffmuir (1715), B. of, 95b
Shiloh (1862), B. of, 207
Siam, see Thailand
Sibir, Khanate of
  16C.: 3
Sicily, K. of
  16C.: 2, 67, 70–1, 144, 156
  17C.: 72–3
  18C.: 35, 42, 74–5, 160
  19C.: 48, 49, 69, 76–9, 161
  20C.: 52, 58, 80, 82, 84
Siena (1555), B. of, 159
Siena, Rep. of
  16C.: 156
  See Tuscany
Sierra Leone
  19C.: 242–5, 253
  20C.: 22, 246–51, 273
Silesia
  15C.: 120
  16C.: 70–1, 121, 123, 125, 126, 145
  17C.: 72–3, 127, 131, 146
  18C.: 39, 40, 42, 74–9, 133, 134, 139a
  19C.: 135–7, 142
Silver mining
  California: 201a
  Scandinavia: 149
  South Africa: 258a
  United States: 209b
Simbach (1743), B. of, 39
Sind
  16C.: 2–3
  18C.: 266, 267

  19C.: 268
  20C.: 270
Singapore
  16C.: 260
  17C.: 261
  18C.: 262
  19C.: 264
  20C.: 277, 280b, 282
Sinkiang
  18–19C.: 274
Sinope (1853), B. of, 51a
Sinsheim (1694), B. of, 33a
Slancamen (1691), B, of, 38a
Slovakia
  20C.: 59, 60, 147, 148a
Slovenia
  20C.: 147, 169a
  See Carinthia, Carniola, Styria
Smolensk (1812), B. of, 45, 46a
Society Is.
  20C.: 16–20, 283
Soissons (1914), B. of, 54
Solomon Is.
  19–20C.: 17–23, 282–3
Somaliland, British, French and Italian
  19C.: 245
  20C.: 23, 174, 175, 246–51, 273
Somosierra Pass (1808), B. of, 44
Soor (1745), B. of, 39
South Africa, Rep. of; Union of
  19C.: 256a
  20C.: 23, 246–51, 256b–9, 273
  See Cape Colony
South America
  16C.: 4, 6a, 234
  17C.: 6b, 235
  18C.: 7a, 8, 10, 236
  19C.: 7b, 12, 14, 233b, 237, 238
  20C.: 16–22, 62, 238, 239
South Australia, State of
  19–20C.: 15, 286–8
South Carolina
  18C.: 196, 198, 200
  19C.: 202, 206, 207
  See United States
Southern Rhodesia
  20C.: 246–51, 255
South-West Africa
  20C.: 23, 247–51
  See German South-West Africa
Southwold (1672), B. of, 29
Spain
  15C.: 162a, b, 163a
  16C.: 2, 66, 70, 144
  17C.: 32b, 33a, b, 72
  18C.: 34, 35, 42, 44, 74

Spain (*cont.*)
  19C.: 46c, 47b, 68, 76, 78, 86, 93
  20C.: 52, 58, 80, 82, 84, 92, 93, 163b
Spain Overseas
  16C.: 70, 229
  17C.: 72, 229, 235, 261
  18C.: 8–11, 43, 74, 196, 198, 230, 236
  19C.: 12–15, 76, 78, 80, 200a, 231, 242–5,
    253, 254, 262–3
  20C.: 16–21, 82, 84, 246–8
Spanish Morocco, *see* Morocco
Spanish Sahara
  20C.: 246, 247, 249–51, 254
Spanish (Adams-Onis) Treaty (1819), 202
Spice Is., *see* Moluccas
Spichern (1870), B. of, 117
Spionkop (1900), B. of, 256b
Stadtlohn (1623), B. of, 30a
Stafforda (1690), B. of, 33a
Stato dei Presidii
  16C.: 144
  17C.: 146
  18C.: 35, 42, 132, 134, 160
Staunton (1862), B. of, 207
Steinau (1633), B. of, 31a
Steinkirk (1692), B. of, 33a
Stockach (1799), B. of, 44
Stockholm (1719), T. of, 37b
Stones River (1862), B. of, 207
Storkyro (1714), B. of, 37a
Stormberg (1899), B. of, 256b
Straits Settlements, 264–5
Studenka (1812), B. of, 45, 46b
Stuhm (1629), B. of, 30b
Styria
  16C.: 70–1, 123, 125, 126, 128
  17C.: 72–3, 127, 131, 145
  18C.: 74–5, 132–5
  19C.: 76–7, 136, 137, 142, 146
Sudan
  19C.: 244
  20C.: 23, 174, 175, 246–9, 273
Suez Canal, 240b
Sulzberg (1525), B. of, 28
Sumatra
  16C.: 5, 260
  17C.: 261
  18C.: 9, 11, 262
  19C.: 13, 15, 264
  20C.: 17–23, 63, 264, 273. 277–9, 280b,
    282
Surinam, *see* Dutch Guiana
Susa (1629), B. of, 159
Swaziland
  19C.: 244–5, 256a
  20C.: 23 246–51, 256b, 257, 273

Sweden
  15C.: 120
  16C.: 2, 67, 70–1, 118–9, 121, 126, 149
  17C.: 32a, 33a, 36a, b, 72–3, 127, 149
  18C.: 37a, b, 49, 74–5, 132, 134
  19C.: 69, 76–9, 86–8, 93, 135–7
  20C.: 52–3, 58, 61, 80–5, 90–3
Sweden Overseas
  17C.: 32a, 72–3, 130, 149, 194–5
  18C.: 74–5, 132, 134
  19C.: 76–7, 135–7, 139b
Switzerland
  16C.: 70, 121–6, 128
  17C.: 32a, 72, 127, 130
  18C.: 39, 48, 74, 132, 134, 154
  19C.: 49, 68, 76, 86, 88, 89, 92, 93, 135–7
    155
  20C.: 52, 57–61, 90–3, 148
Sword, Knights of the, 120
Syria
  16–19C.: 165, 167
  20C.: 59, 167, 174, 175, 273

Tacna (1880), B. of, 238
Taiwan (Formosa)
  17C.: 261
  18C.: 263, 274
  19C.: 265, 274, 275a
  20C.: 276, 277, 279, 280, 282
Talavera (1809), B. of, 46c
Tanganyika
  20C.: 247–51, 255, 273
  See German East Africa
Tangier
  16C.: 70
  17C.: 72
  18C.: 74
  20C.: 58, 82, 84, 247, 248
Tangtu Truce (1933), 276
Tanzania
  20C.: 23, 249
  See Tanganyika
Tarragona (1811), B. of, 44
Tarutino (1812), B. of, 45, 46b
Tasmania
  18C.: 9, 11, 285
  19C.: 13, 15, 285, 287
  20C.: 17–21, 282, 288
Tekna
  20C.: 248
  See Spanish Sahara
Temesvar, Banat of
  18C.: 38b, 146, 166
  19C.: 168
Tenasserim
  19C.: 268, 270

Tennessee
  18C.: 200
  19C.: 202, 206, 207
  See United States
Teutonic Order, 2, 71, 120, 123, 176a
Texas
  19C.: 202, 206, 207, 227
  See United States
Textiles
  England: 92, 97, 102a, 103a
  Europe: 92
  Russia in Asia: 192, 193
  Russia in Europe: 92, 188, 189
  Scotland: 92, 102a, 103a
  United States: 210-11
  Wales: 92, 97, 102a, 103a
Thailand
  16C.: 3, 260
  17C.: 261
  18C.: 9, 11
  19C.: 264
  20C.: 273, 276, 278, 280, 282
Thionville (1639), B. of, 31b
Thrace
  19C.: 77, 79
  20C.: 169b, 170b, 171
Thuringian States
  19C.: 135-7, 140, 141
Tibet
  16C.: 3
  17-18C.: 274
  20C.: 270, 271, 280a
Ticonderoga (1758), B. of, 41a
Tilsit (1807), B. of, 45
Tilsit (1807), T. of, 48
Timor
  16C.: 5, 260
  17C.: 261
  18C.: 9, 11, 263
  19C.: 13, 15, 263, 265
  20C.: 17-23, 265, 273, 277, 279, 282
Tobago
  17C.: 229, 235
  18C.: 43a, 230, 236
  19C.: 12, 14, 231, 237
  20C.: 16-22, 232, 238; 239
Togo
  20C.: 55a, 246, 248-51, 253
Tolentino (1797), T. of, 48
Tonga Is.
  20C.: 16-20, 283
Tongking
  19-20C.: 264, 274, 277, 280b
Tordesillas (1494), T. of, 4, 6, 235
Torgau (1760), B. of, 40
Tortosa (1707), B. of, 34

Tortosa (1811), B. of, 44
Tortuga I. (W. Indies)
  16-20C.: 228-32
Toul, Bp. of
  16C.: 109, 122, 124
  17C.: 32a, 111, 130
  18C.: 115a
Toulouse (1814), B. of, 44, 46c
Trafalgar (1805), B. of, 44, 47b
Transjordan
  20C.: 167, 174
Transvaal
  19C.: 244, 245, 257
  20C.: 256b
Transylvania
  16C.: 71, 144, 164
  17C.: 38b, 73, 146, 166
  18C.: 34, 75, 132
  19C.: 77, 81, 142, 168
Trent, Bp. of
  16C.: 122-5
  17C.: 130-1
  18C.: 132, 134
  19-20C.: 57, 161
Triebel (1647), B. of, 31b
Trier, Abp. of
  16C.: 122, 124, 126
  17C.: 111, 127, 130
  18C.: 132
Trieste
  20C.: 84, 161
Trinidad
  16C.: 228, 229, 234
  17C.: 230, 235
  18C.: 8, 10, 230, 231, 236
  19C.: 12, 14, 231, 237
  20C.: 16-22, 232, 238, 239
Tripoli
  16C.: 164
  17-18C.: 166
  19C.: 242-5
  20C.: 248, 254
Trondheim District
  17C.: 36b, 149
Trucial Oman
  20C.: 174, 175, 273
Tsingtao (Kiaochow)
  19-20C.: 275b
Tsushima (1905), B. of, 276
Tuamotu Arch.
  20C.: 16-20, 283
Tucumán (1812), B. of, 237
Tudela (1808), B. of, 46c
Tunisia
  16C.: 2, 70, 164
  17C.: 72

Tunisia (*cont.*)
18C.: 74
19C.: 76–9, 166, 242–5
20C.: 23, 58, 80, 82, 84, 246–51, 254, 273
Turin (1706), B. of, 34, 159
Turkestan, Turkmenistan
19–20C.: 186b, 273
Turkey
20C.: 56–7, 59, 61, 83, 85, 166–7, 174, 175, 273
See Anatolia, Ottoman Empire
Turnham Green (1643), B. of, 96a
Tuscany
18C.: 42, 132, 134, 146, 160
19C.: 48, 49, 78, 135–7, 142, 161
Tuttlingen (1643), B. of, 31b
Tyrol
16C.: 28, 70, 122–6, 128, 144
17C.: 72, 127, 130–1, 145
18C.: 74, 132, 134
19C.: 135–7, 142, 146
20C.: 161

Uganda
20C.: 23, 246–51, 255, 273
Ukraine, Ukrainian S.S.R.
16C.: 71
17C.: 73, 177a, 181
18C.: 75, 177b, 182, 184
19C.: 183
20C.: 83 85, 148b, 191
Ulm (1805), B. of, 44
Ulster
16–20C.: 94
See Ireland
Ungava, District of
19C.: 223a
20C.: 223b
United Arab Rep.
20C.: 175, 249
See Egypt, Syria
United Kingdom, *see* England, Ireland, Scotland, Wales
United Provinces (Netherlands)
17C.: 29, 32a, 33a, b, 72, 108, 111, 127, 130
18C.: 35, 39, 40, 74, 108, 132
United States
18C.: 199, 200
19C.: 201–8, 210a, 211a, 212a
20C.: 209, 210b, 211b, 212b, 213–5, 217 218
See North America
United States Overseas
19C.: 14–15, 275a
20C.: 16–21, 232, 264–5, 277, 282–3

Uralsk
18–19C.: 183, 184
20C.: 185
Uruguay
19C.: 237
19–20C.: 238, 239
See South America
Uryankhei Terr.
20C.: 184, 274
U.S.S.R.
16C.: 2–3, 6a, 66, 71, 118, 176a, 180–1
17C.: 6b, 36a, b, 73, 180–1
18C.: 7a, 9, 11, 75, 177b, 182
19C.: 7b, 13, 15, 48, 49, 69, 77, 79, 87, 88, 93, 178a, 183, 188
20C.: 17–21, 26, 53, 56–63, 81, 83, 85, 90–3, 184–7, 189–93, 273
Ussuri
19–20C.: 184, 274
Utrecht (1672), B. of, 33a
Utrecht (1713), T. of, 35, 43
Utrecht (1579–81), Union of, 150b

Valeggiò (1630), B. of, 159
Valencia (1808), B. of, 44, 46c
Valmy (1792), B. of, 44
Van Dieman's Land, *see* Tasmania
Venaissin
16C.: 70, 107
17C.: 32b, 72
18C.: 74, 111, 115, 132
19C.: 117
Venezuela
16C.: 234
19C.: 231, 232, 237, 238
20C.: 233a, 238, 239
See South America
Venice, Venetia
16C.: 2, 67, 70–1, 126, 156, 158
17C.: 38, 127, 158
18C.: 39, 132, 134, 158, 160
19C.: 48, 49, 78, 135–7, 142, 146, 161
Vera Cruz (1847), B. of, 227
Vercelli (1615), B. of, 159
Verden
16C.: 122, 124
17C.: 32a, 36b, 129, 130, 149
18C.: 37b, 149
Verdun (1916), B. of, 54
Verdun, Bp. of
16C.: 108, 122, 124
17C.: 32a, 111, 130
18C.: 115a
Vermont
18C.: 200a

Vermont (*cont.*)
  19C.: 202, 206
  See United States
Versailles (1919), T. of, 56–7
Vichy Regime (1942-45), 58
Victoria (in Australia)
  19–20C.: 15, 286–7, 288
Vienna (1683), B. of, 38a, 164
Vienna (1814–15), Congress of, 49
Vienna (1735–38), T. of, 42
Vienna (1864), T. of, 142, 143a
Vietnam
  20C.: 23, 272, 280a
  See Indochina
Vigo (1702), B. of, 34
Vijayanagar
  16C.: 3
Villaviciosa (1710), B. of, 34
Vimeiro (1808), B. of, 46c
Vincennes (1661), T. of, 108–9
Virgin Is. (W. Indies)
  16–20C : 228–32
Virginia
  17C.: 194–5
  18C.: 196–8, 200a
  19C.: 202, 206, 207
  See United States
Vitebsk (1812), B. of, 45, 46a
Vitoria (1808, 1813), B. of, 44, 46c
Vojvodina
  20C.: 169a
  See Banat of Temesvar
Volkovysk (1812), B. of, 45, 46b
Volta
  20C.: 22, 246–51, 253
Wagram (1809), B. of, 45
Wales
  16C.: 66, 70, 118
  17C.: 72, 96a, b
  18C.: 74, 97
  19C.: 76-9, 86, 88, 98–102
  20C.: 52, 58, 80, 82, 84, 90–2, 103, 104
Wallachia
  16C.: 2, 71
  17C.: 73, 164
  18C.: 38, 42, 146, 183
  19C.: 77–9, 166–70a
Walvis Bay
  19C.: 244, 245
  20C.: 246–51
Wandewash (1760), B. of, 41c, 267
Warburg (1760), B. of, 40
Warsaw, Gr. D. of
  19C.: 48, 77, 137
  See Poland
Waterloo (1815), B. of, 44, 47a

Webster-Ashburton (1842), T. of, 219b
Weihaiwei
  19–20C.: 275a, b
Weissenburg (1870), B. of, 117
Wenden (1577), B. of, 176a
Western Australia, State of
  19–20C.: 13, 15, 286–8
Western Samoa
  20C.: 23, 55b, 283
West Indies
  16C.: 4, 228
  17C.: 229, 230
  18C.: 8, 10, 41a, 43a, 230, 231
  19C.: 12, 14, 231, 232
  20C.: 16–22, 62, 232, 233a
Westphalia, K. of
  19C.: 76, 137, 141b, 142
Westphalia (1648), T. of, 32a, 108–9
Wettin possessions
  16C.: 122–5
  17C.: 130–1
  18C.: 132–4
Wexford (1649), B. of, 94a
White Mountain (1620), B. of, 30a
Wiesloch (1622), B. of, 30a
Wilhelmsthal (1762), B. of, 40
Wimpfen (1622), B. of, 30a
Winburg, Rep. of
  19C.: 256a
Winceby (1643), B. of, 96a
Wittelsbach possessions
  16C.: 122–5
  17C.: 130–1
  18C.: 132–3
  19C.: 135
Wittenweier (1638), B. of, 31b
Wittstock (1636), B. of, 31b
Wolfenbüttel (1641), B. of, 31b
Wolgast (1628), B. of, 30b
World
  16C.: 2–6a
  17C.: 6b
  18C.: 7a, 8–11
  19C.: 7b, 12–15
  20C.: 16–23, 62–3, 273
Wörth (1870), B. of, 117
Württemberg
  16C.: 28, 122, 124, 126, 128
  17C.: 127, 129, 130, 145
  18C.: 132, 134
  19C.: 49, 78, 135–7, 140, 141
Wurzach (1525), B. of, 28
Würzburg (1525), B. of, 28

Yemen
  16C.: 2

Yemen (*cont.*)
  20C.: 23, 174, 175, 273
Ypres (1914, 1915), B. of, 54
Yucatan
  16C.: 228
  17C.: 229
  18C.: 230
  19C.: 227, 231
  20C.: 232, 233a
Yugoslavia
  20C.: 57, 61, 83, 85, 92, 93, 147, 169a,
    171, 273
  See Bosnia, Croatia, Dalmatia,
    Herzegovina, Macedonia, Montenegro,
    Serbia, Slovenia
Yukon Terr.
  19–20C.: 223
  See Canada

Zabern (1525), B. of, 28
Zablat (1619), B. of, 30a
Zambia
  20C.: 23, 249
  See Northern Rhodesia
Zanzibar
  16C.: 2
  19C.: 242–5
  20C.: 246–51, 255
Zaporogian Cossacks
  16C.: 71
  17C.: 73, 177a, 181
  18C.: 75, 177b
Zenta (1697), B. of, 38a
Znaim (1809), B. of, 45
Zollverein (1834–88), 140b, 141a
Zorndorf (1758), B. of, 40
Züllichau (1759), B. of, 40
Zusmarshausen (1648), B. of, 31b